Perry Volunteers in the Mexican War
Perry County, Alabama
First Regiment of Alabama Volunteers

1846-1847

and the
Mexican War Diary of
Captain William G. Coleman

J. Hugh LeBaron

HERITAGE BOOKS
2008

HERITAGE BOOKS
AN IMPRINT OF HERITAGE BOOKS, INC.

Books, CDs, and more—Worldwide

For our listing of thousands of titles see our website
at
www.HeritageBooks.com

Published 2008 by
HERITAGE BOOKS, INC.
Publishing Division
100 Railroad Ave. #104
Westminster, Maryland 21157

International Standard Book Numbers
Paperbound: 978-0-7884-2267-6
Clothbound: 978-0-7884-7345-6

Dedication

To my grand children
Brian Houston Flatt and Shannon Caroline Flatt
from Dothan, Alabama

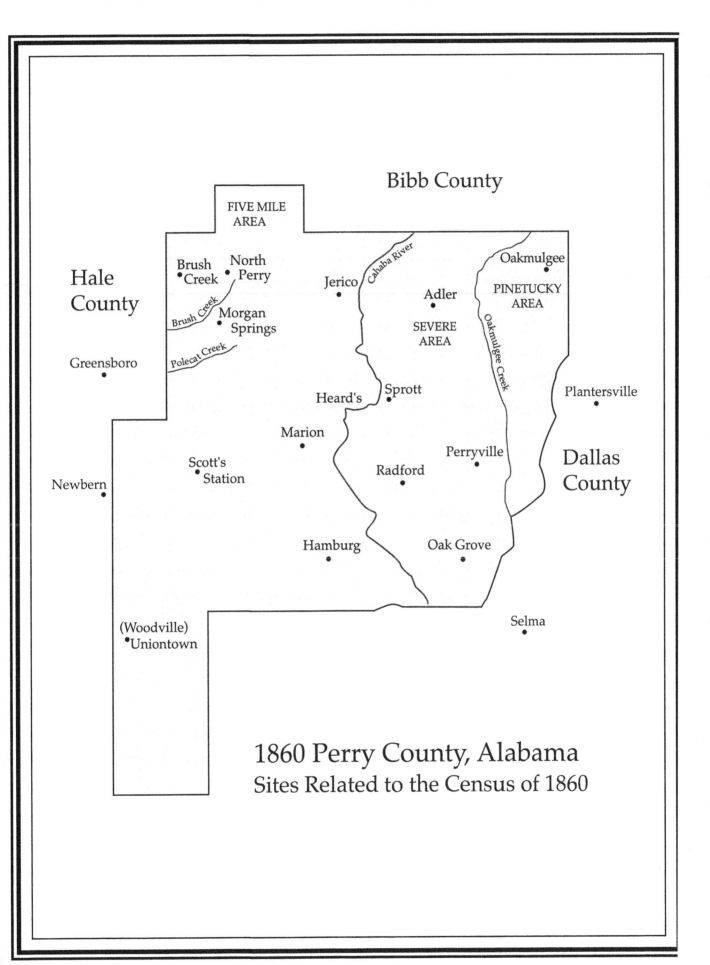

Bibb County

FIVE MILE
AREA

Brush
Creek

North
Perry

Jerico

Cahaba River

Oakmulgee

PINETUCKY
AREA

Hale
County

Brush Creek

Morgan
Springs

Adler

SEVERE
AREA

Oakmulgee Creek

Greensboro

Polecat Creek

Plantersville

Heard's

Sprott

Marion

Scott's
Station

Perryville

Dallas
County

Radford

Newbern

Hamburg

Oak Grove

Selma

(Woodville)
Uniontown

1860 Perry County, Alabama
Sites Related to the Census of 1860

Contents

Illustrations/Photographs

Maps by Amy Richardson

Introduction

The Mexican War has not been a subject of great general interest in the United States although it was America's first foreign war and the land acquisitions made in this conflict gave the country the continental shape we know today. However, in recent years, there has been an increase in the number and variety of volumes about the American adventure in Mexico during the middle years of the 19th Century. Scholars are uncovering new information and developing new perspectives of the war and the men who fought it. Most of these monographs are written using a broad scope to follow the course of the war with considerations of the military, social, political, religious and international implications of the conflict.

The *Perry Volunteers in the Mexican War* is different and is not the type of narrative one normally expects to find about the Mexican War. It is in fact of a rare class because it is concerned principally with the Mexican War adventures of a single company of soldiers who surrendered the comforts of home for a year to serve their country in Texas and Mexico. In mid-1846, ninety-eight men from Perry County, Alabama formed themselves into a military unit for service in Mexico in response to the call of the government for volunteers to rescue, as they believed at the time, the Army of Occupation of General Zachary Taylor reportedly besieged at Matamoros, Mexico along the Rio Grande. The men in the Perry Volunteers have themselves been rescued from near obscurity by the determined investigative efforts of the author. They were spirited citizens who were motivated by patriotism and nationalism to step forward when their country called citizens to arms. Yet their record of service has lain undisturbed in dusty records for over 150 years and is just now brought into the light in this narrative.

Of course, the author does not ignore the general scope of the Mexican War but it as a matter of context for the activities of the men from Perry County, Alabama. Likewise, this narrative considers the movements of the First Regiment of Alabama Volunteers in which the Perry Volunteers served to place the men from Perry County in the proper historical framework. In doing so, the author produces a very readable story about real people in the lower echelons of the army and their adventures in Mexico. The generals of the army appear in this book but only as they interface with the Perry Volunteers. Like all good stories this one has threads that run throughout it. The quest for fame and glory in battle against the Mexicans is such a thread. Thwarted at every turn, the Perry Volunteers found glory elusive. However, the dominant thread in this tale has to do with the heartbreak and painful realities of service in Texas and Mexico and in the Army of 1846-48. Mr. LeBaron tells this saga in rich detail and keeps the reader wondering how the story will end.

The sources used to write this book are of the types that inspire confidence in the reader. The primary sources are the muster rolls of Company C and to a lesser degree the muster rolls of the First Regiment of Alabama Volunteers. A central source is a diary maintained by the captain of the Perry Volunteers in which he recorded many of his experiences during the war from the time he left home until he returned to Alabama. Two journals kept by men in the First Regiment of Alabama Volunteers also contributed to this book. From these three sources, the author gleaned a plethora of meaningful detail about weather, geography, conditions, life, death and other features that are not available elsewhere. The result is a narrative that includes authentic descriptions that relate to the reader the sights, sounds and a visual picture of places and events based on descriptions of people who lived the experience.

Howard S. Linzy, J. D.
New Orleans, Louisiana

Preface

A search for a published history of the men from Perry County, Alabama who served in the Mexican War is an act of frustration. The Mexican War is generally considered the most neglected war in American history and only a few references to individual units such as the Perry Volunteers can be identified. The best of the published sources available for Perry County men is *Alabama Volunteers in the MEXICAN WAR 1846-1848, A History and Annotated Roster*, edited by Steven R. Butler, who is also the Editor of the *MEXICAN WAR Journal* and Corresponding Secretary, former President and founder of the Descendants of Mexican War Veterans. This source consists of the names, ranks and annotations appearing in the official muster rolls of the First Regiment of Alabama Volunteers and a short narrative of the regiment's history. It provides valuable details about the Alabama men in the First Alabama Volunteers.

The author of this narrative used a similar source transcribing microfilms of Alabama soldiers in the Indian and Mexican Wars available in the Family History Centers of the Church of Jesus Christ of Latter Day Saints. Many details were extracted from the Mexican War Journals of Captain Sydenham Moore and Private Stephen F. Nunnalee of The Eutaw Rangers (Company D) and the letters of Captain Moore published in *The Eutaw Rangers in the War With Mexico* transcribed, edited and annotated by Steven R. Butler.[1] Mr. Butler's considerable efforts to make available to the public these journals and his other publications on the Mexican War are of immeasurable value to anyone interested in the war and the genealogy of the men from Alabama who served it. I appreciate the interest of Steven Butler in my efforts and his permission to quote from *The Eutaw Rangers*. The *Mexican War Journal of Captain Franklin Smith* was also a useful source of details about the army while it was at Camargo, Mexico and provided a valuable perspective.

The unpublished Mexican War diary of Captain William G. Coleman is presented to the public in this volume for the first time. It is entirely new to the field of Mexican War scholarship and is the source of an abundance of details used in this volume. Captain Coleman made daily entries in his record beginning on June 11, 1846, the day the Perry Volunteers left Perry County, through June 2, 1847, the day he returned to his home and embraced his family for the first time in a year. It is more appropriate to call the Coleman record a diary than a journal. Unlike the lengthy entries in the journals of Captains Moore and Smith and Private Nunnalee, that are written more in whole sentence narrative form, Coleman's record is made in short, staccato entries with frequently recurring themes such as daily weather and the general observations about his personal health and the health of the men in his company. The absence of explanations in the diary is at times frustrating because of the omission of details. For example, Coleman suggests feuds in the regiment and company but too often fails to explain the cause and provide details. No matter how much more one might wish to know, what is in the diary of William Coleman is a fresh look at the activities of the Perry Volunteers, the First Alabama and the war itself. As such, it is an important addition to the primary source materials about the Mexican conflict.

A range of other primary sources about individual members of the Perry Volunteers was gleaned during nearly a decade of research in Perry County records. The contributions of Perry Volunteer descendants served as the source of some of the materials contained in this account. Considerable effort was made to collate names with various sources to identify people and to correctly interpret cursive writing in original records. Various published sources appearing in

---

[1] Steven R. Butler, transcriber, editor and annotator, *The EUTAW RANGERS in the WAR WITH MEXICO*, the Mexican War Journal & Letters of CAPT. SYDENHAM MOORE and the Mexican War Journal of PVT. STEPHEN F. NUNNALEE (Descendants of Mexican War Veterans, 1998). All quotes and references to Captain Moore and Private Nunnalee were extracted from this volume with permission from the Editor.

the bibliography supplied information to round out this chronicle. Thanks are due to Amy Richardson, a talented artist who prepared maps for this volume; and to Melanie Atkins, Rodger Atkins, Dorothy Dickson LeBaron and Louise Birchfield who shared their proofreading skills, ferreting out errors and suggesting changes. Any errors that remain can in no way be their responsibility. The sheer number has overwhelmed even the most assiduous. A special thanks is due to Howard S. Linzy of New Orleans who wrote the introduction and whose multiple reviews, suggestions, corrections, encouragement, frank and useful criticisms improved the manuscript in copious ways.

My sincere gratitude goes to the descendants of Captain William G. Coleman. While the original diary could not be found, Mrs. Louise Henry Bonin provided a typed transcript of the original. That the diary exists, or once existed, is beyond question, it having at one time been in the possession of descendant T. E. "Gene" Coleman and William Coleman referenced it in a letter to John R. Coffey in 1884. The descendants of William G. Coleman responded with enthusiasm to my requests to locate and share primary source materials from the pen and life of Captain Coleman. Specifically, thanks go to Ben E. Coleman of Shreveport, Louisiana, T. E. "Gene" Coleman of Homer, Louisiana, Mrs. Louise Henry Bonin of Monroe, Louisiana and J. D. "Don" Robinson of Victoria, Texas for their cooperation and permission to publish the materials of their ancestor and the genuine interest in the project. Each of these descendants expressed a strong sense of history and awareness of the role their family had in making America what it is today.

This narrative is an effort to enter into the record the history of the Perry County men who went to Mexico to serve their country, and their contributions to the national composition, in the hope that their service will be remembered and honored. It began as part of a larger project about Perry County, Alabama and evolved because the information was needed for the separate project. The histories of Perry County are for the most part completely mute on the subject of these Mexican War soldiers, and the writer developed a curiosity about the Perry Volunteers. This narrative is the result of that need and natural curiosity. Then there was a personal matter that provided further motivation. My great, great granduncle Charles Green Jackson was a Perry Volunteer, and learning about his part in this venture is important to family history. No attempt is made to make this narrative a general history of the Mexican War. There are ample such histories available to the reader. However, it was necessary to discuss the war in order to put the Perry Volunteers into historical prospective and assist readers not familiar with the subject. In doing so, many contradictions had to be dealt with in the war record. This was especially true when considering army size, causalities, some dates and other data where the official record is missing and conjecture is common among the sources used.

A majority of Perry County Volunteers who served in Mexico were men in their early twenties, and even late teens, with a few in their thirties. Most had never been very far from home before marching off to serve in Mexico. It appears they enlisted, in most cases, for glory and adventure but received something quite different. What these young men experienced, more often than not, was a dose of reality in the form of pain, suffering, heat, boredom, sand, dust, swarming insects, disease, damaged health and, in some cases, death. Soldiering in Mexico was completely unlike the prewar militia drills before an admiring audience at home.

These volunteers enlisted for twelve months although it is possible that they did not know the term of service when they left Perry County, Alabama. Confusion held sway in the military and civil government about the length of the enlistment just before and after war was declared by the United States, with terms of enlistment of three and six months being the announced early lengths of service. However, Congress restricted regiments serving in Mexico to twelve months and many short-term volunteers went home rather than serve for a year. When the time came to be mustered into Federal service, the Perry Volunteers willingly agreed to a term of one year.

The men who assembled in Perry County in 1846 were different from enlistees in the Regular

Army of the United States. They were neither Regular Army soldiers nor state militia, but something in-between that can best be described as a subclass of the state militia. Soldiers in the Regular Army enlisted for five years and were paid $7.00 a month. As a consequence, the Regular Army was composed mostly of immigrants.[2] The Perry Volunteers, on the other hand, were citizen-soldiers who personified the spirit of the young American republic. They were not soldiers by trade but like the noble Roman Cincinnatus set aside their plows to answer their country's call.

Free, non-exempt and able-bodied white men in Perry County between the ages of eighteen and forty-five were in the militia of Alabama as a matter of law.[3] The Governor of Alabama controlled the militia, and he was its commander-in-chief. It was in effect a state army, but the militia was subject to call by the President of the United States in certain circumstances. However, the militia was limited to three-month terms of active duty. This made the militia ineffective as an instrument of national policy because the service term was too limited to allow training and deployment for any meaningful duty. Perry County had militia companies in each political division from its earliest history and held muster days at various places around the county twice a year in April and October. These muster days involved a little drill but were mostly picnics and social events. Militia members also performed patrols in the county to regulate and discipline disorderly persons and roving unruly slaves. In 1837, the militia law was changed in Alabama to provide for volunteers.

Limitations of militias was recognized early in American history and a class of soldiers positioned between the Regular Army and the militia called volunteers arose to fill a need for a way to turn citizen militias into soldiers without limits on the term or places of service in national emergencies. Volunteers were men who were members of the militia that formed themselves into companies and entered the service of the Federal government. They could serve for more than three months, and no permission was needed for them to serve outside of their home state. Thus, the Perry Volunteers were citizens of the county who belonged to the militia and agreed to give up the comforts of home for the perils of service in Mexico.

It is without doubt that patriotism, nationalism and the opportunity for excitement motivated the men who went to the recruiting office at Perryville, Alabama to join the Perry Volunteers. They were also likely to have been enticed by the government's promise of land bounties and pensions. The land bounties were for 160 acres for those men serving a year in Mexico. Not all volunteers made it to Mexico, but patrolled in their home state, replaced Regular Army units that went to Mexico, escorted wagon trains and guarded reservation Indians. In fact, the Perry Volunteers were among only a handful of citizen-soldiers to see service south of the border, and in the beginning, they considered themselves fortunate to be selected to go.

Volunteer companies were democratic in nature, political in practice and selected their own officers. Under an 1832 Alabama law, volunteers were permitted to elect their field officers right up to the regimental level, and every man in the company could cast a ballot for any rank in the regiment. Hailing mostly from the eastern part of Perry County, the Volunteers were friends, neighbors and relatives. A study of the 1850 Census of Perry County and individual genealogies demonstrates clearly that the soldiers in the Company were closely associated with

---

[2] One estimate holds that foreign-born men made up two-thirds of the regular army with men born in Germany, Ireland and Great Britain dominating. Congress repealed a ban on foreigners in the army because it became plain that the ranks could not be filled with native-born Americans. Zachary Taylor's regular army soldiers when he first arrived on the Rio Grande in 1846 contained 840 Irish, 350 Germans, 210 British, 105 Scots and 140 Canadians and western Europeans. George C. Furber, at Tennessee lawyer and Mexican War volunteer, observed that he was "*baffled that any man of intelligence could be induced to enlist in the regular army . . . The pay was poor, the prospects for promotion virtually hopeless. There was no reward for this grim existence . . .*"

[3] At various times in Alabama history, men who were ministers of the Gospels, school teachers, public officials and a few other categories were exempt from serving in the Alabama Militia.

each other before sailing off to Mexico. There were other combinations to show that the volunteers were not only neighbors but some were related by blood and marriage.

With such strong relations and blood kinships among the men, and with the democratic nature of the Perry Volunteers, it is natural that discipline in a company whose officers were elected was lax and less formal than in the Regular Army. Volunteer officers quickly learned that their soldiers expected to be treated as free men and were not eager to give up the rights of citizenship that army life demanded. Officers came to understand that their men could not be regulated with a firm hand and if they did, they encountered trouble from those in the ranks. Lieutenant George B. McClellan of the Regular Army observed that volunteer officers "*were actually afraid to exert their authority upon the Volunteers. Their popularity would be endangered.*" Lenient discipline was at the expense of war readiness, and it appears from subsequent events that the Perry Volunteers' quest for glory in Mexico was partly short-circuited by that loose discipline. The Perry Volunteers were brought into Federal service, but they maintained strong characteristics of Alabama State troops with dominating ties to their home state and community.

In addition to the loose discipline caused by too much familiarity between enlisted men and their officers, elections resulted in officers taking command that had too little experience and lacked many of the technical skills necessary to command troops. In fact, this was a principal complaint about the regimental commander elected by popular vote to lead the Perry County men. Popular commanders often made poor leaders. If the Perry Volunteers lacked soldierly skills such as the manual of arms, forming columns and changing fronts, it was because the regimental officers lacked the skill and dedication to teach them. Nevertheless, in time they became more proficient in the skills of soldiers.

Under the laws enacted by the United States Congress, the complement of the Perry Volunteers was set at 100 men, and they were authorized to serve as infantry. These men were in the first wave of volunteers, having begun to organize themselves just before the declaration of war. They were also among the first twelve-month volunteers on the scene in Texas and Mexico and would have arrived earlier had transportation been available sooner. Eventually, over 73,000 volunteers served in the Mexican War, but the Perry Volunteers went to the scene of the war before all but a small number of volunteers from other states and was one of the first regiments to appear in Texas following the call for twelve-month volunteers.

The Perry Volunteers suffered miserably while in Mexico. Ignorance concerning how disease was spread created insanitary camp conditions. The result was widespread dysentery, diarrhea, mumps, measles, typhoid fever, yellow fever and various other ailments that sent the young men from Perry County to their homes, their bodies racked with infirmities or to their graves. Those who died were usually laid in a shallow grave at the place where they died with only a blanket to cover them and little ceremony to mark their passing. The medical science of the era and the delays in applying treatments accounted for much of the harshness of illnesses and deaths for the young men who left their family and friends as healthy and vigorous specimens of manhood.[4]

The uniforms of the regular United States Army were made of wool or cotton and were light

---

[4] Dr. C. A. Woodruff in a letter to Samuel A. Townes of Perry County dated August 15, 1844, described his belief about the causes of disease. His explanation demonstrates the primitive state of medicine at the time of the Mexican War. Dr. Woodruff wrote about the origins of malaria that, "*poisonous effluvia that emanates from the low grounds . . . where a vast quantity of vegetable matter is acted upon by the midday sun, and decomposition readily generates malaria.*" He further assigned the cause of all disease to rotting matter saying, "*that the cause of disease proceeds from the decomposition either of vegetable or animal matter, induced by moisture and heat . . .*"

blue for privates and navy blue for non-commissioned and commissioned officers. Both wore dark blue forage caps. However, the Perry County men were volunteers and no description survives of their uniforms, if they had uniforms at all. It is assumed that the Perry Volunteers wore no uniform when they entered Federal service. According to regulations, the Perry boys were required to have a dress cap, forage cap, uniform coat, woolen and cotton jackets, woolen and cotton overalls, flannel shirts, drawers, socks and blanket. Whether the Perry Volunteers had the required clothing is not known, but to be accepted into Federal service, they were probably adequately equipped. They eventually received Regular Army uniforms.[5]

Naturally, pay varied with the rank. Each month privates and musicians received $8.00. This pay was quite low for the hardships of military service in Mexico and most of the time their pay arrived on an irregular basis. It was a universal complaint among soldiers, and source of low morale, that pay was inadequate and too often unpaid. The record indicates that the soldiers from Perry County received no pay during the first seven months of service in Mexico.

The Perry Volunteers did not remain in the field until Mexico's capitulation but went home having served out their enlistment. The treaty ending the war was signed in 1848. By that time, the Perry Volunteers had been home for nine months and the continental forty-eight contiguous United States, as we know it today, stretched from sea to shining sea.

---

[5] The journals of Captain Moore and Private Nunnalee recorded that the two Greene County companies in the First Regiment of Alabama Volunteers were the only companies with uniforms when mustered into Federal service in June 1846.

The Texas Connection to Perry County

"The identity, which has existed between the incidents of Texas, the generous sympathies and manly efforts exercised in behalf by the citizens of Alabama is a matter of history, which is chronicled in blood, . . . "
Sam Houston to Marion, Alabama Committee
May 13, 1840

In the 1830s and 1840s, people from Perry County, Alabama migrated to Texas, which until the spring of 1836 was a province of Mexico. Alabama was second only to Tennessee in providing original settlers to Texas where the lure was almost exclusively land.[6] Perry County was well represented among those Alabamians, and the migration of Perry countians to Texas continued throughout the Nineteenth Century. In time, disputes arose between the Texas settlers and the Mexican government. Texas declared its independence and Mexico moved to reclaim the province. War followed and troops led by Sam Houston defeated and captured Mexican General Santa Anna at the Battle of San Jacinto on April 21, 1836. Houston's victory and Texas independence were cheered and celebrated in Perry County and sparked more immigration to the Lone Star State where land was plentiful. Another link was forged with Texas when the hero of San Jacinto fell in love with a girl from Marion, the seat of government in Perry County.

Sam Houston Ten Years After Visiting Perry County
Library of Congress

Sam Houston was badly wounded at the Battle of San Jacinto, and on May 11 he sailed from Galveston to New Orleans on the steamboat *Flora* to receive medical attention for his injury. General Houston landed in the Crescent City on May 22 and was met by a band and a cheering crowd. Seventeen-year-old Margaret Lea from Perry County was visiting the city and happened to be in the crowd the day the renowned Houston came ashore, seeing him for the first time. Marquis James, Houston's respected biographer, described the event:

"General Houston lay in a stupor on the uncovered deck of the Flora. . . . When the Flora touched the wharf a crowd surged on board ... They started to lift Houston from the deck. With a cry of pain and convulsive movement of his powerful arm he flung them off. A band struck up a march: ... His wild appearance stunned the crowd. General Houston's coat was in tatters. He had no hat. His stained and stinking shirt was wound about the shattered ankle. The music stopped, the cheering stopped and a school girl with big violet eyes began to cry. Her name was Margaret Lea."

---

[6] Colonel William Barrett Travis, the Texas leader who heroically refused to surrender the Alamo to Santa Anna, was an Alabamian from Conecuh County. Lancelot Smither of Alabama was at the Alamo but was sent out as a messenger on the first day of the siege and survived. Galba Fuqua and Isaac White were Alabamians who died at the Alamo. Mirabeau Buonaparte Lamar, the first Vice President and second President of the Republic of Texas, migrated there from Selma in Dallas County, Alabama, Perry County's neighbor. William B. Travis' brother, Mark B. Travis, joined Company A of Raiford's Battalion of Alabama Volunteers during the Mexican War saying he wanted *"revenge against the Mexicans"* for his brother's death. When Company A disbanded, Mark Travis joined the Palmetto Regiment from South Carolina when it passed through Conecuh County, Alabama on the way to Mexico.

However, Lea and Houston did not meet, and after a difficult surgery and convalescence, the general returned to Texas on June 12 and was elected President of the Republic of Texas the following September.

Margaret Moffett Lea was the daughter of Temple Lea and Nancy Moffett and took silk and satins for granted in her wealthy father's plantation home near Marion, Alabama. Margaret was the first child born in Perry County after it was legally organized and gained a rare education from her father's wealth. She was educated at home by her parents until her father died and then she attended Pleasant Hill Seminary. Margaret was a lady of rare beauty, refinement and culture. She was one of the first students at Judson Institute (one of the few institutions of higher learning available for females) in Marion, Alabama where she studied Latin, piano, guitar, harp and voice and developed impressive literary skills. Lea met Sam Houston in May 1839 while attending a lawn party in Mobile hosted by her sister, Emily Antoinette Lea Bledsoe.[7] The introduction of Houston and Lea resulted in mutual *"love at first sight."* James described the meeting:

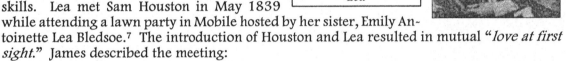

Margaret Moffett
Lea

> *"Houston was in Alabama buying blooded horses and seeking capital for his Texas enterprises. The quest for capital took him to Mobile to interview William Bledsoe, who invited the General to his stately country home, Spring Hill. It was a radiant afternoon in May, and Mrs. Bledsoe was giving a strawberry festival on her lawn. ... In the presence of such a hostess Sam Houston was at his best. They were strolling in the rose garden when a girl came by carrying a dish of strawberries. 'General Houston, my sister, Miss Margaret Lea,' said Emily Antoinette. ... Sam Houston thought he had never seen anything so beautiful ... Margaret's thoughts swept back to the unforgettable Sunday when New Orleans had received the victor of San Jacinto. ... She had been incapable of dispelling the premonition that some time she would meet this romantic man, and the meeting would shape her destiny."*

Antoinette saw little of the General and Margaret that afternoon. They strolled in the garden and fell deeply in love.

Leaving Mobile, Sam Houston traveled to Tennessee, consulted with ailing former President Andrew Jackson at the Hermitage near Nashville and returned to Alabama in midsummer of 1839. Again, he visited the Bledsoe family and their guests Margaret and Nancy Lea. Nancy Lea was interested in investing in Texas and used the occasion of Houston's visit to explore the money-making opportunities in the Lone Star state. Mrs. Lea, a wealthy widow, agreed to visit Texas and make an inspection before investing her money there. Before he left for Texas, Houston proposed marriage and Margaret promised to be his wife. Years later, Margaret was asked how a young well-educated girl from a wealthy Perry County family of high social standing could have risked her happiness with a man so much older and intemperate than herself, and she responded, *"He had won my heart."*

Back in Texas, Houston sent a stream of letters to Margaret asking her to come to Texas with her mother and marry him there. She agreed. Houston went to Galveston in April 1840 to

---

[7] Emily Antoinette Lea was no stranger to Texas. She went to Texas in 1835, as a home missionary for Siloam Church in Marion, Alabama. While in Texas, Antoinette traveled through the Mexican province in an ox wagon or on horseback organizing women's missionary societies. She married William Bledsoe, a wealthy Mobile grocer, in 1839.

meet Margaret at the appointed time. Nancy Lea and William Bledsoe disembarked on schedule but Houston looked for Margaret in vain. The Lea family thought the marriage a bad match. Houston had been married twice before, first to Eliza Allen ending in his resignation as Governor of Tennessee and the other to a Cherokee Indian woman named Tiana.[8] He was at times in his life a heavy drinker and without serious religious affiliation while the Leas were teetotalers and strong church people. Moreover, Houston was nearly three decades older than Margaret.

Strong-minded, plainspoken and independent Nancy Lea liked Houston personally despite herself, but opposed the marriage of her daughter to him. She informed the General upon her arrival in Galveston that Margaret had remained in Perry County and would not be coming to Texas. *"She goes forth in the world to marry no man. The man who receives her hand will receive it in my home and not elsewhere."* While in Texas, Nancy Lea made investments in land and returned to Perry County no more convinced of the suitability of her daughter's suitor and determined to persuade her not to marry Sam. Some of Houston's friends also thought the marriage unwise. Sam's friend, Colonel Bernard B. Bee wrote to another Houston friend, Dr. Ashbel Smith:

> *"I implored him . . . to resort to any expedient rather than marry. I see with great pain in the marriage of Genl Houston to Miss Lea! In all my acquaintance with life I have never met with an individual more totally disqualified for domestic happiness—he will not live with her 6 months."*

Houston would not be discouraged or denied and the Lea family relented to Margaret's steadfast wishes in the end. Obedient to the requirements set by his future mother-in-law and determined to become a reliable husband, Sam arrived in Perry County on May 7, 1840, by stagecoach and checked into the Lafayette Hotel in Marion. Arrangements for the wedding were made, including musicians, but before the ceremonies began, one of the Lea men took Houston aside and demanded an explanation of his separation from his first wife, Eliza Allen. Rumors abounded concerning the failed marriage and Margaret's persistent male relatives were to have the truth this day and, if necessary, save Margaret from herself. Unless Houston was forthcoming, there would be no wedding. In a courteous tone, Houston told his questioner that there was nothing that he would say on the subject of his first marriage, and if this was not satisfactory to the Lea family, then the kinsman should *"call his fiddlers off."*[9] With this, the Lea family opposition to the marriage dissolved

Henry Clinton Lea Home
in Marion, Alabama

---

[8] Houston married Eliza Allen while Governor of Tennessee. After a short time, Eliza left him under a dark cloud of suspicion with wild and vicious rumors in circulation about what happened to the marriage. Demands were made on Houston to explain, but he steadfastly refused as a matter of honor to say anything that would disparage Eliza or the Allen family. Pressure built for him to explain, and he re-signed as governor and went to live with the Cherokee Indians among the wilds along the Hiwassee River in East Tennessee. Houston was popular with the Cherokees who named him "The Raven." He married a Cherokee woman, leaving her years later to move to Texas. Houston bore the scorn of the failed marriage with Eliza and remained silent on the subject all his life. The evidence indicates that Eliza loved another man and married Houston under pressure from her family. Once married, she lapsed into despair about being married to Houston whom she apparently did not love.
[9] This story was related by Judge John Moore, a wedding guest, and recorded by his son, John Trotwood Moore of Marion, Alabama, who became Archivist of Tennessee. The questioner is not identified but

and Houston claimed his bride on Saturday, May 9, 1840, in a wedding ceremony conducted by Reverend Peter Crawford, pastor of Siloam Church, at the Green Street home of Margaret's brother Henry Clinton Lea. The Lea home was six years old at the time of the wedding and Margaret was living here with her mother. When the house was built, the front veranda had four square columns extending from the ground to the gabled roof. To each side of the veranda, brick walks fourteen feet wide extended the width of the house and were covered with latticed arbors. The Henry C. Lea home was quite suitable as a setting for such an important Marion marriage ceremony.

The wedding was an enormous social event in Marion because Sam Houston was as respected and admired as any American in his day. The ceremonies took place in the parlor room upstairs, which was covered in garlanded flowers. Two of Margaret's little Moffett cousins served as flower girls, and Mrs. James L. Goree[10] was the matron of honor. Martin Lea served as Houston's best man and Henry Clinton Lea gave the bride away. The newlyweds remained at the Lafayette Hotel for a week after the wedding before leaving for Texas.

On May 11, a meeting was held at the Perry County court house "*to make arrangements for tendering a public dinner to General Samuel Houston, the distinguished Ex-President of Texas.*" A committee composed of General J. F. Thompson, Dr. Nathaniel W L. Fletcher, R. E. Love, Napoleón Lockett, and Hugh Davis made the official invitation to Houston and set the date for Wednesday, May 13. General Houston accepted and responded in writing making reference to the special bond between the people of Texas and Alabama. He wrote:

> "*The identity, which has existed between the incidents of Texas, the generous sympathies and manly efforts exercised in behalf by the citizens of Alabama is a matter of history, which is chronicled in blood, and can never cease to inspire the patriot and with kindred and grateful emotions.*"

Houston made an address to the people of Perry County at the Siloam Baptist Church at noon on the day selected to honor him. Nearly every man, woman and child in the town was there to hear the famous general speak, including the young ladies of the town's two academies, wearing all white dresses. Houston, six feet three inches tall, made a commanding presence but he kept his remarks brief because of a throat ailment. The reception and a dinner were held under the shade of an oak grove next to the church. The meal had been in preparation for two days and thirteen toasts were given, the last by Samuel A. Townes, Marion attorney and town historian. Townes raised his glass and gallantly said:

> "*I presume our honored guest will not deny, in spite of all his San Jacinto and other victories, that he has been compelled to trail his banner and bow a suppliant knee at the foot of our fair townswoman. I give you, therefore, gentlemen, the health, if not a better man than General Houston, that of one whom he himself will admit to be his 'better half,' the Conqueror of the Conqueror – Mrs. Margaret L. Houston.*"

When Margaret bid adieu to Perry County, she carried trunks packed with linens, silver and clothing, her parlor piano dismantled and crated for shipment, and four slaves she inherited when her father died.

Woodland in Huntsville

Houston and Margaret returned to Texas and to everyone's surprise,

---

Margaret had two adult brothers—Henry Clinton Lea and Martin Lea—at the wedding. [John Trotwood Moore, *Tennessee—The Volunteer State. v. I, p. 401*]

[10] Mrs. James L. Goree was the mother of Lieutenant Robert Thomas Goree of the Perry Volunteers.

Houston became the "*model of propriety*," eventually joined the Baptist Church and devoted himself to Margaret's happiness. He built four homes for Margaret during their marriage and owned them all at one time: Raven Hill Plantation located thirteen miles northeast of Huntsville, a seaside home at Cedar Point on Galveston Bay, a home in Huntsville he called Woodland and another at Independence, Texas near Brenham. Margaret did not like the isolation of Raven Hill, so Houston built her a home in Huntsville. She suffered from asthma and a home was built in Independence because it was thought that the higher altitude would benefit her condition.

Nancy Lea left Perry County and moved to Texas, settling in Independence. When William Bledsoe died, Antoinette married Charles Power, who had a fortune he acquired from diamond mines in Brazil, and also moved to Independence. Margaret bore Houston eight children, the oldest she named Sam and the youngest Temple, after her father. According to Marquis James, *"Margaret was as beautiful as any woman in Texas. She was more intelligent and had been much more carefully educated than the average woman there or elsewhere."*

During her marriage to Sam, Margaret served as first lady of the Republic of Texas and of the State of Texas while her husband was President and the Governor of the State. She was also the first to live in the Texas Governor's Mansion. Sam was one of the state's first two United States Senators during their marriage. Houston died in 1863 of pneumonia at his home in Huntsville, Texas. Barnard Bee had predicted incorrectly. The Houstons were married twenty-three years and were separated only by death. Margaret Lea died of yellow fever at Independence on December 3, 1867, during an epidemic in south Texas.

Republic of Texas Capitol

The union of Houston and Lea was a source of great satisfaction for many Perry County people who took pride that one of their own united with so important a Texas dignitary and national celebrity. Six years after Margaret Lea's marriage to Houston, when war came and Texas needed men to defend her, the need to protect Texas from Mexico went unquestioned among Houston admirers, Margaret's kinfolks and the family's friends in Perry County, Alabama.

War with Mexico

*"Our reliance for protection and defense of
the land must be mainly on our citizen soldiers, who will be ready, as they ever have
been in the times past, to rush with alacrity,
at the call of their country, to her defense."*
James K. Polk, President of the United States

Most Perry countians favored admitting Texas as a state in the Union. Anti-slave opposition in the North prohibited it with the abolitionists in the forefront of the opposition.
William Lloyd Garrison, founder of the American Anti-Slavery Society, put his case against annexation succinctly. *"All who would sympathize with that pseudo-Republic hate liberty, and
would dethrone God."* Northern Senators simply ignored Texas because, as they saw it, the
whole issue was created by the South to gain additional seats in the Senate. With annexation to
the United States in 1837 unlikely, and perhaps impossible for the moment, Republic of Texas
President Sam Houston withdrew Texas' petition for statehood and turned to diplomacy. He
sent Dr. Ashbel Smith as an emissary to England to sound out a possible alliance with Great
Britain and to court the French for support of Texas. Texas' flirtation with England was part of
a well thought out strategy on the part of the Texas President. England saw important eco-
nomic advantages to an independent Texas, including a secure source of cotton for English tex-
tile mills and a market for English goods. With the prospect of a Texas under the influence of
Great Britain looming, U. S. President John Tyler quietly became an advocate of Texas annexation.

The one subject that restrained England from making a move in Texas was the issue of slavery.
Texas law permitted slavery, and England had a consistent anti-slavery policy. Emancipation of
Texas slaves was England's price for recognizing Texas, and English abolitionists hoped to persuade Texas to free its slaves. However, other European powers did not withhold diplomatic
recognition. France acknowledged Texas in 1839. Belgium and Holland followed in 1840.
The United States had made this recognition easy by rebuffing Houston's overtures for annexation. England changed her mind in June 1842 and recognized the Republic of Texas. This action had the effect of renewing United States interest in Texas, and in 1843 President John Tyler
intimated that he would be happy to reopen the question of annexation. Aging Andrew Jackson, who hated England, began to scheme to keep Texas out of England's sphere of influence
and urged annexation.

Houston was the picture of public coolness when dealing with the United States. He set forth
the view that *"Texas . . . could exist without the U States, but the U States can not, without
great hazard . . . exist without Texas."* Many in the United States
agreed with Houston, and on April 12, 1844, President Tyler laid a
treaty of annexation before the Senate. Houston was firm in his deter-
mination to secure a future for Texas and stated, *"If the Treaty is not
ratified, I will require, all future negotiations to be transferred to
Texas."* The Senate did not ratify the treaty. Texas
having been rejected a second time, Houston
announced that Texas *"must work out her own
political salvation."* In 1844, the Democratic Party
nominated James Polk for President of the United States and Houston
finished his final term as President of the Republic, replaced by Anson
Jones. In the United States, Texas was a central issue in the Democratic
Party's campaign supporting annexation, and Polk narrowly won the election. Houston retired
to his home in Huntsville, Texas and faded from the scene.

James K. Polk
of Tennessee

The election of Polk stirred England and France to confer over the fate of Texas. England was
ready to go to war to make Texas a
British protectorate and blunt the
westward expansion of the U. S. In the
United States, the fate of Texas was
critical as Sam Houston had predicted,
and the slavery issue became less vital
than keeping Texas out of foreign control. Northern opposition began to di-
minish and time became precious.
England was on the prowl for Texas
and speed was important if her designs
on Texas were to be thwarted. Another
resolution for annexation was abruptly
laid before Congress; President John
Tyler, President-elect Polk and former
President Andrew Jackson pressured
Congress to act and the pressure was too
much for the opponents of annexation.
The resolution was adopted and signed by

General Zachary Taylor's Army of Occupation
camped on the sandy plain at Corpus Christi, Texas.

Tyler on March 1, 1845, three days before Polk took office.[11] Texas was in the Union at last
with only formalities and details to be worked out for the final consummation.[12] Andrew Jackson wrote to Sam Houston from the Hermitage in Tennessee, "*I now behold the great American
eagle, with her stars and stripes hovering over the lone star of Texas . . . and proclaiming to
Mexico and all foreign governments, 'You must not attempt to tread upon Texas.'*" England
considered going to war over Texas but relented in the end. The British menace, as Houston
expected, had won admission to the Union for Texas and now its security was the responsibility
of the United States.

James Polk took office on March 5, 1845. On March 6, Mexico lodged a formal protest of the
annexation of Texas and severed diplomatic relations with the
United States, notifying the world that she was going to fight
and began preparing armies to take the field. Mexican Minister
General Juan N. Amonte in Washington, D. C. requested his
passports and went home. Several months later, the United
States representative in Mexico City was forced to leave Mexico
and return home. José Joaquín de Herrera, acting President of
the Republic of Mexico, issued a proclamation stating that the
United States has by decree incorporated the territory of Texas
endangering the peace of the world and violating the sover-
eignty of nations and the annexation attacks the rights of Mexico which rights Mexico will defend. A declaration followed
stating in part, "*the government will call to arms all the forces
of the army . . . under the name
'Defenders of the Independence
and of the Laws.'*" The rupture in relations made war more

General Zachary Taylor

---

[11] "*Resolved by the Senate and House of Representatives of the United States of America in Congress Assembled, That Congress doth consent that the Territory properly included within, and rightfully belonging to, the Republic of Texas, may be elected into a new state, to be called the State of Texas, with a republican form of government, to be adopted by the people of said Republic, by deputies in convention
assembled, with consent of the existing government, in order that the same may be admitted as one of
the States of this Union.*" [Joint Resolution of Congress on the question of Texas statehood, Approved
March 1, 1845]

[12] Congress formally accepted Texas into the Union on December 29, 1845.

certain because that action made adjustment of the border of Texas nearly impossible under the circumstances.

Commander-in-chief Polk's only answer was to order 1,500 regular American troops under Brigadier General Zachary Taylor[13] from Fort Jesup in western Louisiana to Corpus Christi, Texas, where they arrived in October 1845. All winter Taylor paced in the sand at Corpus Christi drilling, breaking horses and holding parades. He was reinforced by 2,400 new troops raising the size of the U. S. Army there to 3,900. During this period, the *Picayune*, a New Orleans newspaper, worried about Mexican troops on the Rio Grande and stated, *"It behooves our Government at once to march an efficient force to the frontier of Texas . . . not a single Mexican should set foot on this side of the Rio Grande."* In January 1846, Taylor was ordered to the Rio Grande 200 miles away, but the movement did not begin until March 8, 1846.[14]

Once General Taylor reached the boiling brown waters of the Rio Grande, he began building Fort Texas and mounting siege guns across the river from Matamoros, whereupon Mexican General Pedro de Ampudia[15] notified Taylor to abandon the fort and to withdraw beyond the Nueces River within twenty-four hours. Taylor refused and Ampudia notified him that *"he considered hostilities commenced and should prosecute them."* General Taylor responded to Ampudia on April 25 that he hoped *". . . friendly relations might be maintained on the frontier, until a final settlement of the question of boundary . . . But if such is not to be the case—if hostilities are to ensue—the responsibility must rest with them who actually commence them."* Mexican lancers crossed the river where they killed and brutally mutilated the body of Colonel Truman Cross, Taylor's Assistant Acting Quartermaster General, when he wandered too far from the American camp. Lieutenant Theodoric H. Porter took a detachment out to find Colonel Cross and was ambushed and Porter killed along with one of his troopers.

Battle of Resaca de la Palma
May 9, 1846

The Mexican Army was larger than the U. S. forces, and Mexican troops were confident in their ability to defend Mexico. At the time, the United States Army numbered about 6,600 men in total and sixty per cent of that number was already in Texas with Taylor. Sixteen hundred Mexicans under the command of General Anastasio Torrejón crossed the river and ambushed Captain Seth B. Thornton and fifty-two dragoons on April 25, 1846, killing fourteen and taking the rest prisoner.[16] Two of these dragoons died later from their wounds. American troops had been attacked in force north of the Rio Grande, and this was the beginning of war with Mexico. Mexican forces had drawn first blood and acquitted themselves well attacking with overwhelming odds in their favor. The Mexican commander's next move was to send 4,000

---

[13] Zachary Taylor entered the army as a Lieutenant in the 7th U. S. Infantry on May 3, 1808, served on the frontier, fought in the Seminole War in Florida, was a Colonel of the 6th U. S. Infantry when Congress brevetted him a Brigadier General and placed him in charge of the Army of Occupation in Texas. Taylor did not know much about the art of war. He was careless and neglected intelligence. He too often misunderstood the enemy's action and estimated their strength incorrectly. However, he possessed physical and moral courage, which is an essential quality for generals.

[14] The Army of Occupation consisted of five regiments of infantry, one regiment of dragoons (cavalry) and sixteen companies of artillery.

[15] Pedro de Ampudia was a forty-one year old Cuban who joined the Mexican Revolution in 1821 to fight the Spanish and was made a general in the Army of Mexico. He was made Governor of Nuevo León in 1854 and died in 1868.

[16] Captain Seth B. Thornton was later killed near Churubusco, Mexico while escorting Army engineers studying the defenses there.

men north of the river to cut Taylor's communication with Point Isabel from which the little American army was supplied. Sensing this, Taylor left a detachment at Fort Texas and on May 1 raced the twenty miles to Point Isabel fearing an attack on his vulnerable supply depot. Taylor arrived safely on May 3 and loaded three hundred wagons with supplies and ammunition. On May 7, the American army began the return journey to Fort Texas.

While Taylor was involved in the trip to and from Point Isabel, Fort Texas was besieged by Mexican forces in Matamoros but was successfully defended. The main force of the American army returned on Saturday, May 9. However, during the siege, Major Jacob Brown, in charge of the fort's defense, was killed and the fort was renamed Fort Brown in his honor. The site of the fort later became the city of Brownsville. On the return trip from the coast, in two brisk battles at Palo Alto and Resaca de la Palma, American forces drove the Mexicans back across the Rio Grande, though heavily outnumbered two to one by the enemy. The Americans lost four killed and forty-two wounded men at Palo Alto and thirty-four killed and eighty-nine wounded at Resaca de la Palma.[17] Mexican losses were much higher.[18]

When the news of the attacks on Taylor's army reached New Orleans, the *Picayune* newspaper screamed, "*The war has begun in earnest*" and ran ten-point headlines announcing: "*The Enemy is upon our soil!! Louisiana Volunteers, the Hour has arrived!!*" Other New Orleans newspapers carried headlines such as "*War! War!*" On May 18, 1846, the news of events on the Rio Grande reached Mobile and the *Mobile Daily Advertiser* ran an extra addition with a headline that read: "*From the seat of war—Glorious News!—Triumph of the American Arms!—Gen. Taylor again*

Battle of Palo Alto, Texas

victorious!—Rout of the Mexican army!!" The *Daily Advertiser* printed correspondence from reporters on the scene. These and other stories were repeated across the United States appealing to national pride at the success of American arms when outnumbered far from home. From indications the Mexicans were eager to fight the hated "*Yanquis.*" The Mexican Army was five times larger than that of the United States and one Mexican officer boasted that his horsemen could break the American formations with a lasso. Many Mexicans did not believe the Americans would stand and fight, offering as evidence President Polk's repeated attempts to buy peace. Trouble was brewing between England and the United States over Oregon, and Mexicans were convinced that war would erupt between those countries overwhelming the United States whose total standing army, in size and training, ranked far below the army of either Mexico or England. The English press encouraged the Mexicans. The *Britannia* stated that America as "*an aggressive power is one of the weakest in the world . . . fit for nothing but to fight Indians*" and the London *Times* sarcastically concluded that the conquest of Mexico "*by a state which is without an army*" would be "*a novelty in the history of nations.*"

---

[17] American losses at Resaca de la Palma, Texas demonstrate the international character of the American army with Taylor. Of those killed, seventeen, or half, were born in England, Germany, Ireland, Scotland, and Canada. Among the wounded, thirty-four, or nearly forty per cent were foreign born representing the same countries as among the killed plus Spain, Belgium and France. Most of the killed and wounded were Irish.

[18] Mexican losses at Palo Alto were about 320 killed and 380 wounded, mostly from American artillery fire. At Resaca de la Palma, Mexican losses were reported at 547.

Taylor's dispatch to President Polk about Thornton's capture reached him on May 9. The President addressed the American Congress on May 11, 1846. In the speech, he recounted twenty years of accumulated grievances against Mexico, and all of the American attempts to promote peace with their neighbor to the south, including the Mexican government's rejection "*upon the most frivolous pretexts*" of its Minister John Slidell who went to Mexico with full powers to resolve differences between the two countries.[19] Polk concluded that attempts at peace were a failure and that:

> "*The cup of forbearance had been exhausted even before the recent information from the frontier . . . But now, after reiterated menaces, Mexico has passed the boundary of the United States, has invaded our territory and shed American blood upon American soil. As war exists, and, not withstanding all our efforts to avoid it, exists by the act of Mexico herself, we are called upon by every consideration of duty and patriotism to vindicate with decision the honor, the rights, and the interests of our country.*"

Polk recommended to Congress that he be given authority to "*call into the public service a large body of volunteers*" because this is "*more efficient than any other description of citizen soldiers.*" Congress reacted and war between the United States and Mexico became official on May 13. American troops occupied Burita, Mexico on May 17 and Matamoros the next day.[20] However, Taylor had not anticipated his needs and was without sufficient men, tents, medical supplies, mules, wagons, or steamboats small enough for service on the perilous Rio Grande; he could move the army neither up the river or inland. The Mexico campaign was at a standstill until these matters could be remedied by the unprepared War Department, so Taylor and his army sat at Matamoros until July 1846. President Polk took the first step toward remedying the problem by authorizing a call for 50,000 volunteers, and Americans rushed forward to sign up.[21] Back at Raven Hill Plantation in Texas, Margaret Lea Houston sewed together a flag for Wood's Texas Cavalry that they later followed up the heights in the Battle of Monterrey.

Alabama rushed ahead of the Federal government and began preparations before Congress officially declared war. Alabamians were impressed that General Zachary Taylor's army was in imminent peril and in need of immediate reinforcements to avoid being overwhelmed by the larger Mexican army. An article appearing in the *Mobile Daily Advertiser* emphasized the tone of these early days of the conflict. " *. . . our city was startled by the intelligence that hostilities had commenced on the Rio Grande. Point Isabel was represented to be in the most imminent peril, and the whole "Army of Occupation," in great danger . . .*"

A Mobile diarist recorded on May 6, 1846, seven days before the declaration of war, that

> "*There was much stir and excitement in our streets yesterday, occasioned by an understanding that a requisition had been made on the Governor of this State for troops to repair to the scene of the War. There is a general*

---

[19] John Slidell of Louisiana was authorized to assume Mexico's debt of $4,500,000 owed to Americans if Mexico would recognize the Rio Grande River as the Texas border. The Mexicans refused to talk to Slidell and ordered him to leave the country.

[20] The occupation of Burita and Matamoros was the first time a U. S. Army had occupied foreign territory since 1818 when General Andrew Jackson invaded Spanish Florida. Captain Franklin Smith described Burita as "*a miserable little village of some dozen huts but lies high and fortified by an embankment.*"

[21] Alabama Governor Joshua Lanier Martin jumped the starting gun and issued a call for volunteers on May 10, 1846, three days before the President called for volunteers and assigned a quota to Alabama as required by law. The first request for troops was made to the Governors of Alabama, Arkansas, Georgia, Illinois, Indiana, Kentucky, Mississippi, Missouri, Ohio, Tennessee and Texas. As the war worn on, calls for troops were extended to other states.

heating up for Volunteers and we understand quite a number enrolled their names . . . "

General James W. Lang, caught up in the excitement of the hour, issued a handbill at Mobile before rushing off to Tuscaloosa to see the governor. The handbill was an alarmist call to arms for the men of Alabama and read in part:

TO ARMS! TO ARMS! TO ARMS!

TO THE GALLANT YOUNG MEN OF ALABAMA

Hostilities have actually commenced on the Mexican frontier. Sixty-three of our men have been butchered or taken prisoners. Our army under Gen. Taylor is surrounded by an enemy, reported to be 8 to 10,000 men. His communications have been cut off with Point Isabel, the depot of his provisions, and he has in his camp at Matamoros, rations for only 10 to 15 days, which may perhaps be made to last 20 or 30 days.

I am the bearer of a call to arms from Major Gen. Gaines upon the Governor of Alabama for Volunteers, to be raised and marched immediately to the seat of war, which are to rendezvous at Mobile, there to be equipped and mustered into service.

James W. Lang
Adjutant and Inspector Gen'l of the State of Alabama

Mobile, May 7, 1846

In Tuscaloosa, Joshua L. Martin,[22] Governor and Commander-in-Chief of the Army of Alabama, issued a proclamation on May 10 reading, in part, that he,

"has ascertained that the Army of Occupation on the Rio Grande is in perilous condition . . . therefore, it is earnestly recommended to the citizen soldiers of this State at once to organize themselves into volunteer companies . . . and report themselves as ready . . . to engage in the defense of the country."

These events, and the belief that Americans were in jeopardy on the Rio Grande, resulted in unrestrained passion that became a tide sweeping events along in Alabama that were hard for the governor to control. Volunteer companies waited on no orders or authority but organized at their own expense and proceeded to Mobile, the gathering point for volunteers.

A forty-one year-old farmer and former Indian fighter named William G. Coleman living in Perry County near Perryville heard these calls to arms and responded to events along the Rio Grande. An imperiled United States Army stirred his soul and appealed to his sense of patriotism and love of country. He sprang to action to transform his family, friends and neighbors into volunteer soldiers for service in Mexico.

---

[22] Joshua Martin was born in 1799 in Blount County, Tennessee and moved to Alabama in 1819 settling at Athens, Alabama in Limestone County. He was elected Governor of Alabama in 1845 as the representative of the Democratic Party. Because of the Mexican War, Governor Martin devoted most of his efforts in the office to mustering troops for the war effort and moving the Capitol of the state from Tuscaloosa to Montgomery. His term ended in 1847, and he died in 1856.

Perry Volunteers

*"One regiment of volunteers infan-
try and Riflemen to serve for the
term of twelve months."*
President James K. Polk

Shortly after the declaration of war, William Goforth Coleman and Andrew Barry Moore,[23] a future governor of Alabama, sent out a call across Perry County for volunteers to serve in Mexico and enlisted citizens at Perryville. Perryville was a small community located in the eastern part of the county between the Cahaba River and Oakmulgee Creek, which divides Perry and Dallas counties. It was a modest commercial community that owed its existence as a service center to the farmers living near the village. The principal industry was a gristmill owned and operated by Joel W. England, which provided an essential service to farmers and others by converting corn into meal and wheat into flour. England employed seven or eight men with mechanical skills, five of whom joined the Perry Volunteers[24] leaving England short of experienced workers. The Bernstein brothers, Nathan and Laymond, immigrant German Jews, operated one of two mercantile stores located in Perryville. William F. Ford, a native Alabamian, operated the other store that was about three times the size of the one owned by the Bernsteins. Dr. James Reynolds was the local physician, and Reverend Lewis P. Ramsey served as the neighborhood preacher. Being a farm service community, there was a constant need for blacksmiths and James O. Proctor and Joshua Kelly maintained a shop in Perryville, while Daniel Allen was the village brick mason. In the next decade, Perryville grew into a larger but still modest commercial center as the farmers of the area prospered by growing cotton. In 1860, the village included three stores, a school, a slave trader, four physicians, a schoolteacher, a shoemaker, and three blacksmith shops. It was here at Perryville that

Joshua L. Martin
Governor of Alabama
ADHA

William Coleman and Andrew B. Moore set up a recruiting station, probably at the Ford store, where appeals were made principally to the young men of the area to step forward and join up for service in Mexico. The response was encouraging and in the short span of a few days the enrollment sheets had nearly enough men signed up to form a company of volunteers. The spirit for volunteering was highest around Perryville, which accounted for over thirty per cent of the company, and a good number of men from the south around Oak Grove and Radfordville signed up. Only a few volunteers came from west of the Cahaba River. On May 23, 1846, Andrew B. Moore sent a notice to Alabama Governor Joshua Martin telling him that the Perry County volunteers were organized and ready to place itself under the control and instructions of the governor.

The recruiting was considered an urgent matter because of the belief that the American army was in a critical position on the Rio Grande and likely to be cut to pieces unless rescued. This belief, as well as the belief that national honor was at risk, and patriotic pride in the success in the United States Army in the two victorious battles fought in Texas in the previous month, urged on the recruiting. Recruiting thus fueled caused men in Perry County to come forth rapidly and within less than ten days there were sufficient men to constitute a company of volunteers. These young men lived in a society alive with militia companies and membership carried with it respect and prestige. Little could equal the honor and esteem of carrying the country's

[23] Andrew Barry Moore was born on March 7, 1807, in Spartanburg District, South Carolina. He married Mary Ann Goree the daughter of James L. Goree. He was elected Governor of Alabama in 1857.
[24] One source lists the company's name as the Independent Rangers and another as the Perry Rangers. The primary source of the writer used the name Perry Volunteers.

flag on the field of battle. The Volunteers had ninety-eight enlistments by Monday, May 25, 1846, and held an election to select officers for the company according to Alabama law.[25] It was accepted practice that volunteers, as freeborn citizen-soldiers, should determine who would lead them in time of war. These men assumed that they knew who among their neighbors would make the most efficient leaders. John D. Phelan, Richard Booker Walthall and John P. Graham collected, counted and certified the votes.[26] A complete record of the election outcome is not available and some mystery exists about the election results. The notice sent to Governor Martin on May 23 (two days before the election) is signed by Andrew B. Moore as "Captain" of the "*Perry Legion*" and a list of volunteer companies appearing in a newspaper clipping (date and newspaper are unknown) again identifies Moore as Captain of the Perry Legion. Was Andrew Moore elected captain of the Perry Volunteers and later decided not to serve, or was he acting as a captain in the militia helping the company organize itself? The answer is not known, but it is probable that Moore was acting in the capacity of a militia officer giving official status to the organization of this company of volunteers. What is known is that when the Volunteers assembled at Perryville to move to Mobile, William G. Coleman was commander of the Company; the men listed below served as officers of the unit at various times during the Mexican War.

Officers of the Perry Volunteers[27]

William Goforth Coleman	Captain
[28]Robert Thomas Goree	First Lieutenant
James H. Pitts	First Lieutenant
William Marshall Ford	Second Lieutenant
[29]John B. Fuller	Third Lieutenant
[30]Seaborn Aycock	First Sergeant
Robert M. Holmes	First Sergeant
John G. Heard	Second Sergeant
Robert M. Holmes	Third Sergeant
[31]Young L. Cardin	Third Sergeant
[32]Lewis A. Miree	Fourth Sergeant
[33]John W. Barron	Fourth Sergeant

---

[25] The Act of Congress of May 13, 1846, stated that volunteer "*officers shall be appointed, in the manner prescribed by law in the several States and Territories to which such Companies, Battalions, Squadrons, and Regiments shall belong.*" In Alabama, the election of field officers permitted the men in the company to elect its own officers and those of the regiment to which the company belonged.

[26] The men who certified the election were prominent and respected Perry County officials. Richard Booker Walthall was a state senator and John P. Graham and John D. Phelan were lawyers and judges.

[27] Each volunteer company normally consisted of a captain, two lieutenants, five sergeants and eight corporals. The record of the Perry Volunteers does not show a full complement of non-commissioned officers, having only four sergeants and four corporals at any one time. The sergeants and corporals were responsible for the supervision of privates and needed to know the fundamentals of drill and army regulations.

[28] Robert T. Goree was discharged from Company C on July 15, 1846, ten days after arriving in Texas and was replaced by James H. Pitts as first lieutenant.

[29] John B. Fuller was elected and brevetted a Third Lieutenant on August 1, 1846.

[30] Seaborn Aycock was discharged from the army on February 26, 1847, at Tampico. As First Sergeant, Aycock was responsible for keeping the company's records, conducting roll call and assigning men to details. He was replaced by Robert M. Holmes as First Sergeant on March 1, 1847.

[31] Young L. Cardin replaced Robert M. Holmes as Third Sergeant on March 1, 1847, when Holmes was promoted to First Sergeant, the rank having been vacated by Seaborn Aycock.

[32] Lewis A. Miree was discharged on August 19, 1846, at Camp Alabama and apparently died in New Orleans before he reached home.

[33] John W. Barron was promoted to Fourth Sergeant on August 19, 1846, at Camp Alabama, Texas. He was himself replaced on April 17, 1847, when he was hospitalized at Vera Cruz.

[34]John Pickney Everett	Fourth Sergeant
John W. Barron	First Corporal
John Alfred Fuller	Second Corporal
[35]Samuel P. B. Fuller	Second Corporal
John Pinckney Everett	Third Corporal
Thomas Richard Heard	Fourth Corporal
[36]Wiley W. Fowler	Fourth Corporal
[37]Joseph G. Dennis	Fourth Corporal
James W. Bennett	Fifer
John C. Rogers	Drummer

The volunteers made a good selection for the rank of Captain of their company. Coleman was born in Edgefield District, South Carolina on July 10, 1805, and was the descendant of German immigrants. Physically, he was an attractive man of average height, standing five feet eight inches tall with a dark complexion, gray eyes and black hair. He was educated and intelligent and wrote articles for *Nicholson Encyclopedia* and the South Carolina secular press. Politically, he was a member of the Democratic Party, a follower of John C. Calhoun, a strong advocate of states' rights and a supporter of nullification of Federal laws with which individual states did not agree. Coleman was an ardent, bold and defiant defender of his views. In later years, he would apply the same enthusiasm to secession of Southern states from the Union. In 1846, he had recently married for a second time, was the father of four children and was a warrior from a warrior family.

Coleman's great great and great grandfathers, Jacob and Henry Coleman, immigrated from Switzerland in the 1740s, firmly establishing the family in South Carolina by acquiring tracts of land located between the Saluda and Broad Rivers.[38] Henry was born about 1720 in Switzerland and died in South Carolina about 1767. He married Elizabeth Geiger who died on November 5, 1802, and is buried in the Lutheran Cemetery in Charleston.[39] After Henry's death, Elizabeth married John Horlbeck in 1769. William Coleman's ancestors were martial men and established a family tradition of military service in America that William continued. Henry Coleman held the ranks of captain and major in the Carolina militia. He served in the Cherokee War under Colonel John Chevillette and furnished supplies to the militia during that war. He also engaged in benevolent enterprises and furnished supplies to French Acadians that had been forced from their lands in Nova Scotia in 1755 by the British and forcibly resettled in South Carolina under destitute circumstances.[40] William's grandfather, Casper Coleman,[41] was a patriot soldier during the Revolutionary War. William's father, Benjamin, served during the War of 1812 as a corporal in the company of Captain Jacob Strobel's South Carolina state mili-

---

[34] John P. Everett was promoted to Fourth Sergeant on April 17, 1847, at Vera Cruz.

[35] Samuel P. B. Fuller was promoted to Second Corporal on April 19, 1847, on the road to Jalapa, Mexico.

[36] Wiley W. Fowler was promoted to Fourth Corporal on August 20, 1846, at Camp Alabama, Texas.

[37] Joseph G. Dennis was promoted to Fourth Corporal on March 15, 1847, at Vera Cruz, Mexico.

[38] Coleman's descendants report, and documents show, that Jacob and Henry Coleman came to this country as Gallman and the family name was changed to Coleman. Gallman pronounced in German sounded like Coleman and, like many other European names, was anglicized. Documents related to this family contain the name Gallman as late as 1834 and Coleman as early as 1749. Henry Coleman's last will and testament mentions children that included John Conrad, Henry, Harmon, Casper and Elizabeth. Henry Coleman's parents were Jacob Gallman and Verena Stahell.

[39] Elizabeth Geiger's parents were Herman Geiger and Elizabeth Habluzel.

[40] The British also removed some French Acadians to Louisiana where they established homes in the swamps and prairies of that state and became commonly and widely known as "*Cajuns.*" In later years, some of the South Carolina French Acadians resettled themselves in Louisiana.

[41] Casper Coleman was born about 1749 in Switzerland and died on August 9, 1819, in Edgefield District, South Carolina. His wife was Jemima Sellers who died in November 1827. Their children included Benjamin, Harmon, John, Daniel, Conrad and Elizabeth Coleman. Elizabeth Coleman married Casper Foust.

tia and a sergeant in Captain Samuel Bigham's company of state troops as a substitute for Harvill Casey. At the age of thirty-two, William enlisted in a militia company under the command of Captain Jarnigham and saw service in the Creek War of 1837. William's son, Thomas Bacon Coleman, continued the Coleman family military tradition when he joined Company H of the Second Louisiana Volunteer Infantry Regiment on June 2, 1861, and served with honor in the Confederate Army until the end of the War for Southern Independence.

William Coleman married Frances A. Johnson, the daughter of William S. Johnson of Virginia and Edgefield District, South Carolina, and Anna H. Willis. Frances Johnson was born on July 9, 1813, in Barnwell District, South Carolina, and died near Trenton, South Carolina, on September 9, 1840. Frances' death left William alone and in charge of their four young children and her death was a terrible burden and source of grief for Coleman. Along with the children, William went to live in the home of his parents, Benjamin Coleman and Sarah Ryan,[42] and managed a store for his aging parents. William's oldest son, Benjamin Ryan,[43] ran away from home at a young age, because he could not adjust to Sarah Ryan's regimen in her home. The escapee made his way to Perry County, Alabama where his aunt Elizabeth S. Coleman lived with her husband Middleton Moseley. Benjamin ended up in the care of Thomas Anderson Heard who migrated to Perry County from Wilkes County, Georgia. Heard wrote to Coleman in South Carolina to tell him that Benjamin was at the Heard home, and William traveled to Perry County to retrieve his precocious juvenile son.

At the Heard home, William met Thomas Heard's attractive young daughter Mary Jane and the two developed a fascination with each other even though she was seventeen years younger than Coleman. William and Ben returned to Edgefield District and William began a two-year correspondence with Mary Jane that in time led him to propose marriage. Jane professed love for him, but there were familial problems in the way. Her parents objected to the union, doubtless due to the age difference and a natural inclination of parents to disapprove of any suitor for a treasured daughter; others in the family and friends attempted to persuade her against the marriage attacking the character of Coleman with a busybody's devotion to causing turmoil. To pursue his case, William traveled to Alabama establishing himself in his sister's household from which he attempted to win Jane's hand over the opposition of those allied against him. After a month of anguish, William was tormented as only a frustrated lover can be, and desperate to end his anxiety, he devised a course of action. On Saturday evening, February 3, 1844, after his sister's family had retired to bed for the night, Coleman sat down and wrote Jane a letter in which he set forth his arguments against his critics and the objections of her parents. He ended it saying:

> "My love has been spoken, I must bid you adieu,
> Yet heaven never smiled on affection more true,
> No Heart more devoted earth's compass within,
> Than the Heart of your lover, W. G. Coleman"

The force of his reasoning and expressions of love in this letter persuaded Jane to make her future with Coleman over all objections; she brushed aside the advice of her family, the sniping of William's critics and the objections of her parents, agreeing to marry Coleman. On March 10,

---

[42] Benjamin Coleman was born about 1780 in and died on October 5, 1855. Sarah Ryan was born in 1776, married Benjamin about 1803 and died on June 26, 1860. Benjamin and Sarah were born and lived out their lives in Edgefield District, South Carolina. At the time of their marriage, Sarah was the widow of Colonel George Moore. The children of Sarah Ryan and Colonel Moore were Mary Elder Moore who was born in 1801 and Elizabeth Berryman Moore, born 1803, who married Benjamin Tillman. Her children with Benjamin Coleman were William Goforth, Elizabeth S., who married Middleton Moseley, Susan H., who married Stanmore Butler Ryan, Lucretia Burr, who married Abner Bushnell, Edney F., who married Monroe Augustine Ransom and America F. Coleman, who married John Elder, Francis Ryan and Sidney S. Boyce. Middleton Moseley was living in Perry County, Alabama in 1840.
[43] Benjamin Ryan Coleman was born on May 12, 1832, in Edgefield District, South Carolina.

1844, thirty-five days after Coleman composed his desperate letter, they were married.[44] Jane's family adjusted to the marriage and embraced Coleman into the Heard family. Coleman's union with Jane brought him into the respected Heard family who cast considerable influence in the community, and he profited in the eyes of his acquaintances by his acceptance and association with a prosperous and socially high-ranking neighborhood family. Once married, Coleman turned to farming and lived in Perry County only two years before he recruited the Perry Volunteers, but his popularity and ability as a decisive leader was well established with the people in the community by that time. Coleman's energy in recruiting and organizing the company, and his association with a prominent family, made his election as Captain of the Perry Volunteers almost a foregone conclusion.

What sort of man was elected to lead the Perry Volunteers in the war with Mexico? The writings and life of William G. Coleman reveal something of the nature of the man and his character. He was an intensely loyal family man who cherished his wife and children and honored his parents. He grieved over the death of Frances Johnson, but when he came to love Mary Jane, he transferred his affections just as deeply to her as he had felt for Frances. Throughout the war, he spoke of her only with warmth and devotion for *"my dear Jane"* and wanted most of all to return to her, lamenting after a separation of ten months, *"My Dear Wife, for her my heart will break, O, MY God!"* He gloried in the accomplishments of his children and rejoiced when his son Benjamin joined the Baptist Church in Alabama. The welfare and health of his parents was a matter of constant concern for Coleman, and he grew progressively anxious in Mexico when word from them did not arrive regularly.

Coleman cared genuinely for his friends and was troubled when he did not meet with their approval. He made frequent references in his writings to perceived slights and difficulties from his friend James F. Bailey, and lamented when his duties as commander of the Perry Volunteers interfered with friendships, when he yearned for their approval. So distasteful was the loss of his friends' approval that he considered abandoning his commission more than once. Befriended by his regimental commander, Coleman repaid that friendship with loyal support against acrimonious attacks from others in the regiment. Coleman was apparently blessed with courage and did not flinch or shirk when he was not in the majority opinion among the officers of his regiment, as happened on more than one occasion. He was ambitious to excel and assumed leadership to collect any honors and praise that grew from being in command. He was also a man of honor. After six months in military service, he was plagued with a desire to abandon the war and rush home to his wife and family, but he could not do it because it could not be accomplished *"in a proper manner."* William G. Coleman was a man of his times and, like men of any time, was possessed of many noble virtues and a genuine humanity.

The men who assembled into the military unit at Perryville were a diverse group with a variety of occupations, ages and degrees of education. They were almost universally the products of a rural Protestant culture that was anti-Catholic, the prevalent church in Mexico. Several examples will illustrate the differences in the Company. Charles Green Jackson was four weeks short of his twentieth birthday when he enlisted, and he will serve as a representative of the younger people in the company. His grandfathers, Green B. Jackson and Charles Crow, were born in South Carolina and migrated to Alabama in early 1819 while Alabama was still a Territory. Both were successful farmers, owning considerable land and slaves, prospering as cotton farmers. Crow was also a pioneer Baptist minister and a leader of the church in Alabama having helped organize the Alabama Baptist Convention, serving as its first president and serving faithfully for twenty years as the Moderator of the Cahawba Baptist Association. Charles Green's father was Abraham W. Jackson also a prosperous farmer, a Baptist minister and a leader of the Alabama church.

---

[44] A copy of the original letter is in the possession of the author, courtesy of Ben E. Coleman. A transcription appears in Appendix E. The Coleman marriage ceremony was performed by Reverend John Dennis who was ordained by the congregation at Ocmulgee Baptist Church in Perry County. Mary Jane Heard was born on January 22, 1822, in Wilkes County, Georgia.

Charles Jackson was born in 1826 in Perry County and lived exclusively in the county up to the time of his enlistment in the Volunteers. He was educated in the common schools of the area and was a member of his grandfather Crow's church at Ocmulgee where he made a profession of faith in Jesus Christ five years before the war at the age of fifteen. Four months after returning from Mexico, he moved to DeSoto Parish, Louisiana where he lived out his life, dying at Grand Cane in 1911. During the War for Southern Independence, Jackson served under Confederate General Richard Taylor, the son of General Zachary Taylor, giving Charles the unique circumstance of serving in armies commanded by father and son.

James Francis Bailey was one of the older volunteers enlisting at the age of thirty-five. He was the son of John Guinn Bailey from Georgia, who moved to Perry County about 1818 when James was a lad of seven years, and was reared in the eastern part of the county near Perryville. His father was a prosperous farmer and prominent citizen of the county. James did not follow his father's vocation. Instead, he graduated from the University of Alabama in Tuscaloosa in 1834 and the University of Virginia in 1837 with a law degree. He opened a law office in the county the year he graduated and became an associate of leading Perry County attorney John N. Walthall. Although thirty-five years old when he joined the Volunteers, he was unmarried. Bailey's political views were those of a Southern states' righter Democrat and slave owner, views he staunchly defended with no reservation. In addition to being university educated in the law, James had an intense interest in meteorology and did pioneer work in the field. His writings on the subject were highly intellectual and advanced the science of weather forecasting. After the war, Bailey became an outstanding judge and community leader. He was a personal friend of William G. Coleman, and this relationship may have been part of the reason so exceptional a person as Bailey joined the Volunteers.

Milo Cincinnati Curry was unlike Jackson and Bailey. Curry was poorly educated, not prosperous financially and not from a family that could give him the advantages of even modest affluence. He owned no slaves and was in essence a subsistence farmer living on the margin between modest prosperity and poverty. One suspects that Milo was motivated to join the Volunteers for the pay and land bounty offered by the government. He was the son of Thomas Curry and Rebecca Petty and the grandson of John Curry. Milo was born in Georgia, was married, the father of four children and twenty-eight years old when he enlisted in the Volunteers. He was a member of the Baptist church at Ocmulgee but was excluded or expelled from the membership of that church for the indiscretion of *attending a horserace.* However, when he returned from the Mexican War, he was readmitted to membership in the church and served for the next thirty years as a substantial and respected leader of the church congregation.

William Marshall Ford was a twenty-four year old gentleman of leisure when he joined the Volunteers. The son of John Ford and Elizabeth Farrar, he passed his time in service to the community and the Baptist Church functioning as a member of the Board of Directors of the Alabama Baptist Bible and Colporteur Society, an organization whose purpose was to distribute Bibles and religious literature. He was obviously motivated to enlist by a sense of adventure and patriotism to join the Volunteers since he was secure in a pecuniary sense.

Four men in different circumstances came together in the Perry Volunteers: one from a middle class religious farming family; one a highly educated professional and intellectual; one a poor farmer with a large family to support; and one a young man without much to do. There were other professionals and other poor men but most of the volunteers seem to have been motivated to join the company out of a sense of nationalism and desire for adventure since the monetary rewards for volunteer service were quite small.

The volunteers who traveled to the recruiting station at Perryville were not strangers to each other. They were neighbors and friends, many of whom had known each other all of their lives, having been born in the community or having moved there as young children. John A.

and Samuel P. B. Fuller were brothers and John B. Fuller was their cousin. John and Samuel Fuller were the grandsons of Green B. Jackson who was also the grandfather of Charles Green Jackson. John B. Fuller's son Alfred Franklin Fuller married Mary Elizabeth Jackson who was a granddaughter of Green B. Jackson who was also the great grandfather of John B. Fuller. George H. Hanson and John W. Radford were brothers-in-law, George having married Susannah A. Radford. John, Joseph and Richard Heard were brothers and the brother-in-law of Captain Coleman, and the Tillman boys in the Company were Coleman's nephews. William C. Mayes married Martha Jane Crow, the cousin of Charles Green Jackson. John W. Dacus married Mary Caroline Ramsey, the daughter of the Perryville preacher, Reverend Lewis P. Ramsey. Milo Curry, Joseph Dennis, John Everett, Andrew Harvill, Charles Green Jackson and William C. Mayes were members of the same church congregation, where until 1845, Charles Green Jackson's grandfather, Charles Crow, was the preacher. There were other close relations but the above will serve to demonstrate how the families of the Volunteers were intertwined by blood, friendship, marriage and as citizens of the same community.

Having collected a full company of recruits and elected officers, the Perry Volunteers were prepared to leave Perry County and word was sent out for the men to assemble at Perryville. The recruits arrived early in the morning of Thursday, June 11, 1846, and farewells were painfully made with friends and relatives who gathered in Perryville to see them off. The full range of emotions was displayed, but the men were cheerful about the prospects of a new adventure. They hoped soon to be engaged in the service of their country and in an important mission to rescue the Army of Occupation on the Rio Grande. The goodbyes completed, the Volunteers stepped out on to the dusty road leading south out of Perryville in the mid-afternoon to march to Selma in Dallas County. The objective of the company was Mobile and their intent to offer themselves for service to the United States. The route they traveled was familiar to the volunteers who used it often to travel to Selma, the nearest large commercial center. Marching south, the volunteers stirred up clouds of dust as they tread over the sandy roadbed that paralleled the clear waters of serpentine Oakmulgee Creek that flowed out of the hills to the north. Soon they arrived at Greer's Bridge with Ocmulgee Church on the hill above and crossed to the south side of the meandering, brush crowded creek onto the flat plain leading to the day's objective.

Selma is a short distance from Perryville so the march was fairly easy, and being located on the Alabama River, transportation to Mobile was available there. The Volunteers' entry into Selma was full of pomp with the Selma militia company known as the Selma Rangers providing an honor guard and a martial band adding to the occasion and tempo of the event. Upon arrival, the Volunteers, brimming with pride, observed that a large crowd of people was waiting to greet them and that the spirit of patriotism was strong among the inhabitants of the town. Spread before them under the giant hardwoods along the Alabama River, the men from Perry County observed that the inhabitants of Selma had prepared an evening meal for them. Having enjoyed the food, hospitality, society and well wishes of the citizens of Dallas County, the Perry Volunteers camped for the night in the town and prepared for their journey down river the next day. When the days' activity settled down, William Coleman removed a new bound notebook from among his possessions, dated an entry and wrote a brief summary of the days' activities in his record. Thus began the Mexican War diary of Captain Coleman in which he preserved many of the events and occurrences that were to make up the experiences of the Perry Volunteers during the forthcoming year and preserved a valuable record for future generations.

The next morning the men assembled at the Selma wharf and the crowd there to see them off made warm expressions of friendship and concern for the welfare and safety of the men who were believed to be placing themselves in certain jeopardy against the distant and cruel Mexican foe. They boarded the steamboat *William Bradstreet* to the cheers of those gathered to see them on their way giving the volunteers a sense of pride and important purpose. The *William Bradstreet* steamed away, and the well-wishers were soon out of sight. The Volunteers' thoughts now turned to the dangers to which they were headed, and the strong hope that they would not disgrace themselves, their friends or their county in the battles that surely must lie ahead for them. They also were impressed that the course they had chosen would keep them from their family and friends for the next twelve months and some wondered if they would ever return. But the excitement of events was such that these matters quickly faded from their thoughts as they looked to what lay ahead in Mobile and far-away Mexico. These men, like thousands before and after them, also had a certain vanity and arrogance about how they would perform in battle. The Mexicans would regret the day they met the men from Perry County who would make short work of their impudence in the first battle. Peace would be made, and victorious they would quickly be on their way home to Alabama to receive the accolades and tributes to their courage from friends and family and the gratitude of their county and country.

The Perry Volunteers journeyed down the Alabama River to the Bay City in the hope of being mustered into Federal service and organized with other companies into a regiment. The record is unclear, but it appears that these men may have taken it upon themselves to move to Mobile without being ordered there.[45] When the *Bradstreet* docked in Mobile, the men discovered that their arrival was timed to coincide with a need to fulfill a requisition for Alabama men authorized by President Polk *"for one regiment of volunteer Infantry and Riflemen to serve for the term of twelve months."* The Perry Volunteers went to Camp Martin, named after the governor, located several miles north and west of Mobile, to wait mustering into the army.

Mobile, Alabama
in the 1840s

At Camp Martin, the men began to experience a new comradeship, a new family, a new home in the army, because for the next year they worked, played, slept and ate together in an environment that was highly familial. In later years, they would look back on the experiences of their youth in the army and remember those comrades with a fondness that only the bond of men in mutual support of each other can experience. During the war, these men argued, fought and groused with each other but were bonded tightly by their communal hardships and shared dangers. Thirty-eight years after the war, Captain Coleman wrote to his aging former commander about their difficult days in Mexico and the lingering solidarity among the veterans brought on by their service in the army: *"There are five of my old Company living near me who moved to this country with me and four more of our old regiment living near by. They seem to venerate our old campaign and the lengthening of our shadows brings us into closer order."* Aged men reaching the end of their days often tend to place more emphasis on events than reality would justify. In the case of military men, the feeling of comradeship is most often genuine and persistent, especially when the military experience is particularly difficult. This is doubtless the case of the Perry Volunteers whose service in Texas and Mexico was a trial they could not imagine while they prepared to leave Mobile, and the experience made an indelible impression on them.

---

[45] Alabama Governor Joshua L. Martin reported later that *"a large number of volunteer companies proceed to the city of Mobile without my order."*

First Regiment of Alabama Volunteers

*Every regiment is a miniature army. It has all
the constituents of the largest body of troops.*
Fayette Robinson
Army Officer and Military Historian

Mobile was the leading city in Alabama and one of the most important cities in the South. Founded in 1711 by the French, it was ruled in turn by France, Britain and Spain until 1814 when General Andrew Jackson occupied it for the United States. Located on a sandy plain near the northwest corner of Mobile Bay, it was excellently drained with an enviable road system covered in oyster shells. Mobile was alive with soldiers in late May and June 1846, because the city was the staging point for Alabama volunteers destined for service in Mexico. Here the Perry Volunteers were merged into a regiment consisting of ten companies with each company given a letter designation of A through K with J being omitted. The Perry Volunteers were designated as Company C, and the regiment was named the First Regiment of Alabama Volunteers. Mustering in of these ten companies began on June 8 and continued until June 29 under the direction of Brigadier General Walter Smith, the mustering officer at Mobile who was appointed by Governor Joshua L. Martin to enroll Alabama volunteers into Federal service. The Perry Volunteers were mustered into the army on Saturday, June 13, 1846, the day they arrived in Mobile, and it is from this date that their service officially began. Mustering involved the administration of oaths of allegiance and signing enlistment documents.

The 10 companies that were organized into the First Regiment of Alabama Volunteers were from different parts of the state and, like the Perry Volunteers, were recruited and organized in their home counties.

Company	County	Muster Date	Captain
Company A	Greene County[46]	June 08, 1846	Andrew L. Pickens
Company B	DeKalb County	June 12, 1846	Zechariah Thomason
Company C	Perry County	June 13, 1846	William G. Coleman
Company D	Greene County[47]	June 15, 1846	Sydenham Moore
Company E	Talladega County	June 16, 1846	Jacob D. Shelley
Company F	Jackson County	June 16, 1846	Richard W. Jones
Company G	Pike & Baldwin County	June 16, 1846	Drury P. Baldwin
Company H	Mobile County	June 17, 1846	John B. Youngblood
Company I	Benton County[48]	June 13, 1846	Eli T. Smith
Company K	Talladega County	June 29, 1846	Hugh M. Cunningham

Once mustered into the Army, the Volunteers settled into camp life waiting for the other companies in the regiment to be mustered and the regiment fully organized. On Monday, June 15, a photographer appeared in camp and William Coleman had a miniature made that he sent to his wife. On Tuesday, the Quartermaster issued the Volunteers fifteen company tents, two wall tents, fifteen camp kettles, 30 mess pans and fifteen hatchets. On June 18, the men were given their total clothing allowance for the next year. Captain Coleman recorded that he "*received $36.42 in full payment for 12 months clothing.*" Under the law in 1846, volunteers were not issued uniforms, and privates received a clothing allowance of $21.00 upon muster to purchase

---

[46] Company A (Greensboro Volunteers) was organized in Greensboro in Greene County, Alabama.
[47] Company D was the Eutaw Rangers from Greene County organized in Eutaw, Alabama in May 1846. Lucius J. Lockett from Perry County served as a private in this company. Thomas J. Dale of Perry County was a private in Company D but transferred to the Tennessee Cavalry.
[48] Benton County was formed in 1832 and was renamed Calhoun County in 1858.

their own clothing. However, regimental records indicate that privates in the First Alabama received $36.42 as their annual clothing allowance. The money could be used for other purposes and volunteers sometimes bought cheap clothes.[49] The general result was that volunteers were often poorly clothed. Once in Mexico, General Zachary Taylor ordered that volunteers could buy clothing from government stores and eventually the volunteers were given government uniforms without regard to the law.[50] On Saturday, June 20, the Volunteers were issued eighty-eight muskets,[51] eighty-eight cartridge boxes, eighty-eight scabbard belts, ninety haversacks and ninety canteens. Company C now had all of the fundamental items necessary for a military unit—clothes, tents, cooking utensils, accouterments and arms. They were now equipped to go to war, but had to wait for the government to make final preparations for transportation before they could leave Mobile for Mexico. Poor government planning, however, meant a delay in getting away. The heat and humidity of Mobile in late June made camping out highly disagreeable. While they waited, the camp was marred by tragic events: Augustus Kremmer of Pike County, Alabama died, two volunteers were struck by lightning, measles appeared among the volunteers and the sick piled up in the hospitals and tents in the camps.

Wash Day In Camp
William H. Richardson—1848
Library of Congress

For the next two weeks, the boys from Perry County received their first instructions in the principles of tactics and army life. They were drilled and stood guard as the officers tried to instill unfamiliar rules of military organization and discipline into the men. Squabbles occurred when misbehaving soldiers were arrested and the men in the arrested soldiers' company objected, attempting to have the offenders released by force. The men of Company C also learned that life in the army was much less glamorous than expected. They had to do their own cooking, washing, mending and repugnant duties such as hauling garbage, clearing brush, leveling the ground and digging ditches. This was a big change for men who were accustomed to having their wives, sisters, mothers or servants perform household type duties, and they did not find these camp chores pleasant.

At Mobile, the men from along the Cahaba River in Perry County were introduced to the routine uniformity that was the army in 1846. This erased the initial excitement about being in the army, but they were determined to become good soldiers even with the menial labor sameness and boredom of camp life. The men learned that one day was much like all the other days and that the routine was broken only by unusual or special events. Each day began with a wake up call at five o'clock by the regimental drummer. Upon hearing the regimental drummer beat reveille, John C. Rogers, Company C drummer, joined in to rouse his Company out of their blankets. This signaled the end of rest and the beginning of the Volunteers' day. The

---

[49] A South Carolina volunteer wrote from Mobile to the *Sumter Banner* in 1847 that members of the regiment "*sent the small pittance received from* [the] *government to their needy friends and families.*"
[50] After the Mexican War, Congress changed the law in 1848 and thereafter volunteers were issued uniforms and other clothing of the Regular Army.
[51] The normal firearm of the Mexican War soldier was the Model 1825 smoothbore flintlock musket. This weapon was 57.64 inches long, weighed ten pounds and fired a lead ball slightly less than .69 caliber. A 16 to 18 inch-long bayonet socket at the end of the barrel permitted the musket to be turned into a pike. In addition to firing solid shot, this weapon could fire a cartridge containing twelve buckshots and a cartridge called a buck and ball containing one solid ball and three buckshots. Although often called an inferior weapon, this firearm was deadly. At the time the war began, the army was in the process of shifting to percussion weapons. The First Regiment of Mississippi Volunteers was armed with percussion rifles that the regiment made famous as the "Mississippi Rifle."

camps came alive as the drumming continued and the sounds of the hustle and bustle of active men stirring to arise, wash, put on their clothes and form up in straight lines with their weapon in hand to wait for roll call. All the while, drummer Rogers kept up a rat-a-tat that reverberated and rattled throughout the camp. These sounds could be heard coming from the right and left in the camps surrounding the Perry men, and they were left with the impression of belonging to a mighty army because of the din that could be heard for miles.

As the first business of the day, Sergeant Seaborn Aycock called the roll and reported the status of the company to the officer of the day. Unless on guard duty, ill or excused, every enlisted man was required to attend roll call and answer when his name was announced. At this assembly, Captain Coleman issued instructions for the day, read general orders to the men or made special assignment of duties. This completed, the men were released for breakfast around six o'clock. Breakfast cooked and consumed, men who wanted to see the regimental surgeon reported to his quarters and waited his turn for medical help. The surgeon visited those who could not report to his quarters. All others in the company went on fatigue duty, folding their beds, washing cooking items, putting things in their place and walking over the campgrounds to clean it up. During fatigue time, firewood was cut, drainage ditches dug and other camp chores completed.

At seven-thirty in the morning, First Sergeant Aycock assembled six privates to perform guard duty for the coming day and night. They divided the next twenty-four hours into thirds and two were always on duty to be relieved by two others when their duty time elapsed. Assigning the guards was serious business. Seaborn Aycock inspected the men and their weapons and issued ammunition. They were marched to the parade ground to the sounds of John Rogers' drum and the fife of James Bennett to give the event a somber atmosphere. At the parade ground, those men detailed to guard duty were inspected again and a Corporal of the guard took them to their assigned positions and relieved the men who stood guard during the previous duty period.

Company drill began at eight o'clock. First, the men drilled by squads, then by company. During drills, the soldiers attempted to maintain their alignments as they moved forward, to the rear or in a wheel. All the while, John Rogers kept cadence with his drum to help the men keep in step. Company drill ended, the men marched back to camp for an hour's rest before the noon meal. Food issued, the men cooked and the camp resounded with the clamor and clatter of the cooking and cleaning up from their meals. Around two o'clock in the afternoon, Rogers beat his drum again and was joined by other drummers across the camps. The sound of hundreds of tramping feet signaled regimental assembly where all of the companies in the regiment drilled together. Regimental drill was followed by individual preparation for evening roll call, inspection and dress parade. The men brushed their clothes, shined boots and polished their brass.

Drill was the principal activity in the army.

At about five o'clock, the soldiers assembled in full dress with their arms to be inspected and answer to the roll call after which they were free to prepare and eat their supper. After supper, Sergeant Seaborn Aycock again called the roll, the sergeant of the guard inspected the weapons of the privates and the flag was lowered and folded. Now the men not on guard duty were free for the day, to read or write letters, visit, tell stories and talk about home. At eight thirty, the men assembled for another roll call, thirty minutes later John Rogers beat tattoo, and Sergeant Aycock took the final roll call of the day. The camp was now closed for the privates, and they could not leave without special permission from the officer of the guard. At nine thirty, taps was beat, fires extinguished and the camp went silent.

The regiment had not yet selected its officers, so a primary activity in the camp during free periods was campaigning for Field and Staff officers. Sydenham Moore, Captain of Company D from Greene County and John R. Coffey, a private from Jackson County, were candidates for the rank of colonel. Candidates for regimental offices and their representatives made the rounds of the companies and pressed their qualifications to serve in a leadership role. The weather was hot and during these early days in Mobile some of the men were suffering from the measles, as is often the case with country boys who live isolated lives at home and were infrequently exposed to communicable diseases. On Friday, June 26, regimental elections were announced for the following day.

The election of regimental officers was conducted as scheduled on Saturday at Camp Martin. John Coffee was elected but Sydenham Moore's supporters criticized Coffey as the less qualified of the two. Private Nunnalee recorded in his journal that Coffey was "*a good man, but no officer, nor never will be—a perfect old granny- no energy and but little information.*" Once the election of officers was completed, the regiment was fully organized and ready to be transported to Mexico. Orders were issued on Sunday establishing a line of march to the docks in Mobile on Monday where transportation was waiting to take them to the Rio Grande to reinforce the embattled Army of Occupation.

Officers of the First Regiment of Alabama Volunteers

Colonel	[52]John Reid Coffey
Lieutenant Colonel	[53]Richard G. Earle
Major	[54]Goode Bryan
Adjutant	[55]James D. Parke
Adjutant	[56]Hugh P. Watson
Quartermaster Sgt	[57]Abner H. Hughes
Surgeon	[58]John C. Anderson

[52] John Reid Coffey was born on March 27, 1814, at Wartrace in Bedford County, Tennessee and was the son of Rice Coffey and Sarah Bradford. He moved to Bellefonte, Alabama when he was fourteen. Coffey was thirty-two years old and married to Mary Ann Cross (August 21, 1839) at the time he was elected Colonel of the First Alabama. Before the war, he was a merchant and sheriff but had no known military experience. His lack of military experience and bearing caused controversy in the regiment. He died on March 21, 1896, in Jackson County, Alabama.

[53] Richard G. Earle of Benton County, Alabama was Captain of the Benton Guards (Company I) before his promotion to Lieutenant Colonel of the regiment. Benton County was renamed Calhoun County in 1858.

[54] Goode Bryan was from Tallapoosa County, Alabama. Bryan was an 1829 graduate of the Military Academy at West Point, New York and served in the Regular United States Army from 1829 through 1835.

[55] James D. Parke was appointed Adjutant of the First Alabama with the rank of 2nd Lieutenant. He apparently became ill soon after arriving in Texas and was replaced on July 6, 1846, by Hugh P. Watson at Brazos Santiago, Texas. Parke died on August 19, 1846, at Camp Belknap, Texas and was buried in Texas with a Masonic ceremony. As Adjutant, James D. Parke and Hugh P. Watson acted as the colonel's secretary thereby relieving the commander of dreary paperwork. His duties were important and included marking the regiment's place in line of battle and on the march, training the non-commission officers and managing the regimental band.

[56] Hugh P. Watson was appointed adjutant on June 6, 1846. He was a 2nd Lieutenant in Shelly's Company/Talladega Boys. He resigned as Adjutant on May 1, 1847.

[57] Abner H. Hughes was from DeKalb County, Alabama. As Regimental Quartermaster Sergeant, Hughes was responsible for securing shelter, transportation, uniforms, tents, knapsacks, haversacks, canteens and other items necessary for the regiment. He also had the authority to buy food, fodder, draft animals and similar items in the areas where the regiment operated.

[58] John C. Anderson was originally a 2nd Lieutenant and Surgeon of the Eutaw Rangers from Greene County, Alabama. He was appointed Surgeon of the Regiment on June 29, 1846. Captain Sydenham Moore recorded in his journal that Anderson resigned as surgeon on August 19, 1846, because Colonel

Surgeon	[59]John H. Tilghman
Surgeon's Mate	[60]Anthony B. Green
Sergeant Major	[61]John B. Fuller
Drum Major	[62]Christopher Darrow
Fife Major	Joseph Anderson
Musician	[63]Nathaniel G. Shelly

The First Alabama was the only regiment from Alabama to serve in the war with Mexico. Other Alabamians saw duty in Mexico in 1846 as part of the Battalion of Alabama Volunteers enlisted for three months,[64] three independent companies of volunteers enlisted for six months in 1847, and an independent company of mounted volunteers enlisted for the length of the war. Additionally, there was a battalion consisting of five companies that served in 1847 after enlisting for the length of the war. One of these units under General Robert Desha of Mobile was the first volunteer unit to reach Texas after the call for troops, but the First Regiment of Alabama Volunteers, numbering about 945 men, stands alone as Alabama's full regimental representative of twelve-month troops in Mexico and comprised one third of all Alabama soldiers. Only the Louisville Legion, the First Regiment of Tennessee Volunteers and the Baltimore Battalion (twelve months troops) arrived in Texas before the First Regiment of Alabama Volunteers making their response to the call to arms rather remarkable. The First Alabama would have arrived earlier except for a delay in providing the regiment with transportation. In all nearly 3,000 Alabama men served in the war.

However, the First Alabama followed more than 8,000 militia troops and three-month and six month volunteer soldiers sent to Taylor's aid from Texas and Louisiana or by the unauthorized order of Brevet Major General Edmund P. Gaines, commander of the Department of West. Almost all of these short-term soldiers were sent home without performing any service.

John Coffey had treated him in an "*ungentleman*" way. Army regulations required each regiment to have one surgeon and two assistant surgeons. Moore repeated in his journal on August 31, 1846, that Dr. Moore of Mobile had replaced Anderson.

[59] John H. Tilghman originally served as a private in Crawford's Company of six months volunteers. He was transferred to Company D (Sydenham Moore's Company/Eutaw Rangers) where he was appointed Sergeant Major. Tilghman was appointed Surgeon on August 3, 1846, at Camp Belknap.

[60] Anthony B. Green was made surgeon of the regiment on the certificate of Colonel John R. Coffey dated September 15, 1846, at his headquarters near Camargo, Mexico. Green was originally a 1st Lieutenant in Company B from DeKalb County, Alabama.

[61] John B. Fuller was Perry County's only representative on the list of regimental officers. As Sergeant-Major, he was the regiment's senior enlisted man and acted as the Adjutant's aide. Fuller was brevetted a Second Lieutenant in Company C on August 1, 1846.

[62] Christopher Darrow was originally a drummer in Company I or Earle's Company. As Drum Major, he was the chief musician for the regiment, led the regimental band, prepared entertainment and selected music.

[63] Nathaniel G. Shelly was originally 4th Corporal of Company E (Talladega Boys). He was appointed Musician on October 9, 1846, at Camargo, Mexico.

[64] Battalions are a military units consisting of more than one but less than ten companies.

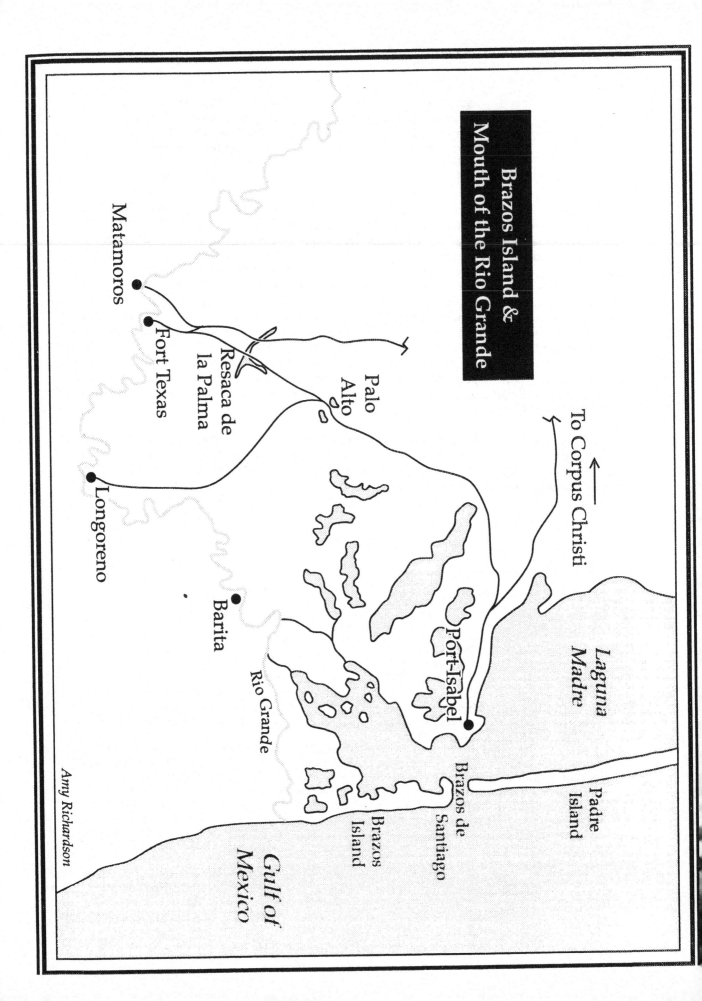

Brazos Island &
Mouth of the Rio Grande

Matamoros

Fort Texas

Resaca de
la Palma

Palo
Alto

Longoreno

Barita

Rio Grande

To Corpus Christi

Laguna
Madre

Port Isabel

Padre
Island

Brazos de
Santiago

Brazos
Island

Gulf of
Mexico

Amy Richardson

Brazos Santiago, Texas

*"Very dry and always windy on this
island, the sun quite hot."*
Captain William G. Coleman

On Saturday, June 27, Captain Coleman received orders that the Perry Volunteers were *"to embark for Point Isabel"* in Texas and preparations to move began in earnest. Monday, June 29, 1846, the Perry Volunteers pulled down their tents, packed their gear and started for the docks of Mobile about noon. Here they boarded the steamship *Fashion*, stowed their baggage away on the ship and made last minute preparations for sailing. The *Fashion* departed Mobile for Texas and Mexico in the afternoon with four companies of the First Alabama on board.[65] Three companies of the regiment boarded the steamship *Telegraph*[66] for the trip that took five days to complete. Two companies were left behind because of the lack of transportation, but these men joined the regiment later.[67] The departure of the regiment was not a mundane affair but a festive event. A large and cheering crowd assembled at the Mobile wharfs to see them off and wish them well. Bands provided martial and cheerful music and politicians provided speeches. Captain Coleman described it as a *"magnificent send off from the wharf at Mobile."*[68] As the *Fashion* cast off its lines some of the soldiers were still on the wharf and had to leap aboard the ship to avoid being left in Mobile. Once underway, as many of the men as could crowded on to the hurricane deck of the ship and stared at the City of Mobile as long as it was in view, their heads doubtless filled with thoughts of home and wondered about what lay ahead. The *Fashion* did not go immediately to sea but stood in Mobile Bay near Mobile Point all night. Departing on the morning of Tuesday, June 30, the ship entered the Gulf of Mexico and headed for Texas.

Sailing on open water was a new experience for the men from rural, land locked Perry County who marveled at the scenery presented by the open sea. The sea was so calm on the first day that scarcely a wave was visible and the air was still. Birds swarmed around the ship, fish could be easily seen in the clear Gulf waters, porpoises in large numbers swam along with the ship repeatedly leaping and diving amazing the travelers, and flying fish presented the greatest curiosity to the men as they sailed over the water like birds. The *Fashion* and *Telegraph*, like most such vessels of that day, were small and the men were housed all over the ship wherever they could find room. Once underway, the Perry Volunteers squeezed themselves below deck with the three other companies on board and guards were posted at the entrances to keep them in their quarters. Here in their lair the volunteers showed a lot of life and brought out fiddles to make music, sang favorite songs heartily and passed the hours telling stories, although they suffered greatly from the heat in the bowels of the ship. Sunrises and sunsets were the most beautiful sights of the day splashing beautiful colors over the water. Two men died during the voyage and were buried at sea but neither was from Perry County.[69] On Thursday, July 2, the fourth day out of Mobile, the sea grew quite rough and the inexperienced sailors from Perry

---

[65] The *Fashion* was a hybrid ship powered by a combination of steam engine and sails.
[66] The steamship *Telegraph* was chartered by General Edmund P. Gaines in May 1846 and was one of the first ships engaged in transporting troops to Mexico. It was fitted with a 12-pounder field gun in case the troops had to fight their way ashore. Before the war, the *Telegraph* was in regular service in the Gulf of Mexico.
[67] Captain William Coleman noted in his diary on July 10, 1846, that *"the Jackson and Talladega companies arrived on Brasos Santiago from Mobile,"* indicating that these were the two companies left in Mobile.
[68] Captain Sydenham Moore described the crowd on the docks as *"immense."*
[69] John Danford of Company H and Robert Marshall of Company G died on board the *Fashion*.

County began to get seasick causing Captain Coleman to record in his diary that *"nearly all hands sick."*

The regiment arrived off Brazos Santiago Island, Texas[70] near the mouth of the Rio Grande on Friday, July 3, after a successful passage across the Gulf of Mexico. Here the Perry boys saw a large number of ships at anchor and passing back and forth around the island as part of the buildup of men, supplies and weapons for Zachary Taylor's army. The tide was too shallow for the *Fashion* to cross the bar into the anchorage that day so the ship lay outside for the night. The next morning, Independence Day in the United States, the *Fashion* carried the Perry Volunteers safely into the anchorage at Brazos Santiago Island.

Not all of the Perry County men who sailed out of Mobile Bay on June 29 were soldiers. Officers were allotted money by the government for personal servants to cook, wash and attend to their needs while on a campaign and in camp. By law, no soldier could be made to act as a servant unless the soldier and his captain consented. Many southern officers brought their slaves with them to take care of camp chores and cook for them. Captain William G. Coleman was one such officer who embarked with a slave. Coleman's slave, Sep, was a remarkable man who endured all of the hardships and privations of Company C and his master.[71] Once in Mexico, a country that abolished slavery in 1824, Sep could have fled and gained his freedom as some other slaves did that accompanied southern regiments to war.[72] Sep did not; he stayed with his master, nursed him in sickness, administered to his wants and needs and extended his ministrations to others in Company C. Sep was so trustworthy that he became a custodian of the little treasures of the men of the Company. He never betrayed a trust, protecting the possessions left in his care. After the war, he returned to Alabama with William Coleman and moved with the Captain to Claiborne Parish, Louisiana where Sep died of old age. Although freed in 1865, Sep remained in the service of Coleman until the end of his days. Captain Coleman told Sep's story over thirty years later, and it was published in the *Memoirs of Northwest Louisiana* in 1890.[73]

Once in Texas, the Perry County men unloaded their baggage, marched inland for about a half mile and set up camp on the hot, barren, wind swept Brazos Island. Colonel Coffey notified General Taylor's staff that eight companies of the regiment were in Texas and *"Ready to receive marching orders."* Tents were pitched on a *"disagreeable sand bank."* According to Captain Coleman, the island was mostly sand dunes void of trees or substantial vegetation and was not

---

[70] Brazos Santiago is a barrier island about four miles long off the coast of Texas bounded on the east and west by Laguna Madre and the Gulf of Mexico and on the north and south by Brazos Santiago Pass and Boca Chica. It was the place where men, equipment and supplies were unloaded from sea vessels and then transported to Point Isabel or the mouth of the Rio Grande. Brazos was about three miles north of the mouth of the Rio Grande. Point Isabel was a small village about five miles from Brazos Santiago Pass where the army maintained an extensive supply depot.

[71] The 1850 Census of Slave Inhabitants of Perry County, Alabama records that William G. Coleman had thirteen slaves on his farm, assumedly his property. Eight of these slaves were males with ages ranging over forty-four years. The oldest slaves were 45, 36, 33, 28, 17 and 16 years old. The youngest were eight and one year old. Which of these slaves was Sep is not known.

[72] The *Matamoros Gazette* reported on April 11, 1846, that six runaway slaves had crossed the Rio Grande at Fort Texas to freedom in Mexico.

[73] According to C. O. Boothe, author of *The Cyclopedia of Colored Baptists in Alabama*, a slave named Samuel Phillips, a Baptist minister, was freed as a reward for his service during the Mexican War. Peter, the slave and servant of Captain Sydenham Moore of the Eutaw Rangers (Company D), died at Camargo, Mexico on November 7, 1846, and was buried there. Four free *"men of color"*—Robert Hopton, James Marshall, Samuel Rivers and Henry Clark—served the South Carolina Palmetto Regiment as servants. The Charleston City Council paid Hopton, Marshall and Rivers for their service and Hopton received a pension from the State Legislature. Other records indicate that the South Carolinians took nine slaves to Mexico. Jim Green, a slave belonging to Joseph Davis, accompanied Jefferson Davis to Mexico as his personal servant. David, a slave, is credited with saving the life of Georgia Surgeon J. T. Lamar by throwing himself in front of the physician and receiving a Mexican lance in his chest that was intended for Dr. Lamar. The story of slaves and free blacks serving in the Mexican War is a largely untold story.

an ideal place for a troop encampment.[74] In fact, the Volunteers had landed in the middle of a merciless environment. The wind blew constantly and covered everything with sand. The sand itself was deep and dry and made simple walking unpleasant and difficult. Flies, mosquitoes and biting insects were a source of misery and irritation. Flies were particularly pesky during the day and turned the tents in the sand black in horde-like numbers. A correspondent to the *Georgia Telegraph* wrote, "*at night the flies give way to the musquitoss, who pursue their vocation of murdering sleep, until the dewey morn . . .*" Securing drinking water was difficult. The Perry Volunteers dug shallow wells in the sand about two feet deep and allowed the water to rise in the hole. The water secured in this way was salty and highly unpleasant to drink. Captain Sydenham Moore of Company D judged the water on the island to be "*intolerable.*" Daytime temperatures were unbearable with no place to escape the sun and night brought only modest relief. Dress parades were held and drills conducted with some of the men fainting in the heat on the island. The drills were badly conducted so the officers made no serious attempt to drill the men in the deep sand leaving them little to do. Freed from most military responsibilities, the Perry boys swam and played in the surf or traveled in groups to Point Isabel to see the sights. Seafood such as fish, crabs and oysters was available on the island for those who could afford to supplement army fare that consisted almost exclusively of hard bread and fat pork. If a soldier wanted sugar and coffee, he had to buy it with his own money.

On Wednesday, July 8, Captain Coleman noted that the camp was "*very dry and always windy on this island, the sun quite hot.*" The sea breezes were delightful in the extreme heat, but it hurled sand into and upon everything in camp. To pass the time, Coleman went to Point Isabel to see the sights there and wrote two letters, one to his parents in South Carolina and the other to "*my dear Jane.*" Nine days later, he observed that it was "*still dry*" and that the camp was nearly out of water to drink. However, later that day it rained and Coleman judged it to be a "*good rain.*" The men of Company C had no way of knowing, but more rain than they wanted was on the way. Two days later on Sunday, July 19, the day began windy and cloudy. Then rain fell in torrents and flooded the camp making life even more miserable for the poor soldiers jammed in this disagreeable place. Coleman observed, "*the rain descended in such torrents as to completely inundate our whole camp from three to ten inches deep; a bad time for poor soldiers.*" Private Nunnalee recorded that ". . . *every tent floor was covered with water, and if there is a dry place on this unfinished portion of creation, it has yet to be found.*" On July 20 Coleman recorded, "*still raining and the whole island on which we are encamped is covered in water.*" Military exercises were suspended and the rainy days were passed in inactivity and abject misery. Coleman was anxious for news from home and noted "*no news from the War, nor none from home and so long deprived of so good a pleasure.*" As Coleman indicates, letters bearing news from home were cherished and much anticipated by the Alabama men. James F. Bailey and John G. Heard regularly went to Point Isabel in search of letters for the Company. During the inactivity, the camp was interlaced with rumors that the war would be short and the principal speculation was that the whole Mexican affair would be over by Christmas.

They were not long on Brazos Island before the men began to sicken and suffer from dysentery. Robert T. Goree, a successful farmer from a prominent Heard's Beat family, was discharged on July 15, 1846, and sent home leaving the Company without a first Lieutenant. James F. Bailey was reported "*quite sick*" on July 17 and Captain Coleman observed on Sunday the nineteenth that "*several fellows very sick.*" The rain continued keeping the entire camp was under water. The Perry Volunteers were anxious to get off the island and to higher ground. After sixteen days there, the regimental commander sent a delegation of officers to see General Zachary Taylor at Matamoros to request permission to move inland to higher ground where wood and water were more accessible. On July 20, they were authorized to leave Brazos Island and set out

---

[74] Captain Sydenham Moore recorded a description in his journal on July 4, 1846: "*The Island is a low, desolate sand Bank-No trees in view & scarce any vegetation whatever.*" The *Georgia Telegraph* reported on July 28, 1846 that the Georgia regiment "*with a regiment of Alabama Volunteers are on a desolate sand bank . . . with not a tree or shrub to temper the fierceness of the tropical heat and hardly a blade of grass to relieve the eye after being fatigued by dwelling on the burning sand.*"

in the rain marching eight miles to the mouth of the Rio Grande.[75] A Baltimore soldier who observed the Alabamians that day noted in his diary *"they are a fine looking set of men."*[76] However, the volunteers' misery continued at the new campsite as the rain was unrelenting for eleven consecutive days after they arrived.

While camped at the mouth of the Rio Grande, the first death among the Perry Volunteers occurred when Jesse W. Heard died on the afternoon of Wednesday, July 22, a victim of pleurisy. He was doubtless buried on the site, as none of the soldiers of Company C that died during the war are known to have been returned to Alabama. During the Mexican War, the United States government did not assume the responsibility of shipping bodies home and the family of the soldier paid for those bodies returned to the United States. There was often too little wood in the area for coffins, so most of the dead were wrapped in a blanket and laid in a shallow grave with a wooden marker or no marker at all. The result is that the location of most of the Mexican War dead is lost forever. More sickness occurred while camped here. Several cases of measles appeared among the men while many of them were distressed with diarrhea. Captain Coleman was very ill, his sickness continuing for over a week, during which time Colonel John Coffey came to his camp and *"staid with me."* To make matters more difficult, the Perry men began to get homesick in the tradition of country boys who go off to war a long way from home.

The mouth of the Rio Grande was a temporary encampment site. The tents of thousands of volunteers dotted the landscape and eventually these camps stretched upriver for twenty miles. The First Alabama camped here for only five days and Coleman recorded on July 22 that the Company was *"able to drill this morning."* However, new cases of measles and diarrhea appeared in camp the next day and Coleman observed, *"a large number of our Company in rather bad health, measles and diarrhea. I have the latter badly myself."* On Friday, July 24 it appears that the regiment divided into two groups: one group consisting of

America troops landing at the mouth of the Rio Grande River

companies from Greene, Talladega, Jackson and Mobile counties marched north of the river to a campsite named Camp Belknap but the Alabamians referred to this place as Camp Alabama.[77] The second group apparently consisting of companies from DeKalb, Pike and Talladega (Company K) counties moved north into Mexico to a place near the Mexican village of Burita where they camped on the opposite side of the river from Camp Alabama. On Saturday, July 25, the Perry Volunteers boarded the rickety old steamboat *Troy* and traveled about two miles up the Rio Grande where they docked for the night and continued upriver the next day arriving at

[75] For reasons not explained, on July 9, 1846, Captain Coleman sent Private James F. Bailey *" to select a camp ground on the Rio Grande near Burrita"* eleven days before the move to the mouth of the river. Bailey returned to camp five days later on July 14, assumingly having selected a campground. The assumption is that the move from Brazos Island was anticipated before permission was given to relocate.
[76] John R. Kenley as quoted in *Alabama Volunteers in the MEXICAN WAR 1846-1848*, Steven R. Butler, Editor.
[77] Camp Belknap was named for Colonel William G. Belknap, a West Point graduate and commander of the 5th Regiment of Infantry in the Regular Army.

their new campsite "*opposite Burita*" on Sunday, July 26.[78] Here they unloaded and on Monday began the process of clearing a camp ground, setting up tents and making a new home for themselves. Bailey and Heard were again sent to Point Isabel in search of mail from Perry County. Coleman noted disappointedly that they "*got none for me*" and six days later again noted his disappointment writing "*never have got any letter from my dear wife or parents since I left Mobile.*"

As soon as the Alabama regiment was settled in their new camps, controversy over the regimental Staff and Field officers arose. Some in the regiment were unhappy with Colonel John R. Coffey from the day of his election in Mobile. This discontent bubbled up again and on July 25, 1846, Lieutenant Stephen H. Hale of the Eutaw Rangers drew up a petition requesting that all of the Field officers resign their commissions to clear the way for the election of new regimental officers. The preparation of this petition was preceded by discussions among officers of the ten companies in an effort to determine in advance who would sign it when it was offered. The response was such that it was placed before the commissioned officers of the ten companies of the regiment and a number of the officers signed it. However, Lieutenant Tynal W. Jones of Company E from Talladega County and William H. Ketchum of Company H of Mobile County refused to sign. In the end, a bare majority of company officers signed the petition.

Among the company commanders, Captain William G. Coleman refused to sign the document. His refusal to endorse the effort to oust the regimental officers led to severe criticism of Coleman because he was said to have loudly opposed the regimental slate of officers in the discussions that preceded the drafting of the petition. Captain Sydenham Moore of Company D recorded his reaction to and conflict with Captain Coleman in his war journal.

> "*Capt Coleman who had always expressed himself as opposed to them* [regimental officers] *and had been loudest in his denunciations of them like a white livered, cowardly miscreant as he is, when the petition was presented to him, refused to sign it, and even pretended to be indignant at it—I heard that he had made some improper remarks about myself, but I called upon him & he positively denied it.*"

Moore's denunciation of Coleman was brutal and harsh and Coleman's defense in the matter is not known, so nothing more can be made of the incident. Coleman's only record possibly related to this feud is a note in his diary made on August 8, "*bad news to my feelings.*" It is possible, perhaps probable, that Captain Moore's disappointment was that he would not have a chance to be elected Colonel of the Regiment since he made no attempt to hide his ambition to excel in that regard. Conversely, Captain Coleman displayed no such ambition. Coleman and Moore were both men of strong views and boldness, which is a formula for an intense conflict between strong personalities. Sydenham Moore voraciously recorded his views in his journal but Coleman was, unfortunately, not inclined to spend time even mentioning the incident in his diary. Nevertheless, the petition was submitted to the regimental officers. For the most part, the regimental commanders ignored it. Major Goode Bryan of Tallapoosa County informed the petitioners that he would immediately write out his resignation and send it forward, but when the petitioners learned that the other officers would not resign their commissions, they urged him to stay since they had no particular grievance against him personally. The privates in the regiment joined the officers with a petition of their own but fear and the influence of officers against the petition, led most privates to decline signing the document. With this, the issue died for the moment.

---

[78] The Mexican War was the first war in which steamboats were used. Along the Rio Grande, steamboats were pressed into service because of the shortage of wagons and draft animals. These boats were collected from towns along the Mississippi and Ohio Rivers and sent to Texas across the Gulf of Mexico. Another adjustment to the shortage of transportation was the use of pack animals, particularly mules.

With the attempt to cast out the officers aborted, Captain Moore was highly critical of the Field officers and wrote in his journal:

> " . . . *Coffey & Earle, are too low & contemptible and have too little pride of character to be induced to give up their offices on any account . . . We will always to be kept back & be regarded as the poorest regiment in the field merely from being judged of by our field officers.*"

Captain Moore's strong opinion notwithstanding, the fact is that the Field and Staff officers remained in place; the actions of the company officers served only to undermine the regiment's standing in the Army of Occupation and to discredit the regimental officers. It also created dissension among company officers that were divided nearly evenly between those for and against the petition. In the long term, the petitions against these officers were unwise and served to thwart the objectives of the petition's purpose in the first place—to secure a place on the battlefield for the Alabama regiment. This incident may have been the source of an opinion in the Army of Occupation that the First Alabama volunteers were a rebellious, undisciplined bunch.

Camp Alabama, Texas

*"The men have to wade waist deep
to get to the river for all the water
that is used for cooking and drinking. It will surely make all hands
sick."*

Captain William G. Coleman

At Camp Alabama, the volunteers drank muddy water carried from the Rio Grande in camp kettles. Here they endured the heat of the Mexican summer, the bites of insects and the pricks and cuts inflicted by the sharp spined vegetation native to the area.[79] On August 4, the rain resumed, water flooded the tents and soaked the blankets on the ground where the men slept. Captain Coleman observed the misery on August 6, *"rainy, bad sleeping on the ground where water is running under a blanket, the only bedding a soldier has."* The next day Captain Coleman received orders that the Volunteers' would move to Camargo, Mexico[80] but that relocation was nearly three weeks away, and there was plenty of misery ahead at Camp Alabama. In the camp, conditions were worsening for the volunteers. Coleman observed that *"the men have to wade waist deep to get to the river for all the water that is used for cooking and drinking. It will surely make all hands sick."* Coffee and sugar were not to be found in this place and provisions were generally scarce. At Camp Alabama the soldiers ate a monotonous daily diet of fat pickled pork, bacon and hardtack at all meals of the day. Fortunately, cayenne pepper grew wild in the area, and when mixed with vinegar, the sauce made an excellent seasoning. This diet combined with the muddy river water and too little attention to sanitation soon led to a massive outbreak of diarrhea. The ranks of the Perry Volunteers started to thin as a result. James H. Irby died during the early nighttime hours of July 29 and John Moore Tillman died at 9:30 in the morning of the same day. Irby was buried at the campsite that day and Tillman was buried the next day *"on the Rio Grand River."* Archibald A. Henry fell ill during this period but did not die until August 18, 1846. Others suffered heavily from diarrhea and fever; their pallid, emaciated faces betrayed their malaise and measles again made an appearance in camp as it did at Mobile to add to the misery of the troops. Other regiments suffered too. The First Georgia reported one hundred men on sick call for the dysentery, colds and fever at a surgeon's call on July 24 and one hundred sixty-two on August 3.

Captain Coleman concerned himself with the discipline of the Perry Volunteers and at Camp Alabama sought to improve compliance with regulations and commands writing on July 30 that he was, *"trying to establish some more discipline in camps."* Trouble occurred when an American insulted the wife of a Mexican and in response her husband knocked the American down for his impudence and was arrested. Coleman was learning the vicissitudes of being in command of citizen-soldiers who were his friends, relatives and neighbors back home before the war and would be again after the war. He was distressed over his role as Captain of the Perry Volunteers. His feelings were injured because some of the men in the company expressed unpleasantly harsh opinions of him. He considered resigning his commission and recorded in

---

[79] Prickly pear grew everywhere in the area rising to heights of ten or fifteen feet. Captain Franklin Smith recorded that the thorns were barbed and could not be pulled out. They had to be extracted by cutting away flesh in which the thorn was embedded. Captain Coleman recorded on October 6 that he *"stuck a thorn in my foot, which pained me smartly."* Few soldiers escaped encounters with these natural hazards during their time in the area.

[80] Camargo was a small town on the east bank of the Rio San Juan about four miles upriver from the junction with the Rio Grande. In 1846, the town had a population of about 2,000 people and the American army occupied it on July 14, 1846. Camargo became a vast supply depot during the war with the tents of thousands of soldiers and huge piles of supplies lining the river's banks.

his diary, "*felt very much like resigning my captaincy in consequence of deep manifest ill feelings entertained by some of the company for me.*"[81] He wanted to be liked but his duties, if he exercised them, would not always allow sustained popularity with the men.

Daniel Sneed and Stephen D. Tillman were granted furloughs to return to Alabama on August 6, William Marshall Ford was furloughed the next day and discharges for disability continued at Camp Alabama: William B. Bailey, Allen Burt, William T. Ford, Dr. Jesse F. Jacobs,[82] Lewis A. Miree, John Owen[83] and Benjamin F. Walker were discharged on August 19, 1846. George W. Smedley and John Miller Tillman were discharged on August 20 and Simon H. Nichols was discharged for disability on August 24. Almost two months after arriving in Texas, four men from Perry County were dead and twelve discharged for disabilities. In the First Regiment of Alabama Volunteers, twenty-five soldiers died and seventy-five were discharged because of disability, reducing the regiment to about 850 men. Captain Sydenham Moore recorded in his journal at Camp Alabama, "*I am growing sick & tired at hearing so often the dead march following to the grave some* [of] *our brave volunteers.*" It was disheartening for the Alabamians to see so much death without having yet engaged the enemy or made a noteworthy contribution to the defeat of Mexico.

There was little to do at Camp Alabama except sit, seek shelter from the rain and heat, bury the dead and care for the ill. William Coleman does not report any drilling, musters, or dress parades during his stay at this camp and begins almost every note in his record with entries such as "*In camps with nothing to do.*" To break the monotony of camp life, Coleman went to visit Matamoros on August 15 to get away from the dullness and stayed there for three days. He rented a room at the America Hotel in town operated by elderly Mrs. Winfield from his native South Carolina and found his chambers warm and clean. For entertainment, he attended a presentation at the local theater and went to the circus. Coleman also walked through the town and observed the Mexican homes that he described as without wooden floors, beds or tables and only a

Matamoros, Mexico
Captain William G. Coleman visited Matamoros in August 1846 to break the monotony of life at Camp Alabama.
Unknown Artist

few chairs. He contrasted the lives of Mexicans with conditions in the United States and observed, "*When the women sit down to work they set flat on the ground.*" While in town, Coleman wrote his "*Dear Wife*" and observed "*excitement in the place in consequence of a report that the Mexicans were intending to retake Matamoros.*"

Captain Sydenham Moore recorded on July 19 that Matamoros was filled with American troops that a short time earlier had been civilians and that they were housed in long lines of tents. The outlying houses around the town were dirty and decaying but that the plaza of the city had some large and substantial buildings. Private Nunnalee remarked in his journal that the houses are old with some built of brick and others of cane or tile with thatched roofs, but that it was a filthy town. He observed that the children go naked and that the lower class Mexican women dressed shabbily. There was much excitement in Matamoros over the arrest and imprisonment

---

[81] Captain Sydenham Moore made a similar entry in his war journal on January 21, 1847, at Tampico stating: "*My position as commander of a company is a responsible one and sometimes a thankless one. Being required to exercise obedience to orders, I often give offense, . . .*"
[82] Dr. Jesse F. Jacobs was married seven months before he sailed for Mexico and his wife was pregnant at the time he left home. The child, a daughter, was born about the time Jacobs was discharged in Mexico, but she died a month later on September 14, 1846. Jacobs died seven years later of tuberculosis.
[83] Four months after returning home, John Owen married his sweetheart Lucinda Weger.

of a Texas Ranger accused of murder. Other Texas Rangers were present making threats to free him by force making a great deal of noise in the process. There could have been a tremendous fight except that the Alcaldé of Matamoros freed the Ranger and restored peace. On the morning of August 18, Coleman boarded the steamboat *Robertson* and returned to camp where he arrived in time to observe the death of private Archibald Henry late that afternoon and took part in his burial the next day.

While the Perry Volunteers were at Camp Alabama, the Army of Occupation was organized to include newly arrived volunteers and prepare for action against the Mexican Army. John B. Fuller was elected, promoted and brevetted Third Lieutenant of Company C on August 3 from his rank as regimental Sergeant Major.[84] Before Fuller's promotion, Company C did not have a Third Lieutenant. John Anthony Quitman was one of Taylor's commanders who arrived in Texas on August 3. Quitman was commissioned a Brigadier General of Volunteers on July 1, 1846, from civilian life and was promoted to Major General on April 13, 1847. He was born in 1799 in Rhinebeck, New York and was a highly educated lawyer. He settled in Natchez, Mississippi, served as a Brigadier General in the Mississippi militia and was a successful politician in the Democratic Party. Overall, Quitman was considered an effective officer who performed his duties well. Winfield Scott appointed him as the military and civil governor of Mexico City after its capture in September 1847. On August 19, the Perry Volunteers were ordered to become part of the Brigade[85] commanded by General Quitman. The First Alabama Regiment was combined with volunteers in the First Mississippi and First Georgia Regiments plus the Battalion of Maryland and District of Columbia volunteers to form Quitman's command. Quitman's Brigade was part of the Second Division of Volunteers along with a regiment of Illinois Volunteers under Division Commander Major General of Volunteers Robert Patterson.[86] Captain Coleman noted in his diary on August 24, "*Majr. Genl. Patterson of Pennsylvania arrived at Point Isabel to command our Division.*" With the appearance of Patterson in Texas, the command structure of the volunteer division was now complete and the move to Camargo could proceed.

Brigadier General
John A. Quitman was the
Brigade Commander of the
Perry Volunteers.
Schultz Collection

As part of the preparation to go into action against the Mexicans, Colonel William G. Belknap, the Inspector General, appeared in the camp of the Perry Volunteers on Wednesday, August 11. He was there to inspect and pass judgment on the suitability of the arms and equipment of the Company. Captain Coleman assisted Belknap in the inspection and noted that muskets, cartridge boxes, scabbards, knapsacks, and haversacks went under review during the inspection

---

[84] Coleman's diary records that Fuller was elected "*3d Lt.*" but the official records state the rank as Second Lieutenant. However, the normal company organization indicates that Coleman was correct.
[85] A Brigade was composed of two or three regiments.
[86] The First Division of Volunteers was composed of volunteers from Kentucky, Ohio and Indiana commanded by William Orlando Butler. Butler served in the War of 1812. Robert Patterson was commissioned a Major General of Volunteers on July 7, 1846, by appointment of President Polk. He was born in County Tyrone, Ireland and served in the Pennsylvania Militia rising to the rank of Colonel. Patterson was commissioned a lieutenant in the 32nd Infantry of the U. S. Army but resigned in 1815 to become a prosperous grocer and commission merchant. He was politically a Democrat and remained active in the Pennsylvania militia until the advent of the Mexican War. Mexican War historian Justin H. Smith described Patterson as "*somewhat in the style of the English squire . . . but . . . lacked a familiar acquaintance with his profession as well as experience in practicing it. He also lacked initiative.*"

and all were condemned as unserviceable except for the muskets. On the same day, Dr. Marion A. Eiland of Radfordville Beat was sent to the hospital at Matamoros where there were an enormous number of sick to serve as acting Assistant Surgeon, and John W. Radford went along as a nurse.[87] Army regulations called for the assignment of one surgeon and two assistant surgeons for each regiment. Dr. Eiland's assignment as an "acting" Assistant Surgeon indicates his assignment was the result of some anomaly rather than a regular, permanent appointment. Eiland and Radford rejoined Company C on November 4, 1846, while stationed at Camargo, the Matamoros hospital emergency having been eliminated by the arrival of additional Regular Army commissioned surgeons from the United States.

On August 20, John W. Barron was promoted to 4th Sergeant and Wiley W. Fowler was appointed 4th Corporal as part of the preparations for moving to Camargo. By the time Company C left Camp Alabama, the unit had shrunk by twenty-two men leaving company strength at about seventy-six men and officers. Four men were dead, and eleven discharged, Eiland and Radford went to work in the hospital at Matamoros, Daniel Sneed, Stephen D. Tillman and William Marshall Ford had been granted furloughs to return to Alabama and George Grissom and William A. Kelly were sent to the hospital at Matamoros due to illness when the Company moved to Camargo. In less than two months, the Perry Volunteers had temporarily lost nearly a quarter of the men that left Perryville on June 11. Seven of the men later returned to the Company, but fifteen men were permanently gone from the Volunteers shortly after arriving in Texas.

During these activities at Camp Alabama, General Zachary Taylor was setting the stage for a move against Monterrey, Mexico. A direct advance from Matamoros to Monterrey was impractical because this route lacked water. General Taylor, therefore, planned to move against Monterrey from Camargo, Mexico at the head of navigation on the Rio Grande. Supplies were forwarded to that place to establish Camargo as the main supply base for the attack on Monterrey. On July 30, he set up the line of march to Camargo with the 7th United States Infantry under General William Worth leading the way, followed by the 5th United States Infantry. The First Regiment of Alabama Volunteers was scheduled to be the eighth unit to break camp and go north making them one of the last units to be moved.

General William J. Worth's
Brigade on the road to Monterrey

General Taylor located his headquarters at Camargo on Monday, August 17 and held a grand review of the Army of Occupation, which the Perry Company missed because they were still at Camp Alabama. Two days later, General William J. Worth's[88] Brigade moved toward Monter-

---

[87] Army regulations made no provision for nurses in the regular establishment of the Medical Department. Nurses were normally enlisted soldiers that were detailed to help in times of medical crisis such as epidemics or following a battle. John Radford's assignment as a nurse indicates that there was a large epidemic among the soldiers camped along the Rio Grande. Private Nunnalee visited the Matamoros hospital and observed that the "*wounded of the battles of the 8th and 9th . . . Some with an arm or leg shot off. Others wounded in the head, &c. Saw a shot taken from one's skull.*"

[88] William Jenkins Worth was born in Hudson, New York on March 1, 1794. He was commissioned a First Lieutenant in 1813 in the 23rd U. S. Infantry. Worth served as an aide to Winfield Scott in the War of 1812 during the Niagara campaign and was almost fatally wounded at Lundy's Lane. He served as commandant of the United States Military Academy for eight years, after which he assumed command of

rey as the advanced element of the army destined to assault the town. Worth set up a forward base sixty miles out of Camargo at Cerralvo[89] and waited for orders to move against Monterrey. General David E. Twiggs and his forces joined him in a few days. After the base at Cerralvo was established, the Quartermaster began to shuttle 1,500 mule pack and wagon trains between Camargo and Cerralvo moving 160,000 rations for the anticipated attack on Monterrey.

In the camps of the First Alabama, E. B. Boast of the Greensboro Volunteers wrote a letter home on August 10 that appeared in the September 5 issue of *The Beacon* newspaper in which he sets forth conditions at the time and the hopes of the regiment:

> *"Col. Coffee received orders from Gen. Taylor on the 7th inst. to hold his regiment in readiness to take the line of march for Camargo as soon as the regiments above us should move, which they are now doing. The object is, as far as we can learn, to get as many troops above Matamoros as possible before Fall . . . The volunteers before the orders for a march came, were discontented and low spirited, but since they learned there would be a chance for a fight, their spirits have risen . . . I believe now that we could live on Gophers the balance of the Campaign provided we could be sure of a fight.*

At Camp Alabama, Company C made final, last minute preparations to depart for what Coleman called *"the seat of the war."* Much of the preparation was already complete—the disabled went home to Alabama, the ill were sent to the hospital, furloughs granted to those needing to return to Alabama, vacancies in the ranks of company officers filled and unserviceable accouterments replaced. On Thursday, August 20, the weather was clear and warm and Captain Coleman noted that he felt fine but that *"the health of the regiment was not very good."* Taking regimental inventory, Coleman noted in his diary on August 25 that, *"there has been 53 men discharged and 27 have died to this date."* Preparations completed, the Volunteers sat with nothing to do but wait on transportation upriver. The prospects of moving closer to the enemy created excitement in the camp and lifted the spirits of the Volunteers, as they were eager for a fight with the Mexicans. The thought of infiltrating the interior of Mexico and desire to win battles and glory cheered them on. While they waited, the camp was rife with rumors, excitement and stories of many types: the Mexicans were suing for peace and everyone was going home; a huge army of Mexicans occupied Monterrey and would attack the Americans soon; General Taylor was angry with the slow movement of volunteers to Camargo; the Quartermaster General was neglecting his duty and so forth, as one rumor piled upon another. Outrageous rumors or not, the Perry Volunteers were pleased to be on the move once again and hopeful of meeting the Mexicans to hasten the end of the war.

---

the 8th Infantry that he led in the Seminole War. He was brevetted a Brigadier General in 1842 and a Major General in September 1846. After the Mexican War, Congress awarded him a sword for his gallantry at Monterrey and the battles involved in the capture of Mexico City. Worth died on May 7, 1849, while commanding the Department of Texas.
[89] Cerralvo, Mexico was about fifty miles southwest of Camargo on the main road used by the American army to advance on Monterrey. In 1846, the town had a population of about 1,800 people and an impressive cathedral with chimes and a towering steeple.

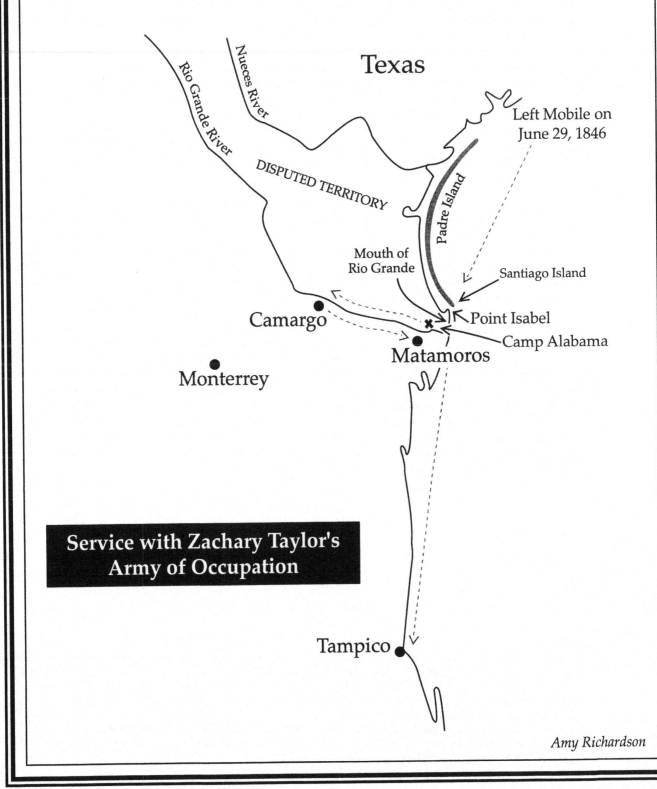

Mexican War Journeys of the Perry Volunteers and the 1st Regiment of Alabama Volunteers

Texas

Nueces River

Rio Grande River

DISPUTED TERRITORY

Padre Island

Left Mobile on
June 29, 1846

Mouth of
Rio Grande

Santiago Island

Camargo

Point Isabel

Camp Alabama

Monterrey

Matamoros

**Service with Zachary Taylor's
Army of Occupation**

Tampico

Amy Richardson

Camargo, Mexico

"Found the place to be a disagree-
able one . . . the town of Camargo
is a bad looking place . . . "
Captain William G. Coleman

Company C stayed at Camp Alabama from July 26 until August 25, 1846. After a month here, the Company again boarded the tired old steamboat *Troy* on the Rio Grande commanded by Captain Wright and began the trip of about 250 river miles up the rain-swollen river to Camargo. The *Troy* stopped at Matamoros the first night and privates George W. Grissom and William A. Kelly were placed in the hospital there. The trip resumed the next day and Captain Coleman recorded his observations on Friday, August 28 and Saturday, August 29:

> *"28th On board steam boat Troy, going to Camargo, hot day, .the country all*
> *the way from the mouth of the river is a low marsh, rich country, inhabited*
> *by the lower classes of Mexicans called Ranchos, a very indolent non-*
> *enterprising people—fine farming lands, but in to small bodies, the country*
> *is flat.*
>
> *29th Still on board the Troy saw little farm houses last evening within 400*
> *yards, fifty four children, the country here is very rich, but desirable only for*
> *cultivation, no resident situations, hot day again, rain every day for several*
> *past, this day passed by Renoso a handsome little town on the west side of the*
> *Rio Grande, above I saw the first table lands, it would be quite a treat if I had*
> *been well enough to have enjoyed it, but I was not."*

Steamboat navigation on the Rio Grande was a tricky business requiring good equipment and experience to maneuver in the riverbed. The *Troy* was a light, shallow draft steamboat and the serpentine nature of the river, plus the strong current of a stream far out of its banks made staying in the riverbed and progress upstream hard to maintain.[90] Only green wood was available for the boilers producing too little steam and the pilot was unacquainted with the difficulties of navigation on the Rio Grande. In making the sharp turns, a boat was frequently caught by the current and swept downstream, upon a sandbar or against the riverbank. The rain-swollen river made matters more difficult, and the *Troy* became stuck hard and fast on a sandbar in the early evening of August 29. Some of the men on board accused the *Troy's* pilot of doing it on purpose to avoid traveling at night, according to Coleman.

The Volunteers passed the hours of darkness on the sandbar until early the next morning when the steamboat *Virginian* appeared and unsuccessfully attempted to rescue the *Troy* by pulling it off the sandbar. The *Troy* was finally extricated from its lodgment after twenty-one hours, resuming the trip upriver a little before sunset the evening of August 30. The boat stopped for the night at Old Reynosa and the Perry Volunteers went ashore where they killed a beef, dividing it among the men. Grounding on this river was a frequent occurrence. The same day that the *Troy* resumed her trip upriver the steamboat *Col. Cross* carrying Mississippi volunteers ran aground and was pulled off a sandbar by the crew of the steamboat *Big Hatchie* ferrying a contingent of the First Regiment of Alabama Volunteers upriver.

---

[90] Captain Franklin Smith recorded in his *Journal* an incident on board the *Col. Cross* when the current struck the steamboat and *"drove it against a tree"* shearing off *"a part of the pilot House guards and some of the staterooms."* He reported another incident when the boat was driven into a corn field by the force of the current.

The rest of the trip went without serious incident, passing great cornfields, cotton plantations and small villages where Mexicans gathered thickly on the riverbank and stared at the unfamiliar riverboats. Most of the riverbank observers were women and children with rarely a man to be seen. Reynosa was two hundred river miles from Camp Alabama. Captain Coleman described it as a "*handsome little town*" resting on a high limestone point and dominated by a large church with a great tower similar to those on an ancient castle. Reynosa was located about a quarter mile off the river, had narrow streets and houses with flat roofs. The Americans maintained a hospital and barracks for soldiers there, and the United States flag flew over the town's highest building.[91] The tablelands referred to by Coleman were broad fertile valleys stretching inland from the river and planted in corn, potatoes, wheat, beans and cotton. While the Perry Volunteers were chugging upriver on the wheezy old *Troy*, other units of the Army of Occupation were marching overland. Due to the many twists and bends in the Rio Grande, the trip overland was considerably shorter at 120 miles compared to the 250 river miles to Camargo from Camp Alabama. Despite not having to march overland, the steamboat ride was, nevertheless, an unpleasant experience and fraught with dangers of its own. About thirty miles above Reynosa a boiler burst on the steamboat *Enterprise* crowded with volunteer soldiers and killed or injured many of the men on board.[92] On Monday, August 31, Coleman again noted his observations of the land through which he passed as, "*poor and marshy. I saw in passing up the river wild vines, water melons, pumpkins, gourds and many other vegetables, such as pamer christals, sunflowers, etc.*"

The Perry Volunteers left the Rio Grande and entered the San Juan River, which was about the size of the Warrior River in Alabama, and continued upstream arriving at their destination below Camargo about one o'clock in the afternoon of September 1, 1846, after six days on the river. Other elements of the First Alabama arrived on the scene around four o'clock that afternoon aboard the steamboat *Big Hatchie*. At Camargo, there was an old church building that was partly falling down. The streets were narrow and the few buildings there were made of mud bricks and covered with straw or palmetto leaves. The citizens of Camargo, accustomed to a quiet pastoral life, were amazed at the army descending upon

Grand Plaza at Camargo, Mexico
Mary Couts Burnett Library-TCU

them in the form of thousands of men in high-pressure steamboats with shrill whistles that they heard for the first time. In a matter of a few days, Camargo was transformed into a bustling center of great activity with large stacks of provisions and rations piled in the public square. The camp was a rock-rimmed place situated upriver where the San Juan River merges with the Rio Grande. This campsite was not an improvement over Brazos Island and Camp Alabama. Exchanging sea breezes that drove sand into every opening for this place void of breezes to provide relief from the relentless heat did nothing to endear the men to military life.

Here the volunteers from Alabama cooked, baked and broiled under the Mexican sun with temperatures over 100 degrees. They discovered that their new home had recently flooded and the San Juan River left a layer of mud about a foot deep that had dried, turning into a fine powdery substance that made its way into and upon everything in the camp. This dust was a constant source of complaint among the soldiers and added to their misery during their sojourn in

---

[91] Reynosa was occupied on June 10, 1846, at the request of the Alcaldé who asked General Taylor for a garrison to protect the town of 1,000 inhabitants from Mexican stragglers and marauders.

[92] The *Enterprise* was an unreliable, worm eaten steamboat that had mechanical trouble on its first trip up the Rio Grande on July 6, 1846, and had to be left at Reynosa. The need for river transportation was such that it was pressed back in service and the boat proved to be a death trap when its boiler ruptured.

Camargo. As if this was not enough, the place was infested with snakes, tarantulas, scorpions, an army of ants and a plague of small green frogs. The glamour and adventure of fighting Mexicans had become a war with some of the most inhospitable creatures in the countryside of Northern Mexico.

Captain Coleman looked around, saw the destruction of the river overflow and was not pleased with what he observed. He noted, in an understatement, his impression in his diary:

> "found the place to be a rather disagreeable one. . . . the town of Camargo is a bad looking place, the location is good enough, the high water washed down all the houses of any importance which ruined the appearance of the place. . . . dry and hot and too much dust for any satisfaction here. . ."

The Perry Volunteers set up as best they could near the river below the grimy town and settled into camp life in what they thought was to be their new home where the tents of the army stretched for three miles along the river. Coleman noted the activity on his first full day in this camp as, "cleaning up and get fixed to live" and clearing a campsite and parade ground for Company drills. Captain Coleman, as part of organizing the Company camp, turned over some surplus muskets, knapsacks, cartridge boxes, scabbards and other extraneous equipment to the Army that were no longer needed due to the recent deaths and discharges in Company C. By September 2, the talk in camp indicated that the First Alabama would not be part of Taylor's advancing army that was expected to leave Camargo any day.

Captain Sydenham Moore of Company D of the First Alabama was expressive with his thoughts at being left behind, noting in his journal on September 2, 1846:

> "Learned with unfeigned regret that we were not be permitted to go on with Gen'l Taylors advance which was about to start to Monterey. We were set aside and other Reg'ts that had arrived long after we did, were sent on. We find preparations going on around us, by those who are chosen to form a part of this expedition, but it only serves to depress us the more. Ours will be a poor destiny. When there is fighting to be done or any chance for gaining glory & honor we will not be allowed to participate in it."

Captain Moore went on to attribute their inactivity to the field officers whom he thought were responsible for the First Alabama being passed over and left inactive in camp. Coleman was more resigned to his fate recording on September 5, "We are to be stationed here God knows how long, for no one else knows, it seems. Today Genl. Taylor, Quitman, and Butler all left Camargo for Monterey."

The weather at Camargo continued to be abominable and the dust insufferable causing Captain Coleman to comment on September 6, "some appearance of rain. It is very much needed to allay the disagreeable dust, which greatly infests our camp. Very hot." The next day the camp talk was that the Perry Volunteers were going to move again and orders to that effect were received that morning. Around noon, the steamboat Corvette[93] arrived on the river to move the Volunteers above the town, so they loaded their camp equipment and other baggage aboard the boat and moved to their new home one mile above Camargo. Upon seeing their new campsite Coleman recorded his impression with a grimace: "arrived at our new encampment . . . at ½

[93] The Corvette was a side-wheeler built at Brownsville, Pennsylvania in 1846 at a cost of $16,000 and was 135 feet long and twenty-six feet wide. It was a soundly built boat with exquisite furnishings and was the most expensive boat bought by the army. The most important feature was that the boat drew only thirty inches of water when loaded. It was captained by Pennsylvania born Mifflin Kenady and his mate Prescott Devot and was used by General Winfield Scott for his visit to Camargo in January 1847.

past 12 o'clock; a bad looking chance for any part of comfort" in this location. The weather continued hot and dry and the Volunteers set themselves to the task of cleaning up a new campground and setting things in order. Coleman went to Camargo to shop where he purchased "*shot, pins, sugar, etc.*" and the cleanup of the campsite and parade grounds continued for a week after they arrived at the new site.

The San Juan River that ran near the camp was used for everything including drinking water, bathing and all other purposes. Sanitary conditions were poor and, as could be expected, the soldiers fell victim to dysentery, measles, mumps, yellow fever and other diseases that ran through the camp. These diseases were an enemy as much as the Mexicans, but disease could not be prevailed against with a volley of musketry. On September 6, the Georgia, Alabama and Second Tennessee regiments reported a huge number of disabilities—Georgia 425 (53 %), Alabama 430 (57 %) and the Second Tennessee 271 (46 %). By the end of September 1846, the First Regiment of Alabama Volunteers had buried twenty-four men and reported 192 still in the hospital or on sick call including twenty-eight officers of the regiment. Shortly after arriving at Camargo, Captain Coleman observed on September 3 that there is "*a great deal of sickness amongst the volunteer army at this time*" and that General Gideon Johnson Pillow[94] had requisitioned the First Alabama "*for men to bury dead in the Tennessee Regiment.*"

General Robert Patterson
Major-General of Volunteers

The men from Perry County were spared excessive illness in large part. After a week at Camargo, Lewis T. Palmer died during the afternoon on September 8. The next month Daniel W. Sneed was discharged from the army at Matamoros on October 13, it is assumed for disability from the hospital there. Hezekiah Filbert was hospitalized on November 24, 1846, and died two days later on November 26, 1846. The death of a soldier is a mournful thing particularly if it appears pointless when no blow is struck against the enemy. Private Stephen Nunnalee, contemplating the death of one of his comrades, made this entry in his journal:

> "*It is painful to die far from home and relatives, where no sister's sweet consoling voice is heard to cheer the flying spirit to another unknown world. Here, when one is taken sick, one indulges only in fruitless hope, for he is too soon hurried into an eternity, where he will hear no more the familiar voices of his fellow-comrades. . . . How perfectly a man can become* [accustom to death]. *He soon loses all of those finer and sympathetic feelings that ennobles his nature. And this is pretty much the case with all. It would not do to be otherwise . . .*"

The illnesses that ran through the army at Camargo caused two deaths in Company C during their three months at this place but no hospitalizations among the men from Perry County. However, Palmer and Filbert's deaths and Sneed's discharge permanently reduced the company by a total of eighteen men. Company strength had declined to about eighty men and officers by

---

[94] Gideon Johnson Pillow was born in Tennessee on June 8, 1806. He graduated from the University of Nashville in 1827, practiced law with James K. Polk, was politically a Democrat and supported Polk for President. The President commissioned him a Brigadier General of Volunteers on July 1, 1846. Pillow had no previous military experience and was an easy target for critics who labeled him as militarily incompetent and a crony of the President. His feuding with General Winfield Scott at the end of the war was scandalous, accusing the successful commander of having little to do with the capture of Mexico City.

Thanksgiving 1846. Many of the Perry boys, including Captain Coleman, were unwell but remained on duty too sick to do much but well enough to stay out of the hospital. It is obvious from Captain Coleman's observations that Volunteer illness was a persistent, ongoing condition throughout the war that was greater than the list of hospitalizations. Since the Alabamians were relatively healthy, they were called upon to assist the Second Tennessee Regiment who reported that about 650 men were hospitalized and many died rapidly at Camargo. These regiments were so enfeebled by illness that in October 1846 men from the First Regiment of Alabama Volunteers were ordered to attend to the ill and bury their dead. About 1,500 Americans died at Camargo—one out of every eight—almost as many as died in battle.[95] At times, thirty per cent of Taylor's army was disabled and the death march was heard in camp from sunrise to sunset.

On September 8, the Perry Volunteers took on a more military appearance. The government gave up the clothing arrangements for volunteers that was prescribed by law and issued them the blue uniforms of the Regular Army.[96] That night there was a false alarm in the camp due to rumors and reports that ten thousand Mexicans were thirty miles away and advancing on the camp at Camargo. The report of an imminent attack by Mexicans lurking around caused the long roll to be furiously beat on drums, the volunteers to form battle lines and discharge a few muskets, but there was no attack, only momentary excitement. Concern that the Mexicans would make an assault on the town, the Volunteers heaped up mounds of dirt into embankments and helped build fortifications in and around Camargo. General Patterson had six pound cannon mounted behind the embankments thrown up by the soldiers and ordered everyone not a resident of the town, a soldier or government employee to leave by September 17, nearly depopulating Camargo of gamblers, whiskey sellers, prostitutes and other camp followers. Rumors were constant that an attack from a large body of Mexicans was probable at any time, but soon the stories faded away when no Mexicans appeared.

The First Alabama began to be detailed out as the regiment settled into garrison duty. On September 7, Company D was moved across the Rio San Juan to guard government stores. Company C was detached from the regiment on Thursday, September 10 and assigned to guard the headquarters of Major General of Volunteers Robert Patterson, which led to more grumbling among the Perry Volunteers because they were not advancing toward the enemy with General Taylor. The distress of the men of Company C was heightened by war preparation activity going on in the camp and at their duty post around Patterson's tent. On September 11, Captain Coleman observed: "*In camps everything in commotion about moving, and fighting Mexicans.*" However, he did not see Company C getting into the fight and stated, "*Exchanged off cartridge boxes, bayonet scabbards and belts; Some appearance of rain but none of fighting in my view.*" He went on to express the unhappiness among the Perry County men: "*this day three months ago we all left our sweet homes and families to take upon ourselves the most miserable and unpleasant life that white men ever lived.*" On September 13, a letter arrived from Lieutenant William Marshall Ford written in New Orleans reporting that Lewis A. Miree, who was discharged for disability at Camp Alabama, had died and never made it home alive. Mexico had claimed another Perry County man. The next day, as part of his duty, Coleman disposed of the property of Lewis T. Palmer and assumedly sent the money home to his family. After over two weeks at Camargo, the Volunteers began to drill a little, but they did it with little skill because they had drilled infrequently since leaving Mobile.

---

[95] In the late summer of 1980, hurricane Allen caused widespread flooding on the Rio San Juan and the erosion of the flood unearthed many of the graves of the Americans buried there.

[96] Volunteer units arrived in Mexico wearing many colors that included blue, gray, green and white trimmed in red, pink and yellow. Between the two Greene County, Alabama companies, one wore a green worsted frock coat and the other a cottonade suit and straw hat. Captain Sydenham Moore noted in his journal that his company received regular army uniforms on November 1, nearly two months after the Perry Volunteers.

After the Perry Volunteers had been in Camargo for about a week, General Taylor put his forces in motion toward Monterrey, the capitol of Nuevo León. Taylor had 15,000 men in camp at Camargo from which he selected units numbering 6,600 men. Among the units selected by Taylor were 3,200 men from the Regular Army including the 1st, 3rd, 5th, 7th and 8th Infantry Regiments, plus the Second Dragoons and five batteries of artillery. The 3,400 volunteers chosen for the advance were the First Volunteer Infantry Regiments from Ohio, Kentucky, Mississippi, Tennessee and two regiments from Texas and the Battalion of Maryland and District of Columbia Volunteer Infantry from Quitman's Brigade.[97] The other 9,000 were not part of the line of march for Monterrey. The volunteers left in camp were under orders to be instructed, perform camp duties and subjected to a *"rigid system of police and discipline."* On September 6, a long line of troops, wagons and pack mules loaded with tents and other equipment headed out of the Camargo camp towards Monterrey and their destiny, giving the appearance of an Arabian caravan as they moved down the road.[98] Captain Sydenham Moore watched the departing army and later penned a letter to his wife, Amanda, expressing the emotions he felt as he observed the scene:

> *"I had my heart on being with that expedition and when I saw the long trains of soldiers marching off in that direction—followed by scores of wagons & pack mules I stood and watched them, as far as my eye could see them, and then turned away and felt for the first time disappointed and sad."*

The reason virtually all of the men had gathered at Camargo was to be part of the expedition moving against the Mexicans. Naturally, the Perry Volunteers expected to be part of the army advancing against the enemy and were deeply disappointed to be left behind. Their only enemy remained the stealthy one of mortal disease and cruel nature. Conditions at Camargo resulted in a large number of ill and disabled soldiers and the First Regiment of Alabama Volunteers cared for the sick while the rest of the army marched off in search of glory. There was great resentment and howls of protest among the Perry Volunteers and others in the regiment. They had traveled thousands of miles, endured disease, watched the death and disabling illness of comrades, suffered the torments of weather and nature and suffered the hardships of travel and camp life. After all this suffering, being left behind was considered an unacceptable outcome for their sacrifices.

The disappointment of those left out of the action was well known in the army and one gallant participant in the battle at Monterrey seemed to understand how the Perry countians felt when he penned a verse about the battle:

> *"We were not many, we who stood*
> *upon the battle-field that day;*
> *But many a gallant spirit would*
> *Give half his life if he but could*
> *Have been with us at Monteray"*

Captain Sydenham Moore in his *Journal* on September 28 expressed perfectly the feelings of those reflecting on the battle and what might have been: *"I would have given any thing in the*

[97] At Monterrey, Quitman's Brigade consisted of the First Tennessee, commanded by William B. Campbell, Mississippi Rifles, commanded by Jefferson Davis and the Maryland and Washington, D. C. Battalion. The First Tennessee lost one quarter of its men at Monterrey and became known as the *"Bloody First."* The Baltimore and Washington, D. C. Battalion suffered six deaths, including Lt. Colonel William H. Watson, and sixteen wounded.

[98] Because of the shortage of wagons, General Taylor acquired nearly 2,000 mules for transport and each of which carried three hundred pounds of supplies and equipment. The Monterrey wagon train consisted about 180 wagons. Each soldier in Taylor's army carried eight days of rations and forty rounds of buck and ball ammunition.

world to have been there, if for nothing else just to have had it to say, . . . that I was at the battle of Monterey."

General Taylor launched a two-pronged attack against Monterrey located in a pass of the Sierra

Madre Mountains on September 21 with 6,600 men but no heavy artillery against 10,000 Mexicans in stone forts bristling with artillery covering every approach to the town. The Mexicans made a fierce and desperate defense firing from barricades in the streets, windows and roofs after their forts were captured. For four days, Taylor's men threw themselves at the forts and fought through the houses and streets of the city in bloody assaults and paid for the American victory with copious amounts of their blood. On September 25, 1846, the Mexican General Pedro de Ampudia agreed to an eight-week armistice, and the Ameri-

Storming of Monterrey
September 21-25, 1846

can flag was raised over Monterrey. The terms of the armistice allowed the Mexicans to retain their arms and march out of the city with their flags flying. General Taylor justified this action to the government in Washington saying: *"The gallant defense of the town, and the fact of a recent change of government in Mexico, believed to be favorable to the interests of peace, induced me to concur with the commission in these terms which will, I trust, receive the approvals of the government."*[99]

Back in the camps at Camargo, the idle Perry County men anxiously waited to hear the outcome of the action at Monterrey. Captain Coleman noted in his diary on September 22, *"Expecting to hear from Monterrey constantly, no news officially from Monterrey, rainy the boys all getting in better health."* The next day he recorded the latest camp activities and rumor making the rounds:

> *"In camp doing nothing but drilling; a little foggy, very warm indeed. All the sick seem to be improving a little. News came into town stating that Canales was killing all sick on the road from here to Monterrey and that he has under his command 500 men."*

During the military actions at Monterrey, the road between there and the base camp at Camargo swarmed with guerrillas that hid in the chaparral and made communication between the two places difficult, dangerous and slow. To get his dispatches through, General Taylor hired Mexicans at forty-five dollars a month and provided them with the swiftest horses. Antonio Canales was a lawyer born in Monterrey who was known as the *"Chaparral Fox"* and had a history of plunder and brutal treatment of Americans in general and Texans in particular. Canales held the rank of Brigadier General in the Mexican Army and led a command of about three hundred irregular soldiers who attacked and ruthlessly killed travelers and soldiers on the Camargo to Monterey road in order to sever communication and pillage supplies flowing to Taylor's army. Canales was adept at killing Texans by knocking their brains out and mutilating their bodies and the Texans in retribution laid waste to Mexican ranches, killing with a brutal-

---

[99] The government in Washington did not approve of the armistice that Taylor negotiated and ordered him to end it and resume offensive operations. President Polk wrote of Taylor in his diary: *" He had the enemy in his power and should have taken them prisoners, depriving them of their arms . . . "*

ity that equaled that of the Mexicans. It was a cruel no quarter war for control of the road and surrounding countryside with neither side relenting nor showing mercy.

On September 29, the bodies of two Tennesseans were found with their throats cut, multiple chest wounds and shot in the back. The volunteers at Camargo swore revenge and sent out a party of horsemen to find the Mexicans responsible for the outrage. Coleman's comments about outlaws killing Americans on the road were in response to this type of guerrilla activity. On October 1, 1846, orders were read at the evening dress parade of the First Alabama that armed Mexicans between the Rio Grande to thirty miles west of the city of Monterrey were to be regarded and treated as outlaws.

A month later an apparently harmless Mexican was murdered in a cornfield near the Alabama and Tennessee encampments and General Robert Patterson swore to hang the "*villain*" responsible if he could be identified. Suspicion fell upon the two nearby regiments, and Private Nunnalee of Company D noted in his journal "*the Alabamians are charged with the whole of it.*" General Gideon Pillow condemned the murder and was determined to blame the Alabamians. However, it was the opinion of others that the death of the Mexican was in retaliation for the brutal murder of the two men from the Tennessee regiment although there is no proof of what happened to the unfortunate Mexican. In November, two more Mexicans were killed near the Alabama camp and again General Pillow accused the Alabama regiment of the crime although he had only supposition and no convincing proof. Like many crimes in this war, the murders of these Mexicans went unpunished.

General Zachary Taylor watched the outcome of the Battle of Monterrey, Mexico while the Perry Volunteers languish in inactivity in their camp in Camargo, Mexico.
Alonso Chappel—1850

While waiting for word from Monterrey, Captain Coleman noted in his diary on September 24 that he had been detailed by General Zachary Taylor as a member of a court martial established to try Captain John McMahon from Georgia[100] for drunkenness and an assault on Colonel Edward Dickinson Baker, commander of Illinois troops.[101] The court martial was the result of an event at Matamoros during a riot among Georgia volunteers. Colonel Baker and a detachment of the Fourth Illinois Volunteers attempted to suppress the disorder and a mêlée resulted with deadly results. Captain John McMahon was the commander of the Jasper Greens, a Georgia Volunteer Regiment company well known for their Irish temperament and violent behavior. Captain Franklin Smith in his wartime *Journal* recorded that he saw "*the celebrated Jasper Greens composed mostly of Irishmen. Of whom a Georgian remarked in my presence 'Give the Jasper Greens some whisky and they will charge into Hell.'*" The *Albany Patriot* (June 3, 1846) wrote of the Jasper Greens, "*most of them are foreigners, and true-hearted Irishmen at that— men who live by their daily labor, and have deprived themselves of the reward of toil, and the blessings of home and family, to serve their adopted country.*" On the night of August 31, 1846, the Jasper Greens were loading on to the steamboat *Corvette* to move upriver to Camargo when the Greens exchanged provocative remarks with the Kennesaw Rangers, a company in

---

[100] Captain Sydenham Moore in his journal noted that he served on the court martial of "*Capt McMahon*" for "*a capital offence—for mutinous conduct, & also for drunkenness.*" George W. Smith and Charles Judah in their book *Chronicles of the Gringos* report the episode as related in this narrative.
[101] Edward Dickinson Baker was Colonel of the Fourth Regiment of Illinois Volunteers. His regiment was mustered into the army in July 1846 and Baker was discharged in May 1847. He was born in 1821 and was twenty-five at the time of the riot incident.

their own regiment, and the infuriated Greens attacked the Kennesaw company with knives, clubs and pistols.

Captain McMahon, his sword drawn, swiftly entered the brawl in an attempt to quell the riot, and Colonel Edward Baker did the same with about twenty-five men in the Fourth Illinois Infantry Regiment. McMahon had been drinking liquor and attacked Colonel Baker and the two men exchanged thrusts with their swords. When the riot ended, Captain McMahon was wounded with a stab wound in his lip and cheek, Colonel Baker had been shot in the back of the head, and three men—a lieutenant, a corporal and a private—were dead. The court martial convicted Captain McMahon of drunkenness on duty and mutinous conduct, but he was "*allowed to keep his sword because of 'the palliating character of the testimony.'*" McMahon's witnesses testified as to his efforts to reduce the violence during the riot and McMahon apologized effectively for his drunken state convincing the court martial to go easy on him.[102] Colonel Baker survived his wounds, served out his Mexican War enlistment and was discharged in May 1847. However, he was killed at the Battle of Ball's Bluff, Virginia on October 21, 1861, while serving as Major General of Union volunteers during the War for Southern Independence. Coleman noted the court martial was adjourned on October 2, having handled a number of cases.[103]

Coleman was still waiting on September 27 to hear the results of the Battle at Monterrey writing in his diary "*still anxiously waiting to hear something from Gen'. Taylor.*" Later that day, he noted:

> "*the news came in that Genl. Taylor has taken Monterrey and lost 500 men and that there was an armistice signed by Taylor and Ampudia for eight weeks, bad arrangement I fear. It is said that Ampudia was allowed to leave town with the honour of War and with colors flying.*"[104]

The report that Mexican General Ampudia was allowed to leave Monterrey with his arms and colors flying was the object of much unhappiness in the U. S. Army and with Captain Coleman. Captain Franklin Smith recorded the reports of "*Texians*" who observed the Mexican army leaving the town: " *. . . they went out in great spirits drums beating flags flying and displaying every evidence of triumph.*" Such descriptions as this disgusted the army and led to unsympathetic criticisms of their commander. General Taylor was accused of throwing the victory away after all of the hard fighting was over and the Mexican surrender a virtual certainty. Although left behind and unhappy with the battle's conclusion, the patriotism of the disappointed Alabama volunteers remained strong. When the news of the American victory reached the garrison at Camargo, a celebration erupted among the troops left behind. A splendid exhibition of fireworks was organized, and bands played national airs such as *Hail Columbia* and the *Star Spangled Banner*. There was much excitement and many expressions of joy at the success of the American army made by the boys

General Pedro de Ampudia
1848

---

[102] Lt. Colonel Thomas Y. Redd, Captain Allison Nelson of the Kennesaw Rangers and Captain Harrison J. Sergent, along with Private C. C. Hammack, testified that McMahon was engaged in suppressing the riot when Colonel Baker rushed into the fray in the darkness without identifying himself and demanded surrender. They further testified that the Jasper Greens acted to defend Captain McMahon.

[103] The officers on the Court Martial were: Major Goode Bryan (Provost); Captain Oscar F. Winship (Judge Advocate) from the Regular Army; Captain Andrew L. Pickens and William G. Coleman from the First Alabama; Captain George W. McCowand and Captain Henry F. Murry of the Second Tennessee; and Captain William T. Willis of the Second Kentucky.

[104] Taylor's casualties at Monterrey were 120 killed, 368 wounded and forty-three missing.

from Alabama in spite of their resentment at losing a chance for personal fame and glory. Private Stephen Nunnalee of Greene County, Alabama recorded the event in his journal, "... *their were great exclamations of joy at the superior valor of our arms and daring heroism of our soldiers.*" Others were joyous because of the bravery of the volunteers at Monterrey. Captain Smith noted the reports of valor in his *Journal* stating, "*all the volunteers fought well every man stood up there is no distinction. The volunteers fought as well as the regulars and they all fought alike but I tell you our losses have been very great...*"

While at Camargo, the Perry Volunteers went through a progression of training activity that improved their military skills. From September 1, the day the Company arrived, through the end of September the Volunteers did little in regard to preparing for combat. For a month, their Captain recorded almost daily in his diary that the Company had, "*little to do*" except to clean the camp, prepare a parade ground and fortify the town of Camargo, while Captain Coleman served on a court martial. Short, poorly executed drills were held on four of the thirty days of the month of September, hardly a suitable schedule to build combat proficiency. The attitude seems to be, why bother with drill if we are not going to meet the enemy? The soldierly training of the Alabama regiment was limited because the officers lacked skill. They drilled the men rarely giving a command and mixing up the execution of military maneuvers. However, things began to change on September 28 when it was circulated in the camps at Camargo that the First Alabama was going to move to Monterrey. Coleman recorded on the 29th that the Volunteers were "*drilling and preparing to meet the Mexicans between Monterey and Saltillo*" and made similar notations in the week that followed. News arrived in camp from General Taylor that Mexican General Antonio López de Santa Anna[105] had fortified Saltillo with 20,000 fresh troops which made the prospects for combat seem more probable than ever before.

General Antonio López de Santa Anna 1835

Drilling of the Perry Volunteers became more intense on October 3 and the pace of war preparations took on a more serious appearance. The Volunteers were roused out of their lethargy and the commanders of the volunteer division began to get serious about the war readiness of the men in their command. From October 5 through October 10, Captain Coleman noted daily that his Company was "*preparing to go to Monterey.*" On October 12, Coleman was clearly waiting to receive orders to proceed to Monterey and on the next day he received orders from General Patterson that he was to conduct drills four times a day. Thereafter, the Company drilled for six hours daily and practiced using the bayonet in double-quick simulated charges during which the men screamed as loud as possible. In November, they began to fire their muskets at targets for what appears to be the first time. General Robert Patterson was profuse in his compliments to Coleman about the efficiency of the First Alabama saying, "*Genl. Patterson complimented our Reg as highly as language could do it. He said our improvement was super human, it was magical and surpassed anything to his knowledge.*" By the end of the second week in October, the Alabamians were "*drilling nearly all of the time.*" The military performance of the regiment slowly improved with time but the soldiers grew progressively restless.

---

[105] Antonio López de Santa Anna Perez de Lebron was born in Jalapa, Mexico. He had a limited education and at sixteen years of age Santa Anna became a cadet in the Fijo de Vera Cruz Regiment and helped to drive the Spanish from Mexico. He was elected President in 1832 and shortly became dictator of Mexico. He marched against Texas in 1836 and was defeated and captured by the Texas army under Sam Houston. He lost a leg expelling the French from Vera Cruz in 1838 and was again elected President of Mexico in 1841, but he was deposed and fled to Cuba. With the beginning of the Mexican War, he returned to power in Mexico and led the Mexican Army against the forces of the United States. Santa Anna died in Mexico City in 1874.

Captain Coleman continued to have difficulties with the men in Company C and his pre-war friendships caused him personal stress. On September 26 and again on October 17, he noted a difficulty with his friend James Francis Bailey recording:

> "26th *My friend Jas F. Bailey became hurt with me for that which I did not intend to be understood as he construed it. I am sorry but cannot satisfy him.*
>
> "*17th again J. F. B. has taken some offense, and treats me coolly, for what I know not. I have given him no cause, knowingly or designedly. It grieves me sorely.*"

The nature of the anguish between the Captain and Bailey is not stated, but it is clear that Captain Coleman and Colonel John R. Coffey developed a strong friendship with each other based on a diary entry on October 5 reading "*Col. Coffee expressed so much friendship for me and in such a manner that I could scarcely keep from shedding a tear of joy.*" Perhaps Coffey was grateful for Coleman's support in the aborted attempt to replace regimental officers earlier in June when he refused to sign the petition calling for officer resignations or perhaps the Colonel just needed a friend and respected the character of William Coleman.

With the arrival of the expanded schedule of drills for the regiment on October 13, Colonel Coffey became seriously ill and did not return to duty until two weeks later.[106] In his absence, command of the regiment devolved to Lt. Colonel Richard G. Earle who was unimpeded in his direction of the regiment by the commanding officer confined to his sick bed. Trouble between the second in command and the officers and men of the regiment began immediately. Earle and Captain Coleman engaged in a serious disagreement about the conduct of regimental drills and the two men "*had a few short words.*" Earle reported Coleman to General Quitman and charged him with "*disobedience of Orders*" leading Coleman to speculate that the incident "*will in all probability cause my arrest.*" Unfortunately, the outcome of the charge associated with this incident is not known and Coleman makes no more comment on the subject. Earle was generally quarrelsome with others and Coleman reports that "*Earle grossly insulted Maj. Bryan a second time and pointedly, I think.*"

On Saturday, October 17, Coleman noted more discontent caused by Earle stating, "*almost mutiny in our Regiment in consequence of Lt. Col. Earls movements in the Regiment.*" The night of this incident, the men in the regiment acted to show their disapproval of their Lieutenant Colonel's treatment. The annoyed and vengeful soldiers erected an effigy of Earle on the parade ground during the night and cut the tail off his horse. The next morning when Earle discovered that he was the object of ridicule, and that his mare's tail was completely pruned, he was in an acrimonious mood. The next day, Earle assembled the regiment and had the men stand in formation while the *Regulations of the Army* were arduously read to them.

It would be difficult to exaggerate the insolence of certain of the volunteers. Some of the men referred to their officers by their first name without any thought of military etiquette or army regulations. After the horsetail incident, Earle was openly referred to by the unflattering name of "*bob tail mare*" and Colonel Coffey was routinely addressed as "*John.*" Lt. Colonel Earle appears to have determined to instill some discipline and military skill in the Alabama Regiment and set out to do it with a firm hand. However, he encountered the universal characteristic of citizen-soldiers to refuse to be treated as anything but free men and to resent anything that offended their sense of equality with officers. They followed orders when it suited them and were indifferent to rank, dress and military protocol. This independent manner stemmed from the

---

[106] The nature of Coffey's illness is not known but Captain Coleman recorded that the colonel "*salivated*" which indicates that he was undergoing mercurial treatment, characterized by excessive discharge of saliva from the mouth. Mercury was used as an element in a variety of internal remedies.

democratic attitude they held as civilians and the notion they were receiving orders from their peers. The cramped caldron in which they lived at Camargo and the constant reminder of death in the camps gave the soldiers ample cause for complaint and irascibility. Earle's activities during his temporary command of the Alabamians made him quite unpopular with his fellow officers and the other soldiers in the regiment.[107]

Still hopeful of getting into the fight against the Mexicans, the Perry Volunteers continued to drill and hold all in readiness to march to Monterrey if orders came. While they drilled and feuded with Lt. Colonel Earle, other events were occurring in Company C. On October 8, Second Lieutenant William Marshall Ford rejoined the Company following a furlough to Alabama, bringing information from their families in Perry County and some little treasures from their loved ones and friends. Coleman's wife sent him "*many things which she thought I needed and among all the rest some biscuits. God Bless her.*"[108] Lieutenant William M. Ford also brought Coleman $80 from Thomas A. Heard, which was welcome because the volunteers had not received any money from the government since mustering into the army at Mobile four months earlier. Word reached the camp on October 9, 1846, through General Gideon Pillow that the Mexican government had "*refused disdainfully*" to consider peace overtures from the United States, irritating the men of Company C and the regiment because of what they considered Mexican arrogance.

On Sunday, October 11, Captain Coleman noted in his diary that four months had passed since the Volunteers marched out of Perryville and down the dusty road to Selma with high spirits and brimming pride in their patriotism. R. T. Grice from Alabama appeared in camp the same day carrying a Mexican sword, gun and lance. He was fresh from the city of Monterrey where he observed the battle between the Mexicans and the Army of Occupation. Grice was impressed by the American losses, numbering them at eight hundred or greater but believed the Mexican losses were larger. The next day First Lieutenant Robert Thomas Goree left the Company's camp for Alabama, having been, according to Coleman, discharged for a second time. Coleman was apparently pleased to see Goree leave noting in his diary, "*Go, I say, and stay there.*" That day a large flock of geese flew over the Alabama camp and the event was thought to be a harbinger of fall weather. Interestingly, it turned cold that night and a harsh, cold and windy "*northeaster*" blew in a few days later. A board of officers appeared in the camp of the Perry Volunteers on October 14 to examine the tents of the Company, which were all condemned as unfit for service. The next day Company C received twelve common tents, and two wall tents to replace the ones judged unserviceable. The old tents were turned over to the quartermaster. The sick seemed to improve in mid October except for those that "*have grown worse to screen themselves from a little duty*" displaying that the malingering soldier is present in every army of every era.

As the month of October grew to a close and the Perry boys were not called to join the army, order and discipline in the company weaken. Without anything to do except tedious continuous drilling, without excitement, diversions or entertainment, without any prospects of meeting the Mexicans in battle, sitting day after day, week after week was enough to try the discipline and fortitude of the best citizen-soldiers. Captain Coleman "*had all of the musicians arrested for neglect of duty*" on Sunday, October 18. The following day there was "*great confusion*" in the Alabama camp because the field officers refused to cooperate with each other. Quarreling among themselves was the principal activity of the men, and they were careless with principles related to military order and punctuality causing Coleman to observe, "*we have come to a low*

[107] The journal of Captain Sydenham Moore provides little illumination about the Lt. Colonel Earle affair. Strangely, Captain Moore's journal has two pages torn out for the dates October 7-31, 1846, giving rise to speculation that these pages may have contained entries about this period of discord in the regiment that Moore was reticent for others to read.
[108] Among the things Coleman received from his Alabama family was a new pair of boots, a waistcoat and an "*old coat that my Dear Old Mother gave me in the winter of 1843.*" Two months later, Coleman still had some his wife's biscuits to eat.

ebb." Taylor's armistice with the Mexicans was still in effect causing inactivity in the U. S. Army. Captain Coleman noted on October 21, *"doing nothing, but drilling and preparing for WAR . . . the army lying on its oars at nothing waiting for the expiration of the Armistice."* Officers of the regiment found some relief from the ennui by having a large dinner prepared in Camargo that was attended by all of the officers except three. While in town for the dinner, Captain Coleman saw Mirabeau Buonaparte Lamar,[109] the first Vice President and second President of the Republic of Texas and a former resident of Dallas County, Alabama. At the Battle of San Jacinto in 1836, Lamar commanded the cavalry of Sam Houston's Army of Texas.

The disobedience of the Alabama men began about two weeks after arriving at Camargo and continued unimpeded while at this camp. Soldiers left their camp without permission and roamed the countryside. James Bennett, the Company fifer from Radfordville Beat in Perry County, was assigned to work as a blacksmith for Captain Franklin Smith. A large train arrived from Monterrey and orders were issued to shoe the mules causing twenty-five men to be detailed to the blacksmith shops, including Bennett. Bennett reported to work on October 10, but left the blacksmith shop refusing to perform any work. He complained that he would not work as a blacksmith for the fifteen cents a day paid by the army. He stated that he had worked hard to acquire the skills of a blacksmith and that a day or two in the blacksmith shop would ruin his clothes, which could not be even replaced by the pay he would receive from the Army for his work. Bennett did not report to work the day after first refusing or the day after that. On October 13, an officer of the First Alabama brought Bennett to Captain Smith and ordered him to do his duty. A few minutes later, Captain Smith saw Bennett walking away and when confronted, Bennett said that he would not work. Later, Captain Smith wrote in a letter to his commanding officer that, *"I sent for the guard and ordered them to the guardhouse"* where they were confined on bread and water. However, due to an amazingly casual attitude toward discipline, Colonel George A. Morgan, commander of the Second Regiment of Ohio Volunteers, released Bennett after only two hours of detention. This example demonstrates the reluctance of volunteer officers to enforce discipline in the ranks of citizen soldiers and, although there was additional discussion of the incident, nothing further was done to punish the insubordination. On November 12, Lieutenant Colonel Richard G. Earle ordered private Duke Nall of the Perry Volunteers into the guardhouse but his offense is not known. Captain Coleman expressed a continuing low opinion of Earle for arresting Nall when he noted the event in his diary, *"Lt. Col. Earle, better known in camp by the name of Canallies, the noted Mexican robber."*

While life in camp was marred by quarreling and waywardness, there were other events occurring that were less dramatic. Daniel Sneed returned from his hospitalization at Matamoros on October 23 having been discharged on the thirteenth and the health of Hezekiah Filbert began its march toward his death, which occurred on November 26. Sneed stayed with the Company until he could arrange for transportation to Alabama but performed no duty. Coleman learned in a message from home that his son Benjamin had joined the church in Alabama. Lucius Lockett from Perry County, serving in a Greene County company, appeared in camp with letters from home for Captain Coleman and others in the Perry Company. The Volunteers continued to fire their muskets at targets as part of their training, and the boys from Perry County proved to be good marksmen and adept at handling firearms, having been raised in a culture where firearms were an essential part of everyday life.

The difficulties of disciplining citizen soldiers was quite evident when at a formation of the Alabama and Tennessee regiments on November 16 addressed by General Gideon J. Pillow and General Robert Patterson, the Alabamians howled and brayed like jackasses in a display of disrespect for the generals and a serious violation of the military code of behavior. General Patterson in a rage immediately sought out Colonel Coffey and lectured him on his regiment's misconduct, which the Colonel endured submissively. Captain Coleman noted the event in his di-

---

[109] Mirabeau B. Lamar's son John Burwell Lamar died in Perry County, Alabama on July 31, 1837, at eleven months of age and is buried on the plantation of Jabez Curry in the Curry family burial ground.

ary stating, "*bad behavior on the part of our Regiment this evening, disrespect shown to our Brig. Genl.*" The next day General Pillow attempted to restore some semblance of order as noted by Coleman in his diary: "*Genl Pillow addressed our Regiment in quite a respectful manner on the treatment he received from it yesterday.*" The poor conduct on the part of the regiment can be attributed to the nature of volunteer soldiers and their inactivity. Camargo was a temporary home for thousands of soldiers who were there to fight Mexicans but who were caught in the idleness of war. War usually consists of short periods of great exertions and activity followed by long periods of absolute boredom. There was little to do at this camp except to attend to the ill, perform uninspiring drill and stand guard duty.

In Mexico, the soldiers from rural Perry County received a lesson in wickedness, immorality, corruption and debauchery that included murder, rape, riot and robbery of Mexican civilians. There is nothing to indicate that the men from Perry County were responsible for any crimes, but regiments from Kentucky, Arkansas and Texas put on a demonstration so odious that a Mexican Catholic priest described them as "*vomit from Hell.*" Lieutenant George Meade wrote home describing the torture of innocent Mexican civilians by American volunteers who "*killed five or six innocent people walking in the streets for no other object than their own amusement . . . they rob and steal cattle and corn from the poor farmers, and in fact are more like a body of hostile Indians than civilized whites.*" People who observed the conduct of the volunteers generally attempted to explain or even obfuscate the behavior. Captain Franklin Smith noted in his *War Journal* that "*honorable men at home*" took on a "*strange sort of morality*" once they entered the army. Colonel Reuben Davis observed in his *Regulations* that he thought the men believed they were free to disregard the law, morality and obligations to God and man when away from the influences of home.

In October 1846, the Baptists in Perry County seemed to understand the moral temptations, hazards and depravity war brings to soldiers. Reverend Abraham W. Jackson, Perry Volunteer Charles Green Jackson's father, was a delegate to the fall meeting of the Cahawba Baptist Association. The assembled delegates prayed for relief from the suffering in the Mexican War and passed a resolution calling for humiliation and prayer for the soldiers and their families:

> "*Whereas, this association is deeply affected by the calamities of war to our common country, and the cause of humanity, and sincerely sympathizing with our fellow citizens who have friends and relations who are now exposed to the temptations of the camp, and the dangers incident to a campaign in the enemy's country—Resolved, that we recommend to the Churches, to assemble at their places of worship on Friday before the next Sabbath in November [1846] and spend the day in fasting, humiliation and prayer before God, that He will incline the hearts of the people of both nations to peace; that an amicable adjustment of existing differences may take place before other fields of battle shall be stained with human gore. And, also, that supplication be fervently made for our exposed relatives and countrymen in Mexico, that God will preserve them from sin, fit them for any emergency which they must meet; and that those hearts which have been lacerated by the death of beloved relations, by the climate or the hand of the foe, may be healed; . . ..*"

During the Mexican War, little attention was paid to the Sabbath in the army. Unlike later wars, chaplains were not uniformly provided to the army and, as a consequence, Sunday services were unusual. The writers of the various journals maintained during the Mexican War made note of the lack of spiritual reinforcement for the volunteers and the disregard of Sunday as a day that was special. Private Nunnalee noted on Sunday, October 4, 1846, "*To-day would be Sunday, if celebrated in a proper manner, or regarded as such.*" Captain Moore recorded that his slave Peter seemed to be the only one who kept Sunday properly and observed on September 6, 1846 that: "*Tho it was Sunday, no one seemed to regard it, except for the Catholic population.*" Captain Coleman mentions preaching only once in his diary on Sunday, June 21,

1846, while at Camp Martin in Mobile. Captain Franklin Smith of the Mississippi volunteers discussing the nature and character of the American army in Mexico noted in his *Journal* that "*never was there a prouder more confident and vain glorious army than this—or one that looks less to God and more to themselves. . . . there are no Sabbaths in war. . .*" and "*In camp. . . but few think of God . . . May the Lord have mercy on us. . .*" Describing the Americans, the Mexican newspaper, *Diario*, recorded that the U. S. Army was: "*made up of adventurers who have no . . . religious creed, no moral principles or sentiments; for whom there are no priests or magistrates and for whom the house of God, the Senate, a drawing room, a theatre and a circus are all the same.*" The evidence is that God did not go to Mexico with this army; the American Army lacked spirituality and its collective behavior in Mexico seems to reflect that lack of sanctity.

On October 24, two companies from the First Alabama were ordered to march to Monterrey with the supply train and the chance to meet the enemy appeared to be improving. Unfortunately, the order to advance was countermanded by General Patterson on the twenty-fifth and Kentucky troops sent instead. The action of ordering Alabama troops forward, and then rescinding the order, was the source of much irritation among the Alabamians. Captain Franklin Smith noted the incident in his *Journal* stating, " *. . . the Alabama companies are ready to march, their subsistence was in their wagons. This looks like a bungling piece of Genl. P*'[Patterson] *work.*" The commissioned officers of the regiment held a meeting to protest being left out of the military action around Monterrey. The assembly was heated with officers taking turns expressing the injustice of their exclusion from the active army. Lieutenant Stephen F. Hale of the Eutaw Rangers seems to have been a principal leader in the effort as he was at Camp Alabama. Private Nunnalee noted in his journal that Hale "*set forth in the strongest language, the rights, duties and privileges of the Regiment as a constituent member of the Army of Mexico*" and detailed the grievances of the men in the regiment. Major Goode Bryan and Captain Sydenham Moore were among those officers making speeches. The officers also explored possible reasons for being left behind and some concluded that the military inexperience of Colonel John Coffey was the reason. A committee was appointed to draft a letter to General Taylor and to send copies to the Governor of Alabama and through him to the citizens of the Alabama.[110] Captain William Coleman did not play a role but recorded in his diary that "*two companies started to Monterey, and then ordered back and some of Kentuckians sent off instead of Alabaman's. Some of the officers held a meeting to remonstrate against the way the reg't had been treated.*"

The protest letter dated October 29, 1846, was composed by some of the Alabama officers and forwarded to General Taylor. This letter stated: (1) that the Alabama regiment sought to maintain its reputation unsullied and that the "*eyes of our friends are upon us*" expecting Alabama to have a place on the battlefield in Mexico; (2) that the Alabama troops were the first troops representing a state to arrive in Texas to rescue Taylor's little army considered in danger from a larger Mexican Army and would have been the first if transportation to Texas had been available; (3) that Alabama's place was taken by late arriving and less senior units from other states that were ordered forward to the battlefield while the Alabama regiment was left in Camargo "*without a purpose to achieve*"; and (4) that the regiment begged for the opportunity to share in the honors and dangers of the campaign in which General Taylor was engaged as a right to be forfeited only by some disqualifying act on the part of the regiment.[111]

The result of the complaining and protest at being left out of the action was to no avail. The Perry Volunteers missed the Battle of Monterrey and the other campaigns in Northern Mexico.

---

[110] The committee was composed of Captain Andrew L. Pickens, Captain Zechariah Thomason, Captain Sydenham Moore, Captain Jacob D. Shelby, Lieutenant William L. Hancock, Lieutenant Reuben T. Thom, Lieutenant William H. Ketchum, Captain Eliphas T. Smith, and Captain Hugh M. Cunningham. The Perry company was not represented on the Committee.
[111] Letter from the Alabama soldiers to General Zachary Taylor, commander of the Army of Occupation in Northern Mexico, dated October 29, 1846, prepared at Camargo, Mexico.

They remained inactive and sullen in the camp at Camargo. To their credit, the men of the First Regiment of Alabama Volunteers did their duty, stood by their colors although their resentment remained. There was no dishonor for them, but they won no glory in battle. Considered from a practical viewpoint, General Taylor wanted to reduce the size of the army he took forward to Monterrey to make it more mobile, easier to handle and less difficult to supply. It is true that units arriving later than the First Alabama went to Monterrey. Among those late arriving units was a regiment from Mississippi commanded by Colonel Jefferson Davis, a West Point graduate, who married Zachary Taylor's daughter. One might consider this favoritism, but it was wisdom. Davis' Mississippians were rigorously trained and disciplined. They performed magnificently at Monterrey and helped save Taylor's little army from disaster at the Battle of Buena Vista, proving the Mississippians were well-led and proficient soldiers.

The circumstance of the Alabama regiment's confinement to camp raises the question as to why. There is no overt information available laying out the reason for the decision from General Taylor or other ranking person in the army. The Alabama men naturally sought answers, and there are existing documents that give some hints about the thinking at the time on this subject. The protest letter of the Alabama regiment contains a sentence that may be revealing. The Alabama officers wrote:

> " it has, as we are informed, been represented to our superior officers that we are a disorderly and rebellious regiment, some times bordering on a state of mutiny; whilst it is represented at home, to our disparagement, that the opportunity of going to Monterrey was tendered to us, and that we ignobly declined."

Was the Alabama regiment really mutinous, disorderly, and rebellious or the victim of surreptitious campaign by junior regiments hoping to get into the action ahead of the Alabamians?

It seems beyond doubt that it was set forth through some source that the Alabamians were unfit. Otherwise, they would not have addressed the subject to General Taylor. As stated earlier, the Alabamians were part of the insolence directed at General Pillow and company officers attempted to arrange the removal of their regimental officers at Camp Alabama. It is also correct to recount that there were incidents of disobedience such as that documented for James Bennett from Perry County, leaving camp without permission and the quarrels with, and ridicule of, Lt. Colonel Earle and the accusations of murdering Mexicans by General Pillow. These incidents could not escape the attention of the army commanders, and it seems rather natural that the reputation of the First Alabama suffered as a result of the regimental discord. In addition, Colonel John Coffey in a letter to General Pillow dated September 12, 1846, states that *some of them* [Alabamians] *now refuse to do duty.*" It appears that the charges of disorder made against the Alabama regiment have some basis in fact.

Reuben Chapman was a member of the United States House of Representatives from the Alabama district of Colonel John Coffey, and Chapman was brought into the controversy. A copy of the protest letter was sent to Congressman Chapman, and he took up the cause of the First Alabama in Congress on February 1, 1847.[112] In the process of calling upon President Polk to answer for the failure of the Alabamians to be placed on the battlefront, he seems to reveal some of the charges made against the men from Alabama. Chapman repeated the charges set forth in the protest letter and like a good

Reuben Chapman

[112] Reuben Chapman was born about 1800 in Caroline County, Virginia and moved to Northwest Alabama in 1824 settling in Huntsville. He moved to Morgan County, Alabama and was elected to Congress in 1835. He was elected Governor of Alabama in 1848 replacing Joshua L. Martin. Chapman's home was burned during the War for Southern Independence, and the Union Army imprisoned him. He died in 1882 in Huntsville, Alabama.

politician refuted them as false and *"destitute of foundation."* He stated that another charge was that General Taylor *"had not sufficient confidence in the officers to take them with him to the battle of Monterrey."*

The record contains evidence that the preparation of Alabama volunteers was lacking due to the deficiency of military skill among the officers. Their own men judged some of the officers as inept. Colonel John R. Coffey's lack of military experience was a controversial point from the time of his election at Mobile. There the matter must lie. The fact is that the First Regiment of Alabama Volunteers was not offered a place in the military actions at Monterrey and other maneuvers of the Army of Occupation in Northern Mexico. They sweltered in inactivity at Camargo for nearly three months.

Meanwhile, President Polk ordered an end to the armistice that General Taylor had negotiated with Ampudia at Monterrey directing the Army to resume offensive operations and General Worth set out to capture Saltillo, eighty miles southeast of Monterrey. The U. S. Navy was busy along the east coast of Mexico and decided to take the port and City of Tampico. When Santa Anna learned of American designs on the city, he ordered it evacuated. The Mexicans left on October 28 after demolishing the defenses and moving the guns. Anna Chase, the English wife of the former American Consul in Tampico who was still in the city, sent word to the Navy that the Mexicans were gone. When the American fleet arrived off Tampico, they saw the Stars and Stripes flying over the city hoisted by the gritty Mrs. Chase. On November 12, Major Robert W. McLane, serving as the personal envoy of President Polk and with orders from the Secretary of War William L. Marcy, arrived in Camargo with oral and written orders for General Taylor. These orders countermanded plans to capture northern Mexico and instructed Taylor to defend Monterrey but not to advance his army beyond that city except as was necessary to defend the town.

Word of the fall of Tampico reached Captain Coleman at Camargo on November 15 and he noted in his diary, *"Rumored in camps that we would all leave for Tampico in a few days."* On November 21, official notice reached the Perry Volunteers at Camargo that the United States Navy had captured Tampico, Mexico's second most important port on the Gulf of Mexico. The ordeal of the Perry Volunteers at Camargo was coming to an end, and they were about to move again.

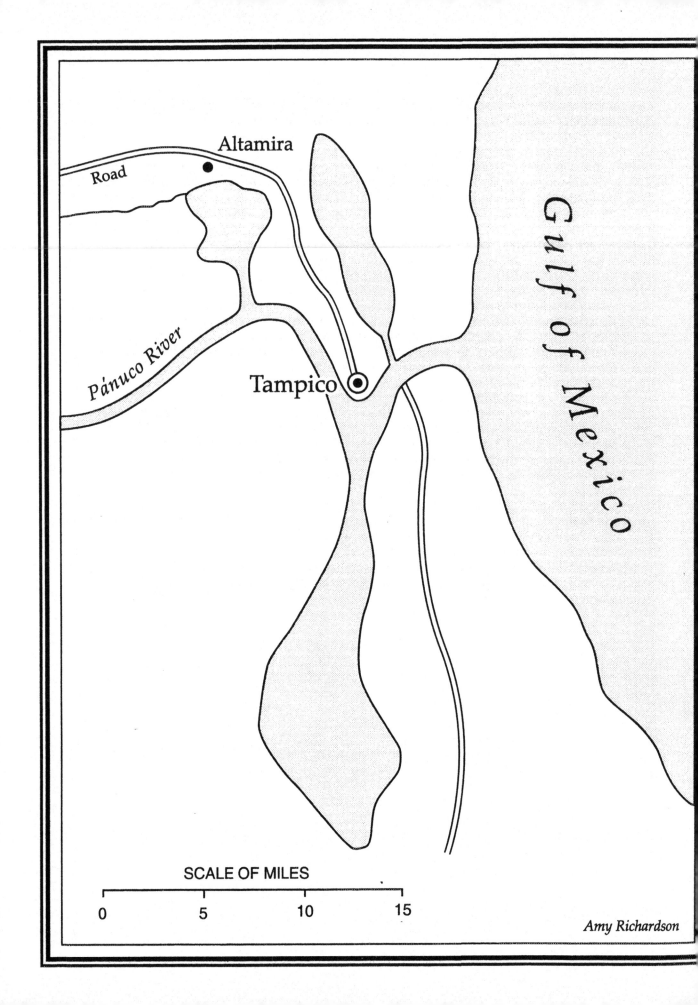

Altamira

Road

Pánuco River

Tampico

Gulf of Mexico

SCALE OF MILES

0   5   10   15

Amy Richardson

Garrison Duty in Tampico

"Found it to be a beautiful town hand-
somely laid off and a great deal of neatness
displayed . . . "
Captain William G. Coleman

When the Mexican War began, President Polk did not have a plan to bring it to an end. After seeing the Mexican resistance along the Rio Grande, at Monterrey, Saltillo and other places in Northern Mexico, it became apparent that the Mexicans would not come to heel without occupying Mexico City. General Taylor's army in Northern Mexico was over 800 rugged miles from the Mexican capitol, and a supply line that long would be too risky or impossible to maintain. Therefore, a second army was formed under General Winfield Scott to approach Mexico City from the coastal town of Vera Cruz about 250 miles from the capital. With this decision made, the focus of the war changed from Northern Mexico to the Gulf coast.

General Winfield Scott
Scott was an imposing figure
standing six feet five inches tall
weighing 230 pounds.

As part of this new approach to the war, the Navy seized the port of Tampico on the east coast of Mexico on November 14, 1846, and presented General Scott with an excellent staging point for the assault on Vera Cruz. The government in Washington was highly anxious to make the port of Tampico secure for the United States. However, the Navy did not have enough men to garrison and defend the place and turned to the army for troops to hold Tampico. The first troops to reach Tampico were 110 Regular Army soldiers who arrived on November 29, 1846. Volunteer Major General Robert Patterson was assigned the responsibility for garrisoning and protecting Tampico and Scott ordered all of the troops of Patterson, Quitman and Twiggs to concentrate there for the move to Vera Cruz.

Among the first volunteer troops ordered by General Patterson to do garrison duty were the Perry Volunteers who received official notification on November 21 to proceed to Tampico without delay. The Alabama men were delighted at the opportunity to leave the scene of so many useless deaths and the Camargo caldron for a happier place with sea breezes. Captain Coleman received orders in the early evening hours of November 23 to embark for Tampico at sunrise the next morning. The Volunteers went to work immediately to prepare for the departure and *"set up all night preparing to meet the order punctually,"* according to Coleman. The men of the Perry Volunteers made the rounds of the camps saying goodbye to their friends who were to remain in Camargo including four companies of the First Alabama.[113] Company C formed up in the early morning hours of November 24 and marched through Camargo to the sound of drum and fife to the departure point four miles from their camp where they boarded the steamboat at sunrise for the trip south. The company's officers, including Captain Coleman and Lieutenants Pitts, Ford and Fuller lagged behind the rest of the Company and had to run much of the distance to the boat to avoid being left in Camargo. General Robert Patterson and his staff came on board the boat at ten o'clock that morning to bid the men farewell in a speech to the soldiers

---

[113] Companies B, E, G and K from DeKalb, Talladega, Pike and Baldwin counties remained in Camargo and rejoined the regiment later.

filled with praise and calls to duty and honor, afterward removing his hat saying, "*hurrah for the Alabamians.*" The Alabamians returned his compliment with three cheers for their Major General.

The Perry Volunteers left Camargo at a quarter after ten o'clock on board the steamboat *Col. Cross*[114] along with companies A, D, F, H and I of the First Alabama bound for the mouth of the Rio Grande. The boat was crowded and the trip downriver was slow. The water level on the Rio Grande was lowest during the months of November, December and January. During these periods, the numerous sandbars in the river protruded into the shallow channels making navigation difficult and life miserable for river captains and pilots. The *Col. Cross* was grounded with annoying frequency, sometimes every few miles, which vexed the soldiers since ramming sand bars often sent them sprawling. During one of these groundings on the first day, some of the men went ashore to hunt game along the river, including Captain Coleman who killed a turkey and wounded another. The richness of wildlife along the Rio Grande in 1846 was evident to the travelers and Coleman reported, "*saw many wild turkeys and geese. More than I ever saw in one day perhaps in my life.*"[115] Coleman fired his rifle so much that he had to clean his gun to keep it serviceable. The first night out of Camargo was spent firmly planted on a sandbar, the *Col. Cross* having made about fifty miles the first day before grounding. By the evening of Thursday, November 26, the boat had passed Reynosa. Life on the *Col. Cross* was not easy or pleasant: the food was poor; the boat fetid, and the health of the Perry men was quite bad—Joseph Heard and James Bailey were especially sick and the health of the Company deteriorated daily; the boat was overcrowded and dirty and the seemingly endless hours stranded on sandbars was tedious for all aboard.

On the third day of the trip down river, the weather turned cold. During the groundings that could last for hours, the Alabamians were allowed to go ashore where on at least one occasion they were responsible for stealing a large number of chickens from a Mexican ranch, according to Private Nunnalee. They arrived at Matamoros in the evening of Friday, November 27, four days after leaving Camargo. While Company C was at Camargo, Matamoros was transformed under the influence of the invading Americans and was greatly improved by the energetic "*Norte Americanos.*" The town was crowded with Americans and Mexicans, but the business energy had a definite American flavor. Merchandise was available at Mobile prices and in great quantity so Captain Coleman went shopping and bought two undershirts and some other shirts for the sum of $3.00. Having depleted his ammunition, he also bought some thirty-two caliber cartridges for his hunting rifle. Liquor was available in the town and some of the men availed themselves of the opportunity to get drunk.

Richard King, Captain of the *Col. Cross*

---

[114] The *Col. Cross* was named in honor of Colonel Truman Cross who was killed when the Army of Occupation arrived on the Rio Grande from Corpus Christi in April 1846. The civilian captain of the *Colonel Cross* was a twenty-two year old New Yorker named Richard King who later founded the famous King Ranch in Texas. King was a veteran of the Seminole War and was recruited by Miffin Kenady to come to Texas as a captain of Rio Grande riverboats. King and Kenady formed a partnership and dominated the Rio Grande steamboat trade for many years after the Mexican War. The *Col. Cross* made the fastest passage from the mouth of the Rio Grande to Camargo of any steamer on the river with a running time, excluding stops, of fifty-one hours and thirty-seven minutes. [Historical Survey-Riverboats of the Rio Grande]

[115] The vast collection of wildlife along the Rio Grande is hard to imagine in modern times. Wolves roamed in large packs, wild turkeys existed in huge flocks, bald eagles, cougars and deer were everywhere, tuft headed partridges, doves, wild pigeons, green parrots, rabbits and quails were abundant in all locations, geese flew in numbers resembling clouds and white-necked or Chihuanhuan crows were known to blacken the sky.

On the morning of Saturday, November 28, the Volunteers climbed aboard their steamboat early in the morning for the trip to the mouth of the Rio Grande passed their former camp near Burita where their friends Archibald Henry, James H. Irby, and John Moore Tillman lay forever buried. The Company arrived at their destination just before dark. At the mouth of the river, they had to transfer their equipment from the *Col. Cross* to another boat for transport to Brazos Island. Captain Coleman was displeased and irritated at the disorder of the move: "*28th—Still on board the Col. Cross arrived at the mouth of the river. Of all confusion that I have ever witnessed in my life was in taking off our equipage and placing it to another boat.*" On Sunday, Company C made its way from the Rio Grande to Brazos Island, arriving at mid morning. Again all was confusion as the Company unloaded their gear and Coleman wrote in disgust, "*Oh! My God how gladly I would be if I could go on home from here in a right and proper manner.*" Five months had passed since leaving Mobile. Captain Coleman was homesick and disappointed that the Perry Volunteers had seen no action and, in the view of the soldiers, made no distinguishing contribution to the war. The Perry County soldiers expected to embark right away for Tampico but faced disappointment again. Like Captain Coleman the men of Company C yearned to go home, but their remaining enlistment time forbade it. They would have to do their duty and meet their obligation—honor required it.

They set up camp on Brazos Island, Texas again and remained there until December 14. However, the first order of business was to care for those most seriously ill in the Company so Captain Coleman went to Point Isabel taking Joseph Heard, Jesse Aycock, Joseph Dennis and Haywood Harvill to the General Hospital. While at Point Isabel, Coleman wrote letters home, and entrusted Colonel Griffin to deliver them to the United States. Coleman started back to his Company the next day but did not succeed. The sailboat he was traveling on to Brazos Island was "*blown back twice and beat off until after 2 o'clock P. M.*" before returning to Point Isabel, but he successfully crossed to the island the next day and rejoined his Company.

Brazos Island had changed some while Company C was away. Houses had been built on the island and large quantities of government provisions were accumulated and stored there, but the sand, the smell, the wind, the rain and the salty drinking water were unchanged from their earlier stay on the island. Once again the sand made its way into everything and the tents were blown down by the wind. Private Nunnalee recorded that "*We can neither eat, sleep, nor drink without having our eyes and mouths full of wet sand.*" At the beginning, the Perry Volunteers did not know how long they would remain on the island, so they drew supplies and waited for orders to move to Tampico. While on the island, there was again nothing much to do but lie in the sand and fight off fleas. Daniel W. Sneed, who was discharged from the Army due to disability on October 13, 1846, at Matamoros, found transportation to Alabama. He exchanged trunks with Captain Coleman and left from Brazos Island on December 7 sayings his farewell to his comrades in the Company. On the occasion of Sneed's departure, Coleman remarked, "*OH! How glad I would be if I was going myself*" betraying his, and doubtless others, ache to return to his family in Alabama. To his credit, honor made him see his enlistment through because he could not consider going home unless it was "*in a right manner.*"

While on Brazos Island, the Perry Volunteers continued to lose men to illness. They were fairly healthy while at Camargo but began to sicken on their way to the coast. As stated, Jesse Aycock, Andrew Haywood Harvill, and John Heard were sent to the hospital at Point Isabel on November 30. Thomas W. Swanson followed on December 2 and Shadrack W. Cardin, James Jones and James Moore on December 10, 1846. More hospitalizations followed with John W. Griffin and John W. Radford going to the hospital at Point Isabel with typhoid fever on December 11 and William J. Liles went the next day. The cause of this surge in illness that claimed twelve of the men from Perry County is not fully known, but it was probably related to the lack of sanitation and clean water that had troubled them during their first stay at this place. Typhoid fever is a filth disease carried by bacteria in food and drinking water and was probably the cause of most of the illness at Brazos Island. When the Volunteers sailed for Tampico, these men were left behind where they remained until at least the end of December 1846. In addition to the sick of Company C, Captain Coleman was concerned for the health of Captain Andrew L. Pickens from Greene County whom he described as *"bad off"* on December 3.

When the Volunteers arrived on the island, the *Virginia*, a large steamship, was anchored off the coast but no orders came to board and depart for Tampico. On December 3, the *Virginia* lowered it sails, began raising steam, displayed her flags and weighed anchor as if preparing to sail but no orders were received to board the vessel. To the contrary, on Friday, December 4, Captain Coleman received orders from General Patterson that the Volunteers were to remain on Brazos Island until further orders, so he abandoned preparations to leave, going to Point Isabel to *"see how the sick were, the boys all getting better that are at the Point."* He remained at Point Isabel the next day waiting for mail to arrive from the United States but, to his disappointment, no letters from home arrived. The Perry Volunteers were disappointed by the news that they were to remain on Brazos Island because they wanted off, having had enough of this desolate place. Life was truly miserable at Brazos with the sand blowing persistently and the drinking water intolerable. During this period, Dr. John W. Moore, Regimental Surgeon, visited Coleman and presented him with a *Prayer Book*, and General Pillow passed through Brazos Island on his way back to the United States. On December 7, a severe storm hit the island with heavy rain and high winds of gale force adding to the suffering of the Volunteers hunkered down in their tents. After the windstorm passed, the Volunteers received the welcome news to prepare to leave Brazos Island. While waiting to depart, Coleman, ever the sportsman, and John Heard went hunting in the high winds to pass the time and shot at wolves without hitting any. Rather than keep up with the muskets and accouterments of the sick men at Point Isabel, Coleman sent them to the Volunteers at the General Hospital there. The men on the island had a dreadful diversion on December 11, when the steamship *Sea* wrecked and sank nearby.[116]

At noon on December 12, 1846, the Perry Volunteers boarded the *Virginia* but did not sail. Instead, the men were confined for two days below decks while the *Virginia* sat bobbing at anchor off of Brazos Island waiting for another storm to pass. On December 14, the *Virginia* set sails for Tampico, departing at mid morning. As soon as the men of Company C went aboard, they learned that they had exchanged their island misery for seasickness and were described by Captain Coleman as *"The sickest set of men I ever saw in my life."* In addition, the *Virginia* was extremely filthy, *"the most I ever saw"* according to Coleman. The rampant sickness continued for the length of the voyage and Captain Coleman noted that he was sick enough to die but could not. The provisions on board were so poor that, combined with the seasickness, many of the men ate nothing during the voyage. The wretchedness of the trip to Tampico was prolonged on December 16 when contrary winds stopped the progress of the *Virginia* and blew it backwards in the morning. A shift in the wind from the northwest later that day again propelled the ship toward its objective. On the morning of Thursday, December 17, Coleman sighted land at daybreak from the deck of the *Virginia* and the Volunteers landed at Tampico that afternoon at four o'clock.[117] Happily, the men recovered from their persistent seasickness as soon as their ship left the Gulf and entered the Pánuco River upon which Tampico is located. Coleman took an immediate liking to the town offering a favorable description:

> *"Found it to be a beautiful town handsomely laid off and a great deal of neatness displayed in the arrangement of this place. The citizens look more like civilized because there are many foreigners located here in business who have I learned much influence on the natives. All hands received us with cordiality."*

Private Nunnalee was also favorably impressed with Tampico and described it with enthusiasm and skill:

---

[116] The *Sea* was returning to Brazos Island after ferrying two companies of Regular Army soldiers to Tampico. At Brazos Island, it ran aground and sank.

[117] Captain Coleman reports in his diary that Captain Jacob D. Shelly's company and Company E from Talladega County arrived in Tampico on Friday, December 18, 1846, on board the steamship *Cincinnati*.

> "*Tampico is a beautiful place, situated on the River, on an elevated ridge, a few miles from the gulf, a fine market, houses well built, and neat, surrounded on three sides by water. . . . It has about 7,000 inhabitants. The streets are paved with stone, . . .Fruit of almost every description and variety—beautiful scenery of evergreens surrounding the town. The inhabitants are quite different from those we have been used to. Quite civil and gentlemanly in their character, more refined, sociable and descent.*"

An anonymous member of the Greensboro Volunteers in a letter published in *The Beacon* newspaper in Greensboro, Alabama on January 16, 1847, compared Tampico to Mobile.

> "*. . . nearly as large as Mobile, and is one of the most beautiful towns I have ever seen. . . . The city is very neatly built, some of the buildings being as handsome as any, . . . that you can see in Mobile. The houses are built of brick, or stone, plastered over and covered with shingles . . . The streets are regularly laid out and paved with stone.*"

Captain Sydenham Moore was also impressed: "*The city presented an imposing appearance . . . & the climate is unsurpassed at this season of the year.*" There was a large crowd of people at the docks to meet them out of curiosity about the first volunteer regiment to reach their city. The people of Tampico were in dread of volunteers, having heard reports of volunteer misconduct, insult and outrage at the other places they had been stationed in Mexico. The men of the First Regiment of Alabama Volunteers were generally well behaved at Tampico, which did much to soften the opinions of the Mexicans in the city toward volunteer regiments.

The landing was made in an atmosphere of great excitement because for two days Tampico had been threatened with attack and the reports of an impending clash with the Mexican Army continued after the landing. The commanders at Tampico spread the arriving volunteers around the outer ring of the town to meet the anticipated assault. The two Greensboro County companies were ordered several miles north of the town. Company C went into a temporary camp below Tampico to wait for a more permanent assignment and mosquitoes made life miserable for the men from Perry County while in the temporary camp. Brigadier General James Shields[118] arrived in Tampico on December 19 to take command of the defense of the city and ordered the town fortified by the occupying troops. A member of the Greensboro Volun-

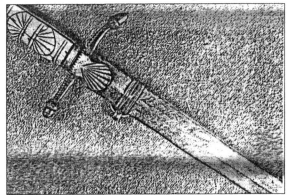

William G. Coleman's sword bearing the inscription "Tampico, Mexico."
Picture courtesy of Ben E. Coleman

teers reported to *The Beacon* back home in Alabama on December 19 that "*There are here at this time some 1,600 men, including the Alabama Regiment—are all busy at work in throwing up breast works for defense, as the Mexicans here assure us we shall soon be attacked, . . The place is strongly fortified by nature, and we are daily adding to its strength . .*"

On December 18 and 23, Coleman recorded that the Perry Volunteers were cleaning their guns and preparing to fight to defend Tampico against Santa Anna whom Coleman called "*Old*

---

[118] Brigadier General James Shields was born on May 12, 1806, in Altmore, County Tyrone, Ireland. Yearning for adventure, he came to America in 1826 and settled in Kaskaskia, Illinois where he entered Democratic politics and practiced law. He was a Catholic, a patriot, fluent in four languages and served three terms in the U. S. Senate. Shields was a militia veteran of the Black Hawk War in 1832 and gained fame in Mexico for his courage.

Santa." During this six-day period the Perry Volunteers fully expected to fight the Mexicans at any moment. Reports and rumors made most volunteers wonder how they would perform in battle when their test of courage came. Mexicans in Tampico pestered the Americans telling them that Santa Anna would eat Christmas dinner in Tampico, but one Greensboro volunteer reported, " . . . *the Mexicans . . . are such notorious liars that we place little reliance on what they say. They seem to take particular pleasure in deceiving us, though they say they would be very sorry for Santa Anna to whip us, as they are making more money out of us than they ever did before.*"[119]

Two days after arriving in Tampico, General James Shields expressed little confidence in the officers of the Alabama regiment to meet the emergency believed to be facing the defenders of Tampico, saying, according to Captain Coleman, that the regiment "*had officers but no commanders as field officers and that he would give us an Officer that would stay with us*" and the regimental officers could "*stay in town and take their pleasure.*" General Shields' remarks are a severe rebuke of the Field and Staff officers of the First Alabama. Shields was a busy man at the time struggling to establish the defenses of Tampico and his remarks may have been the result of distractions and his natural intemperance with volunteer soldiers generally. However, it would appear that the opinion he expressed is a genuine personal assessment doubtless rooted in the reputation the First Alabama established at Camp Alabama and Camargo as well as, perhaps, Shields' own observations. Nevertheless, it should be noted that General Shields' character might have affected his judgment of the officers of the First Alabama. He was described by John Hay as "*a man of inordinate vanity . . .*" Shield's law partner, Gustave Koerner said of him, "*He was exceedingly vain and very ambitious, and like most ambitious men, . . . quite egotistical . . . In his manner he was peculiar, not to say eccentric.*" Before the Mexican War, Shields challenged Abraham Lincoln to a duel in response to a satirical letter Lincoln published in the Sangamo, Illinois *Journal* on September 2, 1842. Shields demanded an apology, Lincoln refused to give it and Shields challenged him to a duel. The two men met on September 22, 1842, on Bloody Island, Missouri where dueling was not illegal. Lincoln never doubted Shields' courage. The future President feared he would be killed but friends intervened to stop the duel pleading desperately "*with the would be combatants to let bygones by bygones.*"[120] With such a confrontational past, Shields' appraisal of the First Alabama Field and Staff officers must be tinctured with considerations of his character and volatility.

Brigadier General
James Shields

On Christmas Eve, the Perry Volunteers were notified to occupy and defend Fort Altamira guarding the road leading north from Tampico. However, by Christmas day, concern about a Mexican attack had faded. December 25 dawned fair, clear and warm and, excepting the guards, the men from Perry County were given the day off to be free and idle. With the concern about combat abated for the moment, the garrison began to relax and went back to doing little of significance militarily except improve the breastworks at the fort. The December weather in Tampico was like summer back in Alabama. Captain Coleman observed that the seasons seemed out of order and that it is "*strange for an Alabamin to see at Christmas green corn, snap beans, green tomatoes, and all kinds of vegetables.*" Two days after Christmas, Colonel Coffey made a visit to the quarters of Captain William Coleman. They discussed the case of Lieutenant John M. McDuff from Coffey's home county in Alabama. General James Shields had ordered McDuff to the United States for "*playing cards*" on duty, according to

[119] Anonymous writer, *The Beacon*, Greensboro, Alabama, January 16, 1847.
[120] Louis Vargo, "When Lincoln Lived By the Sword" *Civil War Times Illustrated*, Vol. XL, Number 7, (Primedia Publication, Harrisburg, PA, February 2002)

Coleman, but McDuff's defense was that he was ill in his tent. The McDuff case caused an enormous controversy in the regiment and in the state of Alabama because McDuff was not allowed a court martial where he could defend himself. The action of General Shields was unusual and an action not provided for in army regulations. The affair seems to further show the intemperate nature of the general.

It is evident that the Perry Volunteers were happy to be in Tampico but were weary of this war. Their only battle to this point in the conflict was with the elements, illness and death with no glory in battle against the army of Santa Anna. In Tampico, they witnessed the arrival of 1847 on a cold, cloudy day, wishing to be at home with their families instead of in distant Mexico. Thoughts drifted to New Year's Day in Alabama, always *"a day for frolicking by the young and gay"* as well as a day for serious meditation with misspent days regretted and a new resolve to amend one's ways and do better in the future.[121] Nevertheless, the Alabama boys settled into life at Tampico, which they found to their liking. Regimental bands gave concerts in the plaza, actors from the army put on plays at the American Theatre to packed houses and a weekly American newspaper named the *Tampico Sentinel* was published. A number of eating, drinking and gambling establishments sprang up for their entertainment and pleasure.[122] All this could be enjoyed because the Perry Volunteers finally received their pay on January 21, 1847, from U. S. Army Paymaster Major Albert G. Bennett after seven months with no money from the government.[123] The pay itself was unhandy as the Volunteers received seven months pay in dimes, quarters and half dollar coins. Captain Coleman was sick and confined to his *"pallet"* so he sent his friend Private James F. Bailey to collect his pay and received $611.85. Pay was again distributed on February 25 and Coleman drew $87.50. The Tampico market offered a seemingly endless array of goods and food that beckoned the freshly paid volunteers.[124] Tampico took on an American look and, if war had to have idle periods, this city was a good place to pass the time. The Alabama regimental band gave concerts and demonstrated precise military movements to the populace and to Tennessee troops stationed in Tampico.

However, Tampico was not paradise and the complaints about mosquitoes were numerous causing Coleman to purchase a *"mosquito bar."* The town seems to have been healthier than Northern Mexico or it may have been that the sickly members of the Perry Volunteers had already been weeded out by disease, a position that the facts support. However, mumps appeared in the camp in early January and at least one Alabama volunteer died of yellow fever according to the journal of Private Nunnalee. On January 5, 1847, a norther hit Tampico sending a cold blast of air through the tents of Company C making life unpleasant.[125] The storm was quite terrible with a fierce wind causing one observer to record, *"Never did I witness such an awful and terrible night! . . . the storm raged with unabated fierceness each puff appearing stronger and stronger while the cold grew more and more intense."* Another norther blew in on January 11 causing increased fear of illness. Consequently, the health difficulties for the Perry Vol-

---

[121] These are the composite thoughts of Sydenham Moore recorded in his journal on January 1, 1847. They may be considered typical reflections upon entering a new year.

[122] One volunteer reported that a café in Tampico served fish, venison, steak, eggs, buckwheat cakes, fried bananas, and coffee for breakfast and soup, baked fish, broiled and roasted duck, lettuce salad, and potatoes for dinner.

[123] Army regulations required that soldiers be paid every two months but the Paymaster failed to fulfill this obligation forcing the soldiers to go unpaid for long periods of time. Private Stephen Nunnalee recorded in his journal at Camargo on October 31, 1846, that *"To-day the Regiment was mustered with a view to being paid off"* but Captain Coleman reports that Company C received their first pay at Tampico on January 21, 1847. In a later entry in his journal on January 21, 1847, Nunnalee records that he was *"paid off yesterday for the first time since we have been in the service, . . . "*

[124] A Regular Army officer reported that the Tampico market offered cakes, chocolate, pots, hats, blankets, peppers, many varieties of beans, eggs, poultry, sugar cane, fish, turtles, rice, corn, salt, soap, raisins, garlic, cabbage, mint, parsley, lard, potatoes, tomatoes, radishes, peas, and dried beef.

[125] The period from October to April was considered the dry season on the coast of Mexico. During this period, northerly gales, known as northers, struck with little warning and were vicious to those on land and distressing to ships at sea.

unteers were not over. On January 17, eighteen Volunteers reported for sick call along with twelve men from other companies. James T. Dacus died of a fever in the hospital at Tampico on January 20, 1847. Seaborn Aycock, the company's first sergeant, James Bennett, the reluctant blacksmith at Camargo, and William H. Jones were discharged on February 26. The Company was thereafter reduced by a total of twenty-seven men, leaving about seventy-one Volunteers on the rolls. The actual number of men available for duty was less than seventy-one because of the twelve men hospitalized at Point Isabel. Brigade Surgeon Dr. John Moore detailed Dr. Marion A. Eiland as Company Surgeon although there was no provision in Army regulations for such a position.[126] On March 1, 1847, John Heard and John W. Radford were released from the hospital at Point Isabel. Other men of Company C fell ill at Tampico and William N. Edwards, Robert Farley, Thomas Richard Heard and Wiley W. Fowler were hospitalized. All of these men were released from the hospital on April 4, but Company C was in Vera Cruz by that time.

Those Perry men not otherwise occupied went hunting in the countryside in January and February 1847. Lieutenant James H. Pitts and Walter Pool, a private in Company F, were hunting partners. Captain Coleman was a well-known hunting sportsman throughout his life and at Tampico hunted on several occasions with a *"Creole from New Orleans"* named Sylvester Peardon who had befriended him. Peardon had lived in Tampico for six years and knew the best hunting areas. On his first hunt Coleman killed a wolf. He and Peardon later traveled ten miles up the Pánuco River where they camped at the mouth of Chile Creek. Coleman killed two bears and *"the Creole"* bagged four geese. Coleman went shopping in Tampico and had a tailor measure him for a *"white linen round coat"* that he ordered made and bought a *"fine French gun"* for which he paid fifty-five dollars. He also bought his wife *"a fine Chinese shawl,"* paying thirty-five dollars for it, and shoes and suspenders for himself.

On Wednesday, January 6, Colonel John Coffey received orders to select two hundred men from the Alabama regiment for an expedition and orders went out from regimental headquarters to the Perry Volunteers to hold themselves in readiness to leave Tampico. The men went to work cleaning their muskets and preparing for an inspection, which was conducted by Captain Harrison on Friday. Where they were going was not explained, so they cooked provisions enough for a hundred mile march as ordered and prepared to leave at a moment's notice. At three o'clock in the afternoon on Sunday, January 10, Company C lined up on the road leading south from Tampico with four other companies from the First Alabama and five companies from the Regular Army. Speculation and rumor indicated that their destination was Tuxpan, a fortified coastal city to the south. Captain William Coleman thought the purpose of the expedition was to *"press horses, mules, and jacks into the service of the U.S."* Captain Sydenham Moore irritably referred to the destination of the expedition

General David E. Twiggs

as *"a precious secret by the Brig. Gen'l."* The expedition marched six miles the first day through rich farmland and passed sugar cane and banana plantations that yielded abundant crops with little labor. Captain Sydenham Moore, always quick to give his opinion, recorded, *"It is* [an] *outrage, for the Mexicans to own such a country. They are too lazy to till the soil; ... In the possession of our people this would soon become one of the choicest regions on the continent."* The march continued on Monday, and by one o'clock in the afternoon the men had covered ten miles when a courier from General James Shields arrived with orders to return to

---

[126] This is according to William G. Coleman's statement to the Mexican War Commissioners dated November 8, 1882. One suspects that the appointment of Dr. Eiland was made in response to a need for more medical oversight due to the large number of ill soldiers. The author has a copy of this statement in his possession.

Tampico to the great disappointment of the men who wanted to see action. There was a fervent hope in the Company to have at least one fight with the Mexicans before going home.

The men from Perry County returned to their encampment in the evening of Tuesday, January 12 having marched nearly twenty miles that day. They were fatigued and complained about sore feet and blisters. Captain Coleman came down with the mumps on the first day of the march and was prostrated by the effects. Unable to march, he was transported in an ambulance for the rest of the trip and lay in his sick bed for the next three weeks before he was well enough to return to duty. Coleman did not enter the hospital but confined himself to his tent where Dr. Marion A. Eiland, Coleman's family physician back in Alabama, ministered to his medical needs. William Coleman recorded in his Mexican War pension statement forty years later that he noted a decline in his health from this incident on the road to Tuxpan with the onset of a condition named hydrocele, which is a collection of fluid within the scrotum. On January 11, a norther blew into Tampico and the weather turned cold again. Back in camp from their tramp, the men learned that General James Shields had ordered their return because Mexican General Santa Anna was in the field with a large army and concern for the safety of Tampico caused the recall.

During their time in Tampico, the ten companies of the First Alabama were posted separately about the outer edge of the town. The fear of attack having subsided, it was decided on January 22 to concentrate the scattered companies nearer the city at Old Tampico. There was an unfortunate incident at the new campsite during the first night there. Peachy Bledsoe and Lafayette Vance were out of the camp and did not return before taps was sounded. When entering the campsite, they were both shot by the sentinels on duty that night but fortunately neither was killed. Bledsoe was seriously injured and required hospitalization at Tampico for seventy-two days in order to recover. Vance escaped serious injury. Captain Coleman was still infirmed with the effects of the mumps so Company C marched off to the rendezvous point and new campsite without him. Coleman lay ill for another two weeks under the care of Dr. M.A. Eiland, James F. Bailey and Robert M. Holmes whom he called "*the best friends and nurses of any man.*" Over the next two weeks, Coleman noted his condition daily with entries such as, "*still sick and very bad,*" "*still sick and confined to my pallet, missed chills for the first day out of 7*" and "*violent pain in my head.*" By January 30, he was well enough to record "*still on my pallet but not much sick*" and the next day, "*mending a little.*"

On January 25, 1847, Generals Robert Patterson, David Twiggs, Gideon Pillow and John Quitman arrived at Tampico with their commands amounting to about 4,000 men. Early in December 1846, most of the Regular Army regiments were removed from Taylor's army and transferred to the command of General Scott. Generals Patterson and Twiggs marched overland to Tampico with their men while General Worth moved forward by sea. Events were moving toward an increase in military activity at Vera Cruz. The First Alabama was again united with the Brigade of General John A. Quitman along with the Tennessee regiment that was garrisoned in Tampico. On February 3, a general review and inspection of the First Alabama was conducted. Coleman was still weak but well enough to attend the review. General Quitman spoke flatteringly to the regiment and was lavish in his praise of the regiment officers and men. For their part, the men from Perry Company and other companies marched with precision and flair at the inspection and came away with a good opinion of their marching ability and military appearance.

The Perry Volunteers promoted Robert M. Holmes from third sergeant to first sergeant to replace Seaborn Aycock and Young Cardin replaced Holmes as third sergeant. The men left ill in the hospital at Point Isabel were mending to the point where they could begin to rejoin the Volunteers. On February 5, Jesse Aycock, James Moore, John Griffin, Thomas Swanson, James Jones, Shadrack Cardin, William Liles and Joseph Dennis arrived in Tampico and rejoined the Company raising the unit's strength by eight men. Four Volunteers remained hospitalized at Point Isabel. Two days later, flashes of light and the sound of cannon along the coast to the

South attracted the attention of the Volunteers. Mexican General Martín Perfecto de Cos with eight hundred soldiers was harassing three hundred ship wrecked Louisiana volunteers under the command of Colonel Lewis G. DeRussey. The sloop of war *St. Mary's* was aiding their escape, creating the sights and sounds that caught the attention of the Perry County men. Captain Coleman recorded the event in his diary stating, "*saw the flashing of powder along the coast south of us. Supposed to be the fighting of some shipwrecked soldiers from Louisiana and the Mexicans.*" The Louisiana volunteers stealthily escaped from danger by leaving behind burning campfires while they slipped away in the darkness to safety, arriving in Tampico the next day. However, 450 valuable horses were lost in the wreck and could not be replaced.

The military preparation and activity in Tampico during February persuaded the Perry Volunteers that peace with Mexico would come only after a long struggle. For the Volunteers, this meant that they would not be going home for another four months when their enlistment expired. General Scott was not yet in Tampico but was expected any day, and it was clear to the Alabamians that they would soon be part of the attack upon Vera Cruz. The men from Perry County had been in Tampico for over two months and were getting tired of the place. It was time to move the war forward, and they would soon get their wish. However, the first part of the month of February was a quiet period for the Volunteers from Perry County as they waited for General Scott to arrive to begin the movement on Vera Cruz. They went hunting, wrote letters home, had their hair cut, went shopping but basically had little to do until their new commander arrived.

General Winfield Scott left Washington, D. C. on November 23, 1846, bound for New Orleans. He stayed only four days in the Crescent City before departing for the mouth of the Rio Grande, from which he proceeded up river on the steamboat *Corvette* to Camargo. At Camargo, he hoped to meet with General Zachary Taylor but Taylor did not appear, so Scott immediately returned downriver to Brazos Island. Scott pressed on arriving in Tampico on Friday, February 19 and left a favorable impression on the troops assembled in the city. Private Nunnalee described him as a "*noble looking old fellow, and stands about as tall as any man. He has the most commanding appearance of any man I ever saw . . . he looks just like a general.*" Scott's arrival was electric in the city, creating excitement and anticipation. Captain Coleman noted, "*Genl. Scott arrived in Tampico. Now for new movements entirely I suppose. Tho be it so.*" The lazy days of February were over for the Perry men and drilling resumed on February 21. Four days later Captain Coleman was "*quite busy making preparations to embark for Vera Cruz. Drew some ordinance stores from Lt. Hayes . . . drew pay for the month of February--$87.50.*" On March 1, Holmes and Cardin were promoted and the monthly returns of men available for duty in Company C was reported as an aggregate of seventy-one, including four commissioned officers.

The Steamboat *Corvette* on the Rio Grande

Anxious to push the campaign forward, Scott stayed in Tampico only one night and departed on Saturday, arriving at Lobos Island on February 21. The General was organizing for an invasion of Mexico through the city of Vera Cruz. His plan was to land troops on the beaches, capture the city and march overland to Mexico City over the same route used by Hernando Cortés over three hundred years earlier in his conquest of the Aztecs in 1519.[127] In the latter part of February 1847, General Scott began to transport troops to Lobos Island located about 180 miles

---

[127] Cortés founded La Villa de Vera Cruz, which was the first mainland settlement created by Europeans. Since it's founding, Vera Cruz had repelled numerous attacks by the English, Spanish and French. After two centuries of attacks, the defenses of Vera Cruz were strong.

north of Vera Cruz in preparation for the invasion. Problems with logistics kept popping up; transports were not where they were needed, troops were delayed and supplies were in abundance in one place while there were shortages in other places. Scott was impatient to get his army ashore and accepted a less than perfect supply arrangement. Although he had less than half the men and supplies he wanted, Scott ordered the invasion preparations to proceed. By the end of February, there were about 10,000 men on Lobos Island who were destined to be part of an invasion force, but the Perry Volunteers were still at Tampico.

Tampico was full of activity and intense excitement. Troops were reviewed daily. Ships continually arrived loaded with goods, merchandise and military stores. The Americans knew the invasion was near, and they rushed to get themselves organized while they waited for orders they knew were to arrive soon. In early March 1847 the men encamped at Tampico began to ship out for Lobos Island. By March 4, Generals Twiggs, Worth and Pillow and their commands had left the city. William H. Fowler, a nineteen-year-old teacher serving with the Greensboro Volunteers, recorded events in Tampico during this period in a letter home.[128]

> *"The head of the column commenced moving on the 20th inst., when General Twiggs' brigade of regulars embarked, followed on the 23d by Col. Bankhead's[129] detachment of Artillery; and Gen. Pillow's brigade is now going on board the transports. Next in order will follow Gen. Quitman's brigade of which the Alabama regiment is attached, and that of Gen. Shields. It is said that we will proceed to Lobos . . . and there organize preparatory to the contemplated attack. So you may now consider us actually en route for the scene of action . . . some argue there will be no battle. These reports however, may prove incorrect—for the majority think the place will not be resigned without a struggle, and the Mexicans themselves say their forces will never 'vamos' again—but, of this time will show. . . . Our company are all in excellent spirits—the most disagreeable hours they pass being during the prevalence of Northers, which are of frequent occurrence, sweeping the country near the coast with great violence."*

An anonymous member of the First Alabama gave his version of events in Tampico in a letter dated March 1, 1847, and demonstrates the hunger for information about what lay ahead for the Alabamians.[130]

> *"I was just at the Colonel's tent, and he told me it was the opinion of all the Generals he had conversed with, that we should have at Vera Cruz one of the hardest fought battles that ever was fought in Mexico. He said that he was under the impression that the Mexicans would dispute our landing as it was the intention of Gen. Scott to land about 8 miles above the city of Vera Cruz, and we would have to fight there, and if we landed at all, continue our fight up to the city. . . . The Surgeon this morning began vaccinating the men of the regiment to prevent them taking the Small Pox, . . . We are to embark for Vera Cruz tomorrow or the next day, and Col. Coffey says he thinks we will be in the fight in about 12 days, but I think that we will be a little longer than that, for you see, the troops that have gone on before us, are now landed at Lobos Island, and it will take them some time to embark again. . . ."*

On March 6 at two o'clock in the afternoon, Company C received orders to make preparations to leave for Vera Cruz. Embarkation began eight hours later and about ten o'clock that evening the Volunteers crowded on board the steamship *New Orleans* with eleven other companies—

---

[128] William H. Fowler, *The Beacon*, March 27, 1847, Greensboro, Alabama.
[129] Colonel James Bankhead of the Second U. S. Artillery. He was brevetted a Brigadier General at Vera Cruz.
[130] Anonymous writer; letter printed in *The Beacon*, March 27, 1847.

six companies from Alabama, three from Georgia and three from Illinois—in all about 900 men. Also on board was Brigadier General Thomas S. Jesup of the Regular Army, General James Shields and Brigade Commander John A. Quitman. At midnight the *New Orleans* set sail from a wharf crowded with Mexicans there to see the Alabamians, whom they liked, cast off.[131] The men of Company C liked Tampico, and its people too, but they had a rendezvous with the defenders of Vera Cruz. At sea, the Perry Volunteers became seasick as soon as they reached the Gulf of Mexico and remained so for the rest of the trip. Even though miserable the Volunteers were in fine spirits as if on a new adventure.

On the morning of March 9, the Perry Volunteers were on the deck of their transport anxiously straining to spot the fortress at San Juan de Ullúa planted on Gallega Reef just offshore from Vera Cruz. About nine o'clock the fortress came into view and by noon the Volunteers were close enough to have a clear, full picture of the *"castle"* and city of Vera Cruz. The San Juan fortress was an impressive sight from the sea with walls sixty feet high and fully capable of repelling any attacks from the sea. It was a large quadrangle bastion with a demi-lune, redoubts and a water battery mounting 135 guns (including thirty-six shell guns) manned by 1,630 men that waited for the American attack. Knowledgeable military experts considered it to be the strongest fortress in North America. The thought of assaulting the *"castle"* was enough to make the blood run cold. In a few weeks, the men would get a look at the inside of the San Juan fortress marveling at its strength, but on this day they could view it only with a sense of dread.

The city too was well fortified by a great wall made of reinforced granite two miles long. Along the waterfront extended a stoutly built massive wall anchored to the north by Fort Concepción and Fort Santiago to the south. On the land side, there were nine forts containing over one hundred pieces of heavy artillery connected by a fifteen-foot high wall that was three feet thick in most places. Outside the city wall, there was a plain about a half-mile wide past which rose sand hills to the north and south. Beyond these hills, the ground rose gradually to a height of three hundred feet. Here the dense forest began, cut only here and there by a road or a cultivated spot. To the southwest of the city lay a series of ponds and marshes that were drained by small streams. It was outside these walls that the Perry Volunteers would operate in coming weeks as the assault of the city of Vera Cruz unfolded.

---

[131] According to an article printed in the *Tampico Sentinel* dated February 27, 1847, the citizens of Tampico petitioned the army to allow the First Regiment of Alabama Volunteers to remain in their city as the garrison force. This action is a testament to the regiment's deportment while in Tampico and a source of pride to the men and officers of the regiment. This article was noted in the March 27, 1847, issue of *The Beacon* published in Greensboro, Alabama. Louisiana volunteers were assigned to garrison Tampico.

Amphibious Assault on Vera Cruz

"Those who seem disposed to keep themselves
out of the danger of battle"
Captain William G. Coleman

General Winfield Scott concentrated on invasion preparations after he left Tampico. On March 5, 1847, he scouted the city's fortifications from the deck of the Navy ship *Petrita* accompanied by a party of young Army engineers that included Robert E. Lee, George G. Meade, Joseph E. Johnson and Pierre G. T. Beauregard, plus Generals Worth, Twiggs and Patterson. They saw the fortress of San Juan spiny with guns and a city enclosed by a high, fortified wall. Scott decided to land his troops three miles to the south of the city out of range of the fortress' guns but not all of his army had yet assembled at Vera Cruz. Scott continued to organize for the landing while he waited anxiously and fitfully for the arrival of those troops not on the scene. The Perry Volunteers skipped Lobos Island and sailed straight for Vera Cruz. They were pleased to see that they arrived in time to be a part of the invasion force. Finally, the long hoped for action against the Mexicans seemed to be at hand. General Scott in full dress uniform came alongside the *New Orleans* on board the steamer *Massachusetts* and spoke to General Quitman saying, according to Private Nunnalee, *"General Quitman we are about landing in an enemy's country. How many men have you?"* Quitman replied *"twelve companies"* and Scott gave directions for the placement of the *New Orleans* in the line of invasion ships. While the Perry countians waited their turn to land, they cleaned their guns and other arms again, drew ammunition and rations, filled their canteens and formed up on the deck to wait for orders to disembark. As the Volunteers stood looking around, they saw every deck and rigging on neighboring ships crowded to capacity with blue and gray uniformed troops with the sun flashing off the polished bayonets and buttons. There were masses of white sails and huffing puffing steam vessels making ready to move in on the target beach. In Vera Cruz, the walls of the city were lined with Mexican spectators waiting to learn the outcome of the American attempt to land on Mexican soil.

Satisfied with his careful preparations, General Scott ordered the ships to take their position. Flares were fired into the air as the signal for the entire invasion fleet to move forward toward the landing beach for the disembarkation of the first troops to go ashore in specially built surfboats. General William Worth and a command of about four hundred Regular Army soldiers were selected to be the first troops to land at Vera Cruz. About four o'clock in the afternoon, a cheer rang out from the thousands of men watching Worth's troops climb into the little surfboats. A second flare signaled the surfboats to go ashore and the sailors leaned into their oars at the order of Mid-

American Troops Landing at Vera Cruz
March 9, 1847
Nathaniel Currier--1847

shipmen in charge of each boat. All eyes were upon the surfboats flying a stern flag as they glided swiftly through the surf in single file with gunboats providing a covering fire. Stillness fell over the onlookers; the excitement and anxiety were almost unbearable for the safety of the first men to touch enemy soil. It was expected that the Mexicans would fire upon the invading Americans at any time, but there was only silence.[132] Worth's men reached shore, quickly formed a battle line, moved inland and raised the American flag—another cheer was raised by the men still on board the ships. The tension broken by the easy establishment of a beachhead, and the absence of Mexican resistance, bands struck up the *Star Spangled Banner* and other patriotic songs. The landings continued all afternoon. General Patterson's troops were in the second wave of landings and the men from Perry County followed General Worth's men ashore.

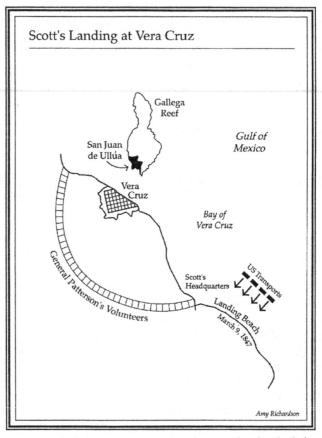

Scott's Landing at Vera Cruz

Gallega Reef

Gulf of Mexico

San Juan de Ullúa

Vera Cruz

Bay of Vera Cruz

General Patterson's Volunteers

Scott's Headquarters

US Transports

Landing Beach March 9, 1847

Amy Richardson

As the sun was fading, the Perry men boarded the landing boats in a calm sea under a cloudless glittering blue sky and were rowed by the sailors to Collado Beach south of the city within sight of the great wall surrounding Vera Cruz. The landing was unprecedented in the history of the world and another like it would not occur until nearly one hundred years later on the coast of France in 1944. The landing was a spectacle with hundreds of ships parading back and forth, flags waving in the light breeze, soldiers cheering, bands playing as the surfboats carved through the sea, creating a grand scene. Captain Coleman was impressed with the visual picture created by the landing and described it as "*a more magnificent sight I never saw in my life.*" Stephen Nunnalee hailed the event as "*. . . one of the grandest sights I ever witnessed.*" Captain Sydenham Moore said of the landing, "*The sight was one of the most imposing I ever saw.*" Coleman recorded in his diary that all of the Perry Volunteers on board the *New Orleans* made it ashore safely.

Just at twilight the surfboats carrying the Alabama men reached the sandy beach with the Eutaw Rangers in the lead. The regiment formed up a short distance from the water's edge. Here they stacked their arms, dined on biscuits and pork and lay down in the sand for the night under the open sky. The night was especially still, the stars beautiful and the moon raised a fiery red on the horizon seeming to emerge out of the water. The surfboats continued to ferry men ashore until by midnight 13,500 soldiers, including late arriving Regulars, were on shore without the loss of a single man.[133] Once all of the men were ashore the surfboats turned to the task of bringing supplies, ammunition and heavy guns ashore. Around two o'clock that night the resting Alabamians heard the cry, "*take arms,*" arose quickly from their slumber and formed a battle line during a clash with Mexican cavalry. The disturbance lasted a short time, and the regiment was soon settled down again for a night's rest only to be aroused around four o'clock in the morning by pickets discharging their muskets. The Perry Volunteers seized their weap-

---

[132] General Juan Morales, the Mexican commander, believed he dare not risk an open fight within range of the Navy guns offshore. General Santa Anna had the Mexican army off doing battle with General Zachary Taylor at Buena Vista leaving General Scott's army free to go ashore unmolested but the men in the invading fleet did not know this or what to expect when they stepped ashore at Vera Cruz.
[133] Six men from the Palmetto Regiment were thought to have drowned when their boat capsized, but they were alive and captured by the Mexicans.

ons and again formed up but order was once more quickly restored, so they returned to their sandy beds. The American army was safely ashore and in control of the landing area. Vera Cruz was a doomed city.

On March 10, 1847, the day began when the American steamboat *U. S. S. Spitfire* commanded by Commodore Josiah Tattnall exchanged volleys with the fortress at San Juan.[134] Observers from Perry County could see the action and thought bombs detonating over the town and fortress was a beautiful sight. They admired the daring little *Spitfire* as it drew nearer and nearer to the fortress, pouring a broadside into it before withdrawing. With Mexican attention diverted, General Patterson's troops passed Worth's division and began to surround Vera Cruz while the Navy was busy bombarding the city and the castle at San Juan from the sea. William Coleman described the encirclement of the town.

> *"The line of march was taken up. General Worth with his division took his position on the right under a severe fire from the Castle Ullúa and from three other points in town; next, General Patterson's division commenced taking positions under a heavy and constant fire of cannon; some skirmish fighting."*

Among the troops taking part in the volunteer encirclement was Private Elias F. Hiney[135] of the First Regiment of Pennsylvania Volunteers who kept a diary of events and on March 10 and 11 described the movement of the Brigade:

> *"Took up our line of march and was in action in a very short time. Mexicans threw bombs and ball with great precision. Though some of us was hurt, we were drawn under the fire of the castle by the Lancers, who retreated and eventually led us into the Chaparral where there was a large party of Mexican lying in ambush near an old cemetery or castle, who fired into us pretty sharp. . . . This was a hard night. Threw up entrenchments. On the morning of the 11th was attacked by lancers and musketry supposed to be 2 thousand strong. Killed several, wounded do [not] know how many Mexican. Supposed 8 killed, several wounded."*

General John Quitman came to the Alabama encampment on the beach around noon on March 10 to dine with the Alabama officers, and they served him hardtack and slices of bacon. Around three o'clock, the Perry Volunteers were ordered to move two miles to the west of the beach and set up camp southeast of the city in an opening near a ruined nunnery surrounded by dense undergrowth. The Alabamians could hear the sound of muskets and cannons firing during the day. Fearing attack from the Mexicans, the Alabama men had trouble sleeping, but the night passed uneventfully.

Death of Colonel
Pierce M. Butler
N. Currier 1847

Volunteer troops from New York and the Palmetto Regiment from South Carolina camped nearby. William Coleman knew that the Palmettos contained a company of men (Company D—Old 96 Boys) from his former home in Edgefield District, and he was interested in visiting them to see some of his relatives, old friends and acquaintances in that regiment. He set out in search of the Edgefield company emblem displaying a palmetto on one side and eagle with the stars and stripes on the other which identified the location of the company containing his friends. He visited his Tillman relatives four of whom were to die in Mexico in the coming

---

[134] Josiah Tattnall was the son of the Governor of Georgia. The *Spitfire* was a small 118 feet side-wheel steamer. Oddly, it was designed by the Mexican Navy for service in the shallow waters of the Mexican coast and appropriated by the Navy from the shipyard.
[135] The source of the Elias Hiney diary is Susanne "Sam" Behling, the great, great granddaughter of Elias Hiney. Quoted with permission.

months and a fifth was discharged for disability before the end of the year. Among Coleman's acquaintances in the Palmetto Regiment were two prominent men from Edgefield District—Colonel Pierce Mason Butler, commander of the Palmetto Regiment and former governor of South Carolina, and Preston Smith Brooks, Captain of Company D. Colonel Butler was to die a hero's death on December 22, 1847, at the battle of Churubusco from a gunshot through the head while leading his men forward against the enemy in battle.[136]

Preston S. Brooks and Coleman grew up in the same community and were well acquainted since they were neighbors when Coleman lived in South Carolina. Brooks was practicing law in Edgefield at the time that Coleman moved to Alabama. Captain Brooks gained fame and notoriety on May 22, 1856, when he entered the United States Senate chamber and clubbed abolitionist Senator Charles Sumner senseless with a walking cane in retaliation for a speech in which Sumner insulted Brooks' cousin Senator Andrew Pickens Butler. However, this was in the future, and on the day of Coleman's visit to the Palmetto Regiment, Preston was simply a twenty-eight year old company captain from Coleman's former home and the order of

Preston
S. Brooks

the day was reminiscing the past and getting an update regarding old acquaintances in South Carolina.[137]

March 11 began cold and rainy and General John Quitman's Brigade comprised of the Palmetto Regiment, Georgia volunteers and the First Alabama was ordered to occupy some sand hills on the western side of Vera Cruz. Captain Coleman noted, "*some sharp fighting . . . several cannon shots at my company,*" that three Americans had been killed and ten wounded in the fighting and recorded that "*this day 9 months I left home and dear wife and children.*" At sunrise, the Perry Volunteers took up a line of advancement. Brigade regiments from South Carolina and Georgia led the way and skirmished with Mexican cavalry while the Alabama regiment waited until the advanced units cleared the way. In the fighting, ten men were wounded in the South Carolina and Georgia regiments. The Volunteers advanced behind a protecting string of sand hills, waded across a shallow lagoon and marched up a long sand hill. Here they encountered General Pillow describing the recently concluded skirmish with a group of Mexicans. From this hill the Perry countians could see the forts of the enemy, the entire city of Vera Cruz and the castle fortification offshore.

The Alabamians again became the target of the Mexicans who hurled cannon shot in their direction and an occasional bullet whizzed overhead. However, the shots mostly fell short although one cannon ball passed through Company D without any effect and a spent musket ball hit Private Simeon A. Maxwell of Greene County but did him no harm. After ten months of waiting, the men from Perry County were finally facing a hostile enemy and the long yearned for fight seemed to be finally at hand. Each man faced his doubts about personal courage and wondered what General Scott had planned for them. Would they be ordered to scale the high foreboding wall around the city under fire from the determined enemy? If so, would they keep

---

[136] Pierce Mason Butler was born on April 11, 1798. He served as a Captain in the U. S. Army, a Lieutenant Colonel of South Carolina Volunteers during the Seminole War and Lieutenant Colonel of the South Carolina Militia before the Mexican War.

[137] Preston Smith Brooks was born on August 5, 1819, and graduated from South Carolina College in 1839. After the war, he was elected to the United States Congress in 1853 and resigned in 1856 under pressure after the Sumner assault; he was promptly reelected to the seat from which he resigned. He died on January 27, 1857, in Washington, D. C. and is buried in Edgefield, South Carolina. Southerners viewed Brooks as a defender of Southern dignity and rights and showered him with gifts of walking canes wherever he went and Georgia named a county after him. Another reaction was that thousands of southern boys born after the Sumner incident were named Preston Brooks including the authors' cousin Preston Brooks Smith of Mississippi. The Smith family continued to use this name for the next four generations. General Quitman said of Brooks that he " . . . *was remarkable for his gallantry . . .*"

their face to the enemy or would they run away to be branded a coward and disgraced forever? The answers did not come on this day, but the men wondered about what lay ahead.

The Alabamians resumed their march around the city to the north taking a road for the next two miles while the Mexicans fired upon their line. General Quitman became the target of one of the Mexicans and only a warning from his aide allowed him to avoid injury as a bullet whizzed over his head. The Alabamians camped along this road on the night of the eleventh and remained there on March 12 to keep possession of it. William Coleman wrote in his diary that the Perry Company spent the night *"lying on our guns behind the highest kind of hills."* The Perry Volunteers had no tents throughout the siege, so they slept on the ground under an open sky with only the poorest, most monotonous food to eat. They were, nevertheless, in good spirits and seemed to enjoy themselves. All the while, the Mexicans kept up a steady fire against Americans in the hills around the city; some Mexicans were taken prisoner and questioned about the defenses around the city. By March 13, Vera Cruz was completely surrounded with the American lines stretching about ten miles from the beach to the north to the beach on the south of the town. With this, the Mexican garrison was locked inside the walls with little hope of additional supplies or reinforcements, although the Mexicans did try to break through the lines to relieve Vera Cruz.

While the Mexican guns of Vera Cruz poured shells down on them, the Alabama boys did the work assigned to them by the engineers. Scott decided to take the city by siege and bombardment. Vera Cruz's fifteen-foot high walls were too strong to scale and mounted over one hundred Mexican cannons that stared menacingly from gun ports along the wall. Scott was anxious to move on to Mexico City but not at the needless cost of American lives. The siege guns could not be landed at first due to a severe north wind that began on March 12 and blew violently for five days, leaving the Volunteers to mark time and shelter themselves from the violent storm. When the guns arrived, the engineers sited them and directed the construction of trenches that approached within a thousand yards of the city. The siege was slow, boring, hot, sweaty, grimy work. Violent rainstorms and blowing sand pelted the Alabamians and insects attacked the men in swarms while they worked and rested.

On March 15, the Perry Volunteers and Captain Coleman were on picket duty on a windy, cold and rainy day when General John Quitman came by their duty station to inform Coleman of General Taylor's victory in northern Mexico saying that:

> *"a battle fought between Genl Santa Anna and Taylor and the victory to the latter. Mexican forces not less than 20,000 of which 4,000 were left dead and wounded on the field of battle. American forces 5009 of which 709 were killed and wounded. All volunteers except for three companies."*

In a demonstration of volunteer soldier pride, Coleman recorded dutifully that all of Taylor's soldiers were volunteers except for about 300 men. He was correct about Taylor's army. In December 1846, all of Taylor's Regular Army soldiers were removed from his command and assigned to General Scott. Thus, Taylor's army was reduced to 4,500 men of all arms. Among the Regulars were three batteries and two squadrons of the 2nd Dragoons. The rest were volunteers like the men from Perry County. Against this small army, General Santa Anna attacked with 23,000 men of which 15,000 were from the Regular Mexican army, but the smaller American army, outnumbered almost three to one, was victorious. The armies clashed on February 22 and 23, 1847. A handful of Regular Army artillerists commanded by Captain Braxton Bragg supported by brave hard fighting volunteers under Colonel Jefferson Davis of Mississippi repulsed a numerically superior force by executing a hastily conceived but successful battle plan. Taylor's losses were high with 746 killed, wounded and missing while Mexican losses were about 1,800 men. It was a superb victory that made Zachary Taylor a national hero and landed him in the White House as President of the United States. Having been smartly whipped at Buena Vista, Santa Anna withdrew his army to the South to oppose Scott's invasion at Buena Vista, Santa Anna withdrew his army to the South to oppose Scott's invasion and the Mexican threat in northern Mexico was over. In celebration, the Navy at Vera Cruz fired a salute in honor of the American victory.

On March 15, there was heavy firing out of the fortress on the Americans making entrenchments and building siege batteries. Occasionally, a musket ball whined by or a bomb burst making a terrible racket, scattering fragments through the trees but doing little harm to the Alabamians. Captain Coleman made an interesting note in his diary during this bombardment: *"Our Col. manifested signs of fear, I think."* This was a reference to Colonel John Coffey whose behavior under fire this day seems to have been the cause of Coleman's diary entry. It is all the more remarkable given the fact that Coffey and Coleman admired each other and remained friends after the war. Coleman also noted on the twenty-first that the only sickness in the company was among *"those who seem disposed to keep themselves out of the dangers of battle."* It appears that not all of the Alabamians were brave men, including the regimental colonel, if Coleman's observations are factual. On May 16, siege activity picked up with constant firing from the city and castle and a skirmish with the Mexicans. During the bombardment, Joseph G. Dennis was promoted to fourth corporal replacing John W. Barron who fell ill and could not perform his duties.

Wednesday, March 17 was the eighth day of the siege of Vera Cruz. Coleman reports that the Perry Volunteers were in fine spirits and that they captured a Mexican messenger carrying dispatches from *"General Morales to the Governor of Vera Cruz regarding men and provisions to be forced across our line into his assistance."* Two days later one of the men in Company C had his *"suspenders shot off of him,"* and while an interesting sight, no harm was done. The building of the siege batteries was a serious matter for the defenders of Vera Cruz, and Mexicans kept up a constant fire on the American sol-

U. S. Artillery at Vera Cruz, Mexico
Nathaniel Currier

diers constructing battery sites and moving the guns into place. Inside the town, the Mexicans knew that the American guns would do staggering damage once they began operating. On March 18 and 19, the Mexicans shelling and firing was particularly intense. Battery construction work close to the city was shifted to the nighttime on March 20 to avoid the withering Mexican gunfire. Guns were placed within 600 yards of the city that night, well within the range of the defending batteries on the wall.

By March 22, the Americans were ready to pummel the city. A demand was made to Mexican General Juan Morales inside the city to surrender. Scott's message was both a warning of impending doom as well as a demand to surrender, and he wrote that he was:

> *"anxious to spare the beautiful city of Vera Cruz from the imminent hazard of demolition, its gallant defenders from the useless effusion of blood, and its peaceful inhabitants—women and children inclusive—from the inevitable horrors of a triumphant assault. ... having now fully invested the said city with an overwhelming army, ... competent to the speedy reduction of the said city, he the undersigned, deem it due to the courtesies of war, ... to summon his excellency ... to surrender the same to the arms*

of the United States, present before the place."

Prideful, General Morales refused to surrender the city. Siege guns opened a bombardment that continued day and night without interruption with the shells falling into the city at a rate of 180 an hour setting the city on fire in several places. The Mexicans answered with their artillery creating a sound rarely heard in warfare of that day. Captain Sydenham Moore recorded in his journal on the day the bombardment began, *"I never heard before such an incessant fire of artillery for several days on both sides. At night the sight was a splendid one— seeing the bombs from the time they left the cannons mouth to the time they fell & burst in town . . ."* The next day Captain Coleman wrote in his diary and was not impressed by the show: *"Our cannon attack is something like ornamental colours added to a perfect figure or picture which can't be bettered by the operation; all I conclude of no avail."*[138] He also noted that the U. S. Navy had been driven away from the Castillo de San Juan by enemy fire but that a captured Mexican said the bombardment was doing great damage inside Vera Cruz. Private Nunnalee described the opening of the bombardment differently:

> *"We could see the bombs soon after they had left our guns, and course them in their arch through the air by the match or fuze, and see it fall into the city, and burst. We could thus hear the pieces crashing the buildings and then hear the report of the bomb, and then the heart-renting wail of the inhabitants that was awful . . . We could not help feeling sorry for them."*

Mexican heavy guns held the Americans at bay at first but the superior firepower was with the Americans. The difference for the Americans was the West Point engineers that Scott valued highly. Their heads were repositories for the latest artillery and ammunition science and were probably the best collection of engineers in the history of the United States. A gloom fell over the Mexican garrison. For five days, American guns put on a loud and spectacular show. They breached the great wall,[139] blew away gun positions and destroyed the morale of the Mexican soldiers and civilians.

Shelling of Vera Cruz
E. B. & E. C. Kellogg—1847

A force of Mexicans made an attempt to break through the American lines and enter Vera Cruz after the bombardment of the city began. To stop this attempted breach, the Perry Volunteers marched out of the trenches in front of Vera Cruz to a place in line about one mile inland on March 23 and encamped there. Captain Coleman noted this move in his diary:

> *"Cannons all ceased firing in consequence of an attack made by the enemy in rear of our right wing. Our brigade was ordered forward, marched about one mile and encamped for the night with Arms in hand expecting an attack from Santa Anna in the rear with 5,000 troops. General Scott*

---

[138] Coleman was correct about the bombardment. The 10-inch mortars were ineffective. Scott brought ashore six naval guns—three 32 inch and three 8-inch shell guns—and these guns effectively pounded the city and the city walls.

[139] The wall around Vera Cruz was made of brick, coral and cement. One American estimated that storming the wall would cost the United States a thousand casualties.

was advised of this move by a prisoner"

Private Hiney recorded in his diary on March 25 that *"an attack from the rear of about 3,000 Mexicans. Drove them back. This night, hard duty lay in our trench at the Battery. . . . There were 6 killed. An attack made on Twiggs by the lancers."* The Second Pennsylvania suffered eleven wounded, but Company C was not engaged in the fighting. When the Perry Volunteers returned to the siege lines, the Mexican guns were silent. On the morning of March 25, General José Juan Landero, who now commanded the Mexican garrison in the city and the fortress at San Juan, sent a flag of truce out to the Americans to discuss armistice but not surrender so the shelling resumed. The next day the army was blasted by a particularly severe norther that created *"A terrible storm of wind and sand"* and wrecked ships off shore according to General Scott's report to the Secretary of War. Captain Coleman characterized the day as a *"Most disagreeable day I ever experienced on account of wind and sand. Sick and cold."* By March 26, 1847, the American shells began to breach the walls at Vera Cruz, and the Mexicans inside the town had had enough and proposed surrendered.

Coleman recorded the particulars of the surrender.

> *"Eighteenth day of the siege. . . . Commissioners appointed by both parties to negotiate a peace, or rather surrender of Vera Cruz, which was agreed to on both sides. Terms are unconditional surrender of both Town and Castle, to lay down all public property, and leave on a parole of honor."*

The American commissioners were Brevet Brigadier General William Worth, Brigadier General Gideon Pillow, Colonel Totten and Captain John H. Aulick representing the Navy. The siege ended when the Mexicans commissioners agreed to surrender the city and the San Juan fortress to the Americans. The American flag was raised over the fortress and the walls of the town on March 29, 1847. At Vera Cruz, the Perry Volunteers faced their first hostile action of the war and had been fired upon with deadly intent by the enemy. They performed all duties required of them and persisted under the heavy fire of the Mexicans. They came through the battle with their honor collectively intact and executed their duties faithfully. None of the Volunteers were killed or wounded and their service outside the city was unremarkable. As it turns out, this was the only hostile action the boys from Perry County would face during the war with the exception of enemy sniping along the road to Jalapa. However, after Vera Cruz the Perry men had something to talk about when they returned home at the end of their term of service. When asked, *"Were you in any battles in Mexico?"* they could now reply, *"Yes, I was at Vera Cruz"* However, their suffering in the service of their county was far from over.

Elias Hiney from Pennsylvania described the Mexican surrender in his diary with uncontrolled enthusiasm on March 29:

> *"This was a glorious day. The most wonderful day ever recorded on the annals of History. We were arrayed in line of Battle whilst the Mexicans marched out of the city and castle to surrender up their arms as prisoners of war. 9,000 arms took from Mexicans. Our line 12,000 strong as the Mexicans marched out, we march into the city and planted the old Stars and Stripes on every fort and castle while the Navy fired a salute and the band struck up Yankee and the variations, of course. Thus, after three weeks of hard fighting, we achieved a glorious victory. . . . We pitched our tents after laying out under the wide canopy of heaven for five weeks. . . . "*

On the morning of the surrender, the Perry Volunteers and their comrades in arms marched to the plain in front of Vera Cruz's main gate to witness the Mexican surrender. They stood in the sun for three hours waiting for the defeated garrison to appear. On the walls of the city, the

Mexicans saluted their flags and then lowered them and the Americans rushed forward with cheer and raised the Stars and Stripes. Twenty-nine guns were fired in a salute to the victors. The final act of surrender occurred when the Mexican garrison left the city from the south gate away from the Perry Volunteers, and they were not allowed to see the Mexicans lay down their arms in front of the American Army. With Vera Cruz evacuated, most of the Americans passed through the gates into the city under the review of General Scott perched on a balcony.

The Perry Volunteers did not get to see inside Vera Cruz right away and, as Captain Coleman said, the boys were "*much wrathy in consequence of not having the privilege to them of visiting the town*" they had helped to capture. The reason they did not get to go into Vera Cruz was because the army had a problem with draft animals and wagons. The United States government failed to send five hundred draft horses needed to pull siege guns and supplies, so Scott had to buy or confiscate Mexican horses and mules. The need for draft and pack animals was desperate, and they had to be acquired if the offensive against Mexico City was to succeed. The transportation problem was so serious that the baggage of the army was cut to a minimum. Each company was allowed only three tents for the use of the sick and each man carried full equipment plus rations for four days in his haversack. Quartermaster General Thomas S. Jesup estimated that it would take 3,000,000 pounds of supplies, 9,303 wagons and 17,413 mules to transport the supplies that General Scott needed to keep the American army in the field. General Scott summarized his intentions in a report to Secretary of War William L. Marcy dated March 29, 1847.

> "*I have commenced organizing an advance into the interior. This may be delayed a few days, waiting the arrival of additional means of transportation. In the meantime, a joint operation, by land and water, will be made upon Alvarado. No lateral expedition, however, shall interfere with the grand movement towards the Capitol.*"

To fill the void for draft animals, and perhaps gather in some beef cattle to serve as ambulatory rations, the Perry Volunteers and the rest of their regiment under the command of General John A. Quitman were sent fifty-five miles to the south to Alvardo, Mexico to collect horses, mules and cattle for the army.[140] The objective of this 2,200 man expedition was to capture the town of Alvarado, which was located at the heart of a flourishing ranching area where it was believed horses and mules could be easily acquired. Peachy Bledsoe did not make the trip. He was hospitalized at Vera Cruz on Tuesday, March 30, the day the expedition to Alvarado left the city. Once again, the Perry Volunteers hoped for at least a little fight with the Mexicans and the honor of capturing the town as a detachment of Scott's Army, thereby garnering all the undiluted praise and honor.

The Volunteers drew provisions for three days and headed for Alvarado. Their advance was near the wall of the city and down to the beach where they marched along the coastline running south out of Vera Cruz, slogging through the deep sand along the water's edge. It was a difficult journey under the harsh sun and was made more disagreeable because drinking water was hard to find. They camped at the little village of Antón Lizardo on the Madelin River the first night after a tramp of twelve miles that did not end until ten o'clock at night. There was a small fishing village at the campsite, but its inhabitants abandoned their homes in fear with the approach of Quitman's Brigade. Coleman described the day's trip and encampment in his diary:

> "*took up the line of march at 8 o'clock a.m., crossed the river following the beach and hard marching indeed. Much fatigue and feet blistered at night. Encamped in a beautiful grove of Palmetto. Saw the greatest curiosity and*

---

[140] Regiments accompanying the First Alabama were from Georgia and South Carolina and these regiments made up Quitman's Brigade.

beauty imaginable—a banyan tree."

After a breakfast of crackers and coffee, they filled their canteens and crossed the Madelin River on a floating bridge constructed by the United States Navy. Again they marched down the sandy beach struggling through sand that seemed to have no bottom. Along this day's march they passed a shrubless, course grass covered plain populated by wild cattle but void of drinking water. Again, Coleman describes a strenuous day of marching: *"Georgia Regiment leading by the left flank. Information came to us that Alvarado had surrendered. Traveled hard, Men much fatigued and feet blistered."* The Volunteers made fifteen miles the second day and camped on an open prairie with little water to be found around the campsite. Most of the men went to sleep without eating a supper of salt pork and crackers because it would only increase their thirst.

The march to Alvarado continued on Thursday, April 1 under the oppressive tropical sun and the Perry Volunteers covered another twelve miles, quickly exhausting their water supply early in the day. The jaunt was through rough prairie that some thought harder than the bottomless sand along the beach. Many of the men saw mirages believing a beautiful lake of clear water lay just ahead but were quickly disappointed when the lake disappeared as they neared the illusion. The only available water during the day's march was from a slimy green colored mud hole occupied by an alligator. The horses refused to drink the water and the men who did were made *"deadly sick."* The trip took them past beautiful palmetto trees and high grass but the struggle in the blistering heat to reach Alvarado continued. They camped on the beach beneath towering palmetto trees that night and dug wells to find water with little success. Nearby wild cattle were killed and the men ate a *"mess of beef."* During the night, salty water rose in the wells dug the previous evening, but it did little to quench their thirst. Some inhabitants from Alvarado showed up in camp after dark with a white flag and invited General Quitman into the town to take possession of the place, destroying the Volunteers hopes for a fight and glory. The General and an escort of dragoons accepted the invitation, leaving the Brigade behind to follow the next day. It was eighteen more miles to Alvarado, but the Volunteers were already worn out with blisters covering their feet. The march resumed the next morning with the First Alabama leading the way but the sick and injured were left behind at the campsite. Again they marched in deep sand and their suffering continued until they reached Alvarado.

General Quitman's objective of acquiring horses and cattle was ruined when a naval attack caused the inhabitants of Alvarado and defending Mexican soldiers to abandon the town, destroy what they could not evacuate and drive off their livestock to keep them away from the Americans.[141] The Volunteers marched into Alvarado in the late afternoon on Friday, April 2, 1847, and they found, as Coleman recorded, *"no Mexicans in the place."* Fast marching, inadequate water, too little rest and extreme heat left many of the men in wrecked physical condition, including Coleman who recorded that he was *"sick of fatigue and sore feet."* Coleman thought that Alvarado was *"a pretty little town"* and estimated the population at 2,500 inhabitants. The 1,000 Mexican soldiers stationed at Alvarado plundered the town before they abandoned it and the formalities of surrender were completed before the Alabamians arrived. There were two crudely built forts on the river above and below the town that were burned and the cannons hauled off by the U. S. Navy.

That night the exhausted Perry Volunteers were assigned to serve as the police for the town and stayed up all night in spite of their fatigue, sore feet, extreme heat, and torture from sand fleas, flies, mosquitoes and gnats. On Saturday, they were again on police duty in Alvarado with instructions to keep order, but Captain Coleman recorded in his diary that they *"did not do it."* The Catholic Church in Alvarado was the best and finest building *"elegantly furnished inside"*

---

[141] Commanding the *Scourge*, Navy Lieutenant Charles G. Hunter, contrary to orders, fired upon the forts at Alvarado and seized the town when the Mexican soldiers ran away. In doing so, he destroyed any chance to secure livestock. Hunter was court martialed for his actions and lightly punished.

that Coleman had seen in Mexico, and he went to inspect it.[142] While Company C was engaged in policing Alvarado, General Quitman went to a nearby town named Tlacotálpam where he negotiated the sale of 500 horses to the U. S. Army. That day Coleman received orders that the Brigade would return to Vera Cruz the next day, Sunday, April 4. The disabled were evacuated by sea but none of the Perry Volunteers are known to be among those returned to Vera Cruz by ship.

The Alvarado expedition was a source of amusement back in the United States. On May 7, the New York *Sun* lampooned it with the following lines:

> *"On came each gay and gallant ship,*
> *On came the troops like mad, oh!*
> *But not a soul was there to whip,*
> *Unless they fought a shadow;*
>
> *Five sailors sat within a fort,*
> *In leading of a lad, oh!*
> *And thus was spoiled the pretty sport*
> *Of taking Alvarado."*

Having helped secure the horses that General Scott desperately needed, the weary Perry Volunteers trudged out of Alvarado on Sunday with the South Carolina regiment leading the way. By forced marching, the brigade covered eighteen miles before stopping and camped at a huge ranch that night with sore feet the collective complaint in the regiment. The next day's marching was an ordeal long remembered by the men from Perry County for its brutal difficulty. Leaving at seven o'clock in the morning, the men marched twenty miles before halting. Several of the Perry Volunteers gave out from fatigue and Captain Coleman *"came near fainting from pain of my feet."* On Tuesday, April 6, the march resumed early with the First Alabama leading the way and arrived at Vera Cruz at noon. The return trip took three days of strained marching and the men suffered greatly from the lack of water along the route and damaged feet were common and nearly universal in the Brigade. The heat was intense and many of the soldiers broke down from their exertions in the harsh condition of the march.[143] Once back in Vera Cruz, the Volunteers went into camp outside the city and Coleman received orders that his Company would be moving out to Jalapa soon but no date of departure was assigned.

On Wednesday, April 7, the Perry Volunteers entered Vera Cruz on an insufferably hot day for the first time and observed the damage of the thousands of shells lobbed into the city. They discovered that it was a charming place with attractive churches, stout white buildings and a beautiful view of the sea. Some of the volunteers thought the streets and buildings reminded them of New Orleans more than any other place. Captain Coleman went to see the fortress San Juan on the reef opposite the city, and he thought it a *"strong place surely. One hundred thirty guns and five large mortars mounted and two hundred more which were not mounted. The Castle I cannot begin to describe. It was commenced in 1602."* On his first outing into the city, Richard Heard was badly hurt in an altercation with a cruel soldier from the Regular Army but Coleman recorded three days later that *"Richard's wounds getting better."* The next day, the Volunteers watched as the Second Division of the Army under the command of General Twiggs march for Jalapa and the interior of Mexico. On Friday, April 9, two brigades, minus the exhausted Quitman brigade, belonging to the Volunteer Division left Vera Cruz for Jalapa following the main body of Scott's army. Captain Coleman went shopping that day and bought silver suspender buckles and a fine gold ring for Jane, paying ten dollars for each item.

---

[142] Captain Sydenham Moore described this church building as *"upon a scale of splendour I had not seen before in any church in Mexico or any country."*
[143] It is not understood why the expedition was not moved to Alvarado by sea. Had this been the case, the suffering caused by the march would have been avoided and the wrecked men saved for further service with the army.

He also reported that a Negro from Tennessee was hanged in camps this day for raping a Mexican woman. On Sunday, April 11, Coleman had another pleasant tour of the city, this time visiting the Cathedral and described it as a *"fine church truly and had seven different characters to worship by these people."*[144]

On April 12, Company C was inspected and issued thirty-three haversacks and twenty-six canteens to replace the worn out accoutrements in the Company. A letter arrived for William Coleman from Private Joseph B. Heard, his brother-in-law. Heard had been hospitalized at Point Isabel in November 1846 but was released in late March 1847, returning to Alabama and writing to let Coleman know he arrived safely. The weather continued hot and disagreeable in the camp at Vera Cruz, and there was little activity except to rest from the exertions of the recent expedition. Captain Coleman had his coattail cut off his uniform in an effort to escape some of the heat. Orders had been issued for the Volunteers to move out of Vera Cruz and join Scott's army on the National Road but no time or date had been set, so the men from Perry County prepared to march and stay in a state of readiness.

The jungle came right up to the walls of the city and the steaming heat brought on fears of *el vómito,* which usually made an appearance at Vera Cruz around mid-April. Right on schedule, the first cases of yellow fever occurred while the Volunteers were there. Now leaving the city's coastal flats to a higher and healthier climate became a concern for the Alabama men. Getting out of Vera Cruz proved impossible for some of the Perry Volunteers. The tramp to Alvarado was severely grueling and many of the men were incapacitated by their exertions there and back. As a result, twelve Perry countians were sent to the hospital and one returned to Alabama with a disability discharge. On April 12, Joseph B. Hale was discharged from the army. Among those Perry Volunteers hospitalized at the Franciscan church in Vera Cruz where the army established a hospital were John W. Barron, Martin Burch, Charles R. Dennis, Joel H. Hunley, George H. Hanson, John W. Griffin, John A. Leach, John B. Martin, Albert G. Melton, William G. Stinson and Lafayette Vance.[145] All of these men remained in Vera Cruz when the Company C headed into the interior of Mexico. In testimony to the difficulty of the march of Alvarado and back, the First Alabama left eighty-eight men behind when the regiment left the city.

First Alabama Regiment Hospitalizations
Following the Alvarado Expedition

Co. A	Co. B	Co. C	Co. D	Co. E	Co. F	Co. G	Co. H	Co. I	Co. K
8	9	12	7	9	7	10	7	9	10

Some of the men left in the hospital at Tampico when the Company moved to Vera Cruz began to be released and were able to return to service. William N. Edwards, Robert Farley and Wiley W. Fowler were returned to duty, but they were in Tampico and would have to catch up with the Company, which departed Vera Cruz on Saturday, April 17 the day that John P. Everett was promoted to fourth sergeant.

[144] Coleman's reference to seven characters worshipped by the Mexican displays a lack of understanding of Catholic beliefs and the purpose of statuary and art in the churches of Mexico. Volunteers in Mexico showed little respect for Catholics, their beliefs or their churches.
[145] Hospitals were an undesirable place to be. Milton Jamieson, an Ohio volunteer, reported that doctors and hospital stewards at the Vera Cruz were cruel to patients and that recovery was more the result of sheer luck than good medicine. The hospital was insanitary. Early Nineteenth Century doctors bled patients and gave them liberal doses of mercury, quinine, zinc and even arsenic. Calomel, pulverized rhubarb, ipecacuanha, camphor, lead acetate, copper sulfate and opium were common medicines. Few doctors saw the connection between illness and poor sanitation, polluted drinking water, contaminated food and lack of personal hygiene.

"Old Hard Crackers and Pickled Pork"

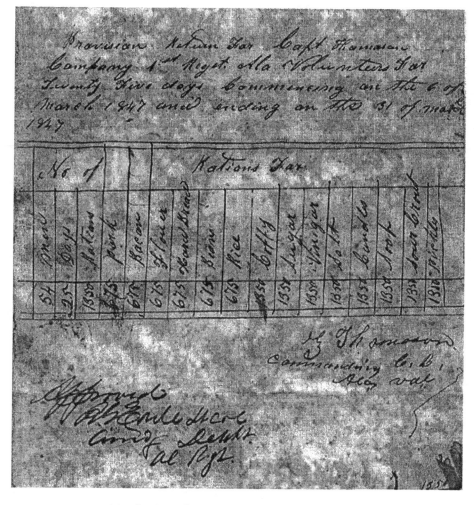

Typical Rations Issued at Vera Cruz, Mexico
March 6, 1847

Following the landing at Vera Cruz, the Perry Volunteers drew rations for the month of March. The above provisions return from the Alabama Department of Archives and History records is for Captain Zechariah Thomason's DeKalb County Company and approved by Lt. Colonel Earle but is typical of the rations issued to all companies. The rations are for the period March 6 through March 31 or 25 days. There were 54 men in Thomason's company and 54 multiplied by the 25 days resulted in 1,350 full daily rations and 675 for half rations. Half ration items included pork, bacon, flour, hard bread, beans, and rice. Full rations were issued for coffee, sugar, vinegar, salt, candles, soap, sour kraut and pickles.

The General Regulations of the U. S. Army (1841) prescribed daily rations of *" three-fourths of a pound of pork or bacon, or one and one fourth pounds of fresh or salt beef, eighteen ounces of bread or flour, or twelve ounces of hard bread, or one fourth pound of cornmeal."* However, because the regulations require it did not mean that it was issued. The Commissary Department of the Army in 1847 usually distributed what they had available and stretched it as far as they could. Captain Coleman described the diet of Company C as *"old hard crackers and pickled pork."*

Perry Volunteers - Service with the Southern Army of Winfield Scott

Gulf of Mexico

Tampico to Vera Cruz March 6, 1847

To New Orleans May 16, 1847

Vera Cruz

Alvardo

Cerro Gordo

Jalapa

Mexico

National Road

Puebla

Mexico City

Amy Richardson

On the Road to Jalapa, Mexico

"There I saw more dead men,
horses, mules, and wounded men
than I have ever before seen."
Captain William G. Coleman

The Volunteers' stay in Vera Cruz lasted over a week after returning from Alvarado. Leaving a garrison force to hold the city, the main body of Scott's army marched out of the city on April 8, 1847, even though he was without sufficient transport to supply the army. The First Regiment of Alabama Volunteers moved out ten days after Scott and headed for the town of Jalapa in the highlands on the route to Mexico City 260 miles away. The pause in Vera Cruz allowed the Volunteers some time to recover from the Alvarado forced march, but the reason for the delay was to permit one hundred wagons to be loaded with provisions for the army. The First Alabama was held in the city, so they could escort and protect the wagon train from Mexican guerillas lurking along the road who's purpose was to cut supplies and communications with the army as they did earlier at Camargo.

The Perry Volunteers trek to catch up with the main army took them through forty miles of deep sand during the first days of their journey carrying full equipment on their backs and four days rations in their haversacks as they struggled over the Mexican National Road first traveled by Europeans three centuries earlier. They left Vera Cruz at six in the afternoon of Saturday, April 17 and covered three miles before going into camp for the night. The next day the line of march was resumed at nine o'clock in the morning constantly moving in the sweltering heat through deep shifting sand and across some *"fine old Spanish bridges"* but Coleman observed that the advance was *"in much confusion."* The Volunteers made fifteen miles the second day and camped by a fine stream of water. However, there was trouble. Some Mexican partisans murdered three America soldiers and were lurking around the road firing upon the train. Traveling along this road the Alabama boys must have been amazed at the natural beauty of the flowers, trees and birds. The area was a gorgeous, exotic paradise to the young men from

along the Cahaba River in Alabama. Their hike took them to the village of Plan de Rio where the road begins to twist and climbs into the highlands leaving *el vómito* safely behind. In the lowlands, the yellow fever season was getting under way but Jalapa was reported as healthy and free of the dreaded disease.

While the Volunteers were traipsing up the mountains, Scott's army encountered Mexican lancers and sent out scouts to find out what was up ahead. Captain Joseph E. Johnson, later of Confederate Army fame, was in the scouting party and came back severely wounded with bullet holes in his thigh and arm to report that Santa Anna was entrenched and posted across the pass

Battle of Cerro Gordo—April 18, 1847
Lithograph by Currier

at Cerro Gordo guarded by a vertical wall on one side and a high cliff on the other. The way to Mexico City was blocked. While the First Alabama strained over the National Road to the high ground and to catch up with the army, the Americans fought the Battle of Cerro Gordo (*El Telégrafo* in Mexico) and dislodged the Mexican army on April 18, 1847. Scott's battle plan called for a two-prong attack against the Mexicans fortified in the narrow mountain pass. The Mexican line bent at first and then crumbled. By mid-morning on the eighteenth, 1,200 Mexicans were killed or wounded and 3,000 men and 200 officers were taken captive. The rest of Santa Anna's army numbering about 7,700 was in a headlong panicked flight toward Mexico City with Santa Anna in the forefront and the U. S. Cavalry in pursuit. At Cerro Gordo, American success came from a flanking movement that made the Mexican's impregnable position ineffective. The American victory was smashing. In the words of General Scott, "*The rout proved to have been complete, the retreating army . . . being dispersed and utterly disorganized.*" On the day of the battle, Samuel P. B. Fuller was promoted to second corporal from private as the Perry Volunteers moved toward the battle scene where they arrived too late to take part in the victory.

The Perry County Company stopped at the hacienda of Santa Anna on April 19 where they waited all day for the wagon train to come up before moving on toward Jalapa and saw that the estate had already been wrecked by the American troops that arrived there before them. Coleman described the Mexican General's summerhouse as "*a fine looking establishment*" and picked up a set of the general's fighting cock gaffs as a souvenir. Ralph W. Kirkman of the Regular Army was more descriptive than Coleman in a letter to his wife dated April 29, 1847.

> "*. . . we stopped . . . at Santa Anna's hacienda and it is really a most beautiful place. A great deal of money has been expended on it. Everything in the house indicates luxury and splendor.*"

While at Santa Anna's estate, Andrew H. C. Harvill and John W. Rogers caught up with the Regiment, having been discharged from the hospital at Point Isabel, Texas and made their way back to Company C. Jalapa was occupied without a fight on the nineteenth. The Perry Volunteers were ordered by General Quitman to lead the regiment forward the next day, and they started toward the town at the head of the column at sunrise on April 20, rapidly covering eighteen miles that day and camping at the one hundred year old National Bridge that night which Coleman described as "*a strong place, both by nature and art.*" The Second Tennessee was camped near the bridge recovering from the battle two days earlier. The camp presented a horrible scene to the men from Alabama. The Second Tennessee, commanded by General Gideon Pillow, had been mauled in the battle and men lay around with amputated arms and legs, hundreds with dangerous body wounds and the graves of the abundant dead were nearby. In all ninety Tennesseans were killed or wounded.

General Quitman came to the camp of the Perry Company on the twentieth and reported the results of the Battle at Cerro Gordo to Captain Coleman. Coleman recorded the General's remarks in his diary:

> "*Genl Quitman reported to me the results of the battle fought between Santa Anna and General Scott on the 18th Inst. Our loss 200. Mexicans loss 2,000 killed. 4,000 prisoners. 10,000 stands of small arms and 23 guns. Several officers prisoners of which LaVega and Herrera[146] were two.*"

Actually, five Mexican generals were captured including Luis Pinson, José María Jarrero, Rómulo Diaz LaVega, Noriega and Obando. General Ciriaco Vasquez was killed. Later that day, the Volunteers watched as the captured Mexican generals were moved down the road on their way to the United States as prisoners of war.

On April 22, the Volunteers resumed their march to Jalapa at one o'clock in the afternoon and soon arrived at the Cerro Gordo battlefield. What the Alabama men saw was the wreckage of

---

[146] General Rómulo Diaz LaVega and General José Joaquín de Herrera, former President of Mexico.

the struggle, and the bloated and mangled corpses of those who were killed. Dead bodies lay in piles and a large amount of arms and ammunition were strewn over the field. Lieutenant Thomas Jackson, later Stonewall, wrote to his sister that the sight *"filled me with as much sickening dismay as if I had been a woman."* Sixty-three Americans died and 337 were wounded. Half of Mexican General Santa Anna's army died or was captured in the fight for possession of the road to Jalapa. Captain Coleman described what he observed in his diary:

> *"Passed the battleground and a stronger position for defenses certainly cannot be in Mexico. There I saw more dead men, horses, mules, and wounded men than I have ever before seen. It is picturesque and magnificent scenery I never have seen. A fine paved road and plenty of water. Our army took a great number of guns, small arms, wagons, mules and ammunition. Battle ground Sierra Gordo. Saw Genl Shields he is very low having been shot through with a grape shot. The mountain pass where the battle was fought is at the head of a deep ravine which runs southeast and is not more than fifty yards wide."*

H. Judge Moore of the Palmetto Regiment recorded his description of the Cerro Gordo battlefield.

> *Here lay, in scattered and terrible confusion, every thing that the mind of man can conceive to be connected with the science and practice of war—dismounted and battered cannon—broken carriages—piles of powder and balls—broken muskets—dead horses and mules—caps and coats—legs and arms, and putrid carcasses of men torn and mangled by cannon balls, and left, half devoured by the beasts and birds of prey; and the whole paraphernalia of war, lying in one mingled and undistinguishable mass, while the putrid stench that rose from every hill and valley, caused a sickening sensation, almost rendered the atmosphere insupportable. . . . while the howl of wolves, and the mournful cries of the jackal were heard from the adjacent hills; and flocks of hungry vultures were hovering near, and perching upon every tree and shrub, ready to whet their barbarous beaks upon the bones of the gallant dead.*

Coleman correctly reports the condition of Brigadier General James Shields who, although blasted completely through his right lung with grapeshot, survived and fought in the battles around Mexico City where he was again wounded, this time in the arm.[147] General Gideon Pillow was wounded in the arm in a futile attack on the main road that cost the Second Regiment of Tennessee Volunteers and the First Regiment of Pennsylvania Volunteers four hundred men killed or wounded. The *Picayune* in New Orleans editorialized that Pillow's *"assault miscarried sole because they were commanded to do an impossible thing . . ."* The Perry Volunteers proceeded on toward Jalapa and camped next to *"a little mountain stream of pure cool free stone water."*

Company C arrived at Jalapa at ten o'clock in the morning of April 23 fatigued and weary from their six-day march from Vera Cruz. Jalapa was a lovely little town on the slope of the mountains resting at 4,800 feet of altitude. The weather was delightful and the town was sprinkled with parks, churches, fountains, winding streets, beautiful residences and squares; it was home to several thousands of people. Some of the soldiers thought it an ideal town and were pleased to learn that it was free of yellow fever and the swarming, biting, stinging insects of Vera Cruz.

---

[147] General Shields was wounded in an attack on a Mexican artillery position on El Telégrafo. When he fell, Colonel Edward Dickinson Baker assumed Shields' command and took possession of the road to Jalapa from the Mexicans. This was the same Colonel Baker involved in the court martial at Camargo with Captain John McMahon. Shields' life was saved by an Irish surgeon in the Mexican Army who cleaned the general's wound by pulling a silk handkerchief through it.

Coleman's description of Jalapa shows his delight with this place and the people he saw. "*It is a splendid looking town, closely built in the edge of the mountain. It contains a dense population of fashionable people of the Castilian stock.*" Captain Sydenham Moore described Jalapa in a letter to his wife as, "*by far the loveliest place & is surrounded by the finest scenery I have ever beheld. The atmosphere is pure and balmy.*" Captain William Blanding of Charleston, South Carolina wrote in a letter home on April 24, "*The town presents quite a romantic appearance . . . Fountains of mountain water are in many parts of the city. Around rise mountains of singular beauty . . . The climate is delicious, the air pure and invigorating.*" The Volunteers camped two miles north of the town on the road to Perote along a small stream near a large stylishly built cotton factory owned by a Scotsman.

Here they remained in camp with little to do except eat "*poor beef and cold water dow cake made of flour, both without salt*" and diarrhea emerged in the Company. The lack of transportation had forced the Volunteers to sleep out in the open without tents since March 6, the day they left for Alvarado. Jalapa was nevertheless a delightful place. The Perry County men must have been fascinated

Jalapa, Mexico

with the delicious fruits of the tropics, and those they could get back in Alabama such as pears, plums and cherries. The scenery at Jalapa took the visitors' breath away. On a clear day, the Gulf of Mexico was almost visible from the heights. The townspeople were friendly and lovely ladies plentiful. Orizaba, a distant lofty perpetually snow covered peak, presented a beautiful and unfamiliar view to the Alabamians. Captain Coleman visited the town on Saturday, April 24 and "*found it to greatly excel any place I have ever seen in any country.*" The Cathedral was magnificent and filled with splendid decorations. The building was large and the halls contained "*rich paintings and images of the saints*" and personified the affluence of Europe in the new world. Like Coleman, the Americans were dazzled by the opulence of the Catholic Church everywhere they went in Mexico. The streets of the town were paved and the houses well made with iron grates over the windows in the Mexican style. Four days later Coleman wandered to the top of a high peak on a warm clear day "*which over looks a beautiful parcel of farms, and the town of Jalapa.*"

The Volunteers stayed here a little over two weeks during the lull of activity ambling over the countryside while General Scott reorganized the army and accumulated supplies for the final push to Mexico City. Coleman received letters from his wife to his utmost satisfaction and he wrote to her. He also received copies of two newspapers, the Marion *Review* and the Hamburg *Journal*, from his brother in law, Monroe Augustine Ransom. Benjamin Tillman, Coleman's brother-in-law and a private in the Palmetto Regiment, came to his camp and stayed overnight. Tillman was seriously ill and would die when his regiment reached Perote, Mexico. Captain Coleman used his time to prepare Company C to march further into the interior of Mexico, although there was much suspense about what would happen to the regiment and where they would move from Jalapa. He secured shoes, pants and a coat for himself and shoes for his mercurial friend James F. Bailey and rounded up some clothes for his men.

On April 29 muster rolls were prepared and the next day Captain George Deas, Assistant Adjutant General, appeared in camp to pay the men. On May 3, orders were received for the Volunteers to draw two days provisions preparatory to moving the next day to Perote on the road to Mexico City. Captain Coleman noted in his diary that his Company was *"fixing to leave for Mexico* [City] *... received orders to take up the line of march tomorrow morning.* On the following day immediately after reveille, wagons were dispersed among the companies of the Brigade to load their baggage for the advance on the capitol city but quite unexpectedly Army headquarters countermanded the orders without any previous warning. The men from Perry County had seen the war, suffered the privations of soldiering and ravages of disease, had seen too much death, had enough of boredom in camp and going long periods without pay, seen exotic Mexico and were now beginning to think seriously of going home. There was no longer any talk about meeting the enemy in battle to show their valor or the importance of winning laurels to parade before the neighbors back home. The talk now was strictly about leaving Jalapa and returning to Alabama. The Perry men had less than sixty days remaining in their enlistment and wanted to go home.

General Scott, however, was thinking about how to get his army to Mexico City. He lacked wagons and horses sufficient to haul the 1,500 tons of military supplies he needed from Vera Cruz. To supply his army, Scott requisitioned *"medicines and hospital stores, clothing for troops, salt, ammunition, shoes for animals, and knapsacks, blankets, hard bread, bacon, and camp kettles."* Other supplies such as *"sugar, flour, rice fresh meat, beans and forage, we hope to find in the country."* Bandits and belligerent civilians attacked the few wagon and pack trains Scott had. It was impossible to guard the supply route from these hit and run attacks. Getting dispatches to Vera Cruz to be forwarded on to the United States was so difficult that the General hired a Mexican cutthroat named Manuel Domínguez and two hundred Mexicans to serve as his couriers.

Another major problem for Scott were the 3,700 volunteers, including those from Perry County, who enlisted for one year and whose enlistments were nearing an end.

Return Home of the Perry Volunteers

"Oh! My Dear God, how bad I feel that I
can't go directly to her."
Captain William G. Coleman

At Jalapa, General Winfield Scott received news on April 27, 1847, that new regiments of volunteers were being diverted from Zachary Taylor's army in Northern Mexico to the Southern Army. Many of the twelve-month volunteers in the Southern Army began to clamor to go home. The Perry Volunteers had six weeks left in their term of enlistment along with most of the other volunteer regiments, including the Tennessee Cavalry, Third and Fourth Illinois Infantry, First and Second Tennessee Infantry, First Georgia Infantry and the First Regiment of Alabama Volunteers. Congress in an Act passed March 27, 1847, asked these volunteers to reenlist until the war ended and offered reenlistment inducements.[148] General Scott personally visited the camps of the regiments eligible for the benefits of the Act and sought to use his influence to secure the reenlistments. Despite his best efforts, only a few men agreed to reenlist. The short term regiments offered to serve for another three months or until Mexico City was captured but Scott refused to accept the volunteers' terms. The *Picayune* reported from a dispatch sent by the newspaper's editor, George W. Kendall, from Jalapa on April 27:

> *"It is not supposed here (Jalapa) that a single regiment can be*
> *formed out of all the twelve months' men now in Mexico . . . The*
> *officers are as little desirous as the men of remaining in the service*
> *. . ."*

These volunteers began to set forth the idea that waiting until their discharge date to leave Mexico would make them pass through Vera Cruz when yellow fever was at its most rampant stage. This they desperately hoped to avoid because yellow fever struck great fear in the hearts of people in the Nineteenth Century. General Scott was in sympathy with the concerns of the Alabamians and could not in good faith hold them any longer although he knew their departure would delay the end of the war. On May 3, he notified Colonel Henry Wilson, commandant of Vera Cruz, to prepare transportation home for over 3,000 men.[149] On May 4, Captain Coleman noted in his diary, *"orders came from headquarters suspending further movement in front for the purpose of discharging the 12th [twelve months] volunteers."* On the same day, Captain Sydenham Moore recorded in his journal, *"orders from Gen'l Scott for us to be disbanded. Owing to the danger to the troops from having to return thro' Vera Cruz while the vomito prevails there, the General was induced to take that course. It came upon all like a thunderclap from a cloudless sky. No one had the least dream of such an order being issued."* Private Nunnalee recorded, on May 4 *"we are to start home in a day or two. I never saw men so changed in my life. Every face seemed lighted up with new life and energy, the happiest set of men ever seen."* The war had suddenly and unexpectedly come to an end for the men from Alabama. All that remained was to make their way to the United States and Alabama.

Over three thousand volunteers in Jalapa from Alabama, Georgia, Tennessee, Louisiana, Illinois and Kentucky, including the Perry Volunteers, prepared to leave Jalapa for Vera Cruz and ships home. General Patterson issued Order No. 17 establishing the line of march for Vera Cruz. In preparation for the trip, the Volunteers were issued ten rounds of ammunition, hard bread for four days and bacon for two days. They were ordered to take their personal effects but to leave

---

[148] Inducements included in the Act were cash bonuses, land bounties and transportation cash from the place of discharge to their homes.
[149] The rigors of the war had reduced seven regiments, normally 7,000 troops strong, to about 3,000 men, a reduction in strength of nearly sixty per cent.

all of their camping equipment except for what was indispensable for the return march. Coleman noted in his diary on May 5, that the Volunteers *"were waiting for the return train from Vera Cruz to escort it back to Vera Cruz where we will take transportation to the City of New Orleans and the U.S.A. to be discharged from the service of the U.S."* Escorts were necessary for the wagon trains running regularly between Vera Cruz and Scott's army since they were continuously passing through country heavily infested with Mexican guerrillas.

The guerrilla Rebolledo boldly attacked a large U. S. military train the month after the Volunteers passed over the road between Jalapa and Vera Cruz. In one attack, Rebolledo killed twenty-four Americans guarding a five hundred pack mule train. The most vicious of the guerrilla leaders was Padre Jarauta who led a large band of well-mounted men in 1847 and ambushed and attacked any American traveling the road including the largest detachments of Scott's soldiers. Couriers or anyone traveling alone or in small groups were in the greatest danger.

On Thursday, May 6, Coleman *"received orders to march to Vera Cruz to start on the morning of 7th inst., Friday morning."* The Alabama men presented a ragged picture in their worn out clothing nearly destroyed by the campaigning. These soldiers were offered captured Mexican uniforms to replace their rags, but they indignantly declined to wear the uniform of the enemy, expressing insult at the offer. Private Nunnalee mockingly attempted to auction off the enemy's uniforms but did not receive a single bid. The Perry Volunteers left Jalapa on Friday, May 7 in fine spirits and anxious to get away as scheduled. They marched past General John Quitman's headquarters and gave three cheers for their general as they passed down the road. The Georgia regiment led the way and covered nine miles the first day.

Mexican guerrilla attacks on supply trains was a constant problem for the U. S. Army in Mexico. *National Archives*

Captain Coleman was sick with the colic, which disabled him so that he had to be transported in a *"spring wagon"* under the care of his friends in the Company. The Volunteers camped at Los Rio that night. The next day started hot and clear and the Volunteers moved out at one o'clock in the morning with the Alabama regiment leading, covering fifteen miles and stopping shortly after noon at Plan del Rio for the night. The third day brought the Volunteers, once again, passed the battlefield at Cerro Gordo where the mutilated bodies of the dead seem to rise from the graves to tell of the horrors of war. Private Nunnalee wrote of the occasion, *" We are becoming more peaceable already and by the time we get home, we will be an entire peace party."* On Sunday, May 9, the march began at 4:00 a.m. and reached the little river town of Obias where they camped for the night. The march began at five o'clock in the morning on Monday with the Alabama regiment leading the way to that night's encampment at Toleta located on a small river. Here they met a military train bound for Scott's Army containing five hundred wagons and four hundred pack mules carrying provisions to the army at Jalapa. Throughout the trip, Coleman remained ill and bounced along in the spring wagon with the others too ill or injured to walk. The final day's march began at midnight and was the most difficult of the trip to Vera Cruz because the men were worn out by their exertions on the previous days. To make matters worse, hostile Mexicans civilians fired upon them. They reached Vera Cruz at eight o'clock in the evening of May 11, 1847, five days after leaving Jalapa and camped outside Vera Cruz at the campsite used by General Twiggs' forces during the siege. Some wandered into town and watched New York volunteers load on board a ship for the United States.

Anxious to go home, Captain Coleman boarded the transport steamer *Fashion* on Tuesday, May 12 leaving the Perry Volunteers in the care of subalterns to come along later on another vessel. On board the *Fashion* with Coleman were friends from South Carolina, including Captain Preston S. Brooks to whom Coleman gave the cock gaffs[150] belonging to Santa Anna that he picked up when visiting the Mexican General's hacienda in April and asked him to deliver them to T. G. Bascom in Edgefield. Brooks was a close neighbor of William's father in South Carolina and was on his way there to enlist new recruits for his regiment's shrinking rolls. When Brooks arrived home, he found little eagerness to go to war because by then most South Carolinians knew about the privations and hardships of service in Mexico. Also, on board was Dr. James Davis, Jr. from Columbia, South Carolina who was the Surgeon for the Palmetto Regiment. Davis had resigned his regimental commission due to ill health and died shortly after reaching South Carolina. During the voyage, Coleman was ill for most of the trip and Dr. Davis supplied him with medication and medical care. Others on board were Captain Sydenham Moore, Coleman's nemesis, Captain Andrew L. Pickens[151] and Major General Robert Patterson and his staff. Patterson returned to the United States when the departure of so many volunteers effectively destroyed his command. The ship was also crammed with the sick of Vera Cruz. The *Fashion* left the docks in mid afternoon and soon Vera Cruz and the castle at San Juan faded from the view of the Alabamians forever.

The *Fashion* reached the wharfs at Tampico about 4:00 p.m. the following afternoon, making the run from Vera Cruz in about twenty-four hours. Some of the Alabamians walked into the familiar town, visited with old acquaintances and enjoyed ice cream, chocolate, and Italian dishes. The *Fashion* lay inside the bar at Tampico for only one night and sailed for New Orleans on Friday, May 14. The trip across the Gulf of Mexico was in clear and pleasant weather and the ship made good time over the calm, smooth sea. The *Fashion* arrived at the mouth of the Mississippi River six days later at ten o'clock in the morning and Captain Coleman expressed his happiness *"to see land belonging to my own Government."* He had been sick most of the trip but recovered quickly once on the Mississippi River. He longed to *"meet my Dear Wife, children, parents, relatives and friends."* Proceeding up the river passed Pilot Town to New Orleans, he admired Fort Jackson and Fort St. Philip as the sun went down. Coleman was in the dark for the forty miles remaining to the Crescent City where he arrived an hour past midnight on Tuesday, May 18.

Coleman went to the *"magnificent"* Hotel St. Charles for breakfast. The Hotel St. Charles is best described as opulent and was one of New Orleans' great landmarks, occupying an entire city block and capable of accommodating 1,000 guest at one time. Built in 1837, the hotel was located between Common and Gravier Streets. However, Coleman did not stay at the St. Charles but paid his breakfast bill and checked into a more modestly priced private boarding house run by a woman named Mrs. Lusk where he had a clean room and bed. He bought a coat and pants, took a bath, donned his new civilian clothes and wrote a letter to his wife and his parents in South Carolina. He then walked about town but his continuing illness marred his enjoyment of the city. Wednesday began clear and calm, but hot, so Coleman settled in to wait for the Perry Volunteers to arrive in New Orleans. He went shopping where he bought his wife a beautiful dress, bonnet, shoes, hose, handkerchief and gloves for which he paid $37.00 and a gift for each of his sons.

On Thursday, Coleman returned to military business and began making out discharge muster rolls for Company C in order to speed up the discharges once the men arrived in the city. Hav-

---

[150] A cock gaff is a metal spur placed on a gamecock or fighting rooster. Cockfights were a popular form of entertainment in early American history and particularly popular in South Carolina. Sumter County's blue battle flag displayed a gamecock gaffed for battle demonstrating the state's strong connection with fighting roosters.

[151] Captain Andrew L. Pickens became quite ill when the regiment reached Tampico. He was left disabled in Vera Cruz when the regiment left for Jalapa and Second Lieutenant Nathaniel M. Murphy assumed command of the Greensboro Volunteers.

ing accomplished that, he wandered through the New Orleans cemetery and noted that it covered about eleven acres and *"it is a splendid fitted up place, finest kind of family vaults, handsomely decorated with wreaths and flowers of every description."* Friday, May 21 began cloudy, then thunder rolled across the city, and it began to rain. Coleman stayed indoors and resumed work on the discharge muster rolls, making four copies before the task was completed. He was ready to leave for home to see his wife and wrote in his diary *"Oh! My Dear God, how bad I feel that I can't go directly to her."* However, his responsibilities as a soldier made him forsake the ache in his heart urging him to head for Perry County, and he lingered in New Orleans as the Perry Volunteers moved slowly toward New Orleans from Mexico. On Saturday Coleman passed the time by climbing and counting the 220 steps of the stairs rising to a height of 147 feet to the top of the Hotel St. Charles spire for an elevated view of the city that he described as *"a fine large and handsome city."*

On Sunday, Coleman's company was still at sea and his anxiety grew as he waited for them. He went to the market where he *"saw a great variety of everything to eat"* and in the afternoon wandered over to the village of Carrollton where he admired the *"finest garden that I have ever seen"* with a water fountain that kept a brass ball bouncing at the top of the fountain spout *"all the time."* When he returned to New Orleans, he learned that his friend and commander Colonel John Coffey and Lieutenant Colonel Richard Earle had arrived in the city.

While Coleman was making his way to New Orleans on the *Fashion*, the Perry Volunteers, Eutaw Rangers and Jones's Company from Jackson County were filling water casts and loading provisions aboard the *Virginia*, the same filthy ship that had transported them from Brazos Island to Tampico. At eight o'clock on the morning of May 16, the *Virginia* was towed out of the harbor and sent on its way by a fair breeze speedily leaving the seat of the war behind. Private Nunnalee noted the occasion with the words, *"Many have been the exciting scenes through which we have passed, but we must leave our nation's flag in the hands of those who know best how to defend it."* The first day at sea was encouraging as the breeze was strong and the *Virginia* carved its way through the Gulf waters at a good clip making Vera Cruz fade quickly but then a calm began on May 17 and the ship sat unmoving upon the sea. The Volunteers on board, however, were not discouraged—they were on the way home and all their trials in Mexico made being becalmed seem a minor event. The next day (the day Coleman reached New Orleans), there was a little breeze in the morning but the ship made only modest progress toward New Orleans.

On May 19, the becalmed, bored volunteers went fishing and caught a large shark as the ship sat on the still Gulf waters. The superstitious *Virginia* seamen said that this was a good omen since a wind always followed when a shark was caught during a calm morning. There was sure to be a breeze shortly. Around noon, the wind came up and the *Virginia* began to move. The current of air continued and the ship made good progress on Thursday, May 20. The calm returned on Friday and a school of porpoises swam around the ship as if doing drills to amuse the men. A volunteer needlessly shot one of the mammals, and they disappeared immediately ending the entertainment. The next day the ship resumed its run toward home and on May 23 and 24, the Volunteers saw seafowls, driftwood and the water changed color, so they reckoned that they were nearing the United States. At nine o'clock in the evening on May 24, the Volunteers saw the lighthouse at the mouth of the Mississippi River and the *Virginia* cast anchor there for the night. The next day was a hot and rainy day in New Orleans when six companies of the Alabama Volunteers arrived at the wharfs. Captain Coleman went to meet the new arrivals hoping his Company was among them, but he was disappointed and grew anxious for the safety of his Company still at sea, recording his fears in his diary that day: *"O Lord! Please deliver them safely on shore this day, I pray thee."* The Perry Volunteers were not far away, but

Coleman had no way of knowing that his men were making their way up the river for a reunion with him.[152]

At sunrise on Tuesday, May 25, the Volunteers saw their native land for the first time in nearly a year and the feeling began to grow that they were actually home at long last. The ship entered the magnificent Mississippi River with all its beauty and the men admired the picturesque farms and plantations along its banks. On Wednesday morning a steam powered towboat arrived alongside the *Virginia* and lashed to it. Freed of dependence upon the wind, the *Virginia* seemed to fly up the river as the towboat huffed, puffed and hissed under the load of the ship and its human cargo. Just as the sun sat in the west, the Volunteers arrived at the New Orleans wharf and the men were satisfied that they were at last back home. Some of the soldiers in the Company were ill and needed immediate medical attention when they arrived. Among the ill Perry Volunteers was Albert G. Melton who died a little over one month later.

On the morning of Thursday, May 27, the Perry Volunteers assembled along with companies D and F, turned in their muskets and other arms and equipment, folded their colors and received their pay, land bounties[153] and discharges. By noon they had been mustered out of the United States Volunteer Army and entered civilian life. They had been in military service so long that being free of the routine of the past year was strange and a little discomforting. Private Nunnalee recorded that the next morning he "*involuntarily thought of reveille and feel lost.*" They took baths, shaved, cut their hair and donned new civilian clothes, discarding what was left of their uniforms. A civilized appearance restored, they took to the streets of New Orleans. Unfortunately, their pay was so small they had little opportunity to take advantages of the delights of the Crescent City. In need of money, some of the soldiers sold their land bounties, the government's reward for their service, for amounts much less than their value. New Orleans and its charms could not offset the longing for home and most of the men set out for Perry County at the first opportunity.

When the war began, the First Alabama mustered in about 945 men and mustered out only 550 a year later, a deficit of 395 men or about a forty percent reduction. Among the Perry Volunteers seven died in Mexico and seventeen were discharged for disability or other causes. There were six desertions in the First Alabama but none among the Perry Volunteers who remained loyal to their oaths under difficult and trying circumstances. None of the Perry men went absent without leave testifying to their patriotism and sense of duty. If these figures are complete, the Perry Volunteers lost less than one-fourth of its original muster and discharged seventy-four men at New Orleans. Since none of the Perry County volunteers died or were wounded in combat, all of the losses were from disease.[154]

Location	Deaths	Discharges
Brazos Island	0	1
Point Isabel	0	0
Mouth of the Rio Grande	1	0
Matamoros	0	1
Camp Alabama/Belknap	3	11
Camargo	2	0
Tampico	1	3
Vera Cruz	0	1
Totals	7	17

[152] The description of the trip from Vera Cruz to New Orleans is based largely on the journal entries of Private Nunnalee.

[153] Bounties, land warrants and pensions were offered to volunteers to entice them into the army. The land bounties were for 160 acres or $100 in land script to those who volunteered for twelve months of service.

[154] Regimental company discharges occurred on different days: Companies I and K on May 25; Companies C, D, and F on May 27, Companies A, B, E and G on May 28; and Company H on May 29, 1847.

Most of the Volunteers made their way swiftly to Perry County and their families. Some of the veterans "*left on the cars for Mobile*" having had enough of the sea to last them forever. Captain Coleman departed New Orleans on Friday, May 28 in the company of James Francis Bailey and John G. Heard. They boarded the packet boat *Mobile* in the late afternoon and sailed for the city of Mobile where they arrived the next day at one o'clock in the afternoon. In Mobile, they met R. G. Cook and immediately bought passage up the Alabama River to Selma on the steamboat *Amasanth* that left at seven o'clock that evening traveling upriver in the dark. The river's water level was high from recent rains creating a current so swift the *Amasanth* poked along agonizingly slowly upstream. Finally, on June 1, 1847, Coleman arrived in Selma at half past midnight.

The final entry in the Coleman diary describes his homecoming:

> "*To my great joy met with many of my friends, which was a meeting long to be remembered by me with feelings of the greatest satisfaction. Got my horse and set out on my way homeward, after having traveled some 12 miles I met through the goodness of God my Dear Wife and children how to contain myself the balance of the day I knew not. Oh, what a day for me, arrived at home at 9 o'clock a.m. and found things in much better condition than I expected to have done. Capt. James B. Harrison sent a team to carry my things home which was quite a favour to me, lest my writing and many little valuable things to me.*"

The returning Volunteers arrived back in Perry County about June 2, 1847, after an absence of one year and three days. There were the traditional country-simple homecoming greetings of heart-felt gratitude around the county as wives, parents, siblings and friends welcomed the soldiers home. Veterans answered questions, told tales of their adventures in Texas and Mexico and tried to catch up regarding events in the county during their long absence. Collations were generously provided and the long-suffering Volunteers struggled to readjust to the food they knew before the war. Individually the members of the Perry Volunteers slipped back into their civilian lives, resuming their occupations and achieving a measure of normality in their lives.

In the four months after the Volunteers left Mexico, the last phase of the war played out. Vigorous Mexican resistance marked the final months of the war as they sought to hold off the Americans, but the United States had superior leadership and more advanced arms and equipment. The American Army was victorious in the battles at Contreras, Churubusco, and Chapultepec. General Santa Anna evacuated Mexico City on September 14, 1847, and retired into exile, replaced by a moderate government that negotiated a peace. The war was effectively over, but one out of every nine American soldiers lay buried in Mexico. The Treaty of Guadalupe Hidalgo was concluded on February 2, 1848, and Mexico ceded all territory north of the irregular line extending along the Rio Grande to El Paso and the Gila River to California, an area consisting of 1.2 million square miles, including the present states of California, Nevada, Utah, Arizona, New Mexico and parts of Wyoming and Colorado. In return, the United States paid Mexico $15,000,000 and assumed Mexico's debt to United States citizens, amounting to another $3,000,000. Five years later, the United States paid Mexico another $10,000,000 to purchase what is today Southern Arizona. After this, the southern border of the United States was permanently fixed.

William Coleman settled into the bosom of his family and the families of his in-laws once back in Alabama. For the next three years, he concentrated on improving his pecuniary affairs and enjoying his family. Two girls, Frances and Sarah, were born to him and Jane after his return and five more children were born in the years that followed. On November 1, 1850, Coleman appeared in court in Perry County before his old friend James F. Bailey, now Probate Judge, to declare in court his eligibility for a land bounty as a Mexican War soldier under an Act of Congress passed a month earlier. Coleman soon left Perry County with his family and in-laws and crossed the Mississippi River heading for Claiborne Parish, Louisiana where unclaimed land was available. He settled his family near the town of Lisbon and lived out his life in this parish.

In his new home, Coleman quickly gained a good measure of status and respect in the community and served on the Police Jury in the parish. In 1854, the Democratic Party made him a successful candidate for the State Legislature in a hotly contested race against J. W. McDonald, the Know Nothing Party candidate. The experience soured Coleman on politics, and he retired after one term. Coleman does not appear to have been a particularly religious man in his earlier years. In Mexico he "*resolved never more to take the name of God in vain,*" and he seems to have been urged to adopt Christianity by Colonel Coffey during their conversations in Mexico. In Claiborne Parish, he made a decision of faith in Jesus Christ and joined the Rocky Springs Baptist Church at Lisbon where members elected him Church Clerk, a position he held for the next twenty-three years. Four years before he died, Coleman addressed the subject of his end and the role of faith in his after life to Colonel Coffey using familiar military terms:

> "*I trust Col. Coffee I have made peace with a merciful God whose goodness you have so kindly invited me to. I joined the Baptist Church . . . and have been constantly striving to be ready for inspection at Resurrection. I hope we will pass muster on that Great Day.*"

While eschewing political office, Coleman was an enthusiastic supporter of the secession movement in Louisiana. Being too old and infirmed for military service during the War for Southern Independence, he became the drillmaster for troops organized locally for service in the State of Louisiana and the Confederate Army. Like others, the war swept away his old life based on cotton culture and slave labor and injected eleven years of oppressive and tyrannical Carpetbagger rule at the point of a bayonet. It was a time of harsh measures as white Southerners sought to reestablish themselves as the dominant political and social power. However, Coleman adjusted to his new status with grace and dignity, setting his hand to the task of building a new South. At the age of seventy-nine, he reminisced with Colonel Coffey summing up some of the years since returning from Mexico and his thoughts about their service with the First Regiment of Alabama Volunteers:

> "*The wreck* [War of Southern Independence] *swept all the property we possessed except our homes which we went to work with willing hands to make our living—with all our Negro property suddenly freed . . . by U. S. muskets and carpet baggers over us for a long time. I actually got to hating the Government for which we had borne the Stars and Stripes on the arid plains of Mexico—and to tell the truth I have but little respect for it as administered since the war . . .*
>
> *I frequently refer to my old Diary that I kept every day during the 12 months . . . I will never forget either those days that we were making history and fame for an ungrateful country that leaves us poor old veterans without a mere stipendiary to supply the ordinary demands of life.*"

In his waning years, he enjoyed the respect of the community as a contemporary observer recorded, "*without enemies, with hosts of friends, he now is serene and happy.*" In a further measure of respect for the old Perry Volunteer, people in his Louisiana community always addressed him as "*Captain*" Coleman in honor of his service to his country in Mexico. William G. Coleman died on October 19, 1888, at the age of eighty-three, having lived a useful life as an active citizen and a soldier in the service of the United States and in behalf of the Confederacy. After his death, Coleman's son Benjamin Ryan Coleman and grandson Thomas A. Coleman were prominent men holding positions of trust and doing honor to their progenitor.

Some former Perry Volunteers left Perry County after returning home settling in other places in Alabama or migrating west to Mississippi, Louisiana, Texas and Arkansas. In 1884, Captain Coleman wrote to his former Colonel, then living in Flackler, Alabama, *"There are five of my old company living near me—moved to this country with me—and four more of our old regiment living near by."* Among those of the *"old company"* were Seaborn Aycock, Jesse Aycock, John G. Heard and Milo Curry. John P. Everett, Charles R. Dennis and John R. Dennis lived nearby in Union Parish and Charles Green Jackson and William C. Mayes in DeSoto Parish. Peachy Bledsoe lived for a while in Union Parish but returned to Texas and lived out his life there. Joseph G. Dennis and John W. Griffin moved to Mississippi. However, most of the discharged members of Company C remained in Alabama. Among the other members of the First Alabama living near Coleman was Benjamin D. Harrison[155] who served as a private in Company E from Talladega County, Alabama and Thomas P. Hamilton[156] of Company D from Greene County, Alabama.

The images of Mexico dimmed with the passing years and family and friends lost interest in the Mexican War as the shadows of the War for Southern Independence lengthened. The government also lost interest in the service of the soldiers in the Mexican War for forty years. Coleman, like most other surviving Mexican War veterans, was interested in continuing and promoting the comradeship with other veterans begun in Mexico. These veterans formed the National Association of Mexican War Veterans in 1874 for the *"promotion of social intercourse, good-fellowship, and all proper assistance."* The organization was especially strong in the South, eventually forming chapters in forty-two states, and was primarily an organization for men in the lower echelons of the Mexican War army. William Coleman and the other veterans living in the area around him in Louisiana took an interest in the organization, attended its sessions and gave their support to the national organization. In 1877, a veterans' convention brought together former Perry Volunteers including Captain William G. Coleman, John G. Heard, Joseph Heard, Jesse Aycock from Claiborne Parish and other veterans from the parish including Thomas P. Hamilton, Benjamin D. Harrison, J. R. Smith, John Cook, M. H. Lippmins, J. A. Witter and J. M. Blackburn.[157] At the convention, the aging veterans reminisced about their days in the army—the marches, musters, voyages on the Gulf and Rio Grande steamboats, the cold bivouacs, the camp fires, the hard beds, the swarming insects, the dreams of home, the gloomy hospitals, gaunt diseases in all its forms, the death march played so often and lost friends and relatives laying buried along the Rio Grande, San Juan River and at Tampico. Following the 1877 convention, a chapter of the of the National Association of Mexican War Veterans was organized in Claiborne Parish on August 10, 1878, with the members electing W. L. Oakes[158] President and A. T. Nelson, Secretary.

---

[155] Benjamin D. Harrison joined Mumford's Company of six months volunteers and was mustered into Federal service on May 23, 1846, at Mobile. When this company was disbanded, he joined the Talladega Boys and became a member of Company E of the First Regiment of Alabama Volunteers and was again mustered into Federal service on May 28, 1846. During the war, he served as a hospital steward and was mustered out on May 28, 1847, at New Orleans. In 1851, he joined the westward migration and moved from Talladega County, Alabama to Claiborne Parish, Louisiana where he became the publisher of the *Claiborne Guardian* newspaper in Homer, Louisiana and later was associated with the *Louisiana Weekly Journal*. At various times, he served as parish clerk and a member of the Claiborne Police Jury. Harrison was born on February 1, 1824, in Alabama and died on April 13, 1889. He became friends with William G. Coleman and submitted an affidavit in behalf of Coleman when he applied for a Mexican War pension. Harrison, although nineteen years younger, died six months after Coleman.

[156] Thomas P. Hamilton was a private in the Eutaw Rangers (Company D) of the First Regiment of Alabama Volunteers. He was born on November 9, 1826, and died on July 2, 1888, in Louisiana. Hamilton is buried in the Old Homer Cemetery in Claiborne Parish, Louisiana. He filed an affidavit in behalf of William G. Coleman when he applied for a Mexican War pension. Hamilton died three months before Coleman.

[157] J. M. Blackburn was born in 1820 in Ohio and was a shoe and boot maker living in Claiborne Parish, Louisiana.

[158] Washington L. Oakes was born in 1827 in Alabama and was a Claiborne Parish farmer.

It was not long until these veterans began to lobby the United States Congress for a pension. However, the National government looked with great suspicion upon the Mexican War organization because of its large Southern membership. Continuing Northern acrimony toward ex-Confederates growing out of the War for Southern Independence made them fear a pension would be aiding their *"enemies"* demonstrating that Southerners had no influence in the National government during the Reconstruction era. The most visible Mexican War veteran of the day was Jefferson Davis, former President of the Confederate States and Colonel of the First Regiment of Mississippi Volunteers during the Mexican War. Consequently, the Federal government delayed a pension for those who served in Mexico leading Captain Coleman to write Colonel Coffey about the Federal government, *"I have but little respect for it as administered since the war . . . "* By 1887, Southern occupation by the North had ended and the radicals in Congress left over from the war had been replaced opening the way for an eight dollar a month pension for Mexican War veterans and widows.[159] However, Mexican War veterans who served in the Confederate Army or other southern forces were disqualified. Membership in the National Association of Mexican War Veterans declined as the veterans died and gradually the organization faded away.

Like the Federal government in those early days, the public today shows little interest in the Mexican War and knows little, if anything about the conflict. Over 150 years later, there is still no National monument to honor these men. Alabama history books rarely mention the service of the volunteers with more than a sentence or two.[160] William Coleman, Charles G. Jackson, Milo Curry, James F. Bailey and William M. Ford were all real people with real families. Their hazardous and arduous service in Texas and Mexico and the sacrifice of these men and their families in behalf of the United States is not trivial. They are not insignificant shadows from the past but people who lived and who live on today in their descendants. These men and the other Perry Volunteers deserve to be remembered, understood and honored.

The Mexican War was America's first foreign war, transforming the North American continent and making the United States into a continental power; every battle was an American victory and men from Perry County were represented there; it was a proving ground for men, materiel and tactics for the War for Southern Independence, training leaders for both sides of that war. Many of these Mexican War veterans from Perry County served in that war too, but the latter conflict would be more trying and terrible than their experience in Mexico. The Perry Volunteers were an eyewitness to history in Mexico where they observed the leaders and future political and military leaders of the nation for at least the next thirty years. For most of the veterans of the Mexican War from Perry County, their service in Texas and Mexico was the great adventure of their youth; it was a chance to see exotic places, meet people in a foreign land and do things that would have been impossible for them without participation in the conflict. In the process, they served their country with resolve and honor and helped to weave their lives into the fabric that is America today.

---

[159] In 1903, the pension amount was increased to twelve dollars and ex-Confederates were included. Eventually, over 17,000 veterans and over 6,000 widows collected pension for service in Mexico.
[160] For example, in *Alabama The History of a Deep South State*, published in 1994, the total discussion of the contribution of Alabama soldiers is succinctly dismissed with the single sentence, *" Alabama responded by sending hundreds of volunteer soldiers."* Less respect could hardly be imagined for the difficult service of the men from Alabama and the disrespect shown by this pithy statement is highly revealing about some historians' view of the Mexican War and the men who fought it.

Headstone of Captain William G. Coleman

Sacred to the Memory of
WILLIAM GOFORTH COLEMAN

Born in
Edgefield Dist., S.C.
July 10, 1805

Died
Oct. 19, 1888

Age
83 yrs. 3 mos. 9 days

Picture by Ben E. Coleman

Summary of Dead, Discharges and Hospitalizations

Seven Perry Volunteers died during the war. Two died shortly after returning to the United States. Six of these deaths occurred during the first four months after arriving the Texas, giving rise to speculation that these deaths were among those least physically able to resist disease and hardship. Seventeen Volunteers were discharged during the war with twelve discharges in the first four months. While the record is uncertain, it is reasonable to assume that disabling disease was responsible for the discharges, and that the affects of the disease were severe enough to preclude further service.

Equally significant, one third of the Perry Volunteers were hospitalized at various times during their service. While hospitalizations do not have the dramatic impact of deaths or the permanence of discharges, they are significant. Illness was common among the men from Perry County. Captain Coleman frequently reported personal illness, including the mumps, but the record does not include information that he was ever hospitalized. Too ill for duty, Coleman languished in his tent under the care of his servant and friends but did not go to the hospital. Hospitalization indicates serious illness or injury, too serious for camp confinement. Not all hospitalizations were for disease. Peachy Bledsoe stayed in the hospital for over two months after being shot by his own sentinels. The 100-mile march to Alvarado in 1847 and back was so severe on the men's body, especially the feet, that twelve Perry County men were hospitalized at Vera Cruz from their exertions on that journey. Additionally, hospitalizations impacted the number of men on duty to meet the enemy.

Deaths[161]

Name	Date of Death	Place of Death
James T. Dacus	January 20, 1847	Tampico, Mexico
Hezekiah Filbert	November 26, 1846	Camargo, Mexico
Jesse W. Heard	July 22, 1846	Mouth of Rio Grande
Archibald A. Henry	August 18, 1846	Camp Alabama, Texas
James H. Irby	July 29, 1846	Camp Alabama, Texas
Lewis T. Palmer	September 8, 1846	Camargo, Mexico
John Moore Tillman	August 29, 1846	Camp Alabama, Texas

Discharges

Name	Date of Discharge	Place of Discharge
Seaborn Aycock	February 26, 1847	Tampico, Mexico
William B. Bailey	August 19, 1846	Camp Alabama, Texas
James Bennett	February 26, 1847	Tampico, Mexico
Allen Burt	August 19, 1846	Camp Alabama, Texas
William T. Ford	August 19, 1846	Camp Alabama, Texas

[161] After his discharge, Lewis A. Miree died in New Orleans in August or September 1846 from a cause related to his service in the Perry Volunteers. Albert G. Melton died a little over a month after he was discharged. James T. Dacus died of fever and Jesse Heard died of pleurisy according to entries in the diary of Captain William G. Coleman.

Robert T. Goree[162]	July 15, 1846	Brazos Santiago, Texas
Joseph B. Hale	April 12, 1847	Vera Cruz, Mexico
Dr. Jesse F. Jacobs	August 19, 1846	Camp Alabama, Texas
William H. Jones	February 26, 1847	Tampico, Mexico
Lewis A. Miree	August 19, 1846	Camp Alabama, Texas
Simon H. Nichols	August 24, 1846	Camp Alabama, Texas
John Owen	August 19, 1846	Camp Alabama, Texas
George W. Smedley	August 29, 1846	Camp Alabama, Texas
Daniel W. Sneed	October 13, 1846	Matamoros, Mexico
John Miller Tillman	August 20, 1846	Camp Alabama, Texas
Benjamin F. Walker	August 19, 1846	Camp Alabama, Texas

Hospitalizations

Name	Date(s) of Hospitalization	Place of Hospitalization
Jesse Aycock	November 30, 1846	
	January 9, 1847	Point Isabel, Texas
John W. Barron	April 12, 1847	
	April 18, 1847	Vera Cruz, Mexico
Peachy Bledsoe	January 23, 1847	
	April 4, 1847	Tampico, Mexico
Martin Burch	March 5, 1847	
	April 17, 1847	Vera Cruz, Mexico
Martin Burnett	April 17, 1847	Vera Cruz, Mexico
Shadrack W. Cardin	December 10, 1846	
	January 9, 1847	Point Isabel, Texas
Charles R. Dennis	April 12, 1847	Vera Cruz, Mexico
	April 17, 1847	
John R. Dennis	April 17, 1847	Vera Cruz, Mexico
Joseph G. Dennis	December 30, 1846	
	January 9, 1847	Point Isabel, Texas
William N. Edwards	Left Hospital April 4, 1847	Tampico, Mexico
Robert Farley	Left Hospital April 4, 1847	Tampico, Mexico
Hezekiah Filbert[163]	November 24, 1846	Camargo, Mexico
Wiley W. Fowler	April 4, 1847	Tampico
George W. Grissom	August 22, 1846	Matamoros, Mexico
John William Griffin	December 11, 1846	
	January 9, 1847	Point Isabel, Texas
	April 12, 1847	Vera Cruz, Mexico
George H. Hanson	April 17, 1847	Vera Cruz, Mexico
Andrew H. Harvill	November 30, 1847	
	April 29, 1847	Point Isabel, Texas
John G. Heard	November 30, 1846	Point Isabel, Texas
Joseph B. Heard	November 30, 1846	
	March 1, 1847	Point Isabel, Texas

[162] According to Captain Coleman, Robert T. Goree was discharged twice. The second discharge was about October 12, 1846.
[163] Filbert died on November 26, 1846.

Thomas Richard Heard	January 9, 1847	Tampico
Joel H. Hunley	April 12, 1847	
	April 17, 1847	Vera Cruz
James Jones	December 10, 1846	
	January 9, 1847	Point Isabel, Texas
William A. Kelly	April 22, 1846	Matamoros, Mexico
John A. Leach	April 12, 1847	Vera Cruz, Mexico
	April 17, 1847	
William J. Liles	December 12, 1846	
	January 9, 1847	Point Isabel, Texas
John B. Martin	April 12, 1847	
	April 17, 1847	Vera Cruz, Mexico
Albert G. Melton	April 12, 1847	
	April 17, 1847	Vera Cruz, Mexico
James A. Moore	December 10, 1846	
	January 19, 1847	Point Isabel, Texas
John W. Radford	December 11, 1846	
	March 1, 1847	Point Isabel, Texas
John W. Rogers	December 2, 1846	
	April 29, 1847	Point Isabel, Texas
William G. Stinson	April 12, 1847	
	April 17, 1847	Vera Cruz, Mexico
Thomas W. Swanson	December 2, 1846	
	January 9, 1847	Point Isabel, Texas
Lafayette Vance	April 12, 1847	
	April 17, 1847	Vera Cruz, Mexico

Pensions

In 1887, the United States Congress provided a pension for Mexican War Veterans. Among the Perry Volunteers, twenty-eight men and/or their widows received pensions valued over the years at $8.00 and $20.00 a month.

Name	Date Pension Began
Angeline M. Aycock, widow of Seaborn Aycock	February 30, 1888
James F. Bailey	March 23, 1887
Susan Caldwell, widow of John K. Caldwell	April 20, 1887
Harriett Cardin, widow of Shadrack Cardin	February 8, 1888
Mary Jane Coleman, widow of W. G. Coleman	December 31, 1888
Jane C. Cook, widow of Hillary T. Cook	June 7, 1887
Milo C. Curry	
Susanna E. Dacus, widow of Rufus W. Dacus	April 23, 1887
Leroy E. Davis and widow Martha Davis	January 24, 1895
Joseph G. Dennis	January 11, 1887
John P. Everett and widow Sarah J. Everett	July 24, 1891
Robert Farley's widow Lavina Sophronia	April 12, 1910
Homer M. Ford's widow Susan E. Ford	October 10, 1887
William Marshall Ford's widow Sarah S. Ford	March 11, 1887
Wiley W. Fowler	September 3, 1887
John Alfred Fuller's widow Cynthia P. Fuller	January 19, 1900
John B. Fuller's widow	April 14, 1887
Samuel P. Burford Fuller	February 11, 1887
John William Griffin	June 27, 1887
George W. Grissom	June 17, 1897
Joseph B. Heard	March 22, 1887
Thomas R. Heard's widow Frances C. Heard	March 21, 1887
Ira J. Horton	February 6, 1888
Joel H. Hunley's widow Martha C. Hunley	September 14, 1894
Charles Green Jackson and his widow	November 1, 1888
David A. Jones & widow Mary A. Jones	February 10, 1906
James Jones & widow Nancy Jones	May 17, 1895
William H. Jones' widow Elizabeth W. Jones	August 21, 1908
John A. Leach and widow Sarah Leach	June 20, 1896
William C. Mayes' widow	
James A. Moore	April 1, 1887
Joseph T. Mount's widow Elizabeth Mount	March 11, 1887
Alfred Muckle	February 26, 1887
James H. Pitt's widow Elizabeth Pitts	
James W. Stanley	April 4, 1887
William G. Stinson's widow	May 14, 1919
Steven D. Tillman's widow Mary P. Tillman	February 10, 1887
Benjamin F. Walker's widow	June 8, 1910

Epilogue

It is the practice of many historians to frame the Mexican War in terms of a training ground for officers of the Confederate and Union armies. This approach, and the overshadowing impact of the War for Southern Independence twelve years later, are the principal reasons the war with Mexico is quickly brushed aside and receives limited attention. Some of the men who served in the Perry Volunteers also served in the Confederate Army, state militia, state reserves and important civil government positions. In some cases, their fellow soldiers recognized the service of these men in Mexico and elected these veterans to positions of leadership. When the Confederate government abolished electing army officers, the military hierarchy rewarded Mexican War veterans with promotions partly on the strength that they had military experience in Mexico.

Some examples of service to the Confederacy by former Perry Volunteers will illustrate the point that veterans with experience in Mexico rose in the ranks and were exemplary soldiers in the struggle for Southern independence. A study of one fourth of former Perry Volunteers who are known to have served in the Confederacy reveals that there was a major, five captains, three lieutenants three sergeants and a corporal represented among them, as well as others who served in the ranks as privates.

Duke Nall
Captain and Major in the 8th Alabama Infantry Regiment

Duke Nall served without particular distinction during the Mexican War. He entered the army as a private and was still a private when he was mustered out at New Orleans. He entered the Mexican War as an unmarried nineteen year old, and like the others in his company, his only battle was the siege at Vera Cruz, which was a long-range conflict conducted by the artillery devoid of the close up fighting in which he engaged in the Confederate Army. When the Mexican War ended, Nall returned to the home of his mother, Margaret Nall (widow of James Nall) near Perryville, Alabama and became a farmer. He later married Sarah Bennett and began to rear a family of his own.[164] When it became apparent that the South had to fight for its independence and repel an invasion from the North, Nall helped to raise a volunteer company named the Southern Guards. On May 16, 1861, he became the Captain of Company K of the 8th Alabama Infantry Regiment. Nall's prior military experience in the Mexican War set him aside from the other candidates for the captaincy of the company. His friends and neighbors remembered that he had served in that conflict and cast their votes for Nall upon the strength of that remembrance. That he had no experience commanding men and had never been in close combat does not appear to have been important to the voters.

Along with his regiment, Duke rushed to the seat of the war in Virginia and went into the defenses at Yorktown, Virginia. In the following years of the war, he led his men through the Virginia battles at Williamsburg, Gaines' Mills, Frazier's Farm, Second Manassas, Fredericksburg, Salem Church and Bristow Station. Early in the war at the Battle of Williamsburg, Nall was put in charge of manning and defending Fort Magruder. He was in the center of the action at the Battle of Sharpsburg, Maryland in 1862 when a bursting artillery shell wounded him just as the battle was beginning.

In 1864, Colonel Young Lea Royston of the 8th Alabama was forced from service in the Confederate Army when he was severely wounded. The regiment's major was elevated to the vacant

[164] After Duke Nall's death, Sarah Bennett married his brother Robert Nall on November 23, 1866.

colonelcy of the regiment leaving the 8th Alabama in need of a major. Although the military authorities had ten company captains from which to choose, Nall was promoted to the rank of major on November 2, 1864, giving evidence of his military acumen. While exercising his duties on the battlefield at the Battle of the Wilderness, Nall was severely injured when he was shot through the lungs. As a result, he was forced to withdraw and turn command over to Henry Clinton Lea, Jr., also from Perry County and a nephew of Margaret Lea. Nall appeared to recover from his lung wound and returned to duty. However, during the winter of 1864 an inflammation occurred in his wound and pneumonia caused his death on November 4, 1864.

Seaborn Aycock
Captain of Company G in the 25th Louisiana Infantry Regiment

Seaborn Aycock served as a first sergeant throughout his service in the Mexican War. He was a married twenty-six year old Perryville farmer when he enlisted. While in Mexico, he became disabled for further service in the army and was discharged at Tampico three months before his regiment was scheduled to be mustered out. As a result, he missed the siege at Vera Cruz and never saw combat. Returning home, he and his family moved to Claiborne Parish, Louisiana in 1850. When war with the North became a fact, Aycock, at age forty-one, offered himself for service in the Confederate Army. His status as a veteran of the Mexican War was well known to the people in his community, and they turned to him for leadership when a military company was organized in Claiborne Parish for service in the war. He enlisted at Lisbon, Louisiana and was elected Captain of Company G of the 25th Louisiana Volunteer Infantry Regiment on March 15, 1862. General William J. Hardee, who served in Mexico, ordered Aycock to Louisiana on conscript duty. Aycock led his company at the battles of Corinth and Farmington, Mississippi, Shiloh and Murfreesboro, Tennessee and Perryville, Kentucky. He was engaged in the defense of Atlanta and was killed leading his men during the Battle of Jonesboro, Georgia on August 31, 1864.

Leroy E. Davis
Captain of the 20th Alabama Infantry Regiment

Leroy E. Davis served as a private in the Mexican War and his service with the Perry Volunteers was unexceptional. When he left active duty, he returned to Perry County, settled down in Heard's Beat and became a farmer. When Alabama seceded from the United States and joined the Confederacy, he enlisted at the age of thirty-six in Company A of the 20th Alabama Infantry Regiment as a private. When his captain, Dr. Alfred S. Pickering, was promoted to major of the regiment, Davis was promoted to captain of Company A. He seems to have been selected because he was a veteran of the Mexican War and was plucked from the ranks of his company because he had military experience. Davis was born on December 27, 1825, and died on June 4, 1894, at the age of sixty-eight. He is buried in Pisgah Cemetery in Perry County.

Homer M. Ford
Sergeant and Captain of Company K of the 28th Alabama Infantry Regiment

Homer M. Ford was born in 1826 in Alabama and marched off to the Mexican War at the age of twenty. He was the son of Absalom Ford and Sarah Ford, his father's cousin. Following his service as a private in Mexico, he returned home and managed the farm of his aging father. When civil war erupted with the bombardment of Fort Sumter, he enlisted as a private in Company K of the 28th Alabama Infantry Regiment at Perryville on March 29, 1862. Seven months later, he was promoted to sergeant and subsequently replaced Charles R. Harris as captain of Company K in November 1862 when Harris resigned. Ford led his company in all of the engagements of the war in the west serving in the invasion of Kentucky, engagements in Tennessee, North Georgia and in defense of Atlanta.

Thomas Richard Heard
Second Lieutenant and Captain of Company A of the 8th Alabama Infantry Regiment

Thomas Richard Heard departed for the war in Mexico with two of his older brothers. All were the sons of Thomas A. Heard, a wealthy Plantersville Beat farmer with extensive slave and land holdings. Thomas R. was born in Georgia in 1827 and held the rank of 4th corporal in Mexico. When the citizens of Perry County formed a company named the Alabama Rangers in 1861, they turned to Heard for a role in the leadership of that company. On May 6, 1861, he was elected as the second lieutenant of Company A of the 8th Alabama Infantry Regiment and was off to Virginia to defend his native land against invasion by the army of the northern states. At Gaines' Mill on June 27, 1862, Heard's company was in the second attacking line behind the 10th and 11th Alabama Regiments assaulting the Yankee entrenchments. The front regiments faltered under the enemy fire and the 8th Alabama moved through their lines, advanced toward the enemy. In a classic roll maneuver, Heard's company help drive the Federals from the field and captured their Napoleón guns, taking many prisoners. It was in this action that Thomas Phelan, Captain of Company A, was killed and Heard was wounded. Although wounded, Heard was promoted on June 30, 1862, to Captain replacing Phelan. Heard was again wounded at the Battle of the Wilderness on May 6, 1864. This time his wounds were so severe that he was forced to leave the army on December 14, 1864.

William T. Ford
Lieutenant in Company K of the 28th Alabama Infantry Regiment

William T. Ford was born in Georgia in 1815, and he was one of the oldest enlistees in the Perry Volunteers at the age of thirty-one. He only served for one and one-half months in Mexico and was discharged for disability on August 19, 1846, at Camp Alabama, Texas. By 1861, Ford was forty-six years old but his status as a veteran of the Mexican War influenced his election as Lieutenant of Company K of the 28th Alabama Infantry Regiment when men from Perry County began to assemble for service in the Confederate Army. He enlisted at Perryville on March 29, 1862, and was appointed lieutenant that same day. However, as in Mexico, his service was short term. After four months service, he resigned his commission on September 7, 1862, and returned home, his age and infirmities precluding further service.

John G. Heard
Lieutenant in Company H of the 17th Louisiana Infantry Regiment

John G. Heard was the son of Thomas Anderson Heard and brother to two other members of the Perry volunteers. He was born in Georgia in 1823 and was a farmer before enlisting in the Perry Volunteers at the age of twenty-three. During his service in Mexico, he was hospitalized at Point Isabel for three months in 1847 but rejoined his company before it mustered out in May. After returning from Mexico, he moved to Claiborne Parish, Louisiana. When the War for Southern Independence began, he joined Company H of the 17th Louisiana Infantry Regiment in October 1861 and was elected lieutenant of the company. He survived the war and returned to his home in Claiborne Parish.

James Francis Bailey
Alabama Committee for Military Affairs

James Francis Bailey joined the Perry Volunteers for service in Mexico as an educated man. He was born in 1811 in Wilkes County, Georgia and lived until April 18, 1889, dying in Marion, Alabama. When the Mexican War began, he was farming near Perryville as his principal occupation, but he was also a lawyer. He graduated from the University of Alabama in 1834 and the University of Virginia in 1837 with an LL.D degree. He maintained a law office in Marion, the county seat of government, and associated with the leading lawyers in that town. He served as a private in Mexico without any particular note in his record. Returning to Perry County after his service in Mexico, he was elected to the Alabama House of Representative in 1847, the year he mustered out, and was elected Probate Judge of the County, a position he held until removed by the Carpetbaggers and Scalawags during Reconstruction. Bailey favored the South's withdrawal from the union with the North and worked to accomplish secession. He was a delegate to the Alabama Secession Convention and voted to leave the union. When war began, he was fifty years old and was appointed to the Alabama Committee of Military Affairs by his friend Alabama Governor Andrew Barry Moore from Perry County. Bailey did not serve in the military but worked with the military affairs committee to oversee the multitude of matters related to defending Alabama and meeting levies for troops from the Confederate government.

William G. Coleman
Drillmaster for Claiborne Parish, Louisiana

Too old and infirmed to serve in the regular Confederate Army, Captain William G. Coleman nevertheless made a contribution to the Confederacy as a drillmaster for companies raised in Claiborne Parish, Louisiana. As the units were formed, Captain Coleman was called upon to drill the men to prepare them for military service in the Louisiana State Troops and the Confederate Army. The old soldier was a highly respected citizen in Claiborne Parish and retained the title of Captain until the end of his life.

John W. Rogers
Third Sergeant in Company K of the 28th Alabama Infantry Regiment

John W. Rogers enlisted in the Perry Volunteers at the age of twenty-six and was detailed as a nurse at the American hospital at Matamoros, Mexico. Returning home to Perry County, he operated a grocery store at Hamburg, Alabama a few miles south of Marion, Alabama in Perry County. With the advent of the War for Southern Independence, he traveled to Perryville, Alabama on March 29, 1862, to enlist in Company K of the 28th Alabama Infantry Regiment at the age of forty-one years. He was elected as the third sergeant of the company. Rogers was killed in battle during the Confederate victory at Chickamauga, Georgia on September 20, 1863. Rogers was one of four Mexican War veterans who served as officers in Company K of the 28th Alabama.

Wiley W. Fowler
Third and First Sergeant in the 4th Regiment of Alabama Militia

Wiley W. Fowler was a sharecropper and lived in Oakmulgee Beat of Perry County. Wiley was born on November 26, 1831, in Alabama. He served as the 3rd and 1st Sergeant in the Perry Guards, 4th Regiment of Alabama Militia, organized on April 10, 1862, in Marion. He died on March 31, 1886, and is buried in the Legal Cemetery in Perry County, Alabama.

John Alfred Fuller
Corporal in the 7th Alabama Cavalry Regiment

John Alfred Fuller served as a corporal in the 7th Alabama Cavalry Regiment. The 7th Alabama Cavalry saw service on the Alabama and Florida coast and with General Nathan Bedford Forrest in Mississippi and Tennessee.

Jesse Aycock
Private in Company C of the 13th Battalion of Louisiana Infantry

Jesse Aycock served as a private in Company C of the 13th Battalion of Louisiana Infantry. Company C was raised in Orleans Parish, Louisiana by Auguste Roche and the Battalion mustered into Confederate service on March 6, 1862, with four companies and 411 men. The Battalion lost heavily at the Battle of Shiloh and disbanded on June 6, 1863, at Tupelo, Mississippi.

John W. Barron
Private in Company D of the 63rd Alabama Infantry Regiment

John W. Barron served as a private in Company D of the 63rd Alabama Infantry Regiment that was organized in July 1864 at Fort Blakely near Mobile and was captured there with the fall of the fortress on April 9, 1865.

James W. Bennett
Private in the 8th Alabama Infantry Regiment

After returning from the war in Mexico, James W. Bennett married, began a family and worked as an overseer of his father's farm. When war with the North began, he left his aged father, wife and two children and joined Company K of the 8th Alabama Infantry Regiment at Radfordville, Alabama. He enlisted as a private on March 17, 1862, and was recruited by Lt. W. L. Fagan. He died of disease on September 15, 1863, while a prisoner of war at Point Lookout, Maryland.

Peachy Bledsoe
Private in Company C of the 22nd Texas Cavalry Regiment

Peachy Bledsoe served as a private in Company C of the 22nd Texas Cavalry Regiment during the War for Southern Independence.

William Coffey
Private in Company K of the 44th Alabama Infantry Regiment

William Coffey served as a private in Company K of the 44th Alabama Infantry Regiment. Company K was raised in Calhoun County, Alabama. The 44th Alabama was organized at Selma, Alabama on May 16, 1862, and surrendered at Appomattox Court House. Coffey died of disease while in the Confederate Army on October 2, 1862.

Rufus W. Dacus
Private in Captain N. L. Breaks' Company of Home Guards

Rufus W. Dacus served as a private in the Home Guards in the company of Captain N. L. Breaks. He enlisted in the company on April 21, 1863, in Lowndes County, Alabama at the age of forty-five years.

Joseph G. Dennis
Private in Company K of the 11th Mississippi Infantry Regiment

Joseph G. Dennis served as a private in Company K of the 11th Mississippi Infantry Regiment. Company K was organized in Carroll County, Mississippi and was named the Carroll Rifles.

Robert Farley
Private in Company C of the 7th Alabama Cavalry Regiment

Robert Farley enlisted as a private Company C of the 7th Alabama Cavalry Regiment at Pollard, Alabama in October 1863. The 7th Alabama Cavalry was organized at Newbern, Alabama on July 22, 1863, and was stationed near Pollard, Alabama for a year afterward. He surrendered with the army of Joseph E. Johnson at Greensboro, North Carolina in June 1865.

Thomas M. Ford
Private in Company K of the 20th Alabama Infantry Regiment

Thomas M. Ford served as a private in the Company K of the 20th Alabama Infantry Regiment. He was captured at Vicksburg, Mississippi on July 4, 1863, and paroled. The 20th Alabama was organized in Montgomery on September 16, 1861, under the command of Colonel Isham W. Garrott of Perry County.

William Marshall Ford
Private in Company G of the 4th Alabama Infantry Regiment

William Marshall Ford was a financially independent man and a gentleman of leisure. He was a member of the board of directors for the Alabama Baptist Bible and Colporteur Society whose purpose was to distribute Bibles and religious literature. He owned three slaves in 1860. Ford was a member of Company C of the 4th Regiment of Alabama Militia before the war. In 1861, he enlisted as a private in the Confederate Army in Company G of the 4th Alabama Infantry Regiment. At the time he was married to Sarah Stinson Miree and was the father of two girls. He was born on September 26, 1822, and died on March 22, 1861, shortly after enlisting in the Confederate army. His parents were John Ford and Elizabeth Farrar.

Andrew Goin
Private in Company I of the 26th Alabama Infantry Regiment

Andrew Goin served as a private in Company I of the 26th Alabama Infantry Regiment. Company I was formed in Fayette County, Alabama and the 26th Alabama was organized on March 27, 1862, by increasing the companies in the 3rd Alabama Infantry Battalion.

Charles Green Jackson
Private in Company B of the 24th Louisiana Infantry and Company B of the Consolidated Crescent Regiment in Louisiana

Charles Green Jackson was the son of a Baptist minister. He was born on October 29, 1826, in Perry County and died on September 13, 1911, in DeSoto Parish, Louisiana. Charles joined the Perry Volunteers at the age of nineteen and turned twenty while his company was at Camargo, Mexico. He returned from Mexico in June 1847, and his family moved to DeSoto Parish three months later where his father, Abraham Wyche Jackson, established a plantation and served as a Baptist missionary to the inhabitants of Northwest Louisiana. Charles worked as an overseer for his father in Louisiana. He married Mary Ann Cowley on September 20, 1855, and was the father of two children when Louisiana seceded from the union. Jackson enlisted in Company B of the 24th Louisiana Infantry Regiment and saw action at the Hornet's Nest during the Battle of Shiloh, Tennessee after which his regiment was disbanded on June 3, 1862. The regiment was reorganized on September 17, 1862, and ordered to report to General Richard Taylor in South Louisiana. He served until his company and regiment were merged with others to form the Consolidated Crescent Regiment. When Union General Nathaniel Banks, invaded central and Northern Louisiana, ravaging the state, robbing, burning and tormenting civilians, the Consolidated Crescent Regiment opposed Banks' advance but retreated to Mansfield, Louisiana which was Charles' hometown. At Mansfield, the Confederate Army of Louisiana under the command of General Richard Taylor, son of Zachary Taylor, turned on Banks and attacked the marauding Yankees on April 8, 1864. Charles Green Jackson's regiment was in the center of the line and took heavy casualties but routed the invaders sending them on a retreat that ended in New Orleans. Charles' service ended on May 19, 1865, at Mansfield when his regiment disbanded. Charles Green Jackson had the distinction of serving under the command of both General Zachary Taylor in Mexico and his son Richard Taylor in the Confederate Army. After the war, Jackson returned to DeSoto Parish and lived out his life at Grand Cane, Louisiana, dying in 1911 a few days short of his eighty-fifth birthday. He married three times.

John William Griffin
Private in Company K of the 8th Alabama Infantry Regiment

During the War for Southern Independence, John William Griffin was conscripted on May 17, 1862, and assigned to Company K of the 8th Alabama Infantry Regiment that was part of the Army of Northern Virginia. During the Battle of Gaines' Mill, Virginia, John displayed exceptional courage and his name was placed on the regimental ROLL OF HONOR for his bravery. He served as a private until the end of the war and surrendered with General Robert E. Lee at Appomattox Court House on April 9, 1865. After the war, Griffin moved to Kemper County, Mississippi where he died on October 26, 1897, and is buried in the Hopewell Methodist Church Cemetery.

William C. Mayes
Private in Company F of the 19th Louisiana Volunteer Infantry

William C. Mayes enlisted as a private in Company F of the 19th Louisiana Volunteer Infantry raised in DeSoto Parish, Louisiana on December 11, 1861. He was discharged on November 1, 1862, after a series of frequent hospitalizations at the Mississippi CSA Hospital in Jackson, Mississippi.

Joseph T. Mount
Private in the Perry Guards and Company H of the
4th Regiment of Alabama Militia and the 3rd Alabama Infantry Reserves

During the War for Southern Independence, Joseph T. Mount served as a private in the Perry Guards in the 4th Regiment of Alabama Militia, organized on April 10, 1862, in Marion. In 1864, he was a private in Company H of the 3rd Infantry Regiment of the Alabama Reserves.

John Owen
Private in the 28th Alabama Infantry Regiment

John Owen was an ordinary man who probably went to Mexico with the Perry Volunteers to break the monotony of his life at the age of twenty-three. He was born in Georgia and worked as a laborer. Owen was in his mid-thirties and married with five children when the War for Southern Independence began. He joined Company K of the 28th Alabama Infantry at Perryville, Alabama as a private on March 29, 1862. He died on December 7, 1863, at Kingston, Georgia while serving in the Confederate Army.

William Wallace
Private in Company K of the 8th Alabama Infantry Regiment

William Wallace was conscripted into Company K of the 8th Alabama Infantry Regiment on February 1, 1863, in Perry County. He was wounded and captured at the Battle of Gettysburg on July 3, 1863, and sent to the Federal hospital on David's Island in New York City harbor. His wounds led to a parole by the enemy, and he was transferred to the Confederacy where he died in Howard's Grove Hospital in Richmond, Virginia on July 4, 1864.

CAMP MOUTON VETERANS—Like many Mexican War Veterans from the South, Charles Green Jackson served the Confederate Army. Jackson (pictured above in the center of the front row with the long white beard) attended a meeting of the Camp Mouton # 41—United Confederate Veterans—in 1900 at Mansfield, Louisiana. His younger brother Adolphus Franklin Jackson, a veteran of the Nineteenth Louisiana Infantry, is pictured in the fourth row.

Who Were These Men?

Information is not available about all of the men identified as members of the Perry Volunteers. In some cases, there is no information available to the compiler beyond their name, rank, muster in and muster out dates. In most cases, some information is available, and there is enough data to form a general picture of the Perry Volunteers and help to improve understanding of the men who served their country in Mexico. Some generalizations about them are:

1) The Volunteers came from the eastern part of Perry County. This is logical since the company was raised in Perryville located in that section; and the Company commander was from that sector of the county; it was here that he conducted his recruiting among his friends and acquaintances. About thirty percent of the volunteers were from Perryville Beat. Only one identified volunteer was from outside the eastern part of Perry County.

2) The Volunteers were men eager to serve their country. Only twelve days elapsed between the declaration of war and the election of officers. Given the delay in communication between Washington, D. C. and Perry County about the declaration of war, the response of the volunteers is remarkable and swift.

3) The Company was made up principally of men in their twenties. Seventy-one percent of the identified Perry Volunteers were between the ages of twenty and twenty-nine. Fourteen percent were under twenty years of age and fifteen percent were thirty or over.

4) Two thirds of the men in this Company were farmers. Since farming was the principal occupation in the county, their numbers among the Volunteers is understandable. Other occupations in rank order are overseer (4), mechanic (2), physician (2) and one each of brick mason, ditch digger, lawyer, pump maker, tailor and laborer.

5) Sixty-five per cent of the Volunteers were born outside of Alabama. Twenty-three of the men were born in Alabama, seventeen in Georgia, eleven in South Carolina, two each from Virginia and North Carolina, and one each from New York and Ireland.

6) After the war, a majority remained in Alabama but nearly half among the known group, moved to other states. Louisiana was the new home for twenty-six per cent; seventeen per cent moved to Texas while eleven percent migrated to Mississippi. One returned to his former home in Tennessee.

DANIEL ALLEN was born in 1810 in Georgia and was a brick mason by trade. He lived in Perryville Beat in Perry County and was thirty-six years old when he enlisted in the Perry Volunteers. His children included William, Joshua, Frances C. and Minerva Allen. [1850 Census of Perry County, Alabama, p. 349B]

JESSE AYCOCK was born in 1826 in Alabama and was an overseer working for Mary Bagley in Heard's Beat in 1850. He was twenty years old when he enlisted for the Mexican War. Aycock was hospitalized at the General Hospital at Point Isabel on November 30, 1846. On February 5, 1847, Captain Coleman noted in his diary that Jesse Aycock rejoined the Company at Tampico after a month in the hospital. After he returned to Alabama from the war, he moved to Claiborne Parish, Louisiana in 1850, where, in September 1877, he attended a convention of Mexican War veterans with his former captain. During the War for Southern Independence, he served as a private in Company C of the 13th Battalion of Louisiana Infantry. Jesse's widow Almede W. Aycock collected a pension for his Mexican War service beginning March 30, 1888. [1850 Census of Perry County, Alabama, p. 355; *Biographical and Historical Memoirs of Northwest Louisiana* (The Southern Publishing Company, Chicago and Nashville, 1890; Roster of Confederate Soldiers; Pension Widow's Certificate-4271; W. G. Coleman Diary]

SEABORN AYCOCK was born on September 27, 1819, in Georgia and was a farmer who owned four slaves. He lived in Perryville Beat and was twenty-six years old and married when he enlisted in the Perry Volunteers. He was elected as the first sergeant of Company C and served until he was discharged from the army on February 26, 1847, at Tampico, Mexico. During Seaborn's service in the Mexican War, he suffered considerably from disease and illness based on the numerous entries in the diary of Captain Coleman although there is no record he was ever hospitalized. In September 1846, he decided to return to Alabama but was too weak and ill to make the trip. His health improved and regressed in cycles until he was finally discharged. Seaborn married Angeline M. Ford on December 19, 1844, and moved to Claiborne Parish, Louisiana in 1850 with Captain Coleman. His children included Seaborn B., Jesse A. and Dorthea Aycock. During the War for Southern Independence, Aycock joined a volunteer company organized in Claiborne Parish in February 1862 that became Company G of the 25th Louisiana Infantry. Seaborn was elected Captain of the company on March 15, 1862, at New Orleans. He led his company at Corinth, Shiloh, Farmington, Perryville, and Murfreesboro. At Jonesboro, Georgia, Aycock was killed on August 31, 1864, while serving in John Bell Hood's army defending Atlanta, Georgia. The Claiborne Parish, Louisiana town of Aycock was named in honor of Seaborn's service to his country in the war. Angeline M. Aycock collected a widow's pension for Seaborn's Mexican War service beginning February 30, 1888. [*Biographical and Historical Memoirs of Northwest Louisiana* (The Southern Publishing Company, Chicago and Nashville, 1890; 1850 Census of Perry County, Alabama, p. 351; Arthur W. Bergeron, Jr., *Guide to Louisiana Confederate Military Units, 1861~1865* (LSU Press, Baton Rouge and London) pp. 133~134; Pension Widow's Certificate-4272; W. G. Coleman Diary; Perry County, Alabama Marriage License # 1619]

JAMES FRANCIS BAILEY was born on January 21, 1811, in Wilkes County, Georgia and died on April 18, 1889, at Marion, Alabama. He was a friend of Captain William G. Coleman but that friendship was strained by the differences in rank and Bailey's personality. Coleman wrote in his diary "*my friend J. F. Bailey attacked with dropsy, much to my grief to discover it*" showing his concern for Bailey's welfare. On other occasions, their friendship was strained as on September 26, 1846, when Coleman wrote, "*my friend Jas F. Bailey became hurt with me for that which I had not intended...*" On October 17, 1847, Coleman wrote, "*J. F. B. has taken some offence and treats me coolly, for what I know not.*" Other entries in Coleman's diary demonstrated difficulties during the war but their friendship survived these difficulties. Bailey's father was John Guinn Bailey of Wilkes County, Georgia who moved to Perry County about 1818 and settled in the eastern part of the county near Perryville, then the county seat of government, where he became a farmer. James graduated from the University of Alabama in 1834 and the University of Virginia in 1837 with an LL.D degree. He opened a law office in Marion in 1837 where he associated himself with attorney John N. Walthall. Bailey married Ellen Amanda Mosley on December 9, 1849. After returning from the Mexican War, he ran for and was elected to the Alabama House of Representatives serving in 1847~48 and was elected the first Probate Judge of the county serving until 1865. Bailey was a secessionist, attended the 1861 Alabama Secession Convention, and voted to withdraw from the Union. After Alabama seceded from the Union, Governor Andrew Barry Moore placed Bailey on the Alabama Committee on Military Affairs. In 1860, Bailey owned seventeen slaves. Judge Bailey was a student of meteorology and developed into a pioneer of the science, writing and publishing theories that stand up well in the weather predictions of today. He was a Democrat and a member of the Siloam Baptist Church in Marion. He was a trustee of Howard College from 1853 through 1880. Bailey collected a pension for his Mexican War service beginning March 23, 1887. [Lovelace, *Siloam History*, p. 18; W. Stuart Harris, *Heritage of Perry County, Alabama*, v. I, p. 180-183; 1860 Slave Census of Perry County; Owen, *Alabama Biography*, v III, p. 72; 1850 Census of Perry County, Alabama, p. 371, Marion Beat; Pension SC-3367; W. G. Coleman Diary; Perry County, Alabama Marriage License # 2119]

WILLIAM B. BAILEY was discharged at Camp Alabama on the Rio Grande on August 19, 1846. He was probably disabled from service due to a severe debilitating diarrhea outbreak along the Rio Grande. Bailey married Mary Jane Mayberry on February 10, 1844, in Perry County. [W. G. Coleman Diary; Perry County, Alabama Marriage License # 1557]

JOHN W. BARRON served as a first corporal of Company C. He was promoted to fourth sergeant on August 19, 1846, at Camp Alabama. Barron was hospitalized at Vera Cruz on April 12, 1847, because of his exertions during a forced march to and from Alvarado and was left behind when his regiment marched into the interior of Mexico to Jalapa. John P. Everett replaced Barron as fourth sergeant on April 19, 1847, due to his inability to serve because of his hospitalization. In the war for Southern Independence, Barron served in Company D of the 63rd Alabama Infantry Regiment. [Roster of Confederate Soldiers]

JAMES BENNETT was the son of Reuben Bennett and Sarah Edwards and lived in the Radfordville Beat in Perry County, Alabama. James was twenty-two when he enlisted in the Perry Volunteers. While stationed at Camargo, Bennett was assigned on Saturday, October 10, 1846, to work as a blacksmith for Captain Franklin Smith. Contrary to orders, James refused to work and did not report at all on Sunday and Monday. He was put on report by Captain Smith and placed in the guardhouse on bread and water for insubordination along with four others who were insubordinate at Smith's blacksmith shop. Captain Franklin Smith of the Commissary Department wrote of Bennett in his *Journal* on October 12, 1846: "*2 Alabamians had reported to him Saturday, Collamer and James Bennet. Collamer worked half a day Saturday—Bennet not at all. Bennet soon left—Collamer (left) at night—and neither of them ever returned.*" On October 13, Smith in a letter to Captain Crosman wrote of Bennett, "*The names of the men are Wm. Robertson George Adams Co. I, J. Bennett Co. C, J. Bird Co. K . . .*" On November 7, 1846, Bennett was "*dangerously*" ill at Camargo and "*very sick*" on January 26, 1847, at Tampico according to notes in the diary of William Coleman. He was discharged from the army on February 26, 1847, at Tampico, Mexico, along with Seaborn Aycock and William H. Jones. After the war, he returned to his father's home, married and became an overseer of his father's slaves. During the War for Southern Independence, Bennett served as a private in the 8th Alabama Infantry Regiment. He was captured at Gettysburg, Pennsylvania on July 3, 1863 and died on September 15, 1863, of disease at Point Lookout, Maryland while a prisoner of war. [1850 Censuses of Perry County, p. 345B and 1860 Censuses of Perry County, Alabama; Alabama Department of Archives and History, Civil War Service Database; Colonel Hillary A. Herbert, "History of the Eighth Alabama Volunteer Regiment," *Alabama Historical Quarterly*, p. 306]

JOHN C. BLASSINGAME's election as Second Lieutenant was certified on May 25, 1846, according to election records. Blassingame was born in 1824 in South Carolina and was the son of William E. Blassingame and Elizabeth P. Townes from Greenville, South Carolina. It is difficult to determine from the records that he actually served in the position to which he was elected, but it appears he did not. In the absence of proof regarding his service, he is included since he appears in the record as a member of the Perry Volunteers. Blassingame was a farmer, enlisted at the age of twenty-two and lived in the Marion Beat in Perry County with his mother after the war. He married Lucy E. Wyatt on June 29, 1856, in Perry County, Alabama. John Blassingame moved to Franklin County, Alabama after his mother died in 1857. [1850 Census of Perry County, Alabama, p. 369; 1860 Census of Franklin County, Alabama, p. 789; *Perry County Heritage*, p. 52]

PEACHY BLEDSOE was born in 1824 in Alabama and worked as an overseer for John S. Ford. He lived in Marion Beat and enlisted at the age of twenty-two and was single at the time of his enlistment. Moses Bledsoe and Polly Turner were his parents and his siblings were William Miller, Phoebe, and Martha Ann. Bledsoe's grandparents were Miller Bledsoe and Jean Elizabeth Bolling. Peachy's father was a veteran of the Indian Wars enlisting in the Alabama Volunteers in 1836. Peachy was shot by his own sentinels at Tampico on January 23, 1847, and hospitalized for over two months due to his wound. After the Mexican War, he moved to Union Parish, Louisiana with his family and later to Texas. He served as a private in Company C of the 22nd Texas Cavalry Regiment during the War for Southern Independence. [1850 Census of Perry County, Alabama, p. 365B; 1860 Census of Perry County, Alabama, p. 697; *Roster of Confederate Soldiers*; Coleman Diary]

MARTIN BURCH was hospitalized at Vera Cruz from March 5 until on April 17, 1847. [W. G. Coleman Diary]

ALLEN L. BURT was discharged at Camp Alabama, Texas on the Rio Grande on August 19 and left camp for Alabama on August 22, 1846.

JOHN K. CALDWELL was twenty-seven when he enlisted in Company C. He was born in 1819 in South Carolina and was a tailor by occupation. He lived in the Radfordville Beat in 1850 and later moved to Mississippi. After the war, he married Susan W. Sansing on December 15, 1850, in Perry County. Susan Caldwell collected a widow's pension for John's Mexican War service beginning on April 20, 1887. [1850 Census of Perry County, Alabama, p. 344; Pension WC-621; Perry County, Alabama Marriage License # 2218]

JAMES CARDIN was born in South Carolina in 1813. He was thirty-three when he enlisted. [1860 Census of Perry County, Alabama, p. 696]

SHADRACK W. CARDIN was hospitalized at Point Isabel, Texas on December 10, 1846, and released on January 9, 1847. He caught up with his Company in Tampico on February 5, 1847. After the Mexican War, he moved to Mississippi. Harriett Cardin collected a widow's pension for Cardin's service in the Mexican War beginning on February 8, 1888. [Pension WC-4923; W. G. Coleman Diary]

YOUNG L. CARDIN was promoted to third sergeant of Company C on March 1, 1847, at Tampico, Mexico to replace Robert M. Holmes who was promoted to first sergeant.

WILLIAM COFFEY served as a private in Company K of the 44th Alabama Infantry Regiment during the War for Southern Independence. He died of disease on October 3, 1862, while serving in the Confederate Army. [44th Alabama Infantry Regiment Muster Roll; *Roster of Confederate Soldiers*; Charles E. Boyd, *The Devil's Den*, 1987]

WILLIAM GOFORTH COLEMAN was born in July 10, 1805, in Edgefield District, South Carolina and was of German descent. Politically, Coleman was a Calhoun Democrat and an outspoken advocate of states right's nullification of Federal laws. He was also a secessionist during the period leading up to the War for Southern Independence. Coleman first experienced war as a soldier under the command of Captain Jarnigham in the Creek War of 1837. He married Frances A. Johnson, the daughter of William S. Johnson of Virginia. Frances bore four children before her death in 1840. Coleman moved to Alabama in 1844 settling in the Plantersville area of eastern Perry County. Two years later, he organized the Perry Volunteers for service in Mexico at the age of forty. He married Mary Jane Heard in Alabama and had eight additional children with his second wife. Coleman was a dedicated sportsman who enjoyed horse racing and hunting. In late 1850, he moved his family to Claiborne Parish in Northwestern Louisiana. Here he had a brief fling with politics running and winning as the Democratic Party's candidate for the Louisiana Legislature in 1854. After serving his term, he eschewed an active role as a political candidate. In Claiborne Parish, he joined the Baptist Church at Lisbon in 1854 and was elected clerk of the church, a position he held for the next twenty-three years. In September 1877, Coleman attended a convention of Mexican War veterans which several members of his old command. In Louisiana, he retained the title of "Captain" all of his life, and the title appears in most records of his day in reference to Coleman. He died in October 19, 1888, at the age of eighty-three, having been a prominent and active citizen throughout his life and is buried in the cemetery at Rocky Springs Baptist Church at Lisbon, Louisiana. Coleman's son, Benjamin Ryan Coleman, and grandson, Thomas A. Coleman were prominent men in Claiborne Parish and the State of Louisiana, both holding many positions of public trust. Mary Jane Coleman collected a widow's pension for William's Mexican War service beginning on December 31, 1888. [1850 Census of Perry County, Alabama, p. 363; *Biographical and Historical Memoirs of Northwest Louisiana* (The Southern Publishing Company, Chicago and Nashville, 1890); Mexican War Pension WC-5979; Perry County Alabama Marriage License # 1804]

HILLARY T. COOK was born in 1822 in South Carolina and was a farmer. He was twenty-four when he enlisted and lived in the Dublin Beat. After the Mexican War, he married Jane C. Terry on March 10, 1850, and moved to Texas. Jane collected a widow's pension beginning on June 7, 1887, for Hillary's service in the Mexican War. [1850 Census of Perry County, Alabama, p. 357; Mexican War Pension WC4641; Perry County Marriage License # 2156]

MICHAEL A. COOK, JR. was born in 1820 in South Carolina and was a farmer living in the Dublin Beat. He was twenty-six when he enlisted in the Perry Volunteers. [1850 Census of Perry County, Alabama, p. 355B]

JOHN CROWLEY was born in Ireland in 1810 and dug and cleaned ditches for a living. Crowley lived in Dublin Beat and worked for William W. Morrow. He was single when he enlisted. Captain Coleman noted in his diary on January 29, 1847, "*J. F. Bailey and John Crowley made bet of $10 aside and put the money in my hands—on Crowley's drinking spirits in one month.*" [1850 Census of Perry County, Alabama, p. 355B; W. G. Coleman Diary]

MILO CINCINNATI CURRY was the son of Thomas Curry and Rebecca Petty and the grandson of John Perry. Milo was born on October 18, 1818, in Putnam County, Georgia and died on April 28, 1903, in Claiborne Parish, Louisiana where he is buried in the Old Friendship Cemetery. He married Clara Henry on February 12, 1836, in Perry County. According to Milo's Mexican War pension papers dated June 6, 1887, he enlisted on June 11, 1846. In his later years, Milo received a pension for his service in Mexico amounting to eight dollars a month. He moved to Louisiana in the 1870s where he settled in the Flat Lick Community in Claiborne Parish. His brother was Berkley Perry Curry and his half brother was James H. Curry. Curry's sisters were Sally, Martha, and Margaret Caroline. Milo was twenty-eight years old when he enlisted and departed for Mexico. He was also married and the father of four children. He lived in the Oak Grove Beat and was a member of Ocmulgee Baptist Church near where he lived in southeastern Perry County. He joined Ocmulgee Church on December 28, 1839, and was excluded from the church on April 24, 1841, for "*attending a horse race.*" He was readmitted to the church on November 27, 1847, six months after returning from Mexico. He subsequently served as the church treasurer and was a respected member of his congregation until his resigned in 1877, to move to Louisiana. Milo's slave, Hannah, was also a member this church, joining the same year as Milo and his wife. [Mrs. Grace T. Watson, Minden, Louisiana; *Alabama Records*, v 241, p. 24; 1850 and 1860 Censuses of Perry County, Alabama, 334B and 701 respectively; Ocmulgee Church Book; Mexican War Pension SC-10180; Perry County Marriage License no. 911; W. G. Coleman Diary; Perry County Marriage License # 911]

Milo Curry in his old age

JAMES T. DACUS died at Tampico, Mexico on January 20, 1847, while his regiment was on garrison duty in that city. Captain Coleman noted in his Mexican War Diary on January 20, 1847, "*James T. Dacus died in Hospital in Tampico of the fever after an illness of about ten days.*"

JOHN W. DACUS was born in 1822 in Alabama and was an overseer. He lived in the Woodville Beat and enlisted at the age of twenty-four. Dacus was single when he enlisted but married Mary Caroline Ramsey on August 26, 1851, in Perry County. Mary Caroline was born in 1834 and seventeen years old when she married Dacus. Her father was Reverend Lewis P. Ramsey from Georgia. [1850 Census of Perry County, Alabama, page 317; Perry County, Alabama Marriage License # 2273]

RUFUS W. DACUS' widow, Susan E. Dacus, collected a pension for his service in the Mexican War beginning on April 23, 1887. During the War for Southern Independence, Rufus enlisted as a private in the Home Guards of Lowndes County, Alabama under the command of Captain N. L. Break on April 21, 1863, at the age of forty-five years. He was born in 1808 and enlisted in the Perry Volunteers at the age of thirty-eight. [Mexican War Pension WC-633; ADAH Civil War Service Database]

LEROY E. DAVIS was born in Alabama on December 27, 1825, and was a farmer. He lived in Heard's Beat in Perry County and enlisted at the age of twenty years. He was not married at the time of his enlistment. During the War for Southern Independence, Leroy enlisted in Company A of the 20th Alabama Infantry Regiment. He was promoted to Captain of his company during the war. Davis died on June 4, 1894, and is buried in Pisgah Cemetery in Perry County, Alabama. Leroy was paid a pension for his service in the Mexican War beginning on January 24, 1895, and his wife Martha J. Davis collected a widow's pension after his death. [1850 Census of Perry County, Alabama, Radfordville Beat, p. 352B; 1860 Census of Perry County, Alabama, page 656; Muster Roll of the 20th Alabama Infantry Regiment; Tracy's Brigade-1862-1865; Headstone Inscriptions; Mexican War Pension SC-13731 and WC-10247]

CHARLES R. DENNIS was born in 1817 and was a twenty-seven year old farmer when he enlisted in the Volunteers. He was hospitalized in Vera Cruz, Mexico on April 12, 1847, when the Perry Volunteers marched to the interior of Mexico to Jalapa, Mexico. On December 28, 1839, Charles joined Ocmulgee Baptist Church and was dismissed by letter on December 23, 1843. He moved to Union Parish, Louisiana after returning from Mexico. [Ocmulgee Church Book; Harry Dill and William Simpson, *Some Slaveowners and their Slaves, Union Parish, Louisiana, 1839-1865*; 1850 Census of Union Parish, Louisiana]

JOHN R. DENNIS was born in 1818 in Georgia. He was a twenty-six year old farmer and the father of three girls when he enlisted. Dennis was hospitalized in Vera Cruz, Mexico on April 17, 1847, when his regiment left that city for the interior of Mexico. John moved to Union Parish, Louisiana after completing his Mexican War service. His children included Nancy (1839), Amanda (1841) and Emily (1846). [1850 Census of Union Parish, Louisiana]

JOSEPH G. DENNIS was hospitalized at Point Isabel, Texas on December 30, 1846. He was promoted to fourth corporal on March 15, 1847, during the assault on Vera Cruz, Mexico. Dennis was a member of the Ocmulgee Baptist Church, which he joined on May 28, 1842. He moved to Mississippi after the Mexican War. He served as a private in Company K of the 11th Mississippi Infantry Regiment during the War for Southern Independence. Dennis survived the war and collected a pension for his Mexican War service beginning January 11, 1887. [*Roster of Confederate Soldiers*; Mexican War Pension SC-646; Ocmulgee Church Book]

WILLIAM N. EDWARDS was hospitalized at Tampico, Mexico and discharged from the hospital on April 4, 1847. He married Cinda Bledsoe in 1842. [Perry County Marriage License 1420]

M. A. EILAND was born in Georgia in 1820 and was a physician. He lived in Radfordville Beat, was single and was twenty-six when he enlisted in the Perry Volunteers. In 1850, he was living in the home of Spencer B. Rutledge. In 1860, he was living in Marion Beat and owned nine slaves. While in Mexico, he served as acting Assistant Surgeon in the hospital at Matamoros, Mexico after October 31, 1846. He rejoined the Perry Volunteers at Camargo on November 4, 1846, and stayed with the Company until they were mustered out. Captain Coleman noted in his pension statement prepared in 1882 that Regimental Surgeon Moore detailed Dr. Eiland as physician of Company C although such a position was not provided for in Army regulations. [1850 Census of Perry County, Alabama, p. 354B and 1860 Census of Perry County, Alabama, p. 722; William G. Coleman Pension Office Statement Dated November 8, 1882, in Claiborne Parish, Louisiana; W. G. Coleman Diary]

JOHN PICKNEY EVERETT was born on March 20, 1826, in Dallas County, Alabama but his parents moved to Perry County the year he was born. His father was Reverend George Everett whose early preaching activities were associated with Ocmulgee Baptist Church in Oak Grove Beat. John made a public profession of his faith at Ocmulgee Baptist Church when he was nineteen years old and was baptized into the church on September 25, 1845, by his father. He joined the Perry Volunteers in his twentieth year. His mother died four months after he returned from Mexico. The family moved to Union Parish, Louisiana in 1849 and settled near the present town of Oakland. In 1851, John married Sarah J. Buckley of Tennessee, and she bore him ten children before dying of yellow fever in Memphis in 1878. John's father died in June 1855 and the care of his twelve siblings devolved to him. As a result, he was deprived of advantages and his education was limited to seven months of school. However he possessed good abilities and by hard work and application of his intellect he overcame some of these disadvantages. In 1853, he was ordained a deacon by the Spring Hill Baptist Church and licensed to preach by that church in 1854 because of his *"boldness in the faith."* In September 1855, he was ordained as a minister and followed in his father's footsteps. In October 1856, John was installed as pastor of the Spring Hill Church and continued in that office until October 1876. During his tenure, he baptized over 500 converts into the fellowship. In December 1876, he moved his family to Shiloh, Louisiana to pastor a church there. John served the Louisiana Baptist State Convention as President and authored periodical literature for the church. He died in Union Parish on June 21, 1891, at the age of sixty-five years and is buried in the Liberty Church Cemetery in that parish. Everett was a founder of the Everett Institute, the first religious school in North Louisiana. His biographer in 1892 described John P. Everett as an *"eminent divine of the Baptist Church, to which worthy calling he devoted the best energies of his life. His many noble characteristics endeared him to a wide circle of friends, and as his was a truly Christian character, his power for good was unlimited."* Everett's children included Laura E., Sallie M., James D., Charles H., Dettie E., L. Etta and Edward. While in Mexico, he was promoted to fourth sergeant on April 19, 1847, to replace John W. Barron while his company was on the Mexican National Road in route to Jalapa, Mexico. Everett received a pension for his service in the Mexican War beginning July 24, 1891, and Sarah J. Everett received a widow's pension after John's death. [Timothy D. Hudson, Winterville, NC; *Louisiana Tombstone Inscriptions*, Vol. VIII and XXIV; Reverend W. E. Paxton, *A History of Baptists in Louisiana From the Earliest Times* (C. R. Barnes Publishing, St. Louis, 1888), pp. 615-616, 580-582; McCord, *Baptists of Bibb County, Alabama*, p. 135; *Southwestern Baptist* Newspaper, April 19, 1860; Glen Lee Greene, *House Upon a Rock, About Southern Baptists in Louisiana* (Parthenon Press, Nashville, Tennessee, 1973), pp. 182-183; Dill and Simpson, *Some Slaveholders in Union Parish, Louisiana*, pp. 21, 95-96; 1850, 1860 and 1880 Census of Union Parish, Louisiana; Ocmulgee Church Book, Perry County, Alabama (unpublished); Mexican War Pension SC-15829 and WC-7660; *Biographical and Historical Memoirs of Louisiana,* Volume 1 (Goodspeed Publishing Company, Chicago, 1892) pp. 405-406; W. G. Coleman Diary]

ROBERT FARLEY was born on December 13, 1822, in Halifax County, Virginia. He joined the Perry Volunteers at the age of twenty-four years and was a farmer. He was hospitalized in

Tampico, Mexico in 1847. In the War for Southern Independence, he enlisted as a private at Pollard, Alabama in October 1863 in Company C of the 7th Alabama Cavalry Regiment. He surrendered at Greensboro, North Carolina at the end of the war. Farley died on February 19, 1910, and is buried in the cemetery at Pine Flat Baptist Church in eastern Perry County. Lavina Sophronia Farley collected a widow's pension for Robert's Mexican War service beginning April 12, 1910. [1907 Confederate Soldier Census; Harris, *Heritage*, v I, p. 230; Muster Roll of the 7th Alabama Cavalry Regiment; Pine Flat Cemetery Headstone Inscription; Mexican War Pension SC-1630]

HEZEKIAH FILBERT fell victim to disease at Camargo, Mexico. Captain Coleman recorded on October 23 and November 22, 1846, "*H. Filbert quite low*" and on November 7, "*Two dangerous cases of sickness in my Company, . . . and Hezekiah Filbert.*" Filbert was hospitalized on November 24, 1846, and died two days later on November 26, 1846. He was probably the son of Mary A. Filbert who lived in Radfordville Beat and the head of the only Filbert family in the county in 1850. There were no Filberts listed in the 1840 Census of Perry County. [1840 and 1850 Census of Perry County, Alabama, p. 344B; W. G. Coleman Diary]

HOMER M. FORD was born in 1826 in Alabama and enlisted at the age of twenty. He was the son of Absalom and Sarah Ford. Sarah was the daughter of William Thomas Ford and Absalom's cousin. After his service in Mexico, Homer returned home and managed the farm for his aging father and married Susannah E. Mims on October 19, 1848, in Perry County. With the commencement of the War for Southern Independence, Homer enlisted as a private in Company K of the 28th Alabama Infantry Regiment at Perryville, Alabama on March 29, 1862. In October 1862, he was promoted to the rank of Sergeant and later to Captain of Company K. He was paroled at Selma, Alabama on June 9, 1865. After the war, he moved to Texas. His wife received a widow's pension for Homer's Mexican War service beginning on October 10, 1887. [28th Alabama Infantry Muster Roll; 1850 Census of Perry County, Alabama, p. 345B; 1860 Census of Perry County, Alabama, p. 723; Mexican War Pension WC-2991; Perry County, Alabama Marriage License # 2003]

THOMAS M. FORD served in Company K of the 20th Alabama Infantry Regiment during the War for Southern Independence. [*Roster of Confederate Soldiers*]

WILLIAM MARSHALL FORD was a member of the board of directors for the Alabama Baptist Bible and Colporteur Society whose purpose was to distribute Bibles and religious literature. Ford was born on September 26, 1822, and died on March 22, 1861. He was the son of John Ford and Elizabeth Farrar. He married Sarah Stinson Miree on July 4, 1844, two years before joining the Perry Volunteers. William's wife received a widow's Mexican War pension beginning on March 11, 1887. He was granted a furlough to return to Alabama on August 22, 1846, while camped at Camp Alabama on the Rio Grande. He returned from furlough on October 8, 1846, bringing news from home and biscuits from Captain Coleman's wife and money from the Captain's father-in-law. He owned three slaves in 1860. In 1861, he enlisted in the Confederate Army in Company G of the 4th Alabama Infantry and was also a member of Company C of the 4th Regiment of Alabama Volunteer Militia. [Harris, *Heritage of Perry County, Alabama*, v I, p. 192; 4th Alabama Muster Roll; 1850 Free and 1860 Slave Census; Owen, *History of Alabama*, p. 108; 4th Militia Muster Roll; Mexican War Pension File WC-1777; W. G. Coleman Diary; Perry County, Alabama Marriage License # 1592]

WILLIAM T. FORD was born in Georgia in 1815 and was the son of John F. Ford. He was a farmer living in Radfordville Beat. William was thirty-one and unmarried when he served in the Mexican War. He was discharged from the army at Camp Alabama, Texas on August 19, 1846, and left for home three days later. During the War for Southern Independence, Ford enlisted in Company K of the 28th Alabama Infantry at Perryville on March 29, 1862, at the age of forty-six. He was appointed a third Lieutenant on March 29, 1862, and resigned five months later on September 7, 1862. In 1860, he owned four slaves. [28th Alabama Infantry

Muster Roll; 1860 Slave Census; 1850 Census of Perry County, Alabama, p. 346B; 1860 Census of Perry County, Alabama, p. 631; Walker, *Gallant 28th Alabama*]

WILEY W. FOWLER was a sharecropper and lived in the Oakmulgee Beat of Perry County. Wiley was born on November 26, 1831, in Alabama and was promoted to 4th Corporal of the Perry Volunteers on August 20, 1846, at Camp Alabama. After the Mexican War, he married Nancy S. Dross in Bibb County, Alabama and served as the Third and First Sergeant in the Perry Guards, 4th Regiment of Alabama Militia, organized for 90 days on April 10, 1862, in Marion. He died on March 31, 1886, and is buried in the Legal Cemetery in Perry County. Wiley received a pension for his Mexican War service beginning on September 3, 1887. [Headstone Inscription; Perry Guards Muster Roll; Mexican War Pension SC-11366; Bibb County, Alabama Marriages 1820-1862]

JOHN ALFRED FULLER was born on July 29, 1824, in Perry County and died on August 21, 1900. He married Cynthia Powell Miree on February 2, 1849, in Perry County. John was the son of Jesse Franklin Fuller and Mary Elizabeth Jackson and the grandson of Green B. Jackson, Elijah Fuller and Sincy Browning. Fuller was a farmer who owned six slaves and was unmarried when he joined the Perry Volunteers at the age of twenty-two years. In 1878-79, John A. Fuller was the representative of Perry County to the Alabama Legislature. Most of his family moved to Union Parish, Louisiana in the years after the Mexican War. During the War for Southern Independence, he served as a corporal in the 7th Alabama Cavalry Regiment. Fuller received a Mexican War pension beginning on January 19, 1900, and his wife received a widow's pension after he died. He held the rank of Second Corporal during the Mexican War. [1850 Censuses of Perry County, Alabama, p. 359; *Roster of Confederate Soldiers*, Mexican War Pensions SC-2576 and WC-12728]

JOHN B. FULLER was mustered into the army on June 13, 1846, was elected regimental Sergeant Major on June 27, 1846, and brevetted a Third Lieutenant on August 1, 1846. Colonel John R. Coffey requested his commission on August 12, 1846. However, Captain Coleman recorded in his diary on August 3, *"had an election for 3rd Lt. John B. Fuller was chosen."* Fuller was the son of John Alfred Fuller and Susannah Burford, the grandson of Elijah Fuller, Sincy Browning, John Browning and Elizabeth Demorest. John married Sarah Elizabeth Roden. He was born in Greene County, Georgia and was a farmer who owned five slaves. He was thirty-five years old, married and the father of eight children when he enlisted. John's sons, Richard and George, served in Company K of the 8th Alabama Infantry Regiment during the War for Southern Independence. Richard was severely wounded and taken a prisoner at Gettysburg on July 3, 1863, but was released due to the severity of his wounds. He surrendered at Appomattox with the Army of Northern Virginia. George was wounded at Gaines Mill, Virginia so severely that he had to be detailed to the Arsenal at Selma, Alabama. Fuller moved to Texas and his wife received a pension for his Mexican War service beginning on April 14, 1887. [1850 Census of Perry County, Alabama, Perryville Beat, p. 347B; 1860 Census of Perry County, Alabama, p. 693; Robert S. Davis, Jr., *Alabama Officers in the Mexican War 1846-1848,* pp. 10-11; 1850 Slave Census of Perry County; Owen, *History of Alabama*, p. 986; Mexican War Pension WC-699; W. G. Coleman Diary]

SAMUEL P. BURFORD FULLER was the son of John Alfred Fuller and Susannah Burford and the grandson of Elijah Fuller and Sincy Browning. He married Delano Heard on February 4, 1845, in Perry County and owned two slaves. Samuel was born in Alabama and was eighteen years old when he enlisted in the Perry Volunteers. He was a member of Ocmulgee Baptist Church in southeast Perry County, which he joined on August 26, 1843. He was excluded from the church on April 26, 1845, for *"fighting and drunkenness."* Fuller was a farmer after the war. In Mexico, he was promoted to second corporal on April 19, 1847, at Cerro Gordo, Mexico. Captain Coleman's diary noted on that date, *"elected . . . one corporal, 2nd S. B. Fuller."* Samuel's son Jesse S. Fuller died of typhoid fever in a Richmond, Virginia hospital while serving in Company K of the 8th Alabama Infantry Regiment during the War for Southern Independence.

Fuller moved to Mississippi and received a pension for his Mexican War service beginning on February 11, 1887. [1850 Census of Perry County, Alabama, p. 349; Bettye Prince Gilbert, Jefferson City, Missouri; Mexican War Pension SC-9397; W. G. Coleman Diary; ; Perry County, Alabama Marriage License; Perry County, Alabama Marriage License #1646]

ANDREW M. GOIN was a pump maker and lived in the Perryville Beat of Perry County. He was born in 1830 in Alabama and owned one slave. He was sixteen and single at the time of his enlistment. Andrew served as a private in Company I of the 26th Alabama Infantry Regiment during the War for Southern Independence. Goin married Arminta Barnett on November 29, 1848, in Perry County, Alabama. [1850 Census of Perry County, Alabama, p. 349; *Roster of Confederate Soldiers*, ; Perry County, Alabama Marriage License # 2020]

ROBERT THOMAS GOREE was the son of James Lyles Goree, a Perry County planter. Robert was elected as first lieutenant of the Perry Volunteers on May 25, 1846, and discharged from the regiment on July 15, 1846, at Brazos Santiago, Texas. William Coleman noted succinctly in his diary on July 14, 1846, "*R. T. Goree discharged from U.S.V*" and again on August 22, 1846, "*R. T. Goree left on the 18th July.*" A third entry on October 11, 1846, reads "*R. T. Goree left our camp for his home in Alabama a second time having been discharged, Go, I say, and stay there.*" He was born in 1823 in Greene County, Alabama and died in 1858. Goree was a farmer living in Barron's Beat and had substantial assets with personal property valued at $10,000 inherited from his father. Robert married Caroline Nelson about 1848 in Greene County, Alabama after he returned from Mexico. He was the nephew of Langston James Goree and the brother of John Rabb Goree (1811-1852) and Dr. James Langston Goree (1819-1866) [1850 Census of Perry County, Alabama, p. 295; Paul R. Goree; Coleman Diary; International Genealogical Index; Harris, *Perry County Heritage*, p. 102, Perry County Will Book A, p. 115]

JOHN WILLIAM GRIFFIN was born in Georgia in 1822 and was the son of Owen Griffin of Wilkes County, Georgia and Elizabeth Heard and the grandson of John Heard, Owen Griffin and Elizabeth Stovall. He was a farmer living in Perryville Beat in 1850 and owned four slaves. He enlisted at the age of twenty-four and married Barbara Harbour on May 24, 1849 when he returned home from the war. Barbara was the daughter of William Harbour and Temperance Radford. Together John and Barbara were the parents of Sarah Frances, William Owen, Elijah Talmon, Nancy Caroline, John Richard and Ardella Hackworth Griffin. John contracted typhoid fever during the Mexican War but served his full enlistment, mustering out with his regiment in New Orleans on May 27, 1847. He was hospitalized at Point Isabel, Texas on December 11, 1846, and rejoined the Company on February 5, 1847, at Tampico. He was again left in the hospital at Vera Cruz on April 17, 1847, having been overly fatigued during a forced march from Vera Cruz to Alvarado, Mexico and back. During the War for Southern Independence, he was conscripted on May 17, 1862, and assigned to Company K of the 8th Alabama Infantry Regiment that was part of the Army of Northern Virginia. Following the Battle of Gaines' Mill, Virginia, he displayed exceptional bravery and his name was placed on the regimental ROLL OF HONOR. He served as a private until the end of the war and surrendered at Appomattox Court House on April 9, 1865. After the war, Griffin moved to Kemper County, Mississippi where he died on October 26, 1897, and is buried in the Hopewell Methodist Church Cemetery. Barbara Anne died in 1887. Griffin received a Mexican War pension for his service beginning on June 27, 1887. [1850 Census of Perry County, Alabama, p. 350B; Herbert, *8th Alabama*, pp. 66 and 310; *Heritage of Bibb; Heritage of Perry*, 1860 Census of Perry County, Alabama, p. 699; Mexican War Pension SC-11598; Perry County, Alabama Marriage License # 2074]

GEORGE W. GRISSOM was born in 1824 in Tennessee. He was a farmer and enlisted at the age of twenty-two. Grissom was left at the hospital in Matamoros on August 27, 1846, when his company moved to Camargo, Mexico from Camp Alabama, Texas. He was detailed for twenty days by Lieutenant Colonel Earle to drive a wagon for the army. After returning from Mexico, he married Elizabeth V. Rogers on September 14, 1848, and moved back to Tennessee. Grissom received a pension for his Mexican War service beginning on June 17, 1897. [1850 Census of Perry County, Alabama, p. 343; Mexican War Pension SC-11272 and WC-11191]

JOSEPH B. HALE was discharged at Vera Cruz, Mexico on April 12, 1847. Captain Coleman noted in his diary on April 11, 1847, *"got a discharge for Joe Hale"* and on April 26, 1847, *"bot cot from J. B. Hale"* [W. G. Coleman Diary]

GEORGE H. HANSON remained behind in the hospital at Vera Cruz, Mexico on April 17, 1847, when his regiment marched into the interior of Mexico to the town of Jalapa. Hanson was a Georgia born farmer living in the Perryville Beat when he enlisted. He was born about 1810 and was about thirty-six and married with three children at the time that he enlisted. He married Susannah A. Radford on July 30, 1829, in Perry County. Susan was the sister of John W. Radford who served in the Perry Volunteers. George died about 1859. According to his descendants, George died while sitting on the porch of his Perry County home, assumedly of a heart attack. Susan Radford was the daughter of William Radford and Nancy James. She was born March 29, 1812, in Georgia and was the mother of seven children by George H. Hanson, three of whom served in the War for Southern Independence. The Hanson children separated after their fathers death: one remained in Perry County; two moved to White County, Arkansas, with one later moving to Texas. Hanson owned at least four slaves at the time of his death. [1850 Census of Perry County, Alabama, p. 351B; Louise Birchfield; Perry County, Alabama Marriage License # 392]

ANDREW C. HAYWOOD HARVILL was the son of Thomas Harvill, a wealthy Perry County planter and slave owner. Andrew married Emily T. Mastin on November 2, 1847, in Dallas County, Alabama. Andrew was born in 1826 in Perry County and enlisted at the age of twenty years. In Mexico, he was hospitalized at Point Isabel, Texas on November 30, 1846, and rejoined his company at Jalapa, Mexico on April 29, 1847. Harvill was a member of Ocmulgee Baptist Church in southeastern Perry County, joining on December 4, 1852, and was excluded on April 24, 1853, for *"excessive and frequent drunkenness."* Harvill appears to have been a wastrel squandering his inheritance. [1850 Census of Perry County, Alabama, p. 333B; Ocmulgee Church Book (unpublished); 1860 Census of Perry County, Alabama, p. 681; Harvill Estate Papers]

JESSE W. HEARD died on July 22, 1846, of pleurisy while Company C was camped at the mouth of the Rio Grande in Texas. [W. G. Coleman Diary]

JOHN G. HEARD was the son of Thomas A. Heard and the brother of Joseph and Thomas R. Heard who were also members of the Perry Volunteers. He was the brother-in-law of Captain William G. Coleman and is mentioned frequently in the Captain's diary of his war experiences. John was born in Georgia in 1823 and farmed his father's property along with his brothers. He was twenty-three when he enlisted and lived in the Plantersville Beat in Perry County. In Mexico, he was hospitalized at Point Isabel, Texas on November 30, 1846, and did not rejoin his regiment until March 1, 1847. He married Susan Martin on June 2, 1851. She was born in 1832 and was the daughter of Robert Martin, a Baptist preacher from North Carolina. During the War for Southern Independence, Heard joined Company H of the 17th Louisiana Infantry in October 1861 and was elected Lieutenant of his company. In September 1877, he attended a convention of Mexican War veterans with others from his regiment. [1850 Census of Perry County, Alabama, p. 363; Madge Pettit, *Pioneers and Residents of West Central Alabama*, (Heritage Books, Inc., Bowie, Maryland, 1988), p. 165; W. G. Coleman Diary; Perry County, Alabama Marriage License # 2229]

JOSEPH B. HEARD was the son of Thomas A. Heard and the brother of John G. and Thomas R. Heard. Joseph was born in Alabama in 1824 and lived with his father in Plantersville Beat of Perry County. He was hospitalized at Point Isabel, Texas from November 30, 1846, until March 1, 1847. During his service in the Mexican War, Joseph was frequently ill as reported in wartime diary of his brother-in-law William Coleman. Joseph moved to Louisiana after returning from Mexico. Heard received a pension for his service in Mexico beginning March 22, 1887. [1850 Census of Perry County, Alabama, p. 363; Mexican War Pension SC-13341; W. G. Coleman Diary]

THOMAS RICHARD HEARD was born in 1827 in Georgia and was the son of Thomas A. Heard, a wealthy farmer who owned over fifty slaves, and the brother of John G. and Joseph Heard. During the Mexican War, he was the subject of numerous diary entries by Captain Coleman, his brother-in-law. All of the diary notations mentioned Heard's health except for an unexplained entry made on April 7, 1847, at Vera Cruz that read, *"Richard Heard got badly hurt by a trifling Regular Soldier."* During the War for Southern Independence, Heard served as a second lieutenant beginning on May 8, 1861, and Captain beginning on June 30, 1862, in Company A of the 8th Alabama Infantry Regiment. He was wounded at the Battle of Gaines' Mill, Virginia on June 27, 1862, and again at the Battle of the Wilderness on May 6, 1864. He retired from the Confederate Army on December 14, 1864, due to his Wilderness wounds. Heard's widow, Frances C. Heard, received a widow's pension for his service in the Mexican War beginning on March 21, 1887. [1850 Census of Perry County, Alabama, p. 363; Hilary Herbert, History of the 8th Alabama, *Alabama Historical Quarterly*, 1977, Vol. XXXIX, p. 662; *Roster of Confederate Soldiers*, Mexican War Pension WC-1447; W. G. Coleman Diary]

WILLIAM C. HEARD was the son of Charles Heard. William was born in Alabama in 1828. He was eighteen at the time of his enlistment and living with his father in Marion Beat. Captain Coleman noted in his diary on December 18, 1846, *"Bot a hat and shoes Mexican made—gave them to W. C. Heard."* Heard married Amarintha Crawford on December 15, 1850. [1850 Census of Perry County, Alabama, p. 367B; W. G. Coleman Diary; Marriage License # 2217]

ARCHIBALD A. HENRY died at Camp Alabama, Texas on the Rio Grande on August 18, 1846, at six o'clock in the afternoon. Captain Coleman noted in his diary on August 19 at Camp Alabama *"buried A. Henry."* [W. G. Coleman Diary]

ROBERT M. HOLMES was the son of John Holmes and lived in the Perryville Beat in Perry County. He was a mechanic, was born in Alabama in 1823 and was twenty-three years old when he enlisted for service in Mexico. Holmes was promoted to first sergeant from third sergeant at Tampico, Mexico on March 1, 1847. Captain Coleman noted in his diary on January 23, 1847, that Robert Holmes' brother John Holmes visited the Perry Volunteers at Tampico and on January 29 that Holmes had nursed him through an illness and was a good friend. Coleman recorded Holmes' promotion on March 1, stating, *"appointed R. M. Holmes 1st Sergt."* [1850 Censuses of Perry County, Alabama, Perryville Beat, p. 348B; W. G. Coleman Diary]

IRA J. HORTON received a pension for his service in the Mexican War beginning on February 6, 1888. [Pension SC-14004]

JOEL H. HUNLEY was left in the hospital at Vera Cruz, Mexico on April 17, 1847, when the Perry Volunteers marched to the interior of Mexico. Hunley was a Radfordville Beat farmer who was born in Virginia in 1800. He was the old man of the company being forty-six when he enlisted. Hunley moved to Texas after returning from Mexico. Joel received a Mexican War pension beginning on September 14, 1894, and his wife, Martha C. Hunley, received a widow's pension after he died. [1850 Census of Perry County, Alabama, p. 346; Mexican War Pensions SC-6920 and WC-10721]

JAMES H. IRBY died at Camp Alabama, Texas on July 29, 1846, which was twenty-five days after arriving in Texas. Captain Coleman noted the event in his diary on July 29, 1846, *"James H. Irby died at 3 o'clock a. m."* and *"buried J. Irby, Camp Alabama."* Irby married Mary Hill in Greene County, Alabama on June 21, 1839, and was the son of Moses Irby. [Greene County, Alabama Marriages 1823-1860; W. G. Coleman Diary]

CHARLES GREEN JACKSON was born on October 29, 1826, in Perry County, Alabama. He was the oldest son of Abraham Wyche Jackson and Jane F. Crow, the grandson of Reverend Charles Crow, Sarah Harlan, Green B. Jackson and Clara Yeates and the great grandson of John Jackson and Elizabeth Lloyd of South Carolina. Charles' grandfather Green B. Jackson was born on May 6, 1767 in Lexington District, South Carolina but moved to Greene County, Georgia shortly after his father, John Jackson, died in 1794. Green left Georgia for Alabama in 1819 and died in Perry County on November 20, 1849. During his life, Green B. Jackson was quite prosperous. Charles' father Abraham was a prosperous planter, slave owner, and an ordained Baptist Minister. Charles Green was educated in the common schools of Perry County and lived his entire life in the county before joining the Perry Volunteers and sailing for Mexico. Three months after returning from Mexico, he left Perry County and moved to DeSoto Parish, Louisiana with his family. Charles married in Louisiana and fathered two children by his first wife, Mary Ann Cowley, the daughter of James Cowley and Susan Russell. He married twice more to Laura Virginia Oliver and Anne E. Connevey. During the War for Southern Independence, he fought with Company B of the 24th Louisiana Infantry Regiment until that regiment was merged with other regiments to form the Consolidated Crescent Regiment. At the Battle of Mansfield, Louisiana, he was among the Confederates commanded by General Richard Taylor, the son of Zachary Taylor, Charles' commander in Texas and Northern Mexico. Charles had the distinction of serving under both father and son. He was described as 5' 9 " tall, light complexion, gray eyes, and black hair at the age of twenty. Jackson died on September 13, 1911, at Grand Cane in DeSoto Parish, Louisiana. He received a pension for his service in Mexico. It amounted to $8.00 a month in 1888 and increased to $20.00 a month by the time of his death. Copies of some of his pension records are attached as Appendices including a note from his former commander, William G. Coleman. [Mexican War Pensions SC-17323 and WC-15841]

Charles Green Jackson about 1900

JESSE F. JACOBS was a physician. He was discharged from the army on August 19, 1846, at Camp Alabama, Texas and died of consumption in Perry County, Alabama on January 24, 1852, at the home of his father-in-law Seth B. Ford at the age of thirty-three years. Jacobs was born on February 14, 1818, in Greenville District, South Carolina and migrated to Alabama in 1841 where he set up a medical practice in Perryville. He married Nancy E. Ford on November 12, 1845, and volunteered for service in the Mexican War in May 1846. Jacobs is buried in the Ford family cemetery in Perry County. Captain Coleman noted in his diary on August 19, 1846, that *"Doctor Jacobs . . . called for a discharge to go home"* and on August 22 that *"the following men belonging to the Indt. Rangers left for home with their discharges: . . . J. F. Jacobs . . ."* [*South Western Baptist*, March 24, 1852; 1850 Censuses of Perry County, Alabama, Heard's Beat, p. 354; Ford Cemetery Headstone Inscriptions; W. G. Coleman Diary; Perry County, Alabama Marriage License # 1734]

DAVID A. JONES received a pension for his service in Mexico beginning on February 10, 1906. His wife Mary A. Jones received a widow's pension after David's death. Captain Coleman noted in his diary on March 16, 1847, that *"got sword belt from D. A. Jones."* [Pensions SC-6089 and WC-14462]

JAMES JONES was born in Georgia in 1824 and was a farmer living in the Perryville Beat of Perry County. He was twenty-two years old when he enlisted. Jones was hospitalized at Point Isabel, Texas on December 10, 1846. After the war, Jones married Nancy Crawley on December 19, 1847, and moved to Louisiana. He received a pension for his service in Mexico beginning on May 17, 1895 and his wife Nancy received a widow's pension. Captain Coleman noted in his diary on December 10, 1846, that he *"sent James Jones . . . to P. Isabel with their guns and accoutrements"* and on February 5, 1847, *"some of my Company joined us which was left at Point Isabel . . . James Jones . . . "* [1850 Census of Perry County, Alabama, p. 351; Pensions SC-8760 and WC-9794; W. G. Coleman Diary; Perry County, Alabama Marriage License # 1947]

WILLIAM H. JONES was born in 1826 in Alabama and enlisted at the age of twenty. Jones lived in the Pinetucky Beat of Perry County and was discharged from the army at Tampico, Mexico on February 26, 1847. He married Elizabeth W. Cross on September 21, 1847. Jones moved to Louisiana after the war and received a pension for his Mexican War service beginning on August 21, 1908. After his death, his wife, Elizabeth received a widow's pension. An entry in Coleman's diary dated February 26, 1847, reads, *"discharged . . . W. H. Jones."* [1850 Census of Perry County, Alabama, p. 289; Mexican War Pensions SC-52246 and WC-15129; W. G. Coleman Diary; Perry County, Alabama Marriage License # 1999]

WILLIAM A. KELLY was born in Georgia in 1827 and was a mechanic. He lived in Perryville Beat and was nineteen when he enlisted. Kelly was hospitalized at Matamoros, Mexico on August 24, 1846. A Coleman diary entry dated August 27, 1846, reads *"Kelley to go to the hospital."* William married Martha Perry on November 29, 1848. [1850 Census of Perry County, Alabama, p. 349B; W. G. Coleman Diary; Perry County, Alabama Marriage License # 2022]

JOHN A. LEACH was born in 1823 in Georgia and was a farmer that owned one slave. He was twenty-four when he enlisted and lived in the Pinetucky Beat. Leach remained in the hospital at Vera Cruz, Mexico on April 17, 1847, when his regiment marched into the interior of Mexico. After returning from Mexico, Leach married Sarah Barnett on November 28, 1848, and moved to Union Parish, Louisiana, later moving to Texas where he received a pension for his Mexican War service beginning on June, 20, 1896. His wife Sarah received a widow's pension after John died. [1850 Census of Perry County, Alabama, p. 292; Mexican War Pensions SC-15840 and WC-10393; Dill, *Some Slaves*, 1860 Census of Union Parish, Louisiana; ; Perry County, Alabama Marriage License # 2021]

WILLIAM J. LILES was hospitalized at Point Isabel, Texas on December 12, 1846. He was born in 1823 in Alabama and was a mechanic. He lived in Perryville, was single and was twenty-three when he enlisted. Captain Coleman noted in his diary on December 12, 1846, *" W. Liles went to Point Isabel sick"* and on February 5, 1847, at Tampico, Mexico *"some of the sick of my Company joined us which was left at Point Isabel . . . Wm. Liles . . ."* [1850 Census of Perry County, Alabama, p. 349B; W. G. Coleman Diary]

JOHN B. MARTIN was the son of Buckley and Susan Martin who lived in the Perryville Beat. John enlisted at the age of eighteen and was born in Georgia in 1828. After the war, he returned to his father's home and became a farmer. He was hospitalized at Vera Cruz, Mexico on April 17, 1847, when his regiment left for Jalapa, Mexico. [1850 Census of Perry County, Alabama, p. 349; W. G. Coleman Diary]

WILLIAM C. MAYES was born about 1838 in Marion, Alabama and was the son of Thomas Mayes and Jane G. Burleson. William married Martha Jane Crow, the daughter of Silas Harlan Crow and Sarah A. Martin, on December 7, 1847, six months after returning from Mexico. Mayes was a member of Ocmulgee Baptist Church in Perry County. Mayes' wife received a widow's pension for his service in the Mexican War. He moved to DeSoto Parish, Louisiana and served as a private in Company F of the 19th Louisiana Volunteer Infantry during the War for Southern Independence. Mayes's wife was a first cousin of Charles G. Jackson. [Mayes Family Newsletter; Mexican War Pension WC-3317; International Genealogical Index; ; Perry County, Alabama Marriage License # 1938]

THOMAS EDWARD McCRAW, JR. was the son of Thomas Edward McCraw, Sr. and Sarah Mitchell. Thomas, Jr. was born on December 13, 1826, in Alabama and was nineteen when he enlisted. He was the grandson of Edward McCraw and Mary Owen. Thomas Edward McCraw,

Sr. was born on December 4, 1787 in Virginia and died on February 1, 1854 in Perry County. Thomas' was one of eleven children; his siblings included Lemuel J., Ruhamy, Nathaniel Mitchell, Chloe Elizabeth, Nancy Carolina, Mary Elizabeth, Sarah Ann, Selinda Catharine, William Smith and James W. McCraw. [*It's McCraw not McGraw*, compiled by Carol Joyce McCune McCraw]

ALBERT G. MELTON was left behind in the hospital at Vera Cruz on April 17, 1847, when his regiment marched into the interior of Mexico. He died on July 3, 1847, one month after he returned from Mexico. He was the son of Nancy Haynes and William Allen Melton, a native of Edgefield District, South Carolina who died in Perry County on May 16, 1864.

LEWIS A. MIREE was discharged from the army on August 19, 1846, at Camp Alabama, Texas. Captain Coleman noted in his diary that Miree left Mexico on August 22 and on September 13, 1846, Coleman recorded that he *"got a letter from Lt. Ford yesterday written from New Orleans stating the death of Lewis A. Miree."* It appears that Miree died on the way to the United States or in New Orleans before reaching home. [W. G. Coleman Diary]

JAMES A. MOORE was the son of James B. Moore. James A. was born in 1825 in Alabama and became a farmer like his father after the war and lived in Barron's Beat. He was hospitalized at Point Isabel, Texas on December 10, 1846. Moore received a pension for his Mexican War service beginning on April 1, 1887. Captain Coleman noted in his diary on December 10, 1846, *"sent . . . James Moore to P. Isabel with . . . guns and accoutrements"* and on February 5, 1847, *"some of the sick of my Company joined us which was left at Point Isabel . . . James Moore . . ."* [1850 Census of Perry County, Alabama, Barron's Beat, p. 294; *Alabama Records*, v 241, p. 19; Mexican War Pension SC-1496; W. G. Coleman Diary]

JOSEPH T. MOUNT was born in 1819 in New York and was twenty-seven when he enlisted. He married Elizabeth Ann Davis on January 17, 1850, and was a tailor by trade. During the War for Southern Independence, Mount served as a private in the Perry Guards in the 4th Regiment of Alabama Militia, organized on April 10, 1862, in Marion. In 1864, he served as a private in Company H of the 3rd Infantry Regiment of the Alabama Reserves. Joseph's wife Elizabeth received a widow's pension for Mount's Mexican War service beginning on March 11, 1887. [Perry Guards, 3rd Alabama and Perry Volunteers Muster Rolls; 1860 Census of Perry County, Alabama, p. 663; Pension WC-3414; ; Perry County, Alabama Marriage License # 2139]

ALFRED MUCKLE was born in 1824 in South Carolina. He was the son of William Muckle and enlisted at the age of twenty-two. William Muckle was a native of England, owned over seventy slaves and was quite wealthy. Alfred moved to Texas after the war and received a pension for his service in Mexico beginning February 26, 1887. Muckle married L. J. Tubb in Perry County on March 30, 1869. [1850 Census of Perry County, Alabama, p 343; 1860 Census of Perry County, Alabama, p. 632; Pension SC-2915; International Genealogical Index]

DUKE NALL was born in 1827 in Alabama and was a farmer. Duke was nineteen when he enlisted in the Perry Volunteers. After his service in Mexico, he returned to his mother's home, operated her farm and married Sarah A. Bennett. In the War for Southern Independence, he was the Captain of Company K of the 8th Alabama Infantry, the Southern Guards, from May 16, 1861, until November 2, 1864. On November 2, 1864, he was promoted to Major of the 8th Alabama Infantry Regiment when Colonel Young Lea Royston was forced to retire from the army due to battle wounds. This left an open officer position in the regiment and Nall filled the Major's vacancy. An artillery shell wounded him as the 8th Alabama was moving into position at the Battle of Sharpsburg, Maryland on September 17, 1862, and seriously wounded at the Battle of the Wilderness in Virginia on May 6, 1864. At the Wilderness fight, Nall briefly commanded the 8th Alabama but was shot through the lungs. Henry Clinton Lea, Jr., replaced Nall as commander. Nall died on November 4, 1864, of complications caused by his Wilderness lung wound. He was assumed to have recovered and returned to the regiment. However in the winter of 1863-64, he was attacked by pneumonia and inflammation set up in his old wound resulting in his death. During his Confederate service, Nall was present at the Siege of Yorktown, and the battles of Williamsburg, Gaines' Mill, Frazier's Farm, Second Manassas, Fredericksburg, Salem Church and Bristow Station. At the Battle of Williamsburg, Nall was in charge of two companies occupying Fort Magruder. He was the son of Margaret Nall and the brother of Robert Nall. In 1860, he owned twelve slaves. [Microfilm number 1462787 Family History Center LDS Church; Herbert, *8th Alabama*, pp. 56, 79, 110, 139, 176, 178, 202 and 306; 1860 Slave Census of Perry County, Alabama; 1850 Free Censuses of Perry County, Alabama, Perryville Beat, p. 347B]

SIMON H. NICHOLS was discharged from the army at Camp Alabama, Texas on August 24, 1846.

JOHN OWEN was born in 1823 in Georgia and worked as a laborer. He enlisted in the Perry Volunteers at the age of twenty-three and lived in Severe Beat. His Mexican War service was short, and he was discharged at Camp Alabama, Texas on August 19, 1846. Once home, he married Lucinda Weger on December 22, 1846. John died on December 7, 1863, at Kingston, Georgia during the War for Southern Independence. He joined Company K of the 28th Alabama Infantry Regiment on March 29, 1862, at Perryville, Alabama as a private. [28th Alabama Infantry Muster Roll; 1850 Free Census of Perry County, Alabama; Walker, *Gallant 28th Alabama*, p. 329; ; Perry County, Alabama Marriage License # 1882]

LEWIS T. PALMER died at Camargo, Mexico on September 8, 1846. Captain Coleman noted on September 1, "*Lewis T. Palmer died at ½ past 1 o'clock p.m.*" and "*sold L. T. Palmer things*" on September 16, 1846. [W. G. Coleman Diary]

JAMES H. PITTS was born in 1820 in South Carolina. He was a farmer who owned seventeen slaves and lived in the Perryville Beat. He was twenty-six and married with one child when he enlisted. Pitts became the Company's first lieutenant after Robert T. Goree was discharged on July 15, 1846. He moved to Texas after the war and his wife Elizabeth received a widow's pension for his service in Mexico. James' son, John A. Pitts, was born on June 21, 1848, and died on May 31, 1851, at the age of two years and eleven months. [1850 Censuses of Perry County, Alabama, Perryville Beat, p. 348B; Pension WC-3518; W. G. Coleman Diary]

JOHN W. RADFORD was born on April 18, 1825, in Alabama and worked as an overseer. He enlisted at the age of twenty-one and lived in the Radfordville Beat. He was assigned as a nurse in the hospital at Matamoros, Mexico from August 10 until November 4, 1846. Radford was a patient in the hospital at Point Isabel, Texas on December 11, 1846, where he remained until March 1, 1847. He was the son of William Radford and a brother-in-law of George H. Hanson. [Louise Birchfield; W. G. Coleman Diary]

JOHN C. ROGERS was born in 1818 in Tennessee. He was a farmer and lived in the Pinetucky Beat of Perry County. He served as the drummer of Company C during the Mexican War. In 1836, Rogers served in a militia company known as the Selma Rangers during the Creek Indian War, leaving Selma on May 25, 1836, and served for eight weeks. He married Mary Ann Jones on October 16, 1845. [1850 Censuses of Perry County, Alabama, Pinetucky Beat, p. 287; Selma *Free Press*, May 28, 1836; Walker, *Gallant 28th Alabama*, p. 330; ; Perry County, Alabama Marriage License # 1703]

JOHN WILLIAM ROGERS was born in 1820 in Perry County, Alabama and was twenty-six years old when he enlisted in the Perry Volunteers. John was the son of Reuben John Rogers and Elizabeth Watters and married Nancy Richardson on January 20, 1848. Rogers' Mexican War record contains a note that he was sick at Point Isabel, Texas on December 2, 1846. Another note sets the date of his hospitalization on December 11. He remained behind as a nurse in the hospital at Point Isabel, Texas, but he rejoined the Perry Volunteers on April 23, 1847, at Jalapa, Mexico. Rogers was killed at the Battle of Chickamauga, Georgia on September 20, 1863, while serving as 3rd Sergeant in Company K of the 28th Alabama Infantry during the War for Southern Independence. He enlisted at Perryville on March 29, 1862, at the age of forty-one. After his death, his wife Nancy H. Rogers filed a claim for $165.09 owed to John. In 1860, he owned one slave. [28th Alabama Infantry Muster Roll; 1850 Free Census of Perry County, Alabama, Radfordville Beat, p. 346B; 1860 Slave Census of Perry County, Alabama; LDS Pedigree Resource File; Perry County, Alabama Marriage License # 1959]

GEORGE W. SMEDLEY was discharged from the army at Camp Alabama, Texas on August 29, 1846. After returning to Alabama, he moved to Lauderdale County, Alabama. [1850 Free Census of Lauderdale County, Alabama, p.36; W. G. Coleman Diary]

DANIEL W. SNEED was born in 1819 in Bibb County, Alabama and was the son of Daniel Sneed and Margaret Graham. Sneed was twenty-eight years old when he joined the Perry Volunteers. He was discharged from the army at Matamoros, Mexico, on October 13, 1846. Captain William Coleman noted in his diary under the date December 7, 1846, "*Mr. Snead took leave of us all for Alabama.*" [International Genealogical Index, Coleman Diary]

JAMES WILSON STANLEY was born on November 27, 1819, in Bibb County, Alabama. He married Elizabeth G. Griffin in November 1848 in Perry County. Elizabeth G. Griffin was the daughter of Bird O. Griffin and Alsira Autrey. Elizabeth Griffin was born September 18, 1832, and died on September 5, 1907. Stanley was twenty-eight years old and single when he joined the Perry Volunteers. He received a pension for his service during the Mexican War beginning on April 4, 1887. He died March 12, 1919, in Whitehouse, Smith County, Texas and is buried in the Whitehouse Cemetery. [Pension SC-4747; Perry County, Alabama Marriage License # 2017]

WILLIAM G. STINSON was left behind in the hospital at Vera Cruz, Mexico on April 17, 1847, when his regiment marched to the interior of Mexico. Beginning on May 11, 1919, his wife received a widow's pension for William's service in Mexico. [Pension WC-15274]

THOMAS W. SWANSON was hospitalized at Point Isabel, Texas on December 2, 1846.

GEORGE CLEMENT TILLMAN was the son of Mary Tillman and lived in the Oak Grove Beat. He was born in 1826 in South Carolina and was twenty when he enlisted. His mother owned twelve slaves and was a farmer. After returning from the Mexican War, he married Sarah E. Fincher on November 29, 1849, in Perry County, Alabama. George Clement moved to Texas after the war and received a pension for his service in the Mexican War and his wife Sarah E. received a widow's pension after his death. [1850 Censuses of Perry County, Alabama, p. 334; Pensions SC-11323 and WC-14212; Perry County, Alabama Marriage License # 2121]

JOHN MILLER TILLMAN was discharged from the army at Camp Alabama, Texas on August 20, 1846. He married Mary Elizabeth Plummer in May 1847 after returning from Mexico. Tillman's wife received a widow's pension for his service in Mexico beginning February 19, 1887. Their son John Plummer Tillman was born on January 25, 1849, at Perryville, Alabama, and he married Sarah Hurt in 1876. Three other children of John Tillman lived tragically short lives: Frederick Jacob Tillman was born on October 1, 1856, but lived only one year and a day; George Clement Tillman was born February 25, 1864, and died on November 8, 1868. Robert Henry Tillman was born December 20, 1866, and died on October 20, 1868. [Pension WC-822; International Genealogical Index; Headstone Inscriptions; Perry County, Alabama Marriage License # 2016]

JOHN MOORE TILLMAN married Martha F. Mitchell on May 7, 1845, in Perry County, Alabama and died at Camp Alabama, Texas on July 29, 1846, at nine o'clock in the morning. He was buried on July 30 "*on the Rio Grande River*" according to an entry in the wartime diary of Captain William G. Coleman, Tillman's uncle. [W. G. Coleman Diary]

STEPHEN D. TILLMAN moved to Texas after returning from Mexico. His wife Mary P. Tillman received a widow's pension for his service in Mexico beginning February 10, 1887. [Pension WC-4475]

LAFAYETTE VANCE was left in the hospital at Vera Cruz on April 17, 1847, when his regiment moved into the interior of Mexico to the town of Jalapa. He was shot by his own sentinels on January 23, 1847, at Tampico, Mexico but was not seriously injured. Captain Coleman noted in his diary on January 23, 1847, "*at night Peachy Bledsoe and Lafayette Vance both got shot by their own sentinel, truly sorry to learn the fact.*" [W. G. Coleman Diary]

BENJAMIN F. WALKER was discharged from the army at Camp Alabama, Texas on August 19, 1846. He moved to Mississippi after returning from Mexico. His widow received a pension for Benjamin's service in Mexico beginning June 8, 1901. [Pension WC-13074; Coleman Diary]

WILLIAM WALLACE was born in North Carolina in 1829, joined the Perry Volunteers at the age of eighteen and lived in Radfordville Beat. During the War for Southern Independence, Wallace was conscripted into Company K of the 8th Alabama Infantry Regiment on February 1, 1863, in Perry County. He was wounded and captured at the Battle of Gettysburg on July 3, 1863, and sent to the Federal hospital on David's Island in New York City harbor. His wounds led to a parole by the enemy and he was transferred to the Confederacy where he died in Howard's Grove Hospital in Richmond, Virginia on July 4, 1864. [Herbert, 8th Alabama, *AHQ*, p. 316; 1860 Census of Perry County, Alabama, p. 642]

ALFRED W. WEST was born in 1823 in North Carolina and was a farmer. He lived in Radfordville Beat, owned one slave and was twenty-three when he enlisted. West married Asa Ann Wilson on December 11, 1851, in Perry County, Alabama. [1850 Free and Slave Censuses of Perry County, Alabama; Perry County, Alabama Marriage Records]

SEP was not officially a member of the Perry Volunteers but served Company C for the year they were in Texas and Mexico. Sep made all of the marches and suffered the hardships and privations of the Company with no pay for his efforts. He was the black body servant of Captain William G. Coleman and a slave. His service to the captain took him into Mexico, a free country, and he could have fled as some other slaves did that accompanied Southern regiments to the war. Yet he stood fast by his master, nursed him in sickness, administered to his wants and extended his ministrations to others in the Company C. Sep was the trusted custodian of the men of Company C who left their little treasures in his care. He never betrayed a trust, taking great care with their possessions. He returned to Alabama with Captain Coleman after the war and moved to Louisiana with his master where he died of old age in Claiborne Parish.

The Roster of Perry Volunteers

Name	Rank	Muster Date
Allen, Daniel	Private	June 13, 1846
Aycock, Jesse	Private	June 13, 1846
Aycock, Seaborn	1st Sergeant	June 13, 1846
Bailey, James Francis	Private	Unknown
Bailey, William B.	Private	June 13, 1846
Barron, John W.	1st Corporal, 4th Sergeant	June 13, 1846
Bennett, James W.	Fifer	June 13, 1846
Blassingame, John C.	2nd Lieutenant	Not Dated
Bledsoe, Peachy	Private	June 13, 1846
Burch, Martin	Private	June 13, 1846
Burt, Allen L.	Private	June 13, 1846
Caldwell, John K.	Private	June 13, 1846
Cardin, James	Private	June 13, 1846
Cardin, Shadrack W.	Private	June 13, 1846
Cardin, Young L.	Private	June 13, 1846
Coffey, William	Private, 3rd Sergeant	June 13, 1846
Coleman, William Goforth	Captain	June 13, 1846
Cook, Hillary T.	Private	June 13, 1846
Cook, Michael A.	Private	June 13, 1846
Crowley, John	Private	June 13, 1846
Curry, Milo Cincinnati	Private	June 13, 1846
Dacus, James T.	Private	June 13, 1846
Dacus, John W.	Private	June 13, 1846
Dacus, Rufus W.	Private	Unknown
Davis, Leroy E.	Private	June 13, 1846
Dennis, Charles R.	Private	June 13, 1846
Dennis, John R.	Private	June 13, 1846
Dennis, Joseph G.	Private, 4th Corporal	June 13, 1846
Edwards, William N.	Private	June 13, 1846
Eiland, Dr. Marion A.	Private	June 13, 1846
Everett, John Pinckney	3rd Corporal, 4th Sergeant	June 13, 1846
Farley, Robert	Private	June 13, 1846
Filbert, Hezekiah	Private	June 13, 1846
Ford, Homer M.	Private	Unknown
Ford, Thomas M.	Private	June 13, 1846
Ford, William Marshall	Private, 2nd Lieutenant	June 13, 1846
Ford, William T.	Private	June 13, 1846
Fowler, Wiley W.	Private; 4th Corporal	June 13, 1846
Fuller, John Alfred	2nd Corporal	June 13, 1846
Fuller, John B.	Private, Sgt. Major, 3rd Lt.	June 13, 1846
Fuller, Samuel P. Buford	2nd Corporal	Unknown
Goin, Andrew	Private	June 13, 1846
Goree, Robert Thomas	Private, 1st Lieutenant	June 13, 1846
Griffin, John William	Private	June 13, 1846
Grissom, George W.	Private	June 13, 1846
Hale, Joseph B.	Private	June 13, 1846

Hanson, George H.	Private	Unknown
Harvill, Andrew C. Haywood	Private	June 13, 1846
Heard, Jesse W.	Private	June 13, 1846
Heard, John G.	2nd Sergeant	June 13, 1846
Heard, Joseph B.	Private	Unknown
Heard, Thomas Richard	4th Corporal	June 13, 1846
Heard, William C.	Private	June 13, 1846
Heard, William M.	Private	June 13, 1846
Henry, Archibald A.	Private	June 13, 1846
Holmes, Robert M.	3rd Sergeant, 1st Sergeant	June 13, 1846
Horton, Ira J.	Private	June 13, 1846
Hunley, Joel H.	Private	June 13, 1846
Irby, James H.	Private	June 13, 1846
Jackson, Charles Green	Private	June 13, 1846
Jacobs, Jesse F.	Private	June 13, 1846
Jones, David A.	Private	June 13, 1846
Jones, James	Private	June 13, 1846
Jones, John S.	Private	June 13, 1846
Jones, William H.	Private	June 13, 1846
Kelly, William A.	Private	June 13, 1846
Leach, John A.	Private	June 13, 1846
Leslie, George W.	Private	June 13, 1846
Liles, William J.	Private	Unknown
Martin, John B.	Private	June 13, 1846
Mays, William C.	Private	June 13, 1846
McCraw, Thomas Edward, Jr.	Private	June 13, 1846
Melton, Albert G.	Private	June 13, 1846
Miree, Lewis A.	Private, 4th Sergeant	June 13, 1846
Moore, James A.	Private	June 13, 1846
Mount, Joseph T.	Private	June 13, 1846
Muckle, Alfred	Private	June 13, 1846
Nall, Duke	Private	June 13, 1846
Nichols, Simon H.	Private	June 13, 1846
Owen, John	Private	June 13, 1846
Palmer, Lewis T.	Private	June 13, 1846
Pitts, James H.	1st Lieutenant	June 13, 1846
Radford, John W. Jr.	Private	June 13, 1846
Ratliff, Moses	Private	June 13, 1846
Rogers, John C.	Drummer	June 13, 1846
Rogers, John W.	Private	June 13, 1846
Smedley, George W.	Private	June 13, 1846
Sneed, Daniel W.	Private	June 13, 1846
Stanley, James W.	Private	June 13, 1846
Stinson, William G.	Private	June 13, 1846
Swanson, Thomas W.	Private	June 13, 1846
Tillman, George Clement	Private	June 13, 1846
Tillman, John Miller	Private	June 13, 1846
Tillman, John Moore	Private	June 13, 1846
Tillman, Stephen D.	Private	June 13, 1846
Vance, Lafayette	Private	June 13, 1846
Walker, Benjamin F.	Private	June 13, 1846
Wallace, William	Private	June 13, 1846
West, Alfred W.	Private	June 13, 1846

The Mexican War Diary
of
William G. Coleman
June 11, 1846 through June 1, 1847

Introduction

When William G. Coleman left home on June 11 for Mobile, he had a bound notebook in his possession, so it was his intent to record his experiences in Mexico from the beginning. He spent the first night in Selma where he made his initial diary entry. On each of the succeeding days, Coleman faithfully recorded something of each day's events even when he was ill to the point of disability. Coleman's record over the twelve months sheds heretofore hidden light on the Perry Volunteers and the Mexican War. The histories of the war and the journals and diaries of others who served in the war consistently support the accuracy of Coleman's record.

However, there are many points in the diary where the reader wishes that Coleman would give more information on an entry or subject. He notes the arrest of Duke Nall but does not reveal the reason for the arrest. When some company officers attempted to remove the regimental officers, Coleman was a part of a controversy, but he is silent in his diary as to his part in the matter. He also notes the death of men in the Company as well as discharges but except in two cases does not give the cause of death or discharge. Conversely, he provides information about promotions and illness in the Company that do not appear in the official muster records.

Coleman used reoccurring themes in his daily entries after about a month of keeping the diary. He noted the daily weather, his personal health and the health of his company. He also regularly noted the length of time since he and the company left Perry County and the arrival of each letter from home. From his notations, one quickly concludes that members of the Perry Volunteers suffered from illness almost all of their enlistment although they were not hospitalized.

The original diary cannot be located but a transcript was preserved. It is from this transcript that the writer organized Coleman's diary. Some minor changes were made. Among those was the addition of full dates (month, date and year) including the day of the week to assist the reader's understanding. A very few words in the transcript were altered where spelling corrections helped improve understanding and some punctuation was injected or altered where the transcriber made obvious interruption errors. The reader will also note the presence of footnotes in the diary transcript. The diary may be used separately from the narrative of the Perry Volunteers and the footnotes will be helpful in this event. Also, there are items appearing in the diary that are not directly referenced in the narrative making footnotes valuable. Existing examples of Coleman's handwriting show that he wrote with a neat and lucid hand. The result is that his diary must have been highly readable. There are not more than a dozen words in the document that could not be easily read by the transcriber of the original diary thereby preserving Coleman's work almost entirely as written.

Unfortunately, the name of the transcriber is not known and sadly credit cannot be given to this person for their work. However, gratitude is extended to Mrs. Louise Henry Bonin who preserved the typed transcription and generously provided it to the author.

1846

June 11, 1846 [Thursday]

Commencing on the 11th June left Perryville at 3 O'clock P.M. with the Perry Company Independent Rangers under my command, was escorted into Selma by Rangers,[165] was furnished a supper by the inhabitants of Selma.

June 12, 1846 [Friday]

Took passage on the Steamboat *Bradstreet* for Mobile[166]

June 13, 1846 [Saturday]

Arrived in Mobile received by the Governor Joshua L. Martin,[167] mustered into the service of the United States by Genl. Smith.[168]

June 14, 1846 [Sunday]

Sunday, all day in camps

June 15, 1846 [Monday]

In camps doing nothing, had miniature taken to send home to my Dear Wife

June 16, 1846 [Tuesday]

In camps doing nothing[169]

June 17, 1846 [Wednesday]

In camps doing nothing. S. B. Ford left us went home[170]

June18, 1846 [Thursday]

In camps; company received $36.42 in full payment for 12 months clothing.[171]

June 19, 1846 [Friday]

---

[165] The Selma Rangers were formed in the 1830s and served in the Indian Wars of 1836 and 1837. The unit contained the sons of the most prominent families in Selma and Dallas County, Alabama.

[166] The name *William Bradstreet* appears on the Selma register of steamboats in regular service on the Alabama River between Selma and Mobile, Alabama.

[167] Joshua Lanier Martin was born in 1799 in Blount County, Tennessee and moved to Alabama in 1819. He was elected Governor of Alabama in 1845 and died in Tuscaloosa in 1856.

[168] Brigadier General Walter Smith was appointed by Alabama Governor Joshua L. Martin to enroll Alabama troops into Federal service.

[169] The records indicate that the Quartermaster issued tents, kettles, mess pans and hatchets to Company C on this day. Coleman apparently did not consider it significant enough to record the event.

[170] This is probably Seth B. Ford of Perry County who was the father-in-law of Dr. Jesse F. Jacobs.

[171] Regulations required that privates received a clothing allowance of $21.00 for twelve months but the muster records of the First Alabama indicate that privates serving in Texas and Mexico received the same clothing allowance as Captain Coleman.

In camps, T. R. Heard[172] sick

June 20, 1846 [Saturday]

In camps, health generally good[173]

June 21, 1846 [Sunday]

Sunday, In camps heard preaching, one volunteer died.[174]

June 22, 1846 [Monday]

In camps; some sickness; two men struck by lightening, several taken to the hospital with measles

June 23, 1846 [Tuesday]

In camps, sick myself

June 24, 1846 [Wednesday]

In camps; nothing doing but office seeking; measles in camps; very hot

June 25, 1846 [Thursday]

In camps; settle rank of Captains and their positions in line;[175] got letter from wife.

June 26, 1846 [Friday]

In camps; election ordered for field officers to command the 1st Regiment Ala. volunteers.[176]

June 27, 1846 [Saturday]

In camps, election came off, the following gentlemen were elected, John R. Coffey Col.[177] commandant of 1st Regiment Volunteers Ala; Lt. Col. R. G. Earle[178] of the first Battalion; Majr. Good Bryant[179] of the second Battalion; orders came to embark for Point Isabel,[180] Joseph Heard sick.[181]

---

[172] Thomas Richard Heard was the son of Thomas A. Heard and the brother-in-law of William G. Coleman. Richard was born in 1827 in Georgia.

[173] The records indicate that the Perry Volunteers received muskets, cartridge boxes, scabbard belts, haversacks and canteens on this day.

[174] Augustus Kremmer of Company H from Pike County, Alabama died on June 21.

[175] Captain Coleman is referring to the seniority ranking among the captains of the regiment.

[176] Under Alabama law, members of volunteer units had the right to elect their company and regimental officers.

[177] John Reid Coffey was born March 27, 1814, in Bedford County, Tennessee and was the son of Rice Coffey and Sarah Bradford. Before the war, John was a merchant and sheriff but had no military experience.

[178] Robert G. Earle was captain of the Benton Guards (Company I) before his election to Lieutenant Colonel of the First Alabama.

[179] Goode Bryan was from Tallapoosa County, Alabama and was an 1829 graduate of the U. S. Military Academy at West Point and served in the Regular Army from 1829 through 1835.

[180] Point Isabel, Texas was the supply depot for General Zachary Taylor's Army of Occupation.

[181] Joseph B. Heard was the son of Thomas A. Heard and the brother-in-law of William G. Coleman. Joseph was born in 1824 in Georgia.

<u>June 28, 1846</u> [Sunday]

Sunday in camps, received orders to take up the line of march to the Rio Grande; not much sickness in the Regiment.

<u>June 29, 1846</u> [Monday]

The Regiment took transports on the steam vessels *Fashion* & *Telegraph* for the seat of war.[182] We had a magnificent send off from the wharfs at Mobile.

<u>June 30, 1846</u> [Tuesday]

On sea nothing of importance occurred.

<u>July 1, 1846</u> [Wednesday]

On sea; several fellows sea sick, I amongst the rest; one poor fellow died belonging to the Wilcox Company.[183]

<u>JULY 2, 1846</u> [Thursday]

On sea nearly all hands sick, sea quite rough.

<u>July 3, 1846</u> [Friday]

On sea; all improving in health

<u>July 4, 1846</u> [Saturday]

Saturday landed on the Island Santiago[184] near the mouth of the Rio Grande; pitched tents on a disagreeable sand bank.

<u>July 5, 1846</u> [Sunday]

In camp, many troops stationed on the Island Santiago

<u>July 6, 1846</u> [Monday]

In camps, doing but little, drilling a little. In camps, some of our Company down with the measles, wrote to my Dear Wife.

<u>July 7, 1846</u> [Tuesday]

In camps, the Tennessee Regiment commanded by Col Campbell[185] left Santiago for Bareta[186]

<u>July 8, 1846</u> [Wednesday]

---

[182] Before and after the war, the *Fashion* and *Telegraph* were in regular service in the Gulf of Mexico.
[183] Robert Marshall of Company G died at sea on July 1, 1846.
[184] Brazos Santiago Island, Texas measured about two miles wide and four miles long.
[185] Colonel William B. Campbell, Commander of the First Regiment of Tennessee Volunteers. He led the Tennesseans at the battles of Monterrey and Cerro Gordo.
[186] Burita, Mexico was a small insignificant village located on the Rio Grande above Matamoros.

In camps; very dry and always windy on this island, the sun quite hot; went over to Point Isabel; wrote two letters, one to Father and Mother in South Carolina the other to my Dear Jane[187] and Father and Mother in Ala.[188]

July 9, 1846 [Thursday]

In camp on Brasos Santiago Island; Sent J. F. Bailey,[189] esq. To select a camp ground on the Rio Grande near Burrita.

July 10, 1846 [Friday]

In camps, dry and unpleasant, the Jackson and Talladega companies[190] arrived on Brazos Santiago from Mobile. My birthday.

July 11, 1846 [Saturday]

In camps, nothing of importance

July 12, 1846 [Sunday]

In camps, nothing of importance amongst the troops

July 13, 1846 [Monday]

In camps, we have been mustered into service one month this day. Still dry on the Island (wrote to my dear wife)

July 14, 1846 [Tuesday]

In camps, nothing of any importance has yet come to us. James F. Bailey returned back to camp Brazos Santiago. R. T. Goree[191] discharged from U.S.V.

July 15, 1846 [Wednesday]

In camps, nothing much doing, some sickness amongst our troops, dry and warm

July 16, 1846 [Thursday]

In camps, nothing doing, very dry in this country; J. F. Bailey, Joe Heard, Richard Heard, and myself all more or less sick.

July 17, 1846 [Friday]

---

[187] Coleman married Mary Jane Heard, daughter of Thomas A. Heard. She was born on January 22, 1822, in Wilkes County, Georgia.

[188] Coleman referred to his father and mother in Alabama, by which he meant Jane's parents, his mother-in-law and father-in-law.

[189] James Francis Bailey, a Marion attorney, was born January 21, 1811, in Wilkes County, Georgia and died April 18, 1889, in Marion. His father was John Guinn Bailey. After the war, he married Ellen Amanda Mosley and served as probate judge of Perry County.

[190] These companies stayed in Mobile when the other eight companies sailed for Texas on June 29, 1846 and arrived at Brazos Island six days after the other companies.

[191] Robert Thomas Goree was the son of James Lyles Goree and was born in 1823 in Greene County, Alabama. He married Caroline Nelson of Greene County, Alabama.

In camps; still dry; water about to fail entirely; Bailey quite sick; today we had on the Island a good rain.

July 18, 1846 [Saturday]

In camps, rainy, sick with bad headache and bowel complaint, R. T. Goree discharged

July 19, 1846 [Sunday]

Sunday in camp; cloudy and windy, no news from the War,[192] nor none from home and a long time to be deprived of so good a pleasure; the rain descended in such torrents as to completely inundate our whole camp from three to ten inches deep; a bad time for poor soldiers; several fellows very sick.

July 20, 1846 [Monday]

Still raining and the whole Island on which we are encamped is covered in water; this evening our Regiment left for the mouth of the Rio Grande; sick.[193]

July 21, 1846 [Tuesday]

In camps at the mouth Rio Grande; quite sick; several cases measles in our camp many sick with diarrhea.

July 22, 1846 [Wednesday]

In camps, much better in health myself; able to drill this morning; fine, pleasant weather, several new cases of measles in my company. The sick generally better, wrote to Major W. S. Miree.[194] Jesse W. Heard died about 5 o'clock P.M. of pleurisy (wrote to my dear wife)

July 23, 1846 [Thursday]

In camps, at the mouth of the Rio Grande doing nothing but talking about moving up the river, a large number of our company in rather bad health, measles and diarrhea, I have the latter badly myself. Coffey staid with me, still bad off with the diarrhea, many others in the same fix

July 24, 1846 [Friday]

In camp at the mouth Rio Grande, sick all day taking medicine, felt a little better at night, no letter from home yet, much depressed in spirits and feelings

---

[192] After the battles at Palo Alto and Resaca de la Palma, the war ground to a halt because General Taylor did not have steamboats, wagons, horses or pack animals with which to supply the army. He delayed his advance into Mexico for three months while the War Department assembled transportation for the Army.

[193] The First Alabama sent a delegation of officers to General Zachary Taylor to request permission to leave Brazos Island because the conditions there were so abysmal. Taylor granted the request and the regiment moved to the mouth of the Rio Grande.

[194] William S. Miree was born in 1803 in South Carolina and moved to Alabama in 1822. He represented Perry County in the Alabama Legislature on four occasions between 1832 and 1863. Miree lived in the Perryville area and was an active Baptist serving as clerk of the Cahawba Association in 1850 and as clerk at Pisgah Church from 1837 until 1866. William's wife, Elizabeth P. McLendon, daughter of Louis and Cynthia McLendon of Georgia, died of pulmonary disease on June 3, 1860, at the age of fifty-four years. Elizabeth McLendon was born on November 13, 1805, and was baptized into Shiloh Church in Perry County in 1826 and joined Pisgah Church in 1834. Miree owned 44 slaves in 1860.

July 25, 1846 [Saturday]

Left the mouth Rio Grande on an old steamboat *Troy*, lay out about 2 miles from where we started.

July 26, 1846 [Sunday]

Sunday on our way up the River Rio Grande arrived at our new camp opposite Burita, felt better than I have for the last 10 days.

July 27, 1846 [Monday]

In camp at Camp Belknap,[195] cleaning up the camp ground acting as officer of the day, clear, but some appearance of rain. James F. Bailey and John G. Heard[196] went to Point Isabel after letters, got none for me.

July 28, 1846 [Tuesday]

In camps, idling away our time, doing little or nothing, no news from my family, heard of the death sister's little son, Stanmore,[197] and Cousin Elizabeth Covar's[198] infant, Carolinians.

July 29, 1846 [Wednesday]

In camps, James H. Irby[199] died at 3 O'clock A.M. some appearance of rain, warm and sultry, much sickness in camps and some in my company, my nephew John Moore Tillman[200] died at half-past 9 o'clock A.M.; buried J. Irby, Camp Alabama.

July 30, 1846 [Thursday]

In camps, trying to establish some more discipline in camps, Mexican taken prisoner for knocking down a white man who was insulting his wife, buried John Moore Tillman on the Rio Grand River, sick myself.

July 31, 1846 [Friday]

In camps; doing but little; very warm where we are now stationed, heard F. T. Tillman died.

AUGUST 1, 1846 [Saturday]

In camps, nothing doing, saw Amon Farrow and old Carolina acquaintance[201]

---

[195] Camp Belknap was the official name of the camp but the Alabamians usually referred to it as Camp Alabama.
[196] John G. Heard was the son of Thomas A. Heard and the brother-in-law of Captain William G. Coleman. John was a farmer who was born in 1823 in Georgia.
[197] Coleman's sister Susan H. Coleman married Stanmore Butler Ryan and the dead child is theirs.
[198] Elizabeth Covar was born in 1805 in South Carolina. She was married to John Covar who was born in South Carolina in 1797 and lived in Edgefield District, South Carolina. Their surviving children included Isabella, born 1832, Nancy, born 1834, and a son, J. L. Covar, born 1843.
[199] James H. Irby married Mary Hill in Greene County, Alabama on June 21, 1839, and was the son of Moses Irby.
[200] William Coleman's half sister Elizabeth B. Moore married Benjamin Tillman.
[201] The identity of Amon Farrow is not known, but the Farrow family had representatives living in Edgefield District, South Carolina in 1850.

August 2, 1846 [Sunday]

Sunday in camps, Clear & warm, nothing doing, nothing of consequence; never have got any letter from my dear wife or parents since I left Mobile

August 3, 1846 [Monday]

In camps; cloudy and pleasant; had an election for 3d Lt. John B. Fuller[202] was chosen, Brig. Genl Quitman arrived at Brazos; Our commander[203]

August 4, 1846 [Tuesday]

In camps, rainy, bad sleeping on the ground where the water is running under a blanket, the only bedding a soldier has.

August 5, 1846 [Wednesday]

In camps; rec'd orders to leave for Camargo,[204] warm weather; some fever in camps, rainy.

August 6, 1846 [Thursday]

In camps, rainy, wrote home; Sneed[205] and Tillman[206] got furlough to go home, sick with a violent pain in my head.

August 7, 1846 [Friday]

In camps, clear and warm, Sneed and Tillman left at 8 o'clock for Ala, sick; General Taylor[207] left yesterday for Camargo

August 8, 1846 [Saturday]

In camps, doing nothing, Majr. Goode Bryan resigned his commission as Majr.[208] Clear and warm weather, got letter from home and one from So. Ca., bad news to my feelings

August 9, 1846 [Sunday]

In camps, felt bad all day without being much sick. Richard Heard sick. Got the Marion News

August 10, 1846 [Monday]

---

[202] John B. Fuller was the son of John Alfred Fuller and Susannah Burford. Coleman list his rank as Third Lieutenant but the muster rolls record that he held the rank of Second Lieutenant. The normal company officer arrangement indicates the rank should be Third Lieutenant. He was elected on August 1, 1846 according to official records.

[203] John Anthony Quitman from Mississippi was the brigade commander of the Perry Volunteers.

[204] Camargo, Mexico was located at the head of navigation where the San Juan River merges with the Rio Grande.

[205] Daniel W. Sneed was born in 1819 in Bibb County, Alabama and was the son of Daniel Sneed and Margaret Graham.

[206] This is probably Stephen D. Tillman.

[207] General Zachary Taylor, commander of the Army of Occupation, was moving to assault Monterrey.

[208] Major Goode Bryan offered to resign his commission in response to a petition by some of the company commissioned officers asking for the resignation of all regimental officers. Bryan was the only regimental officer who offered to resign but, in the end, none of the officers, including Bryan, resigned.

In camps, felt bad, but not sick, dreamed last night a dream that disturbed my feelings some. R. Heard sick. J. F. Bailey unwell. 12th man in the Ala. Regiment died. John W. Radford[209] detailed as nurse in hospital by Col. Coffey.

August 11, 1846 [Tuesday]

In camps; felt very much like resigning my captaincy in consequence of clear manifest ill feeling entertained by some of the company for me;[210] not well. Helped to inspect the muskets, cartridge boxes, scabbards, knapsacks, canteens and haversacks. Condemned all in the Regiment except muskets. 2 months since I left home. Resolved never more to take the name of God in vain.

August 12, 1846 [Wednesday]

In camps; at nothing and nothing to do, but to eat pickle pork and old hard crackers

August 13, 1846 [Thursday]

In camps, this day two months we were mustered into the service of the U. S. A., very warm

August 14, 1846 [Friday]

In camps, nothing doing and going down hill as fast as practicable, warm weather in this country.

August 15, 1846 [Saturday]

In camps; nothing doing, weather cooler, more like fall; much sickness in camps; The men have to wade waist deep to get to the river for all the water that is used for cooking and drinking; it will certainly make all hands sick. Went on a visit to Matamoros spent the time more pleasantly than I expected to do. Staid at the American hotel kept by an old South Carolinian, Mrs. Winfield, clean and warm. Went to theatre and circus. Dr. Eiland[211] went to hospital by appointment.

August 16, 1846 [Sunday]

In the town of Matamoros; spent my time in looking about amongst the Mexicans; they have no plank floors, scarcely no chairs, no beds and no tables. When the women sit down to work they set flat on the ground.

August 17, 1846 [Monday]

In Matamoros, wrote to my Dear Wife, was quite an excitement in the place in consequence of a report that the Mexicans were intending to retake Matamoros.

August 18, 1846 [Tuesday]

Arrived in Camps by the steam boat *Robertson*, found some of the boys quite sick; Archibald Henry died about six o'clock P.M., got a letter from home stating all were well

---

[209] John W. Radford was born on April 18, 1825, in Alabama.
[210] The Volunteers had come to Mexico to fight and, if there was no enemy to fight, the men were ready to fight their friends. Every good officer lived in fear of letters written home about them or revenge that might be taken when they reached home if discipline were enforced.
[211] Dr. M. A. Eiland was born in Georgia in 1820. He served as Acting Assistant Surgeon in the hospital at Matamoros, Mexico for three month in 1846.

August 19, 1846 [Wednesday]

In camps, clear and very hot, buried A. Henry. J. F. B & T. R. H. & S. A.[212] sick; Lewis Miree, Jno Owen, Doctor Jacobs and T. Ford all called for a discharge to go home, W. Bailey and A. Burt, got a discharge on Thursday last,[213] the following members of the Indt. Rangers were discharged by request from the service of the U. States service—John [Miller] Tillman, J. F. Jacobs,[214] W. T. Ford,[215] A. L. Burt,[216] John Owen,[217] Louis A. Miree,[218] B. F. Walker, [219]W. B. Bailey[220]

August 20, 1846 [Thursday]

In camps; preparing to move on to the seat of war, Camargo; clear and warm; the health of the Regiment is not very good, my health fine. J. W. Barron[221] promoted to 4th Sergt., W. W. Fowler[222] appointed 4th Corp.

August 21, 1846 [Friday]

In camps, expecting to move constantly on toward the wars. James F. Bailey quite sick, clear and pleasant

August 22, 1846 [Saturday]

In camps, doing nothing, several of the fellows left for home, clear and pleasant, the following men belonging to the Indt. Rangers left for home with their discharges: L. A. Miree, W. B. Bailey, W. T. Ford, J. F. Jacobs, John Owen, A. L. Burt, G. W. Smedley,[223] B. F. Walker. R. T. Goree left on the 18th July. John Miller Tillman left on the 7th August. M. Ford[224] went on furlough home.

August 23, 1846 [Sunday]

Sunday in camps at Camp Ala., Clear and warm, Bailey, Aycock and R. Heard all a little sick. Robert _____ commissary appointed by the President.

August 24, 1846 [Monday]

[212] James F. Bailey, Thomas Richard Heard and Seaborn Aycock
[213] The discharge date was August 13, 1846.
[214] Dr. Jesse F. Jacobs died of consumption in Perry County on January 24, 1852. He was born on February 14, 1818, in Greenville District, South Carolina and migrated to Alabama in 1841. He married Nancy E. Ford, the daughter of Seth B. Ford.
[215] William T. Ford was born in 1815 in Georgia and was the son of John S. Ford.
[216] Allen L. Burt
[217] John Owen was born in 1823 in Georgia.
[218] Lewis A. Miree died shortly after returning to the United States from disease acquired in Mexico.
[219] Benjamin F. Walker
[220] William B. Bailey
[221] John W. Barron
[222] Wiley W. Fowler was born on November 26, 1831, in Alabama and died on March 31, 1886. He is buried in the Legal Cemetery in Perry County, Alabama.
[223] George W. Smedley
[224] William Marshall Ford

In camps doing but little in the way of improvement, cloudy and raining, Majr Genl. Patterson of Pennsylvania[225] arrived at Point Isabel to command our Division. S. H. Nichols discharged. Simon H. Nichols discharged. Got letter from Wife.

August 25, 1846 [Tuesday]

In camps; doing nothing; there has been 53 men discharged, and 27 died up to this date,[226] hot indeed. Left Camp Ala. for Camargo on the Steamer *Troy*. Captain Right

August 26, 1846 [Wednesday]

10 o'clock—On our way to Camargo, not very well, pain in my head, very hot day. Stop'd at Matamoros over night.

August 27, 1846 [Thursday]

On board boat, left at Matamoros, Grissom and Kelley[227] to go into the hospital, clear and warm

August 28, 1846 [Friday]

On board steam boat *Troy*, going to Camargo, hot day, the country all the way from the mouth of the river is a low marsh, rich country, inhabited by the lower classes of Mexicans called Ranchos, a very indolent non-enterprising people—fine farming lands, but in to small bodies, the country is too flat.

August 29, 1846 [Saturday]

Still on board the *Troy* saw three little farm houses last evening within 400 yds, fifty four children, the country here is very rich, but desirable only for cultivation, no resident situations, hot day again, rain every day for several past, this day passed by Renoso[228] a handsome little town on the west side of the Rio Grande, above I saw the first table lands, it would have been quite a treat if I had been well enough to have enjoyed it, but I was not. At 8 o'clock P.M. stuck fast on a sand bar, said to have been done purposely by the pilot.

August 30, 1846 [Sunday]

The health of my company improving a little I think and am truly glad to see it so. The *Virginian* tried to pull the *Troy* out of the mud, but failed to do so. My friend J. F. Bailey attacked with the dropsy,[229] much to my grief to discover it. To our great surprise the *Troy* got off the sand bar at half past 5 o'clock P.M., remained 21 hours, on up a short distance and stop'd at Old Renoso, I was quite sick all night.

August 31, 1846 [Monday]

---

[225] President James K. Polk commissioned Robert Patterson a Major General of Volunteers on July 7, 1846. He was born in Ireland and was a Colonel in the Pennsylvania Militia before the war.
[226] These numbers refer to discharges and deaths in the First Regiment of Alabama Volunteers.
[227] George W. Grissom and William A. Kelley
[228] Reynosa was a Mexican city located about seventy miles northwest of Matamoros on the Rio Grande. Reynosa was occupied without resistance by the First U. S. Infantry, Braxton Bragg's artillery and Price's Texas Rangers in June 1846.
[229] Dropsy is a contraction of the word hydropsy, which is the presence of an abnormally large amount of fluids.

Still on the old *Troy* going on to the seat of war, in bad health, also S. A., R. H.[230] and some few others, left old Renoso at 20 min. after 8 o'clock A.M., paid $2.50 for one quarter old beef killed by the company. From the mouth Rio Grande to Matamoros by land 30 miles; by water 100 from thence to Reneso by land . . . by water 170 miles to old Renoso; by land 42 miles by water 25 from old Renoso; to Camargo by land 40 miles by water; 55 (or 35) the greater part of the latter had poor and marshy. I saw in passing up the river wild vines, watermelons, pumpkins, gourds and many other domestic vegetables, such as pamer christals,[231] sunflowers, etc.

SEPTEMBER 1, 1846 [Tuesday]

Arrived at Camargo at 1 o'clock P.M., found the place to be rather a disagreeable one. Our mess[232] all split in two, no disadvantage to me; the town of Camargo is a bad looking place, the location is good enough, the high water washed down all the houses of any importance which ruined the appearance of the place.

September 2, 1846 [Wednesday]

In camps, cleaning up and get fixed to live, our whole life times I fear, dry and hot, too much dust[233] for any satisfaction here, turned over to Mgr. Bryan one tent and poles.

September 3, 1846 [Thursday]

In camps at Camargo, Mexico, dry and hot, turned over some surplus guns, knapsacks, cartridge boxes, scabbards, etc.,[234] quite sick at night; the troops leaving for Monterey.[235]

September 4, 1846 [Friday]

In camps at Camargo, Mexico, dry and hot, a requisition made this day by Brig. Genl. Pillow on our Regiment for men to bury dead in the Tennessee Regiment.[236] a great deal of sickness amongst the volunteer army at this time. I am in bad feeling today.

September 5, 1846 [Saturday]

In camps at Camargo, dry and hot, doing nothing, We are to be stationed here God knows how long for know one else knows it seems, today Genl. Taylor, Quitman, and Butler[237] all left Camargo for Monterey.

---

[230] Seaborn Aycock and Thomas Richard Heard

[231] Pamer Christals cannot be identified. The spelling is probably a transcriber's error.

[232] A mess is a collection of soldiers (usually 4-6) who eat together sharing cooking and clean up duties. Officers normally had servants that performed mess duties such as Coleman's slave Sep.

[233] The San Juan River overflowed and deposited a layer of mud over the campsite that dried and became a powdery dust that plagued the soldiers during their entire stay at Camargo.

[234] Coleman had surplus weapons and accoutrements because of the deaths and discharges of his men at Camp Alabama.

[235] General Zachary Taylor left Camargo with part of the Army of Occupation to assault the town of Monterrey.

[236] The Second Regiment of Tennessee Volunteers reported 650 men as ill and many died. Professor Justin Smith records in his classic work on the Mexican War that the First Tennessee brought 1040 men to Mexico and through deaths and discharges that number was reduced to less than 500.

[237] William Orlando Butler was born in Jessamin County, Kentucky on April 19, 1791, graduated from Transylvania College in 1812 and joined the army as a private when the War of 1812 began and was brevetted a major by Andrew Jackson at the Battle of New Orleans. In 1846, he was appointed a major general of volunteers by President Polk and was second in command at the Battle of Monterrey, Mexico where he was wounded in the leg on the first day. In 1848, he was the Democratic candidate for vice-

September 6, 1846 [Sunday]

Sunday some appearance of rain, it is very much needed to allay the disagreeable dust which greatly infests our camp, very hot. Wrote to Father Heard yesterday and to wife the day before—I am in bad health, also Richard and Aycock. A thunderstorm in sight of us

September 7, 1846 [Monday]

In camps below Camargo, some talk of moving above town, cloudy and more pleasant than yesterday, turned over to Col. Coffey one tent and poles, left the camp below Camargo at ½ past 10 o'clock A.M. in steamboat *Corvette*, still dry and hot, arrived at our new encampment one mile above Camargo at ½ past 12 o'clock, a bad looking chance for any part of comfort. Sick with headache, got letter from my Dear wife which gave me pleasure and pain in turn, got one from W. W. Garrison.[238]

September 8, 1846 [Tuesday]

In camps near Camargo, dry and hot but more pleasant than for several days past, cleaning out camp grounds, bot some shot, pins, sugar, etc. at Camargo. Lewis T. Palmer died at ½ past 1 O'clock P.M.

September 9, 1846 [Wednesday]

In camps, cleaning up a parade ground, wrote home, clear and very hot. Unwell myself also several of the company, the encampment alarmed but no fighting; my whole company detailed on detached service to guard the Majr-Gen. Patterson

September 10, 1846 [Thursday]

In camps, moving and fixing up for a fight, clear and a little cooler than some days, rest somewhat sick

September 11, 1846 [Friday]

In camps everything in commotion about moving, and fighting Mexicans, this day three months ago we all left our sweet homes and families to take upon ourselves the most miserable and unpleasant life that white men ever lived. Clear, hot and dry. Exchanged off cartridge boxes, bayonet scabbards and belts, some appearance of rain but none of fighting to my view, very sick at night. Aycock and Richard agreed to go home.

September 12, 1846 [Saturday]

In camps, doing nothing, cloudy, and some appearance of rain, a pleasant shower of rain in the course of the night.

September 13, 1846 [Sunday]

---

president of the United States with Lewis Cass but the ticket was defeated. He died in Carrollton, Kentucky on August 6, 1880.
[238] This is probably Edward W. Garrison, a Perry County farmer and close neighbor of William G. Coleman. Garrison was born in 1810 in South Carolina. The transcription of W. W. Garrison may be an error by the transcriber.

Sunday, in camps, sick and taking medicine, three months of service today, Government indebted to me for three months service, Warm weather in this country, Aycock and Richard both sick and weak, got letter from Doctor M. A. Eiland.

September 14, 1846 [Monday]

In camps, cleanup parade ground, got letter from Lt. Ford[239] yesterday written in New Orleans stating the death of Lewis A. Miree, hot and calm, taking medicine myself and Richard, Aycock weak—Aycock declined the idea of trying to get a discharge for a while.

September 15, 1846 [Tuesday]

In camps, doing but little in camps, cloudy and warm, got five new papers from my wife (God bless her heart) Dress parade first since the 24th August, and company drill also.

September 16, 1846 [Wednesday]

In camps, sold L. T. Palmer things, clear and warm, Capt. Shelly[240] of Talladega, Co. and Capt. Smith[241] of Benton County returned to the camps after an absence of six weeks. I was sick all day with a high fever. Aycock and Richard improving in health I hope.

September 17, 1846 [Thursday]

In camps, fortifying Camargo, slight change in the weather, morning cool clear; sick, feel better than I did yesterday. Aycock and Richard slowly improving.

September 18, 1846 [Friday]

In camps, fortifying the town,[242] wrote to wife, Farther & Mother, and Thomas Melton,[243] clear and hot, low spirited and sick.

September 19, 1846 [Saturday]

In camps, drilling a little badly done generally, clear and hot, sick Aycock and Richard improving a little, rained late in the after part of the day.

September 20, 1846 [Sunday]

Sunday, In camps, quite foggy, the 1st fog I have ever seen in this country, it is very thick indeed, the sick all getting better. Got 2 letters from home, one from my dear wife & one from my son Benjamin[244] and through them heard from my parents in So. Ca. John Heard one from Father . . . all were well, a good rain, and rainy night.

---

[239] Lieutenant William Marshall Ford who was on furlough in Alabama.

[240] Jacob D. Shelley was the Captain of Shelley's Company (Company F) in Withers' Regiment of six months volunteers. When the regiment was disbanded, Shelley became Captain of Company E—the Talladega Boys—in the First Regiment of Alabama Volunteers of twelve months troops.

[241] Captain Eliphas T. Smith was the commander of Company I.

[242] Military authorities at Camargo were concerned about a Mexican attack during September 1846 and fortified the town principally by digging trenches and heaping earth into mounds.

[243] Possibly Thomas Haynes Melton who moved to Scott County, Mississippi and was the son of William Allen Melton who lived near Perryville. Thomas Melton was born November 15, 1807, in Greene County, Georgia, and was the older brother of Alfred G. Melton, a Perry Volunteer.

[244] Benjamin Ryan Coleman was born on May 12, 1832, in Edgefield District, South Carolina. He was educated at Edgefield Academy until he was thirteen years old and then moved to Alabama where he attended the best schools in the county. In 1850, he moved to Claiborne Parish, Louisiana and married

September 21, 1846 [Monday]

In camps doing but little, looking for news from Monterey,[245] cloudy and warm

September 22, 1846 [Tuesday]

In camps, cloudy and warm, wrote to my Dear Wife and parents. Expecting to hear from Monterey constantly, no news officially from Monterey, rainy; the boys all getting in better health.

September 23, 1846 [Wednesday]

In camps doing nothing but drilling; a little foggy, very warm Indeed. All the sick seem to be improving a little. News came into town stating that Canales[246] was killing all sick on the road from here to Monterey and that he has under his command 500 men.

September 24, 1846 [Thursday]

In camps, drilling, I was detailed by Genl. Taylor, to set on court martial, clear and hot, wrote to Father Heard, set on the court, not much done more than organise the court, bad off with colic or something similar.

September 25, 1846 [Friday]

In camps, drilling, sitting on the ct. Martial, clear and hot, no news from Genl. Taylor yet, much anxiety among the troops to hear from Monterey, turned a little cooler.

September 26, 1846 [Saturday]

In camps; I am still sitting as a member of the Court Martial, just through examining witnesses in the 1st case that Capt McMahan of the Geo. troops for drunkenness and assault on Col. Baker of the Illinois Troops[247] My friend Jas. F. Bailey became hurt with me for that which I did not intend to be understood as he construed it. I am sorry but cannot satisfy him, disclaimed at the time any such construction as he placed upon, some little cooler than common, cloudy, the sick all getting better except S. Aycock. Some of the field officers became quite enraged with me but I stuck close to my point and was sustained by my Col.

September 27, 1846 [Sunday]

Fedelia N. Melton, the daughter of William Allen Melton, and together they were the parents of eleven children. In Louisiana, Benjamin rose to prominence as the parish surveyor, a planter, school director, and teacher. He also served as the Clerk of the District Court until removed by Carpetbaggers during the reconstruction era after the War for Southern Independence. With the end of radical reconstruction in Louisiana, he was elected Minute Clerk for the State Legislature and worked as an assistant engineer for the Vicksburg, Shreveport and Pacific Railroad. In 1890, he was the census enumerator for Claiborne Parish. Benjamin was a member of the Baptist Church and a Mason. Politically, he was a Jefferson Democrat and a noted parliamentarian.

[245] The battle of Monterrey was fought on September 21-25, 1846. The soldiers left at Camargo were anxious to know the outcome and waited tensely to learn the fate of American arms.

[246] Mexican Brigadier General Antonio Canales led a command of guerillas that attacked travelers, couriers and supply trains on the Camargo to Monterrey road in order to sever communications and supplies with Taylor's Army of Occupation.

[247] The court martial of Captain John McMahon grew out of an incident that occurred on August 31, 1846, at Matamoros when Colonel Edward D. Baker and his Illinois troops suppressed a riot by Georgia volunteers. In the mêlée, McMahon assaulted Colonel Baker resulting in McMahan's court martial.

Sunday, clear and warm. Done nothing still anxiously waiting to hear something from Genl. Taylor; the news came in that Genl. Taylor has taken Monterey and lost 500 men and that there was an Armistice signed by Taylor and Ampudia for eight weeks, bad arrangement I fear. It is said that Ampudia[248] was allowed to leave town with the honour of War and with colors flying.[249]

September 28, 1846 [Monday]

In camps, learned that we were to go on to Monterey—still sitting on the Court Martial. Our sick all getting better. Aycock and Richard improving, already disposed of two cases in Court, clear and warm.

September 29, 1846 [Tuesday]

In camps drilling and preparing to meet the Mexicans between Monterey and Saltillo; Still sitting on the Court Martial, clear and warm, M. L. McMahan[250] came directly to us from Perryville to our Camp, sick with the head ache, an alarm made without a cause

September 30, 1846 [Wednesday]

In camps, fixing to fight, clear and warm, still on the Court Martial, have disposed of 3 cases and commenced on the fourth case.

OCTOBER 1, 1846 [Thursday]

In camps, doing but little, still on the court martial, nights cool and days, very warm, adjourned the Court Martial on account of my being sick

OCTOBER 2, 1846 [Friday]

In camps; still sitting on Court Martial, adjourned the Court Martial *sine die*. Sick with jaundice.[251] Dispatch from Genl. Taylor stating that Santana was fortifying at Saltillo with 20,000 fresh troops.

October 3, 1846 [Saturday]

In camps, drilling, and preparing to meet old Santana at Saltillo. Sick with the jaundice. Aycock and Rich'd improving slowly. Orders from Genl. Taylor complimenting himself and others on his getting whipped at Monterey[252]

October 4, 1846 [Sunday]

Sunday. The foggiest morning I ever saw in my life I think, sick, Aycock, Rich'd & John also, nothing new in circulation. Learned from Brigadier Genl. that our Reg. would leave this camp for Monterey some time during the present week; Clear and hot. Sick bed with pain in my head; Aycock too all night, John & Rich'd all sick

---

[248] Major General Pedro de Ampudia was the commander of Mexican troops defending Monterrey.
[249] The Mexican army was allowed to march out of Monterrey with colors flying and carrying their arms. This decision caused much unhappiness in the American army and the disapproval by the U. S. government.
[250] M. L. McMahan married Sarah Wilbanks Radford.
[251] Jaundice is a yellowing of the skin and eyes caused by liver and gall bladder disorders.
[252] The battle of Monterrey ended in an armistice rather than a surrender causing General Zachary Taylor to be criticized for his decision to let the Mexican army go free.

October 5, 1846 [Monday]

In camp preparing to go to Monterey; clear and very hot, all sick but Joe[253] and Bailey who both keep in fine health. Got a letter from my Dear old Parents from South Carolina, such sickness in that country; My Dear old father was in fine health together with my two little Boys Thos & Frank;[254] I am truly thankful, and proud to hear from them. Col. Coffey expressed so much friendship for me and in such a manner that I could scarcely keep from shedding a tear of joy. Feel some better in the evening.

October 6, 1846 [Tuesday]

In camps, washing up, and preparing to go to Monterey, Clear and hot, the sick all a little better or I think. Stuck a thorn in my foot, which pained me smartly.

October 7, 1846 [Wednesday]

In camps preparing to go to Monterey; Clear, hot and dry, this day Sneeds furlough is out. Genl. Patterson complimented our Reg. as highly as language could do it. He said our improvement was super human, it was magical and surpass'd anything of his knowledge.

October 8, 1846 [Thursday]

In camps preparing to march to Monterey; I had an interview with Genl. Patterson yesterday on some special and important business. Clear and warm, all our sick a little improved I think; Considerable sickness in the Regiment, not many very bad cases, I hope, W. M. Ford returned Ala. By him I got direct information from my Dear Wife who sent me many things, which she thought I needed and among all the rest some biscuits. God bless her.

October 9, 1846 [Friday]

In camps, preparing to march to Monterey. Clear and warm. Turned over to the Quarter Master's store some canteens and other articles. Some little rain, Got information from Genl. Pillow that the Mexican Government had refused disdainfully to treat with our Government on our present difficulties with the Nation; Col. Coffey sick.

October 10, 1846 [Saturday]

In camps, still thinking of going on to Monterey. The weather some more pleasant, wrote to my wife.

October 11, 1846 [Sunday]

In camps, this day four months we left Perryville in high and low spirits. R.T. Girce came into our camps from Monterey. He states that the contest between Taylor and Ampudia was severe that Taylor's loss of killed and wounded must have been some seven or eight hundred, and the Mexicans much greater. He was in the engagement. He had with him a Mexican sword, a gun and a lance. Some appearance of rain, quite warm, Col. Coffee sick, salivated[255]

October 12, 1846 [Monday]

---

[253] Joseph B. Heard
[254] Thomas Coleman was twelve years old and Frank (Francis) Coleman was ten at the time of this entry.
[255] Salivation was associated with the administration of mercury as a medicine.

In camps, still expecting to receive instructions to go to Monterey R. T. Goree left our camp for his home in Ala. A second time having been discharged; Go, I say, and stay there, very warm weather. All the sick getting better except John H.,[256] Wrote to Father and mother, also to my Dear (Wife) Caldwell m do John H. a pr. Pants, fine rain in the afternoon, a quantity of wild gees passing about. Ominous, I hope of cold weather, a fine rain, turned cold

October 13, 1846 [Tuesday]

In camps, clear and cool, put on my new boots that my wife and Father sent me, put on a waistcoat, and an Old coat that my Dear Old Mother[257] gave me in the winter of 1843, still talking about going to Monterey. This day 4 months we were mustered into the service of the U. S. A. Got orders from Genl. Patterson to drill 4 times a day. Col. Coffey salivated.

October 14, 1846 [Wednesday]

In camps, commenced drilling under the new and above order, and confusion began with the drill. Lt. Col. Earl and myself had a few short words, which will in all probability cause my arrest. Clear and warm. Was reported to the Genl. in command by Lt. Col. Earl for disobedience of Orders, had the Tents of my company examined by a board of Officers and condemned as unfit for service. Wrote to Doctor J. N. Gradic.

October 15, 1846 [Thursday]

In camps, drilling four times per day. Clear, coolish nights, and warm day, received for the Company under my command twelve common tents, and two hundred pins and two wall tents, forty-two poles. Col. Coffey badly salivated.

October 16, 1846 [Friday]

In camps, drilling nearly all the time. The sick all improving particularly of my mess. Some I fear have grown worse to screen themselves from a little duty. However, I hope not. Clear and warm, nights cool. Turned over 13 common tents, 13 sets of poles, 2 wall tents, and 2 sets wall tent poles to L. F. Jimison A. M S. K., Received $80.00 by the hand of Lt. Wm. M. Ford from Father Heard, James Bailey put in my hands $50.00. Lt. Col. Earl grossly insulted Maj. Bryan a second time and pointedly, I think.

October 17, 1846 [Saturday]

In camps and I think likely to be for the next eight months, drilling and . . . ., Cloudy and a little coolish, again J. F. B. has taken some offence, and treats me coolly, for what I know not. I have given him no cause, knowingly or designedly. It grieves me sorely. Quite windy all day, almost mutiny in our Regiment in consequence of Lt. Col. Earls movements in the Regiment . . . . horses tail cut off. . . . agreeable to his Col. . . . . own statement.

October 18, 1846 [Sunday]

Sunday. In camps, it is reported that we are to be sent back to the mouth of the Rio Grande, and then Tampico on the coast. Cloudy and cold, a northeaster; Officer the day, had all the musicians arrested for neglect of their duty. Wrote to wife; Maj. Goode Bryan made in my estimation a very pointed and partial remark which I am much opposed to, it was that he would have reported any of his Captains for neglect of duty . . . . Battalion, I would ask

[256] John G. Heard
[257] Sarah Ryan Coleman was born in 1776 in South Carolina.

Col. Earl's effigy put up in front of the Col's tent, with these words, upon it WAIT FOR THE WORD . . . COOL . . .ALAS POOR YORICK . . . COL EARl . . . .

October 19, 1846 [Monday]

In camps, clear and warm in the day and cold at night. Great confusion in our Regiment at this time among the field officers

October 20, 1846 [Tuesday]

In camps, cloudy and pleasant; to my sorrow James F. Bailey has not . . . . and if I have done any thing to justify such treatment I am ignorant of it, and am sorry for it. All our sick getting better except Richard; I fear that he is not much improved. Nothing new from the War or the States that we can learn here in camps

October 21, 1846 [Wednesday]

In camps doing nothing, but drilling, and preparing for WAR and Army lying on its Oars at nothing waiting the expiration of the Armistice.[258] A big dinner prepared in the town of Camargo for the officers of the Alabama Volunteers. Warm and some appearance of rain which is much needed to lay the dust. I attended the dinner in Camargo every officer present except three or four was tolerably much. How cum you so; Oh, what a day to some, and Oh, what a day to some others; saw President M. B. Lamar[259]

October 22, 1846 [Thursday]

In camps, doing but little except quarreling among ourselves; Alas, we have come to a low ebb for there is but little good order as regards punctuality. Cloudy and pleasant, Daniel Sneed returned to our camp from Ala at ½ past two o'clock P.M. in a low state of health but improving, G. W. Grissom furloughed for 20 days to wagon by Lt. Col. Earl.

October 23, 1846 [Friday]

In camps, drilling four times per day. Preparing to meet Old Santa Anna in Dec., Cloudy and pleasant. H. Filbert quite low, all others improving in health. Col. Coffey took command of the Reg't. I have a bad cold.

October 24, 1846 [Saturday]

In camps, Clear and warm, doing but little. A little in hope of going with a train wagons to Monterey.[260] Unwell with a pain in my head, and have a bad cold; two companies of our Reg't rec'd orders to march to Monterey. Maj. Bryan order on with those two companies, received a

---

[258] The armistice negotiated by General Zachary Taylor was for eight weeks and was scheduled to end in late November 1846.

[259] Mirabeau Buonaparte Lamar, the first Vice President and second President of the Republic of Texas. Before moving the Texas, Lamar practiced law in Selma, Alabama. He was born near Louisville, Georgia on August 16, 1789. After a brief trip to Texas in 1835, he moved permanently to Texas and joined the Army of the Republic as a private and rose to the rank of colonel of cavalry through his gallantry and heroism. In the Mexican War, he served as an inspector and adjutant for J. Pinckney Henderson's Texas division and served with gallantry at Monterrey. Thirty years later, Jefferson Davis said of Lamar, "*At Monterrey, with a bright red vest, heedless of danger,* [Lamar] *rushed into the thickest of the fray . . . charged home to victory. He was an ideal Texan—a man of rare genius and tender affection.*"

[260] Wagon and mule trains hauled supplies to the Army of Occupation in Monterrey from the supply base at Camargo. Because of Mexican guerilla activity along the road to Monterrey, soldiers guarded these trains, but they were frequently attacked even when guarded.

letter from John N. Walthall,[261] esq., heard from my Dear Wife and Son, learned that Benjamin had joined the Church in Alabama.[262] sick with headache and cold.

October 25, 1846 [Sunday]

Sunday, clear and little coolish early in the day, sick bad headache, two companies started to Monterey, and then ordered back and some of Kentuckians sent off instead of Alabaman's. Some of the officers held a meeting to remonstrate against the way the reg't had been treated.[263] Clear and warm. I have a bad cold and headache.

October 26, 1846 [Monday]

In camps doing but little drilling, windy, dry, and hot; wrote to my Dear Wife but Oh, God, cannot get any letter from her.

October 27, 1846 [Tuesday]

In camps, drilling four times a day. Cloudy and some appearance of rain, Warm, James F. Bailey and Sep[264] got letters from my folks, and through their letters I heard from them. I got none of my own. L. Locket returned to camp.[265]

October 28, 1846 [Wednesday]

In camps, acting officer of the day, Cloudy and warm, wanting rain very much, the health of the Reg't much improved. Mailed a letter to my Dear Wife, and rec'd one from by the hand of L. Lockett

October 29, 1846 [Thursday]

In camps drilling, sick with cold, head ache, and tooth ache. Clear and cloudy by turns, warm weather

October 30, 1846 [Friday]

In camps, drilling and washing up for a muster for pay on tomorrow. Making out Muster Roll, Clear, hot and dry. Wrote to Father Heard and John N. Walthall. I have a bad cold.

October 31, 1846 [Saturday]

In camps, was mustered for pay by Capt. O. F. Winship U.S. Officer.[266] Dry and windy, quite disagreeable in consequence of the dust, and hot sunshine

---

[261] John N. Walthall was a prominent Marion, Alabama attorney.
[262] Benjamin Ryan Coleman was apparently living with his stepmother in Alabama during the war. The 1850 Census of Edgefield District, South Carolina shows William Coleman's sons—Thomas, Francis and Benjamin—living with his parents in South Carolina while his daughter Francis was living with William in Perry County, Alabama.
[263] This meeting of "*some of the officers*" resulted in a letter of remonstration to General Zachary Taylor about not being allowed to advance against the enemy or take some active role in the war. The complaining did not have any effect and the Alabama regiment languished distraught in Camargo with no purpose to accomplish. Coleman's entry indicates that he did not take part in the meeting and subsequent letter to General Taylor.
[264] Sep was a slave of William Coleman who accompanied him to Mexico and served as his body servant throughout the war.
[265] Lucius Lockett was a private in Company D of the First Regiment of Alabama Volunteers and a prewar resident of Perry County, Alabama serving as a private in the Eutaw Rangers.

NOVEMBER 1, 1846 [Sunday]

Sunday, cloudy and pleasant, bad cold, and pain in my head; wrote to my Dear Wife

November 2, 1846 [Monday]

In camps, very busy making our Muster Rolls for the purpose of payment. Commenced firing at targets

November 3, 1846 [Tuesday]

In camps, finished making out Muster Rolls. Hot and dry, handed in my Muster Rolls to Captain O. F. Winship mustering officer for payment.

November 4, 1846 [Wednesday]

In camps, warm and dry, Doctor Eiland and John W. Radford joined us from Matamoros yesterday. The health of the Reg't generally improving; I have a bad cold and head ache.

November 5, 1846 [Thursday]

In camps, practicing at targets, Dry and warm, also some good shooting in my company.

November 6, 1846 [Friday]

In camps, doing but little, waiting the return of the express from Genl. Taylor, clear dry and warm, bad cold, wrote to my Dear Wife

November 7, 1846 [Saturday]

In camps, doing but little, cleaning up our equipment; Clear, hot and dry, health improving generally in the regiment; Two dangerous cases of sickness in my company, James Bennett and Hezekiah Filbert.

November 8, 1846 [Sunday]

Sunday, clear, dry, and windy; such a review I never have witnessed under the same circumstances, Oh, what a balk. The health of my company improving; I am sick with cold, and head ache.

November 9, 1846 [Monday]

In camps, doing but little, drilling and anxiously waiting orders to leave this place. Cloudy, and some appearance of rain, which add much to our comfort in camps, if not our health,[267] also—wrote to my Dear Wife.

---

[266] Brevetted Captain Oscar F. Winship, Assistant Adjutant-General in the Adjutant-General's Department. Winship was a graduate of the Military Academy at West Point, New York and entered the U.S Army on September 13, 1844, as a First Lieutenant in the 2nd United States Dragoons. He was brevetted Captain for meritorious service during the Battles of Palo Alto and Resaca de la Palma and was brevetted a Major on August 20, 1847, for gallant service at the Battle of Churubusco, Mexico. He died at Troy, New York in 1855 at the age of thirty-eight.

[267] Rain was welcome at Camargo because of the enormous clouds of dust indigenous to the place.

November 10, 1846 [Tuesday]

In camps, ordered to drill as light infantry, all hands tolerably green in it as well as myself, the health of my Company much improved, only three sick and unfit for duty. Cloudy, and warm, very dry, rain much needed. Wrote to sister Isabella.[268] Sent her a song ballad. J. F. Bailey stood guard for the 1st time.

November 11, 1846 [Wednesday]

In camps, doing nothing but awaiting marching orders from Camargo, Clear, hot and dry. Wrote to Father Heard. Sent the foregoing named letters by Lt. Pope[269] of Benton County. The health of my Company still improving this day five months since we left our homes to proceed to the seat of War in Mexico

November 12, 1846 [Thursday]

In camps, doing but little, clear, dry, and hot, D.N.[270] sent to the guard by Lt, Col. Earl, better known in camps by the name of Canallies, the noted MEXICAN ROBBER.

November 13, 1846 [Friday]

In camps, doing but little, still in waiting orders from head quarters to march. Clear, hot and dry. Oh God! That I could hear from My Dear Wife, children and friends. This day five months we mustered into service of the U.S. for 12 months; heard more bad news from Ala. of myself. General Pillow threw two Regiments of his Brigade together and maneuvered them in an evolution or two of the line, badly done.

November 14, 1846 [Saturday]

In camp, clear, hot and dry, very dusty. Nothing doing, wrote to John Bailey[271] last evening. Can't hear from home, Oh how it hurts me.

November 15, 1846 [Sunday]

Sunday in camps, very windy day and dusty, J. F. Bailey got 3 letters from home through which I learned that my Dear Wife and Children were well at the time the letters were written. Rumoured in camps that we would all leave for Tampico in a few days—the health of my Company much improved—I have a bad cold and headache.

November 16, 1846 [Monday]

In camps, drilling and preparing to go on to the seat of War, orders came in to our camps from the Genl. in command for the Rolls of each company to he called every two hours, health improving in my Company, bad behavior in part of our Regiment this evening, disrespect shown to our Brig. Genl.

---

[268] Coleman is referring to his sister-in-law Nancy Isabella Heard who was eighteen in 1846. Isabella later married John Robert Fuller, the son of Jesse Franklin Fuller and Mary Elizabeth Jackson. John Robert Fuller was the brother of Perry Volunteers John Alfred Fuller and Samuel P. Burford Fuller and a cousin of Lt. John B. Fuller.

[269] First Lieutenant R. M. "Bill" Pope resigned his commission on November 14, 1846, due to personal illness. He was doubtless taking Coleman's letters to Alabama on his way home. Pope was a member of Company I of the First Regiment of Alabama Volunteers.

[270] Private Duke Nall from Perry County, Alabama.

[271] John Bailey was born in 1802 in Georgia and was the father of Coleman's friend James Francis Bailey. He was a farmer living in Heard's Beat in Perry County, Alabama.

November 17, 1846 [Tuesday]

In camps, doing but little, clear, hot and dry, wrote to my Dear Wife; Genl. Pillow addressed our Regiment in quite a respectful manner-on the treatment he received from it yesterday

November 18, 1846 [Wednesday]

In camps, preparing to leave this place, cloudy and cold, a northwest wind upon us which in disagreeable, more dust than is pleasant.

November 19, 1846 [Thursday]

In camps, doing but little only trying to leave Camargo; Cold night, warm or rather pleasant through the day, a violent cold and pain in my head and in my eyes, our marching orders countermanded by Genl. R. Patterson.

November 20 1846 [Friday]

In camps, doing nothing, quite unwell with cold, and pain in my head, clear and pleasant.

November 21, 1846 [Saturday]

In camps, clear and pleasant; sick with cold and sun pain in my eyes. Oh'. God how I have suffered, this forenoon, I eat one of the biscuits my dear Wife sent me, which was baked in Ala two months and a day. News reached our camp officially that Tampico had been taken possession of by our Navy

November 22, 1846 [Sunday]

Sunday, in camps, preparing our Muster Rolls, to receive pay, and then take shipping to Tampico to meet Santa Anna's troops. Clear, windy and dry and very dusty, sick with cold and sun pain in my head, more indisposition in my Company than has been for some time. Filbert's quite low. Col. Coffey received orders to put on board the *Col. Cross*, a steam boat, 5 companies of his Regiment for Tampico. Joseph Heard sick with chills and fever.

November 23, 1846 [Monday]

In camps; doing nothing all day, dry and very windy; at night 9 o'clock, I received orders to embark on the steamboat *Col Cross* bound for the mouth of the Rio Grande which was to leave by sunrise on the following morning; we immediately went to work and set up all night preparing to meet the order punctually.

November 24, 1846 [Tuesday]

Took leave of my friends in camps, which were left behind (4 companies) of the 2nd Battalion to which I belong about sunrise, and marched my Company to the boat. All got on board except myself, Lt. Pitts, Lt. Ford and Lt. Fuller. I had a severe walk and run together, about four miles to reach the boat. I however did reach it, and so did the others—I received for one months services from Capt. Brime Paymaster $90.50.[272] Done but little traveling today on sand bar nearly all the time. I killed 1 turkey and wounded another with a rifle gun.

[272] A subsequent entry on January 25, 1847, indicates that Capt. Brime is actually Archibald W. Burns, paymaster. Archibald Burns is also referenced as the Camargo paymaster in Captain Franklin Smith's *Journal*. The name Brime is probably a transcriber's error. No Captain Brime is listed in the records as an officer in the U. S. Army during the germane time period.

November 25, 1846 [Wednesday]

On board the steam boat *Col. Cross*. Saw many wild turkeys and geese more than I ever saw in one day perhaps in my life, cleaned up my gun pretty well. Clear and cool lay all night on a sand bar about 200 miles above the mouth of the River. Considerable sickness in my company, Joseph Heard quite sick, J. F. Bailey also.

November 26, 1846 [Thursday]

On board the Steamer *Col. Cross* between Reinoso and Matamoros on the Rio Grande, poor fair on this boat as I ever saw, and at the small tune of $1.00 per day, cool and windy. Joseph Heard quite sick. J. F. Bailey looks very badly, the health of my Company not so good as it has been recently. One poor fellow died on board the boat.

November 27, 1846 [Friday]

Still on board the *Col. Cross*, sickness increasing in our ranks, arrived at Matamoros about 5 O'clock went into town, got two undershirts, and other shirt $3.00, got of Capt. McLaughlin [273] 32 Rifle Cartridges, clear and windy, saw Majr Bryan at Matamoros.

November 28, 1846 [Saturday]

Still on board the *Col. Cross*, arrived at the mouth of the river of all confusion that I have ever witnessed in my life was in taking off our equipage and placing it upon another boat.

November 29, 1846 [Sunday]

Sunday on our way from the mouth of the Rio Grande; landed at Brazos Santiago at 10 o'clock A.M, then again confusion took place. Oh! My God how gladly I would be if I could go on home from here in a right and proper manner.

November 30, 1846 [Monday]

Went to Point Isabel with four of my company to be left in the Genl. Hospital—Joseph Heard, Jesse Aycock, Joseph Dennis and Haywood Harvile. Wrote to my Dear Wife and mailed the letter at the Point. J. F. Bailey with me. Sent letters by Col. Griffin to my dear wife, Jane.

DECEMBER 1, 1846 [Tuesday]

Started from the Point early after breakfast, was blown back twice, and beat off until after 2 O'clock P.M. when we again succeeded in getting ashore at the Point, windy and clear.

December 2, 1846 [Wednesday]

Got over from the Point, preparing to leave for Tampico, drew stationary for 3 months beginning on the December 1846 to Feby 28th 1847, cloudy and warm, sick all better but Swanson, who is bad off—exchanged trunks with Mr. Sneed, he concluded to return to Ala.

December 3, 1846 [Thursday]

---

[273] The only Captain McLaughlin listed among the officers in the Mexican War is Captain William McLaughlin commander of Company A of the 3rd Regiment of Ohio Volunteers.

On Brasos Island preparing to leave for Tampico, fine weather and wind for sailing in that direction. Sickness I fear increasing, Capt. Pickens[274] bad off, in fine health myself. Wrote a letter to my Dear Wife.

December 4, 1846 [Friday]

On Brasos, orders reached us to remain here until further orders, sorrowful indeed, cloudy, warm and rainy, went over to Point Isabel to see how the sick were, the boys all getting better that are at the Point.

December 5, 1846 [Saturday]

Staid at the Point all day waiting for the mail, but alas, none came. Genl. Pillow arrived on Brasos on his way home, clear and windy.

December 6, 1846 [Sunday]

Sunday, In camps, on Brasos Island, how long we are to remain, we do not know. Doctor Moore Surgeon[275] of the Ala. Regiment presented me a Prayer Book. Clear and windy; the sand blowing about badly, the Steamship *Sea*[276] arrived from Tampico, and lodged on a sand bar at Brasos Santiago Texas.[277]

December 7, 1846 [Monday]

In camps, on Brazos Island, doing nothing but lying in the sand, up to our knees, clear and windy; Mr. Snead took leave of us all for Ala. OH! how glad I would be if I was going myself in a right manner.

December 8, 1846 [Tuesday]

In camps on Brasos, very windy so much so that we cannot get off to Tampico, went over to Point Isabel to get letters for my company, the mail not opened. Genl Shields sent on by Genl. Taylor to take command of our Regiment and the forces at Tampico.

December 9, 1846 [Wednesday]

In camps on Brasos, still windy and we Brasos sand bank. Got letter from my Dear Wife, and a number for the company.

December 10. 1846 [Thursday]

---

[274] Captain Andrew L. Pickens was commander of Company A (Greensboro Volunteers) of the First Regiment of Alabama Volunteers. His record shows that he arrived ill at Tampico and lingered in poor health while there. He remained at Vera Cruz when the regiment marched for Jalapa.
[275] Dr. John W. Moore was from Mobile and replaced John H. Tilghman as Surgeon of the regiment when the latter resigned after a disagreement with Colonel John Coffey. Nothing much is known about Dr. Moore.
[276] The *Sea* was returning to Brazos Island after ferrying two companies of regular army soldiers to Tampico. At Brazos, it ran aground and sank.
[277] Brazos Santiago is a small channel connecting the Gulf of Mexico and Laguna Madre. The channel passes between the south end of Padre Island and Brazos Island.

In camps on Brasos, doing nothing by lying here in suspense. John & myself went out hunting, shot three times at wolves,[278] clear and windy, too much so for us to leave for Tampico, sent James Jones, Shack Cardin and James Moore to P. Isabel with their guns and accoutrements.

December 11, 1846 [Friday]

Still on Brazos preparing to go to Tampico, cloudy and windy, this day six months ago I left my home and Dear Wife to come to Mexico, sent John W. Griffin[279] and John Radford with their guns and accoutrements, Steamship *Sea* wrecked and entirely lost.

December 12, 1846 [Saturday]

Got on board the Steamship *Virginia* for Tampico. The sickest set of men I ever saw in my life. W. Liles[280] went to Point Isabel, sick. L. Vance left us very strangely, lying at anchor.

December 13, 1846 [Sunday]

Sunday on board the Steam Ship *Virginia* all hands sick, what a filthy place, the most so I ever saw, this day six months we were mustered into the service, hot and disagreeable.

December 14, 1846 [Monday]

On board the *Virginia*, raised steam and set out for Tampico at 10 o'clock A.M. I have not set up ten minutes since I arrived on board and have eat nothing.

December 15, 1846 [Tuesday]

On board the *Virginia*, sick enough, but could not die, nothing of importance except stealing on board took place today.

December 16, 1846 [Wednesday]

On board the *Virginia*, no gain on our way to Tampico, blown back, Oh, how sick I am at this time, after noon a fine breeze arose from the northwest, which assisted us very much on our way.

December 17, 1846 [Thursday]

On board the *Virginia* at day light in sight of land, still sick, entered the mouth of Pánuco River at ¾ after 2 o'clock, arrive at Tampico at 4 o'clock P.M. Found it to be a beautiful town handsomely laid off and a great deal of neatness displayed in the arrangement of this place. The citizens look more like civilized because there are many foreigners located here in business who has I learn much influence on the natives. All hands so soon as they left the Gulf got well of their Sea Sickness.

December 18, 1846 [Friday]

Lying a little below town cleaning up guns and preparing to fight for this is a place that all hands received us with cordiality. They are expecting an attack from a part of Old Santa Troops constantly. Troops constantly, clear and hot, Capt. Shelly and his company arrived by

---

[278] There were large packs of wolves that inhabited the Rio Grande valley as well as large numbers of other wildlife. American journalist frequently mentioned their mournful and incessant howls at night.
[279] John William Griffin contracted typhoid fever, causing his hospitalization.
[280] Private William J. Liles of Company C was born in 1823 and was a mechanic living in Perryville, Alabama before the war.

the Steamship *Cincinnati*, Majr. . . . also arrived. Bot a hat and shoes Mexican made—gave them to W. C. Heard.

December 19, 1846 [Saturday]

In camps a little below Tampico doing nothing and likely to continue, Genl. Shields intended to inspect arms and assign to us a situation, but being all out of fix, done nothing, but said that we had officers but no commanders as field officers, and that he would give us an Officer that would stay with us, and let gentlemen stay in town and take their pleasure. Cloudy and cool, kind of a north wind.[281]

December 20, 1846 [Sunday]

Sunday, all hands of the Independent Rangers, worked hard on their guns, cloudy and cool, all well, or rather up and at work, do not yet know where we are to be located.

December 21, 1846 [Monday]

In camps at Tampico, drilling, and preparing to fight, some appearance of falling weather, had our several posts assigned to us. My command was ordered to a point, commanding one of the passes into town—wrote to my Dear Wife, and Oh my God that I could hear this day that she was in good health.

December 22, 1846 [Tuesday]

In camps, preparing to move to our places where we are to remain some time, cloudy and warm, hard rain at night. Nothing of importance took place. The troops throwing up fortifications

December 23, 1846 [Wednesday]

In camps doing nothing but fortifying the town of Tampico, cloudy and warm.

December 24, 1846 [Thursday]

Moved my Company to Ft. Altamira, cloudy and very hot, had the toothache very badly, bought pr. Shoes and suspenders.

December 25, 1846 [Friday]

Christmas Day, Clear and very warm; all hands idle or free today except the guard.

December 26, 1846 [Saturday]

In camps doing nothing but working on breast works, some appearance of falling weather, sick

December 27, 1846 [Sunday]

In camps at Fort Altamira doing nothing. Clear and quite warm, Weather having very much the appearance of summer. Strange for an Alabamin to see at Christmas green corn, snap beans, green tomatoes, and all kinds or vegetables. Col. Coffee made me a visit to my Quarters;

---

[281] General James Shields, commander of the Tampico garrison, had no confidence in the command ability of the First Alabama field officers.

Capt. Shelly's company was removed from my command. Lt. McDuff[282] of Jackson County was relieved from his company and regiment and ordered to the U. S. for playing cards—by Genl Shields. Have the jaw ache. very bad abscess forming on my jaw----had my jaw lanced at 12 P.M.

December 28, 1846 Monday]

In camps, doing but little, company generally well what is present with us here at Tampico, clear and hot, the weather very much resembles summer in the States of the U. S., wrote to my Dear wife, bot mosquito bar.

December 29, 1846 [Tuesday]

In camps, clear and warm, all my company improving in health, borrowed of Lt. McC. . .[283] fifty dollars, Col. J. R. Coffey move him to my quarters

December 30, 1846 [Wednesday]

In camps, was mustered by Lt. Austin U. S. Officer for pay. Clear and hot;

December 31, 1846 [Thursday]

Last day of the year 1846, in camps last muster for pay. Clear and hot.

End of the Year 1846

1847

JANUARY 1, 1847 [FRIDAY]

In camps, cold and cloudy, busy making returns, monthly and quarterly. My Company generally well, drilling a little. Wrote to my Dear Wife

January 2, 1847 [Saturday]

In camps; went hunting with a Creole from New Orleans, he has been here six years at Tampico. I killed a wolf, nothing else killed, drilling but little, had measure taken to make white linen round coat. R. Heard had chill.

January 3, 1847 [Sunday]

Sunday. In camps, doing no harm I hope, cloudy and cool, R. H. Sick, bot venison small back. Wrote to Father Heard

January 4, 1847 [Monday]

---

[282] Second Lieutenant John M. McDuff of Company F of the First Regiment of Alabama Volunteers. General James Shields ordered him to the U. S. without a court martial on December 27, 1846, and the men from Alabama vigorously protested this action. Alabama Representative Reuben Chapman took the McDuff controversy to the floor of the U. S. House of Representatives.

[283] Probably Second Lieutenant Garner M. McConnico of Company G (Baldwin's Company) of the First Regiment of Alabama Volunteers.

In camps doing nothing, clear and windy. Richard sick. I have either the mumps or the glands enlarged which gives me much pain. Bought fine French gun, paid for it $55.

January 5, 1847 [Tuesday]

In camps, doing nothing, clear and cool, sick with the mumps. Richard also, J. F. Daily complaining today

January 6, 1847 [Wednesday]

In camps, doing nothing, clear and warm. Sick with the mumps. Richard, and J. F. Bailey sick. Our Col. rec'd orders to raise 200 effective men from his regiment to go.

January 7, 1847 [Thursday]

In camp, doing nothing but cleaning up guns for the above trip. Cloudy and cold, very windy, Sick, Bailey & Richard sick to; the health of my Company not in the best of health, several down with the mumps

January 8, 1847 [Friday]

In camps, was inspected by Capt. Harrison to take up the line of march to parts unknown. Cloudy and pleasant, sick

January 9, 1847 [Saturday]

In camps preparing to march from Tampico on some unknown expedition, pressing horses, mules and jacks into the service of the U.S. Richard Heard went to hospital and others, clear and pleasant

January 10, 1847 [Sunday]

Sunday, cold and windy, at 3 o'clock a detachment of 10 companies of Regulars and 5 of Vols. Took up the line of march, to where no one know, marched 4 miles and camped for the night.

January 11, 1847 [Monday]

On the road toward Altamira, marched 10 miles from town and was ordered back to Tampico. Ordered back at 5 o'clock P.M., this day 7 months we left our homes and Dear wives and families. Several of my Company failed in consequence of chills and fever. I with the mumps

January 12, 1847 [Tuesday]

In camps at Tampico, Cold and cloudy, Ten of my Company had chills. Bailey, Aycock and J. G. Heard all sick. I with the mumps

January 13, 1847 [Wednesday]

In camps, several sick, cloudy and unpleasant. This day seven months, I was mustered into the service of the United States for twelve months, a long time too, write to my Dear Wife.

January 14, 1847 [Thursday]

In camps, doing nothing, in our Regiment as fast as people can. Clear and pleasant. Several sick with chills and fevers in my Company. Bailey, R. Heard and Aycock. Wrote to Wm. ... Bailey, esq. of Perry County, Alabama.

January 15, 1847 [Friday]

In camps, cloudy and a little cool, several case chills, and fever in my Company, wrote to Father and Grand Mother Bailey

January 16, 1847 [Saturday]

In camps, doing nothing, Capt. Shelly being a busy old body, had our Regiment in confusion by wanting some changes to take place among the companies. Warm

January 17, 1847 [Sunday]

Sunday, Cloudy and rainy, cool, the number of sick report this morning is 18 and 12 behind us makes 30.

January 18, 1847 [Monday]

In camps, clear and pleasant an order came to the Col. to prepare four of his Companies to march. Several sick. I had chill. Got letter from my Dear Wife and one from parents in South Carolina.

January 19, 1847 [Tuesday]

In camps preparing to leave Tampico taking Muster Rolls. Sick myself with chills, a very cold day, what is called here a Norther. Wrote to my Dear Wife.

January 20, 1847 [Wednesday]

James T. Dacus died in Hospital in Tampico of the fever after an illness of about ten days. Considerable sickness in the Company

January 21, 1847 [Thursday]

The Company was paid off today for the first time since entering the service. I was very sick with chills and fever. Paid by Major Bennet.[284]

January 22, 1847 [Friday]

All my company that was able was marched to Old Tampico a distance of about four miles. I myself left behind with some others too sick to go. I kept with me Doctor Eiland, J.F. Bailey and R. M. Holmes.

January 23, 1847 [Saturday]

Still sick and very bad, at night Peachy Bledsoe and Lafayette Vance both got shot by being out at an improper time at night by their own sentinel, truly sorry I am to learn the fact. John Holmes, R. M.s brother came to see us.

---

[284] Major Albert G. Bennett, Paymaster for the United States Army. He was brevet a Lt. Colonel at National Bridge, Mexico. Bennett died in 1857.

January 24, 1847 [Sunday]

Sunday, Still sick and confined to my pallet, missed the chills for the first day out of 7. Warm and clear.

January 25, 1847 [Monday]

Still sick and confined to my pallet, My friend J.F. Bailey drew for me my pay up to the 31st Dec. 1846, amount $611.85 deduct from that one months pay which I drew from Majr. Burns[285] $521.35, this drawn from Majr. Bennett. Genl. Patterson, Genl. Twiggs and Genl. Quitman all arrived here with their commands of about 4000 men.

January 26, 1847 [Tuesday]

Still sick, but no chill, Bennett very sick, had some work done on my sword[286]

January 27, 1847 [Wednesday]

Still Sick, but no chill, violent pain in my head, all of our folks better.

January 28, 1847 [Thursday]

Still sick, and on my Pallet, a little improved. Cloudy, and cool, all the sick getting better, heard that Father[287] was to leave Ala. for Tampico, Mexico about the 15th inst. Oh! God, I would be so glad to see him, then I could hear from My Dear Wife.

January 29, 1847 [Friday]

Still sick, quite weak, no particular pain, but in my head, all the sick getting better. I have some of the best friends, and nurses of any other man. I must name some: J. F. Bailey and R. M. Holmes, cloudy and a little coolish. J. F. Bailey and John Crowley made a bet of $10 aside and put the money in my hands—on Crowley's drinking spirits in one month.

January 30, 1847 [Saturday]

Still on my pallet but not sick much. Pain in head, and weakness, cloudy and cool, got two letters from my Dear Wife

January 31, 1847 [Sunday]

Sunday, still on my pallet, mending a little, My Company rec'd orders to move back from Old Tampico, also Majr. Bryan's command, Cloudy and disagreeable, wrote to my Dear Wife.

FEBRUARY 1, 1847 [Monday]

My health improving slowly, all the sick getting better. Cloudy but war, all the Companies which was encamped at old Tampico was moved back, and joined the regiment, borrowed some cavalry tactics of Capt. Wm. R. Caswell,[288] Tennessee Volunteers.

[285] Major Archibald W. Burns was born in New Jersey where he enlisted as a volunteer on July 2, 1846, and served as a paymaster. He was discharged on April 1, 1849.
[286] Coleman's sword is in the possession of his descendant T. E. "Gene" Coleman and the sword bears the engraving "Tampico, Mexico."
[287] There is no record that Thomas A. Heard actually visited Coleman and his sons in Tampico, although such visits from people in Alabama were known to occur.

February 2, 1847 [Tuesday]

My health improving, and so is all the Company, clear and hot.

February 3, 1847 [Wednesday]

Cleaned up my fine gun, getting well, I hope, cloudy and cool, had a little work on the ramrod of my gun, bot fine vest of . . . Capers, borrowed mattress of the same.

February 4, 1847 [Thursday]

Still weak, and a pain in my head, our Regiment was reviewed by Brigr. Genl. Quitman and nobly complimented by him for the great acquirement made by the Regiment, Cloudy and warm

February 5, 1847 [Friday]

Improving in health, warm day, exchanged off with Majr. Capers $350 in silver for Gold, received pay for the month January, got Mexican gold doubloons $16 each, got $9 Mexican Gold, got letter from my Dear Wife. Some of the sick of my Company joined us, which was left at Point Isabel, Jesse Aycock, James Moore, John W. Griffin, Thomas Swanson, James Jones, Shadr. Cardin, Wm. Liles and Joseph Dennis, leaving four behind, which I expect are gone home.

February 6, 1847 [Saturday]

My health still improving, Cloudy and warm, the above 8 men drew their pay up to15th of Nov. 1846.

February 7, 1847 [Sunday]

Still improving in health, feel able now for duty. The health of the Company improving, Clear and very warm, wrote to My Dear Wife. Sent John W. Radford a descriptive roll, Saw the flashing of powder along the coast south of us. Supposed to be the fighting of some ship-wrecked soldiers from Louisiana and the Mexicans,[289] sick all day, pain in my head.

February 8, 1847 [Monday]

Sick all day with a pain in my head and slight fever, very warm, several sick in my Company, and many more in the regiment. Louisianans came into Tampico[290]

February 9, 1847 [Tuesday]

Improving some little in health, Aycock down with the . . . , very hot and clear.

February 10, 1847 [Wednesday]

[288] Captain William R. Caswell, Tennessee Mounted Volunteer Regiment, was discharged May 1847. Captain Franklin Smith notes that Caswell was an aid to General Gideon J. Pillow at Camargo. Caswell was born in 1810 in Jefferson, Tennessee and married Elizabeth C. Gillespie on September 15, 1831.
[289] On February 1, 1847, the transport carrying 300 Louisiana volunteers under the command of Colonel Lewis G. DeRussey ran ashore about forty miles south of Tampico. The Louisianans were in danger from Mexican General Martín Perfecto de Cos and his 800 men. St. Mary's, a sloop-of-war, came to the aid of the volunteers, but they craftily escaped during the night leaving behind burning campfires while they slipped away from harm and danger.
[290] This is a reference to the ship wrecked Louisiana troops who escaped General Cos.

Cloudy, cold and very windy, blowing from the north, nothing doing all the sick getting better.

February 11, 1847 [Thursday]

Still cold, cloudy and windy, nothing doing, waiting for the arrival of Genl. Scott, this day eight months ago we all left our homes, wives, children and friends for the Republic of Mexico and here we are now Tampico, Mexico.

February 12, 1847 [Friday]

Cold, cloudy and rainy, doing nothing but waiting for Genl. Scott to say what we shall do.

February 13, 1847 [Saturday]

Cold, cloudy and rainy, had my hair cut off very short, doing nothing at all

February 14, 1847 [Sunday]

Still cloudy, and cool, doing nothing it being Sunday I have spent a part of the day in writing to my Dear Wife, I don't feel very well today. Got letter from my Dear Wife rec'd a paper from M. A. Ransom[291] So. Ca., Lt. Murphy[292] returned.

February 15, 1847 [Monday]

Clear and pleasant, mailed a letter to my Dear Jane, bot one pr. pantaloons, one shirt, one pr. shoes, and three pr. socks.

February 16, 1847 [Tuesday]

Clear and pleasant, doing little or nothing, all the sick getting better.

February 17, 1847 [Wednesday]

Clear and hot, went up the Pánuco River hunting with the Creole Sylvester Peardon, camped at the mouth Chile Creek about 10 miles from Tampico.

February 18, 1847 [Thursday]

Cloudy and pleasant, commenced hunting, killed two bear myself. Creole four geese ...., a little piece of timbered land.

February 19, 1847 [Friday]

Cloudy and warm, in camps doing but little towards closing the War. Genl. Scott arrived in Tampico, now for new movements entirely I suppose. Tho be it so'

February 20, 1847 [Saturday]

---

[291] Monroe Augustine Ransom married Edney F. Coleman, William Coleman's sister.
[292] First Lieutenant Nathaniel M. Murphy of Company A (Greensboro Volunteers) was left ill at Point Isabel in December 1846 and rejoined the regiment at Tampico. He was promoted to First Lieutenant from Second Lieutenant on August 5, 1846. Lieutenant Murphy assumed command of the company on April 17, 1847, at Vera Cruz when Captain Andrew L. Pickens was left ill in that town when the regiment left for Jalapa.

Clear and pleasant, Genl. Twiggs division ordered to embark for the Island Lobos.

February 21, 1847 [Sunday]

Sunday in Camps doing but little, I understand that Genl. Quitman's Brigade has orders to go to Vera Cruz. Sent several papers to my friends in Ala. Clear and warm.

February 22, 1847 [Monday]

In camps drilling, making preparations for Vera Cruz, clear and pleasant. Lt. Pitts and Pool[293] went hunting.

February 23, 1847 [Tuesday]

In camps drilling a little, clear and warm, learned that the So. Carolinian Regiment of Volunteers for the whole tour[294] was upon Lobos Island, J. F. Bailey and John Heard sick.

February 24, 1847 [Wednesday]

In camps doing little, clear and pleasant.

February 25, 1847 [Thursday]

In camps quite busy making preparations for to embark for Vera Cruz. Drew some ordinance stores from Lt Hayes 3rd . . . drew pay for the month of February—$87.50

February 26, 1847 [Friday]

In camps, bought for my Dear Wife a Chinese Shawl* (fine) gave thirty five dollars for it; Discharged S. Aycock, James Bennett and W. H. Jones; clear and pleasant, windy

February 27, 1847 [Saturday]

In camps, bought some little shoes for Willie and Buddy and a bridle for Ben gave for them $13.25, cloudy and cool

February 28, 1847 [Sunday]

Sunday inn camps, Company mustered for pay by Col. Coffey. Cloudy and cold, got letter from my Dear Wife, dated 15th inst.

MARCH 1, 1847 [Monday]

In camps, appointed R. M. Holmes 1st Sergt., Young L. Cardin 2nd Sergt., made monthly returns for duty; 45 pvts no. of 4 C. O., total present about . . . Aggregate 71, cloudy and pleasant; 4 Companies of our Brigade embarked for Vera Cruz.

March 2, 1847 [Tuesday]

---

[293] Walter Pool who was a private in the company of Captain Richard W. Jones (Company F) from Jackson County, Alabama.
[294] Coleman means that the South Carolina Palmetto Regiment had enlisted for the duration of the war.

In camps, preparing to leave for Vera Crus at night. I went to the Theatre, clear and warm. J. F. Bailey wrote to my Dear Jane. Mr. Atkinson from Edgefield So Ca. arrived at Tampico, Mexico.

March 3, 1847 [Wednesday]

In camps, Cloudy and warm. 3 Companies more of our Brigade embarked for Vera Crus.

March 4, 1847 [Thursday]

In camps, clear and pleasant, win so high as to prevent our embarking for Vera Crus, sent 5 men to the hospital in town.

March 5, 1847 [Friday]

In camps, clear and windy, expecting every minute when we will embark for the scene of Arms which is expected to take place at Vera Cruz.

March 6, 1847 [Saturday]

Embarked on board of Steamship *New Orleans* for Vera Crus. Clear and windy, Steamer very crowded 900 men on board.

March 7, 1847 [Sunday]

On board the Steamer *New Orleans* anchored in the harbor Tampico. Cloudy and looks very much like rain. Set sail at 2 o'clock P.M. for Vera Cruz—seasick.

March 8, 1847 [Monday]

On board the Steamer *New Orleans*, at sea and sea sick all the time.

March 9, 1847 [Tuesday]

Still on board the Steamer *New Orleans*. Cloudy and warm. Sea sick, All hands went ashore and a more magnificent sight I never saw in my life, 11,500 troops were landed on the beach about 6 miles below Vera Cruz in surf boats prepared for that purpose. The first five were from the *Vixen*,[295] a small man of war.

March 10, 1847 [Wednesday]

The line of march was taken up. General Worth with his division took his position on the right under a severe fire from the Castle San Juan do Ullen and three other points in town, next Genl. Patterson's division commenced taking position under a heavy and constant fire of cannon, some skirmish fighting. Met with several of my old friends and acquaintances from E.D.S.C.[296]

March 11, 1847 [Thursday]

---

[295] The famous Brown and Bell shipyards in New York constructed the *Vixen*. The ship was designed for use by the Mexican Navy and was bought by the U.S. Navy for service in the shallow waters of the Mexican coast. It was a small side-wheel steamer measuring 118 feet long and twenty-two feet at the beam. The ship was armed with three 32-pound carronades.

[296] Edgefield District, South Carolina

Second day of the siege, establishing a line around the town, some sharp fighting . . . Three Americans killed and 10 wounded. Several cannon shots at my company, this day 9 months I left my home and dear wife and children, very hot indeed.

March 12, 1847 [Friday]

Lying on our guns behind the highest kind of sand hills, not much firing today, the wind very high, planting some batteries

March 13, 1847 [Saturday]

Fourth day of the siege, succeeded in getting our troops entirely around Vera Cruz. Gen. Twiggs on extreme left, firing on us all day. This day 9 months we were mustered into the Service of the U. S. Cold and windy

March 14, 1847 [Sunday]

Sunday, 5th day of the siege, planting batteries, wind very high, can't get anything ashore, firing on us all day, cold and rainy

March 15, 1847 [Monday]

Sixth day of the siege, wind very high, I with my company on Pickett guard. Genl. Quitman came to inform me of the battle fought between Genl. Santa Anna and Taylor and the victory of the latter. Mexican forces not less than 20,000 of which 4,000 was left dead, and wounded, on the field of battle. American forces 5,000 of which 700 was killed, and wounded, all Volunteers except three companies. Our Col. manifested signs of fear, I think. Cold and rainy. Appointed Joseph G. Dennis 4th Corporal

March 16, 1847 [Tuesday]

Seventh day of the Siege, Mexican balls and bombs flying all about us in a very unwelcomed manner, Several fell directly amongst us, firing at the Alabama Regiment. Troops in good health, got sword Belt from D. A. Jones. Cold, cloudy and rainy

March 17, 1847 [Wednesday]

Eighth day of the siege, Still under the fire of the enemy, Troops in fine spirits generally. A salute was fired from the Navy in HONOR of the Victory achieved by Genl. Taylor over Santa Anna. Had my feelings hurt by one of my best friends, speaking of officers without any exceptions, Took up a man bearing dispatches from Genl. Moralles [297] to the Governor of Vera Cruz regarding men and provisions to he forced across our line into his assistance.

March 18, 1847 [Thursday]

Ninth day of the siege preparing to turn loose our guns on the City, enemy still firing at us, J. F. B. said in my presence that he never would think as much of me again, because I spoke to a man that he did not like, and by the by I think as little of the man (Lt. Thorn) [298] as I do of any man in the Army, be it so, I don't feel myself to blame, I am sorry that my friendship is of so little importance to him. I knew that I would go as far for him as any other man living. Stood guard. Cloudy and rainy.

---

[297] Brigadier General Juan Morales was the commander of the Mexican defenders at Vera Cruz.
[298] Possibly James D. Thorne of Company D in the First Battalion of Alabama Volunteers.

March 19, 1847 [Friday]

Tenth day of the siege, a heavy firing from the enemy at the right wing of the army. Gen Worth's division, at least 200 guns fired, moving part of our provisions stores north of the City, got my bedding from the beach. very warm day, calm, one man's suspenders shot off of him

March 20, 1847 [Saturday]

eleventh day of the siege, a heavy firing from the enemy all day, at least 400 guns fired, only one killed, went to see Col. Butler,[299] clear, calm and warm, the health of the Army very good at this time, clear, very windy, sun crossing the equator. Col. Butler showed me two letters from his daughter and nephew.

March 21, 1847 [Sunday]

Sunday, twelfth day of the siege, Clear and windy, extremely so, the enemy firing on us all day without effect. Not much sickness among the troops except those who seem disposed to keep themselves out of the dangers of battle. Sent out piquet guard. Found Capt. Moore[300] to be the kind of man that Majr Bryan long since said to me he was . . . . . Stood on picket.

March 22, 1847 [Monday]

Thirteenth day of the siege, clear, calm and hot. the enemy still firing at us. Genl Scott fired a few guns at the enemy commenced at 4 O'clock in the afternoon. some sharp firing from that time until dark. The element was of smoke, and thunder like report. both parties continued firing all night.

March 23, 1847 [Tuesday]

Fourteenth day of the siege; some shooting on both sides, our cannon attack is something like ornamental colours added to a perfect figure or picture which can't be bettered by the operation, All I conclude of no avail. Our Navy driven by the enemy from the Castle. Saw the snow covered mountain peak called the Orzimbo (Orizaba) 60 miles west of the city of Vera Cruz 4000 feet from the level of the Gulf. Clear, very windy, blowing a norther. Quite sick all night. One man killed and one man wounded.

March 24, 1847 [Wednesday]

Fifteenth day of the siege, a constant firing kept up from both sides without much effect I fear. Wrote to my Dear Wife. Our forces very busy mounting cannon.

March 25, 1847 [Thursday]

Sixteenth day of the siege, firing kept up from both sides regularly, what damage has been done to Mexicans I know not, we have lost about six men killed and fifteen wounded. Cloudy

---

[299] Colonel Pierce Mason Butler commander of the Palmetto Regiment of volunteers from Coleman's home state of South Carolina. He was born on April 11, 1798, and educated at Moses Waddel's Academy in Abbeville, S.C. He was a banker by profession, served as a Captain in the United States Army and as a Lieutenant Colonel in the South Carolina Militia. Butler was elected governor of South Carolina in 1836 and served until 1838. Colonel Butler was mustered into the army in December 1846 and killed at the Battle of Churubusco, Mexico on December 22, 1846. He is buried in Edgefield, South Carolina.
[300] Probably Captain Sydenham Moore who was the commander of the Eutaw Rangers, from Greene County, Alabama. Coleman and Moore had animosity between them as the result of an attempt to force the resignation of the regiment's officers while stationed at Camp Alabama. Coleman opposed the attempt to remove the officers.

and pleasant. Cannons all ceased firing in consequence of an attack made by the enemy in rear of our right wing. Our brigade was ordered forward, marched about one mile and encamped for the night with Arms in hand expecting an attack from Santa Anna, in the rear with 5,000 troops. Genl. Scott was advised of this move by a prisoner taken; much damage said to have been done to town by our guns. Mexican guns all silenced.

March 26, 1847 [Friday]

Seventeenth day of the siege, Very little firing done on either side. Most disagreeable day I ever experience on account of wind and sand. Sick with cold. Capitulation proposed by the Mexicans. Firing ceased on both sides.

March 27, 1847 [Saturday]

Eighteenth day of the siege, clear and pleasant, still unwell with cold, no firing at all. Commissioners appointed by both parties to negotiate a peace, or rather a surrender of Vera Cruz which was agreed to on both sides. Terms are unconditional surrender of both Town and Castle, to lay down all public property, and leave on a parole of honor. Warm and cloudy.

March 28, 1847 [Sunday]

Sunday, clear and pleasant, doing nothing all day, received one letter from my parents in So. Ca. and one from J. Bailey, I wrote to J. Bailey.

March 29, 1847 [Monday]

Clear and pleasant, received orders to march on tomorrow to Alvarado, a distance of about fifty miles from Vera Cruz S. East, The American Flags was raised on the great Castle San Juan De Ulloa at 12 o'clock, and on the forts and walls of the City Vera Cruz. Pain in my head, The soldiers much wrathy in consequence of not having had the privilege granted to them of visiting the town.

March 30, 1847 [Tuesday]

Clear and very hot indeed, several of my Company reported themselves sick, at 3 o'clock P.M. Genl. Quitman's Brigade took up the line of march by the left flank, Ala. Regiment leading, pass through town, and to the mouth of the Boco Del Rio river, where we encamped for the night in a little village called Auto Lizards,[301] Got letter from my Dear Wife.

March 31, 1847 [Wednesday]

Took up the line of march at 8 o'clock A.M., crossed the river following the beach and hard marching indeed. Marched by the right flank So Ca. Regiment leading, warm and dry, much fatigued and feet blistered at night. Encamped in a beautiful grove of Palmetto. Saw the greatest curiosity and beauty imaginable, a banyan tree.

APRIL 1, 1847 [Thursday]

Took the line of march at 8 o'clock A.M. Georgia Regiment leading by the left flank in formation; came to us that Alvarado had surrendered, traveled hard, men much fatigued and feet blistered.

---

[301] This is Antón Lizardo. Coleman either spelled the name erroneously or the transcriber interpreted the cursive writing incorrectly.

April 2, 1847 [Friday]

Took up the line of march by the right flank, Ala. Regiment leading, marched into the town, Alvarado at 4 O'clock P.M., found no Mexicans in the place, a very pretty little town, the population of the place is said to be about 2,500 inhabitants, so soon as we arrived I was with my company detailed for Police up all night, I was sick of fatigue and sore feet; extremely hot.

April 3, 1847 [Saturday]

In town all day busy keeping order and then did not do it, visited the church, the best and finest building that I have seen in Mexico, elegantly furnished inside, received orders to take up the line of march back to Vera Cruz tomorrow, extremely hot, sand flies, mosquitoes and gnats in abundance.

April 4, 1847 [Sunday]

Sunday, took up the line of march by the left flank S. Co. Regiment leading, hard march 18 miles with sore feet, very hot, encamped for the night at a ranche in the prairie which is 10 miles across.

April 5, 1847 [Monday]

Took up the line of march at 7 o'clock by the right flank Georgia Regiment leading march 20 miles, Several gave out through fatigue. I came near fainting from pain of my feet, hot, extremely so, camped at the river.

April 6, 1847 [Tuesday]

Took up the line of march at 7 o'clock, Ala. Regiment leading, arrived in town at 12 o'clock, very hot, men much fatigued indeed, visited the town in part, orders issued for the Army to march in a few days to Jalapa.

April 7, 1847 [Wednesday]

In camps near Vera Cruz, very hot indeed, made a visit to the Castle San Wan and indeed it is a strong place surely, one hundred and thirty guns and five large mortars mounted and two hundred more which was not mounted, the Castle I cannot begin to describe, it was commenced in 1602, Richard Heard got badly hurt by a trifling Regular Soldier.

April 8, 1847 [Thursday]

In camps near Vera Cruz, 2nd Division of the Army, Genl. Twiggs command, took up the line of march for Jalapa, the interior towards Mexico City, wrote to My Dear Wife, sent some newspapers to the States, very dry, and hot, orders to turn over all surplus ordnance stores to the proper authorities.

April 9, 1847 [Friday]

In camps, two Brigades of Genl. Patterson's Division took up the line of march for Jalapa, very hot day, bought silver suspender buckles $10 and one fine gold ring for My Dear Wife for $10.

April 10, 1847 [Saturday]

In camps, extremely hot, good health in Ala. Regiment, So Ca. dying up fast, sick with a head ache, Richard's wounds getting well, hung a Negro who was from Tennessee for committing a rape on a Mexican woman.

April 11, 1847 [Sunday]

Sunday in camps, this day ten months I left my home and Dear Wife, children and friends, tours more pleasant than common, visited the Cathedral, it is a fine church truly, and had seven different characters to worship by these people Mexicans, Got a discharge for Joe Hale.

April 12, 1847 [Monday]

In camps, very hot, drew 33 haversacks and 26 canteens under orders to take up the line of march towards the City of Mexico. Got letter from Joseph Heard which I gladly received and was glad to learn that he got home, also got one from Father Heard, I was equally glad to receive, very much disappointed in not getting a letter from My Dear Wife, for her my heart will break, O, MY God!

April 13, 1847 [Tuesday]

In camps, extremely hot and disagreeably so, wrote to Benjm[302] and Joseph Heard, very low spirited, on several occasions sent papers to my acquaintances in the States, I feel today as though I am forsaken by almost every body. bot pr. paints.

April 14, 1847 [Wednesday]

In camps, extremely hot, some appearance of rain, preparing to go on up the country to Jalapa, boot coat, felt badly all day.

April 15, 1847 [Thursday]

In camps doing nothing, hot, had coattail cut off, wrote to my Dear Wife, expecting constantly when we will take up the line of march to reinforce the Army now at the National Bridge,[303] lost my keys, three companies of the Ala. Regiment ordered to march tomorrow morning up the country.

April 16, 1847 [Friday]

In camps, the morning is Norther, cool, three companies of our Regiment left Jalapa, found my keys—this I want to remember.

April 17, 1847 [Saturday]

Turned into Quarter Master department mess chess, etc., hot and calm, took up the line of march for Jalapa at 6 o'clock P.M. Georgia Regiment leading, encamped at the bridge 3 miles from the city of Vera Cruz, stopped as usual without any command.

April 18, 1847 [Sunday]

Sunday, Took up the line of march by the right flank the So. Ca. Regiment leading at 9 o'clock A.M. Marched over some heavy sand, saw some fine old built Spanish bridges, march in much

[302] This is probably Benjamin Ryan Coleman, William's son.
[303] The National Bridge was on the National Road between Vera Cruz and Jalapa, Mexico and was a fortification guarding that road. It was a magnificent structure more than fifty feet high and nearly a quarter of a mile long with a commanding view of the river.

confusion, hot, cloudy. Encamped after a few fires from the enemy at a fine running stream of water about 15 miles from Vera Cruz.

April 19, 1847 [Monday]

Took up the line of march by the left flank, ... leading at ... , cloudy and warm, clouds look lowering, report reached us that the army was routed by our troops, our loss considerable. Saw Santa Anna's favorite residence,[304] it is a fine looking establishment, Elected one 4th Sgt. J. P. Everett and one corporal 2nd S. B. Fuller. received orders from Genl. Quitman to be ready with my company to march in advance of the Brigade at day light tomorrow morning.

April 20, 1847 [Tuesday]

Took up the line of march at sunrise Ala. leading by the left flank, Marched 18 miles cross several of the best stone bridges I ever saw, encamped at the National bridge on the Qntijua River, a strong place, both by nature and by art, Genl. Quitman reported to me the result of the battle fought between Santa Ana and Genl. Scott on the 16th Inst. Our loss 200. Mexican less 2,000 killed 4,000 prisoners 10,000 stand of small arms, and 23 guns, several officer prisoners of which LaVega and Herrera were two. Saw them on their way to the states as prisoners of war.

April 21, 1847 [Wednesday]

Took up the line of march at ½ past o'clock A. M. Georgia leading, marched hard over a level country, dry and hot, encamped for the night at Plan del Rio, a little village place on a small river where the battle commenced on the 16th inst., I have crossed 10 very fine bridges.

April 22, 1847 [Thursday]

Took up the line of march at 1 o'clock, Pa. Regiment leading by the left flank, passed the battle ground and stronger position for defense certainly cannot be Mexico, there I saw more dead men, horses, mules, and wounded men than I have ever before seen, it a picturesque and magnificent scenery I never have seen, a fine paved road and plenty of water, our army took a great number of guns, small arms, waggons, mules and ammunition. Battle ground Sierra Gorda. Saw Genl. Shields. he is very low having been shot through with a grape shot, the mountain pass where the battle was fought is at the head of a deep ravine which runs southeast and is not more than fifty yards wide. Encamped on a little mountain stream of pure cool free stone water, have crossed thirteen stone bridges; have marched in sight of a mountain peak (the Orizaba) on our left from Vera Cruz. It had a fine appearance.

April 23, 1847 [Friday]

Took up the line of march at 5:30 A. M., So. Ca. leading by the right flank, crossed three stone bridges, arrived at Jalapa at 10 o'clock A.M., it is a splendid looking town, closely built in the edge of the mountains, it contains a dense population of fashionable people of the Castilian stock, encamped two miles north of town on a small stream near a cotton factory, built in good style. Have not heard from My Dear Wife in one month. Cloudy and cool, quite cold tonight

April 24, 1847 [Saturday]

In camps near Jalapa, visited town and found it to greatly excel any place I have ever seen in any country. Got a letter from my Dear Wife which gives me much satisfaction, wrote to her. Clear and pleasant in this country, had pr. pants made.

---

[304] Santa Anna had two dwellings on the National Road; one located at Mango de Clavo about sixteen miles from Vera Cruz and another more elaborate country seat at El Encero near Jalapa.

April 25, 1847 [Sunday]

Sunday, in camps, Clear and warm, about twelve o'clock began to cloud up at night, rained, received two papers—the *Marion News*[305] from My Dear Wife, the *Hamburg Journal*[306] from M. A. Ransom.

April 26, 1847 [Monday]

In camps, cloudy but pleasant, some ran fell, had coat cleaned and pr. shoes, bot cot from J. B. Hale, the health of my Company not so good. Diarrhea among us

April 27, 1847 [Tuesday]

In camps doing nothing but eating poor beef and cold water dow cake made of flour, both without salt. Wrote to my Dear Wife, my brother-in-law Benj. Tillman[307] staid all night with me, he was quite sick, cloudy and rainy.

April 28, 1847 [Wednesday]

In camps, clear and warm, went on top of a high peak of a hill which over looks a beautiful parcel of farms, and the town of Jalapa, at 12 o'clock clouded up then thunder and rain.

April 29, 1847 [Thursday]

In camps, very warm early in the morning, made out muster rolls. John W. Rogers & H. Harvill[308] rejoined our company at Jalapa, got pants.

April 30, 1847 [Friday]

In camps, cloudy and rainy, company mustered for pay by Capt. Deas A. A. G.,[309] health of the company generally good. Some lancers lurking round about our camps, killed one, idle, Watson[310] resigned the adjutancy.

MAY 1, 1847 [Saturday]

In camps, sent some little papers to the states.

May 2, 1847 [Sunday]

---

[305] This may have been the *Marion Review* published in Marion, Alabama in 1847.

[306] Hamburg was a small community located a short distance directly south of Marion, Alabama in Perry County. Hamburg was a farming community with one schoolteacher, a grocery store operated by Adolph Wolfe from Poland, a well digger, and one brick mason.

[307] Benjamin Tillman died a short time later at Perote, Mexico.

[308] Rogers and Harvill were hospitalized at Point Isabel during the period when the Company was on Brazos Island, Texas.

[309] Captain George Deas was Assistant Adjutant-General in the Adjutant-General's Department. He served as a First Lieutenant in the Fifth Infantry of the Regular Army and was Brevetted a Major after the battles of Contreras and Churubusco. He served as a Lieutenant in the Confederate Army and died in 1870.

[310] Hugh P. Watson served as Adjutant of the First Alabama. He was appointed on July 6, 1846, at Brazos Island.

In camps preparing to take up the line of march, still further into the interior. Got shoes for self and J.F.B. some captured Mexican clothing sent into camps to be divided among the soldiers. Rainy.

May 3, 1847 [Monday]

In camps, fixing to leave for Mexico, cloudy and rainy, clothing distributed among the companies of the Brigade, received orders to take up the line of march tomorrow morning.

May 4, 1847 [Tuesday]

Immediately after reveille wagons were ordered to companies for baggage trains for the Brigadier, General packing up, took place, but before the wagons loaded, or the tents struck, orders came from headquarters suspending further movement in front for the purpose of discharging the 12th Volunteers.[311] Cloudy and rainy

May 5, 1847 [Wednesday]

In camps waiting for the return train from Vera Cruz to escort it back to Vera Cruz where we will take transportation to the City of New Orleans and U.S.A. to be discharged from the service of the U.S. Clear and warm, Received orders to march to Vera Cruz to start on the morning of 7th inst. Friday morning.

May 6, 1847 [Thursday]

In camps preparing to leave for Vera Cruz, clear and warm, four Regiments left Jalapa for Vera Cruz, Taken very sick; worse off at night with the colic than I ever was before, Good attention to me by my friends.

May 7, 1847 [Friday]

Took up the line of march for Vera Cruz, Georgia leading. Clear and warm, I very sick all day, was conveyed on a spring wagon, encamped at Los Rio only 9 miles from Jalapa.

May 8, 1847 [Saturday]

Took up line of march at 1 o'clock Alabama leading, Clear and hot, encamped at Plain Del Rio at 1 o'clock, quite sick all day, 12 mos since the battle of Palo Alto.

May 9, 1847 [Sunday]

Took up the line of march at 4 o'clock Georgia leading, clear and hot, encamped at a little town Obias on a little river, quite sick all day, anniversary of the Resaca del a Palma battle.

May 10, 1847 [Monday]

Took up the line of march at 5 o'clock Ala leading, Very clear and hot, encamped at Toleta on a small river. Getting better, quite sick all day. 12 month troops embarking for N. Y.

May 11, 1847 [Tuesday]

Took up line of march at 12 o'clock A.M. and arrived at Vera Cruz at 8 o'clock and encamped at Twiggs old campground. Clear and hot, quite weak, This day eleven months since I left my

---

[311] Coleman means the volunteers that enlisted for twelve months.

home, friends, My Dear Wife and children. Got 3 letters from my Dear Wife, Volunteers embarking for New York

May 12, 1847 [Wednesday]

Embarked on board the transport steamer *Fashion* with Genl. Patterson[312] bound for New Orleans. Clear and hot, left my company at Vera Cruz, quite to my reluctance, quite unwell.

May 13, 1847 [Thursday]

On board the *Fashion*, quite pleasant, still sick, arrived at Tampico at 3 o'clock P.M. making the run in 24 hours. Very sick on landing, left at 1:30 o'clock P.M. lay inside the bar all night. This day 11 mos, Since I was mustered into service for 12 mos.

May 14, 1847 [Friday]

On board the *Fashion*, pleasant and clear, very sick all day, gave Capt. P. S. Brooks[313] Santa Anna's Cock gaffs[314] for T. G. Bascom; Dr. Davis[315] gave me medicine.

May 15, 1847 [Saturday]

On board the *Fashion*, pleasant and clear, fine running, sick but a little better.

May 16, 1847 [Sunday]

On board the *Fashion*, pleasant and clear, not so sick as I have been. Still on board the *Fashion*, nothing of importance took place during the day, clear and calm, some better of my sickness.

May 17, 1847 [Monday]

Still on board the *Fashion*, arrived at the mouth of the Mississippi at 10 o'clock A.M. and well pleased I was to see land belonging to my own Government, past a small town name unknown near the mouth.[316] Clear and warm. Getting much better, begin to feel well to what I have felt, I hope soon to meet my Dear Wife, children, parents, relatives and friends after passing the mouth of the river 35 miles I reached a beautiful construction, Fort, called Fort Jackson standing on both sides of the river, well built.[317] At sunset was 40 miles below New Orleans, saw no more of the country. Some fine sugar plantations below New Orleans, arrived at the great city N.O. at 1 o'clock A.M. on the morning of the 18th.

May 18, 1847 [Tuesday]

[312] General Robert Patterson returned to the United States from Mexico because the departure of so many volunteers effectively destroyed his command.

[313] Captain Preston Smith Brooks was the commander of Company D of the Palmetto Regiment of Volunteers from South Carolina. He was mustered into the army in December 1846. Brooks later gained fame by clubbing Senator Charles Sumner senseless on the Senate floor with a walking cane in response to a speech Sumner made in which he gave insult to a kinsman of Brooks. Brooks became a Southern celebrity after the incident.

[314] A cock gaff is a metal spur placed on a gamecock (i. e., fighting rooster). Santa Anna was addicted to fighting gamecocks and kept large flocks of the birds.

[315] This is Dr. James Davis, Jr. who was the Surgeon for the Palmetto Regiment of South Carolina Volunteers. He resigned from the army on June 28, 1847, due to poor health and died after he reached South Carolina.

[316] This is Pilot Town located near the south pass entrance into the river. As its name implies, it was where the river pilots lived to be accessible to river traffic.

[317] Coleman is in error because the forts were not both Fort Jackson. Fort Jackson was located on the west side of the Mississippi River and Fort St. Philip on the east side.

Found myself in the magnificent Hotel St. Charles,[318] took breakfast, paid my bill and left the St, Charles and sought out a private boarding house, found a good house and that is well kept by Mrs. Lusk, bot me a coat and pants put on some clean clothes after taking a bath. Wrote home to my Dear Wife also to my So. Ca. Parents, then walked a little about town. Clear, hot and calm, Quite unwell.

May 19, 1847 [Wednesday]

In New Orleans, awaiting the arrival of my company. Bot some beautiful things for my Dear Wife, Dress, bonnet and shoes, hose, handkerchief and gloves for $37.00, Bot Will a pr. of boots, and half hose, sent Tommy and Frank a whip each. Clear, hot and calm. Sick.

May 20, 1847 [Thursday]

In New Orleans, making out Discharge Muster Rolls, to have my company discharged as soon as it arrives here. Warm, a little cloudy, visited the N.O. graveyard, it covers about 11 acres of land, it is a splendid fitted up place, finest kind of family vaults, handsomely decorated with wreaths and flowers of every description. Sick.

May 21, 1847 [Friday]

In New Orleans, making discharge rolls completed them 4 in number. Oh! How anxious I am to see my company arrive in N. Orleans, Cloudy and some rain, thunder, got letter from my Dear Wife written on the 15th inst. Oh!, my Dear God, how bad I feel that I can't go directly to her.

May 22, 1847 [Saturday]

In New Orleans still waiting the arrival of my company, went up stairs on the St. Charles spire to take a view of the city went up 220 steps 8 inches each step,[319] New Orleans is a fine large and handsome city. Clear and hot, sick.

May 23, 1847 [Sunday]

In New Orleans anxiously waiting the arrival of my company, went to market early, saw a great variety of everything to eat, visited in the afternoon a little village place Carrollton where I saw the finest garden that I have ever before seen, a curiosity in a water fountain which kept up all the time a brass ball. Col. Coffee, Lt. Col. Earl arrived in N. Orleans. Had chill.

May 24, 1847 [Monday]

In New Orleans still anxiously waiting the arrival of my Company, very hot and clear.

May 25, 1847 [Tuesday]

In New Orleans, still waiting the arrival of my Company, taking medicine, sick, raining all day. 11 companies of the Ala. Regiment arrived leaving 4 yet behind, and mine one of them. O Lord! Please deliver them safely on shore this day, I pray Thee.

May 26, 1847 [Wednesday]

---

[318] The Hotel St. Charles is best described as opulent. Its restaurants, bars and shops have been chronicled as small cities, and the hotel occupied an entire city block. The St. Charles had accommodations to sleep and feed one thousand guests at a time.
[319] The steps of the St. Charles spire rose to a height of 147 feet.

In New Orleans, still anxiously waiting for my Company to arrive, quite feeble, this morning and becoming uneasy on account of my Company, Clear and warm, rained at night, My Company arrived in New Orleans some of the men, and my friends quite sick.

May 27, 1847 [Thursday]

In New Orleans, very sick, my Company was mustered out of the service of the United States, and paid off. Clear and warm, had a bad spell of cramps pleurisy[320] or something else that I thought would almost kill me, suffered much, taken again at night 10 o'clock bad all night.

May 28, 1847 [Friday]

In New Orleans, very sick all day, had acts of friendship shown to me by Mr. Forbes that places me under obligation to him. Left New Orleans at five o'clock on board the packet *Mobile*[321] for Mobile. James F. Bailey, John G. Heard, and myself

May 29, 1847 [Saturday]

On board the packet *Mobile*, quite sick but some better, arrived at Mobile at one o'clock P.M. met with my old friend R.G. Cook, left Mobile on the steamboat *Amasanth* at 7 o'clock bound for Selma.

May 30, 1847 [Sunday]

Sunday on board the *Amasanth*, clear and hot, had great attention paid me by Col. P. I. Weaver,[322] quite sick all day, and several of the company also sick.

May 31, 1847 [Monday]

Still on board the *Amasanth* beating along against the current of the Ala. River very slowly, and quite sick.

JUNE 1, 1847 [Tuesday]

Arrived at Selma at ½ past one o'clock A.M. There to my great joy met with many of my friends, which was a meeting long to be remembered by me with feelings of the greatest satisfaction. Got my horse and set out on my way homeward, after having traveled some 12 miles I met through the goodness of God my Dear Wife and children how to contain myself the balance of the day I knew not, Oh, what a day for me, arrived at home at 9 o'clock A.M. and found things in a much better condition than I expected to have done. Capt. James B. Harrison sent a team to carry my things home which was quite a favour to me, lest my writing and many little valuable things to me.

---

[320] Pleurisy is an inflammation of the pleura, a membrane that covers the lungs, characterized by a dry cough and pain in the affected area.
[321] The *Mobile* was a small vessel that ran regularly between Mobile, Alabama and New Orleans carrying mail, passengers and goods.
[322] This is probably P. J. Weaver, a wealthy Selma, Alabama merchant and civic leader.

Appendix A
MEXICAN WAR PENSIONS
Act January 29, 1887
AFFIDAVIT OF WITNESS

State of _Louisiana,_ County of _DeSoto,_ SS:

Before me, a _Clerk of Court_ in and for the county of _DeSoto_ on this _1,_ day of _November,_ A. D. _1888,_ personally appeared _A. F. Jackson,_ who, being duly sworn, deposes and says;

I have known _C. G. Jackson_ For the space of _44 years_ years, and I was requested by said _C. G. Jackson_ to sign my name as a witness to the declaration for pension under the Act of January 29, 1887, sworn to by him on the _First_ day of _November,_ A. D. _1888;_ and that at his request I so signed my name as witness; that the said _C. G. Jackson_ is the identical person who signed the foregoing declaration, and who is therein described, and who was enlisted in the company of Captain _W. G. Coleman_ In the regiment commanded by _John R. Coffee,_ in the Mexican War, as in the said declaration set out.

No. 1. That the said _C. G. Jackson_ actually served sixty days with the Army or Navy of the United States in Mexico, or on the coast or frontier, or en route thereto, in the war with that Nation, that I swear to these facts from knowledge obtained as follows: _I have been raised up with him and know it from family History._

No. 2. That the said _C. G. Jackson_ was actually engaged in a battle in said war, to wit: in the battle of _Vera Cruz,_ at _Vera Cruz, Mexico_ on the _9 to 29ᵗ_ ~~day~~ of _March,_ A. D. _1847,_ and was honorably discharged, and these facts I swear to from knowledge obtained as follows: _Having been raised up with him. Know it from family History._

No. 3. That said _____ is disabled by reason of _____ which said disability was not incurred while the said _____ was in any manner voluntarily engaged in, or aiding or abetting, the late rebellion against the authority of the United States, but was incurred on or about the _____ day of _____ A. D. _____ At _____ and this fact I swear to from knowledge as follows: _____

No. 4. That the said _____ is dependent in whole or in part for his support and is incapacitated from the performance of manual labor, and I swear to the fact of dependence from knowledge obtained from and based upon the following facts: _____

No. 5. That the said _C. G. Jackson_ is sixty-two years of age, having been born on or about the _29_ day of _October,_ A. D. _1826,_ at _Perry County,_ in the State of _Alabama_ and that I swear to these fact from knowledge obtained as follows: _from the family records_

That I have no interest in the prosecution of this claim.

A. F. Jackson

Subscribed and sworn to before me this _First_ day of _Nov_ A. D. 188~~78~~. And I hereby certify the person who signed and executed the foregoing affidavit to be a credible person, and of good repute for truth and veracity in the community in which he lives, and that the contents of the above were fully made known to h*im* before signing.
[Seal]

Geo. H. Sutherlin

Clerk of the District Court

Note—The witness should strike out all the allegations of this affidavit which h does not personally know to be true.

(8527-190 M.)   _for Desoto Parish Louisiana_

Appendix B

State of Louisiana }
Parish of Claiborne}

Before me the undersigned authority this day personally appeared W. G. Coleman a resident of Claiborne Parish, Louisiana and to me well known who being duly sworn deposes that he was Captain of Company "C" First Regiment Alabama Volunteers in the United States service in the war between The United States & Mexico, and that C. G. Jackson was a member of said company & served therein as a private in 1846 and 1847 and that John R. Coffee was Colonel of said Regiment, R. G. Earle Lieutenant Colonel and Goode Bryant Major.

W. G. Coleman

Sworn to & Subscribed
Before me this the 19ᵗʰ
of January 1887
          Drew Ferguson
          Clerk D. C.

Mr. C. G. Jackson
Dear Sir:
   I take pleasure in
forwarding this Certificate
to you hoping it may be of
benefit to you.
          W. G. Coleman

Appendix C

3—014

ACT OF FEBRUARY 6, 1907

DECLARATION FOR PENSION

THE PENSION CERTIFICATE SHOULD NOT BE FORWARDED WITH THE APPLICATION.

State of *Louisiana* }

County of *DeSoto* } ss

On this **26** day of *February* A. D. one thousand nine hundred and **Seven** personally appeared before me, a *Notary Public* Within and for the county and state aforesaid *Charles G Jackson,* Who being duly sworn according to law, declares that he is **80** years of age, and a resident of ~~DeSoto~~ *Grand Cane* County of *DeSoto,* State of *Louisiana;* and that he is the identical person who ENROLLED at *Mobile, Ala* under the name of *Charles G. Jackson,* on the -- day of *June,* 18 **46,** as a *Private,* in *Co. C First Alabama Regiment Volunteers* in the service of the United States, in the *Mexican* War, and was HONORABLY DISCHARGED at *New Orleans,*

(State name of war, Civil or Mexican)

on the -- day of *June,* 18 **47** That he also served _____

(Here give a complete statement of all other services, if any)

That he was not employed in the military or naval service of the United States otherwise than as stated above. That his personal description at enlistment was as follows: Height **5** feet **9** inches; Complexion, *Light;* Color of eyes, *Gray;* Color of hair, *Black;* that his occupation was *Farmer;* that he was born *Oct. 19ᵗ* 18 **＃26** at *Perry Co., Ala*

That his several places of residence since leaving the service has been as follows:

(State date of each change, as nearly as possible.)

DeSoto Parish, Louisiana, Left Alabama Last of Nov. 1847

That he is -- a pensioner. That he has -- heretofore applied for pension _____

No. of Pension Certificate 17323

(If a pensioner, the certificate number only need be given. If not the number of the former application, if one was made)

That he makes this declaration for the purpose of being placed on the pension roll of the United States under the provisions of the act of February 6, 1907.

That his post-office address is *Grand Cane,* County of *DeSoto,*

State of *Louisiana*

Charles G. Jackson

(Claimant's Signature in Full)

Attest: (1) *R. S. Pickett*

(2) *L. Y. Tidwell*

Also personally appeared *R. S. Pickett,* residing in *Grand Cane, La* and *L. Y. Tidwell,* residing in, *Grand Cane, La,* Persons who I certify to be respectable and entitled to credit, and who, being by me duly sworn, say that they were present and saw *Charles G. Jackson* the claimant, sign his name (or make his mark) to the foregoing declaration; that they have every reason to believe, from the appearance of the claimant and their acquaintance with him of **one** years and **30** years, respectively, that he is the identical person he represents himself to be, and that they have no interest in the prosecution of this claim.

R. S. Pickett

L. Y. Tidwell

(Signatures of witnesses)

SUBSCRIBED and sworn to before me this **26ᵗ** day of *Feby,* A. D. 190 **7** and I hereby certify that the contents of the above declaration, etc., were fully made known and explained to the applicant and witnesses before swearing, including the words *DeSoto and 4,* erased, and the words *Grand Cane and 26,* added; and that I have no interest, direct or indirect, in the prosecution of this claim.

William H. Smith

(Signature)

Notary Public

(Official Character)

Appendix D

MEXICAN WAR
3-798

DROP ORDER AND REPORT

Department of the Interior

BUREAU OF PENSIONS

FINANCE DIVISION

Washington, D. C., Sep 26, 1911

Charles G. Jackson

(Pensioner)

17,323

(Certificate Number)

Act February 6, 1907

(Class)

(Soldier)

MEXICAN WAR

(Service)

U. S. Pension Agent

Knoxville

Sir: You are hereby directed to drop from the roll the name of the above-described pensioner, who died *Sept 13,* 19 *11*

J. L. Davenport

Commissioner

REPORT

Commissioner of Pensions
Sir: The name of the above-described pensioner, who was last paid at $ *20* month to *4 Aug* 19 *11,* has this day been dropped from the roll of this agency.

William Rute

U. S. Pension Agent

Sept 28, 19 *11*   6--833

Appendix E
William G. Coleman Letter to Mary Jane Heard

February 3rd 1844

My Dearest:

I have seated myself this evening after the retirement of all of the family, to pen down an idea or two that has been presenting themselves to my mind for several days. 1st You have perhaps heard so much said against me that you do not think me worthy of so pure a heart and hand, as yours, Dearest. 2nd If you have any fears that I am capable of deserving you be candid and tell me so, for under existing circumstances plain and candid dealing will certainly be best for us both. 3rd Dear Jane you are of sufficient age to judge of such qualities as a gentleman ought to possess for you to enjoy life with, you know my person, my disposition, my habits, and so on and so on; now Dearest if you do not think a combination of all you know of me, would give you ease, comfort, and that you could feel yourself happy by uniting your destiny with that of your fond lover, then Dearest you would wrong yourself and me, to marry me. 4th Can you not pity me for the abuse and slander that is so maliciously hurled at me—and all, and only because—I <u>love you</u>. I may be represented to you as a deceiver, a swindler, a gambler, a murderer, and even a thief, and I can bear it with calmness and quietly, but not willingly, and will after all love you. 5th I have had some hints that my reputation as a gentleman is doubted. It seems to be with your informant, I assure you Dearest that I have yet to learn that my reputation as a gentleman, has ever been questioned, until your informant reported it to you, I will if you are not satisfied with my statement ~~I will~~ give you references (both in this state and So. Ca.) so that you may learn my parentage, my character, and my habits, the charges which has been alleged and reported to you Dearest against me are without authority, the reasons why reported against me none has been given I presume, none can be given, only that I love you, and that you ought not to love me in return. 6th You know Dearest, That Christ was accused of hypocrisy, and other offenses, for which he even suffered death, we then need not look or expect better luck than God himself met with. Now Dear Jane look at all these things carefully and I think you must think with me that it is all done through design. Remember that I am doomed to love you so long as I live, then can't you love me for pity's sake, and marry, and make me happy for love's sake. Don't let the prejudices of others deter and prevent the execution of your wishes, when it may accord with your judgment. Oh, Dearest, then let us consummate our anticipated happiness, for I hope our souls have formed an inseparable union, is it not so. I have indisputable evidence that you do love me, in return for my devoted affection for you, and Oh God that your judgment may still direct you to love me so that our happiness may ere long be consummated is the prayer of your faithful admirer, and afflicted lover. I would visit you weekly, had you not requested of me not to do so. You say you regard my feelings too highly to suffer me to have them injured, -- and that I regard your feelings so much higher than I do my own, is all that could prevent my visiting you, for I know if I was to visit you at your Father's you would as you love me have to suffer for it. Now under all these circumstances will you not Dearest tell me that you will be mine, and content my tortured and almost distracted mind. You told me that if your Parents were willing you would marry me. You know they will not consent willingly that you may marry any gentleman. Why not then marry the man you say you love better, and prefer to all others. I am sure you will never have cause to regret it unless I out live your affection, which I hope never would, or could be. If you will not promise me now, that you will marry me under the present circumstances, must I conclude that you never will, and cease to interrogate you on this subject. You may be assured Dear Jane that if you will marry me that your Parents will soon become reconciled to your own choice. You have some relations that will never forsake you in consequence of your taking such a step, but will continue their friendship, and commend you for your course and principles, because they delight in an independent principle. Dearest do not keep me longer in suspense, for days appear to have the length of weeks, weeks months, and months years. Then, Oh, imagine my feelings, knowing that you are the only earthly object of my desire and that upwards of four long weeks have elapsed since I have had the pleasure of enjoying a sight of you, much less than the enjoyment of your society, which is far dearer to me than any thing can be. Now let me close by desiring a candid answer to the above questions. Give me a direct answer.

I will because I can subscribe myself in truth. Yours devotedly, beyond expression
W. G. Coleman

Miss M. J. Heard, Oh let it be Mrs. M. J. Coleman

My love has been spoken, I must bid you adieu,
Yet heaven never smiled on affection more true,
No Heart more devoted earth's compass within,
Than the Heart of your lover, W. G. Coleman

Appendix F
William G. Coleman Letter to John R. Coffey

Aycock, P. O. Claiborne Parish La.
June 1884

Col. John R. Coffee, Flackler, Alabama

Dear Friend and Comrade:

I received your very welcome message on June 2, and I assure you it was as astonishing as it was agreeably surprising, for I had "long since mourned your death" and proud indeed was I to learn of your prolonged existence, and I am sure of your valuable usefulness to your country and friends—in this scroll I can only express my feelings toward you as one finding a long lost friend and a page will have to suffice for the sudden emotion—and as our shadows lengthen we can write often and be closer together by frequent communication. I will give you some of my experiences since the Mexican war. I returned to my farm in 1947 and remained in Alabama until 1850, when I purchased land and moved to this Parish, North La. where I have resided since.

This country was comparatively new when I moved here, land was good and productive, plenty of game and inviting, and until the War we were doing well, successfully planting with a good society built up in 1856 and 1857. I was elected to the legislature with large majority, served that Term out, have filled all the positions I would accept until too old—and feeble—Since I had the mumps in Mexico I have been afflicted with Hydrocile, and as I get older locomotion is more difficult and riding painful. I have raised 11 grown children seven living—all married but one son, all possessed of good sense and energy to make a living above want. My boys entered the army early (except my eldest who was clerk of the court and exempted) passed through the terrible struggle and God spared them all to get home alive and honorable. The wreck swept all the property we possessed except our homes which we went to work with willing hands to make our living—with all our Negro property suddenly freed—in their brazen effrontery and stupidity backed up to U. S. muskets and carpet baggers over us for a long time. I actually got to hating the Government for which we had borne the Stars and Stripes on the arid plains of Mexico—and to tell the truth I have but little respect for it as administered since the war.

There is five of my old Company live near me moved to this country with me—and four more of our old regiment living near by. They seem to venerate our old Campaign and the lengthening of our shadows brings us into closer order. I trust Col. Coffee I have made peace with a merciful God whose goodness you have so kindly invited me to. I joined the Baptist Church in ___ and have been constantly striving to be ready for inspection, at Resurrection. I hope we will pass muster on that Great day.

You speak of being fearful of worrying me by the length of your letter—far from that. I could have read a book though written by you—now as we have the road blazed out lets keep up the communication. I frequently refer to my old Diary that I kept every day during the 12 months. I know you would love to read it. You speak of what we enjoined on each other at Veny, Ariz. I remember it well. I will never forget either of those days that we were making history and fame for an ungrateful country—that leaves us poor old veterans without a mere stipendiary to supply the ordinary demands of life. Now I am done—No. 1—and ask you to answer immediately—and then we can go into a communication of detail. I have the good luck and honor of having the company of my careful good wife down the declivity of life who with the balance of my family and old soldiers join me in love abundant to you and your family. God bless you.

W. G. Coleman

Appendix G

Appendix to the Congressional Globe
p. 186-188
29th Congress .... 2n Session
Alabama Volunteers-Mr. Reuben Chapman

Alabama Volunteers
Speech by Mr. R. Chapman
of Alabama
In the House of Representatives
February 1, 1847

The rules having been suspended, on the motion of Mr. Chapman, of Alabama, he submitted the following resolutions, to wit:

"Resolved, That the President of the United States be requested to communicate to this House any information in his possession, or in the War Department, showing reasons why the Alabama regiment of Volunteers under the command of Colonel John R. Coffey, was retained on the Rio Grand, and not allowed to advance to participate in the battle at Monterrey, while other regiments from other states who arrived long subsequent to the Alabama regiment in the hostile county, were permitted to go in advance and take part in the battle.

Resolved further, That the President of the United States be requested to inform this House of what offense and what laws or regulations of the army, Brigadier General Shields commanding at Tampico, Mexico deprived Lieutenant John McDuff, of the Jackson County company of the Alabama volunteer regiment, commanded by Colonel John R. Coffey of this command, and ordered him home without giving him the benefit of a court of inquiry or a court martial to inquire into the charges, if any, against him.

Mr. CHAPMAN said:

Mr. Speaker: I am at all times adverse to consuming the time of this House more particularly in relation to subjects that may not be as interesting elsewhere as in my own district. Heretofore as all who observed my course will bear me witness, I have taken up as little of the time of the House as any member in it. On the present occasion, I feel myself called upon to explain the object I have in submitting the resolutions just read to the House: it is due to myself as well as to this body that I shall do so. And first, Mr. Speaker I will remark, that I do not expect this House to remedy the evils set forth in the resolutions except as far as the publication of the information call for may affect the object. I do not propose that the General Taylor shall be censured by this House for the injustice to the Alabama volunteers referred to in the first resolution, or that General Shields shall be, for the oppression he has been guilty of towards Lieutenant McDuff in the second. I do call upon this House to exercise the power, the existence of which no one can deny, to obtaining the information from the executive department on the subjects referred to with a view of publishing it to the people in order that the wrongs, if wrongs have been committed may come in an authorative form under their observation; that the high military officers who committed them may be at least punish by their condemnation, if their acts warrant condemnation.

It is due to myself, Mr. Speaker to say further that before I left Alabama last fall I saw many newspaper paragraphs, and heard much said among the people of the State, on the subject referred to in the first resolution—of the injustice to the Alabama volunteers, by keeping them at Camargo on the Rio Grand, while the volunteers from other States, who reached the seat of war long subsequent to them, were allowed to go in advance and participate in the battle of Monterrey. This could not fail to attract attention among the people of the State, and call forth speculations and opinions sometimes quite unfavorable to the regiment and the officers. These reports have so generally circulated, that they have made impressions upon the minds of the people of Alabama, such as can only be removed by the publication of the official reports on the subject, if any have been made.

Mr. Speaker, I have been pained to hear these slanderous reports so freely circulated, and I regret to say so often credited against the Alabama regiment, including the officers, and more especially to the injury of the colonel commanding that regiment. How those slanderous reports originated, whether by the indiscreet zeal of General Taylor's friends, for the purpose of excusing him with the people of the

State for what otherwise would have been universally condemned as gross injustice towards these volunteers, or by persons entertaining envious feelings toward Colonel Coffey and the other officers in the regiment, on account of their having succeeded in obtaining the rank they respectively hold, I will not undertake now to decide. Nevertheless, great injury has been inflicted: by falsehoods, the character of the regiment has suffered, and the reputation of the officers has, for the time at least, been grossly traduced. It is my purpose, Mr. Speaker, as far as I can do so by eliciting the truth in an authorative form, to put down these slanders, and vindicate the character of the regiment and the reputation of the officers.

Those persons who turned out so promptly on the first call of their country, and now compose that regiment, are the noblest and most gallant spirits in their State. If any are to be considered above the reach of envy, or saved from the shafts of the slanderer and the defamer, the patriot who takes up arms in his country's cause ought to feel so while engaged in the service. Certainly there is no class of citizens who have a higher claim upon all good men to protect their reputation, or who ought with more confidence to expect the aid of this House to vindicate them, as far as it is in our power to do so, than they have. The volunteers from Alabama asked from General Taylor nothing but justice: They claimed for themselves no privileges, nothing beyond what was due to that description of troops, under like circumstances, form other States. They did not turn out in the service of their country without having a full knowledge of the hardships of the campaign before them; of the dangers and difficulties that would beset them; and, above all, they well understood the responsibility and duties of a soldier. But they expected, as the reward for all their sufferings, to share the honors of the campaign. They went to meet in mortal strife the enemies of their county—to participate in the battles, and reap their portion of the laurels won. It was this hope that smoothed their path and buoyed up their spirits. They were willing to perform their full part in the more arduous but less glorious duties of a soldier's life. Not a word of complaint would have been uttered by them on account of the order under which they were detained in the loathsome and sickly valley of the Rio Grande, guarding stores and provisions, instead of marching forward to participate in the honors of the battle of Monterrey, if there had not been selected for that service in their place volunteers from other States who were less prompt in turning out in their country's cause, and who reached the seat of war long subsequent to them.

I am well aware, Mr. Speaker, that it is not the business of Congress, nor would it be prudent in the Executive, to embarrass the commanding general by limiting his power in the selection of the troops for a particular service; but in making his selections for the more honorable as well as the less agreeable, he ought to observe such rules as will dispense justice in the army. When there is necessity for departing from that rule, which all will agree to be a just one, he ought to give his reasons—state why the exception was made. This is the information I desire. It may be that reasons has been assigned that will exempt General Taylor from blame, and relieve the Alabama volunteers from the injury they have suffered in their reputation, and their State from the seeming indignity consequent upon making our regiment the exception to a just and equitable rule. Because of this apparent injustice unexplained, the Alabama volunteers do complain, their friends are mortified, and their State feels the indignity that they were kept back when ardently desiring an opportunity to meet the enemy, and their proper position assigned to others who were long subsequent to them in reaching the hostile county.

I have, Mr. Speaker, to ask the indulgence of the House while I read at the Clerk's desk a remonstrance, the result of a meeting composed of the officers of the Alabama regiment, held at Camargo the 25th of October last, on the subject mentioned in the resolution. This remonstrance was, as I am informed, adopted unanimously. It is addressed to General Taylor, in language as respectful as possible, but at the same time it sets out the causes of their grievances so fully, so plainly, and so much better than I could do for them, that I prefer their own statement of all the facts. If the remonstrance has ever been answered, I am not informed it.

The remonstrance was then read as follows:

"Camp Near Camargo, Mexico
October 23, 1846

"At a meeting of the officers of the Alabama regiment, to take into consideration their grievances, and, if possible, suggest a remedy for the same, Colonel John R. Coffey was called to the chair, and Lieutenant Ketchum appointed Secretary. Whereupon the chairman, in a few remarks, stated the objective of the meeting.
"On motion of Captain Smith, it was
"*Resolved*, That a committee be appointed to draft a remonstrance to send to General Taylor, and a copy of the same to be forwarded to the Governor of the State of Alabama, setting forth our griev-

ances, seek out, as far as possible, the causes thereof, and, in the name of the Alabama Regiment, in a respectful manner, to ask for an explanation.

"On motion of Captain Moore, it was

"*Resolved*, That a committee of ten be appointed, to comprised of one member from each company.

"Whereupon the following gentlemen were appointed on said committee: Captain Pickens, Captain Thomason, Captain Moore, Captain Shelby, Lieutenant Hancock, Lieutenant Thom, Lieutenant Ketchum, Captain Smith, and Captain Cunningham.

"On motion, the meeting adjourned till Thursday evening.

Thursday, October 29, 1846

"Pursuant to adjournment, the committee made the following report:

"To Major General Z. Taylor, Commander-in-chief of the Army of Occupation:

"Although it is an unpleasant task, as well as an unusual liberty in military etiquette, for subordinate officers to lay their grievances before and remonstrate with their superiors, yet a solemn sense of duty we owe to ourselves, as well as to the State from which we came, that high sense of obligation that rests upon ever gentleman and soldier to preserve unsullied this reputation, compels us, on the present occasion, to forgo those considerations of mere delicacy and military etiquette, and avail ourselves of that high constitutional right, guaranteed to every American citizen, to present his complaints and grievances in a manly, dignified, and respectful manner to his superiors, of whatever grade or character, whilst we, in a spirit of truth, candor, and the most perfect respect, call your attention to some of the grievances to which our regiment has been subjected, and vindicate ourselves against certain erroneous impressions, alike prejudicial to our rights, and derogatory to our character as a regiment, and to us as officers.

"In order to a just appreciation of our grievances, we desire to call your attention to the history of the Alabama regiment, and to the disappointments to which we have been subjected. You may remember, for such are the facts, that in the month of May last, two regiments of volunteers were called from Alabama by General Gaines, and soon after the battles of the 8th and 9th of that month; and whilst it was generally understood, throughout the whole country, that our little army, then on the Rio Grande, under your command, was in the most imminent danger, by his order mustered into the service of the United States for six months. A part of both these regiments reached Mexico; the first led by Captain Desha – the first of all of to gird on the sword and fly to the rescue when his country called; the second by Colonel Raiford. These detachments were afterwards disbanded here, by order from the War Department; and the portion of these two regiments which were detained in Mobile, the place of rendezvous, for want of transportation, were disbanded there by virtue of the same order. Still, however, unwilling to abandon the objects they held steadily in view when they left their homes, they proceeded forthwith, not only as individuals, but as companies, to be mustered into the service for twelve months; and at this time composed a large part of the Alabama regiment in the service.

"After various perplexing delays, we finally embarked for the seat of war in the later part of June, and arrived on the sands of Brazos on the 4th day of July, and found in advance of us only three detachments of twelve months troops, to wit: the Louisville legion, first regiment of Tennessee troops, and the Baltimore battalion. There we remained, patiently enduring all the sufferings and privations incident to the season and place, for three weeks, confidently supposing that we would be carried forward into actual service, in the order in which we arrived at the scene of war.

"We were then removed up the Rio Grande some seven or eight miles, to Camp Belknap, where we remained until about the last of August, and until many who had arrived here after us had preceded us up the river. We were then removed to Camargo, where we arrived about the first of September. In the meantime our brigade had been arranged: composed of the Alabama regiment on the right, the Georgia regiment and the Mississippi regiment on the left. We felt sure, then, that we should soon be in active service, and the tedious disappointment and sufferings of the past would soon be forgotten. We had left our homes and friends to fight the battles our country; the eyes of our friends were upon us, they knew that our regiment was among the first at the seat of war, and felt sure that Alabama, the first State in the Union that had troops on the Rio Grande, would have place on the first battle-field in Mexico – the very thing that our regiment, officers and men, of all others, most desired.

"But here again we were doomed to a new mortification. We were halted and posted without a purpose to achieve, whilst the Ohio and Mississippi regiments that had arrived in the field long since we had, were placed in our front and en route to Monterrey, and Alabama's place there was filled by another. Since then, the Georgia regiment has been ordered on, and two companies of our regiment, which started for Monterrey to-day, were ordered back, and the second Kentucky regiment were ordered on in our place; some of whom are on their march. Though our whole brigade is now at Monterrey, we are still left behind, although the right of the brigade. We have been more than twice decimated by the diseases of the camp. Of this we do not complain; it is incident to a soldier's life. At Camp Belknap, we were compelled to carry our provisions and water a mile, and for weeks through salt lakes waist deep; this, it is true, was an unusual hardship; but of this we do not complain. The men under command have been now near five months in the service without receiving one dollar of pay; but still of this we do not complain – for it was for higher and more elevated considerations that induced us to embark in the service. Nor do we claim superiority over any other regiment in the field, either in patriotism or chivalry; but we do claim, in both of these respects, equality with any corps in the service. We do think we are entitled to move on in order in which we came into the field, and to our proper place in the brigade in which we were assigned, until by some act of our own we forfeit that right. And it is that we have been passed by whilst others have been advanced over us, that we do complain. Is this a grievance of which may justly complain? We must leave that with you to determine. We only ask to share in the dangers and honors of the campaign, whatever they may be. But, as if the above grievances were not enough, it has, as we are informed, been represented to our superior officers that we are a disorderly and rebellious regiment, sometimes bordering on a state of mutiny; whilst it is represented at home, to our disparagement, that the opportunity of going to Monterrey was tendered to us, and that we ignobly declined.

"In relation to the first charge, if it has made any impression upon your mind prejudicial to our interests, we beg leave to undeceive you upon that subject, and positively assure you that it has no foundation in truth; and challenge the accuser to point his finger to one legal order that has been disobeyed, one outrage that has been committed in which any considerable number either of officers or men has been engaged, or one act that even savors of mutiny or rebellion; and if the opportunity was tendered to this regiment or any part or parcel of it, either to advance to Monterrey or to any other place beyond the point at which we now are, you best know the fact and to whom the tender was made, and we most respectfully request you, as our commanding officer, and as an act of justice to us, to the State from which we come, and in order to place us in a proper position before our friends at home, to respond to this communication, and to say whether any such offer was ever made to our regiment, or any part thereof, and if so, to whom. We pledge ourselves that was, of all things, what we most desired; and we would hold in most ineffable contempt, any man or set of men, who has or would, on our behalf, for one moment decline such an overture.

"Notwithstanding all the ravages of disease, we are able now to bring into active service more than five hundred men of those under our command, we can speak without delicacy, and we positively assert, that in all the qualifications that constitute gentlemen, patriots, and soldiers, they are unsurpassed by any volunteer troops in the field. Whatever may be the deficiencies of our field and or company officers, and of that is not proper that we should now speak, it is certainly not just that a whole regiment should be consigned to disgrace on account of the weakness, folly, inefficiency, of one, two, or more men. Whilst we have deemed it alike due to you our superior officer, to ourselves, and to our friends at home, who are at a loss to account for our position, to say this much, we beg leave in conclusion to assure you, that in what we have said, we intend not the slightest disrespect to you or any other superior officer; that we will, to our utmost, discharge our duty in whatever position you may be pleased to assign us.

"Please receive assurance of our highest respect and regard."

Besides the charges so extensively circulated as set forth in the remonstrance just read, that the Alabama regiment was a disorderly, rebellious body of men, sometimes bordering on a state of mutiny; and that an opportunity of going forward to the attack on Monterrey had been tendered to the officers of the regiment, who ignobly refuses, I had heard of others, which I sincerely believe to be as destitute of foundation as those mentioned in the remonstrance. One only I will mention; it is this: that General Taylor has assigned as his reason for ordering the Alabama regiment to remain on the Rio Grande, that he had not sufficient confidence in the officers to take them with him to the battle of Monterrey. I say, Mr. Speaker, that I do not believe General Taylor ever assigned such a reason. Nothing had ever occurred to justify him in making such a statement, and I will not believe that he would in the absence of any cause add insult to injury by so expressing himself. I am so well assured myself that there has been no cause heretofore to impair General Taylor's confidence in the officers or the soldiers of the regiment, that I will undertake to say, that if an opportunity had ever occurred to test their valor and their conduct on the field of battle, previous to the movement I have made in their behalf to-day, I would have been relieved altogether from the necessity. The colonel, as well as a considerable proportion of his men, reside in my district. I have known Colonel Coffey intimately for many years, and I take great pleasure in bearing my humble testimony to his high character as a gentleman, and his bravery and every other qualification that belongs to the gallant officer. No man has, or deserves more than he does, the confidence and respect of those who know him. True it is, that he is quite a reserved and unassuming gentleman in his deportment. Perhaps in this age of the world, when men are, I regret to say, more favored in the estimation of many by their vanity and egotism, than by that modesty and reserve that ought to belong to every gentleman, Colonel Coffey may lose caste on that account of his not practicing the usual quantity of presumption in his intercourse among men; but those who know him best appreciate him most. I have an acquaintance with most of the officers in the regiment, and take equal pleasure in saying as much in their behalf—no regiment in the service, I feel confident, has truer or more patriotic officers or who will render more service to the country, and give a better account of themselves when ever an opportunity presents itself. The regiment only requires a proper occasion to prove to General Taylor and the world, that they are fit for any and all the duties that belong to the soldier, and brave and determined enough for any emergency however desperate. Why, then, I ask, Mr. Speaker, was the Alabama regiment, who was the first, or among the first, to respond to the call of their country, and hasten to the seat of war before the others, kept back on the Rio Grande, to suffer so severely by the diseases of that fatal climate, while volunteers from other States, long subsequent to them in the enemy's country, were carried in advance, and in their stead, to fight the battle at Monterrey—as one of the officers of the regiment (Captain Smith) has said, "to win and wear laurels that ought to entwine our brows:"

It has been truly stated in the remonstrance, that a portion of the two regiments at first called out, under the orders of General Gaines, from Alabama, were the first volunteers that reached the seat of war. That gallant officer, General Desha, of Mobile, (whose patriotism on the occasion does him so much honor,) with his company of volunteers, was the first to reach the Rio Grande, after the call for volunteers to relieve General Taylor, when he and his army were supposed to be in imminent danger of falling into the hands of the enemy. The next to arrive there was Colonel Raiford, of Alabama, and his command. It does seem to me, Mr. Speaker, that these circumstances ought to have entitled them, if not to General Taylor's favor, at least to expect full justice from him. I have frequently heard it charged, that the Mexican war has been carried on by the General, or some of those who are supposed to have too much control in his counsels, with a view of making political capital—of breaking the dominant party down, and raising the other party in the estimation of the people. I am not disposed to believe this, Mr. Speaker: it surely cannot be so: but the apparent injustice done to Alabama in this matter, while unexplained, is certainly calculated to encourage the belief among the people of the State. It is well known, Mr. Speaker, that of all the States in the Union, no one has stood more firm in the Democratic faith than Alabama; there, the banner of our party has never trailed in the dust: there, the strong citadel of Democracy has always stood, and I will, I trust, continue to stand proof against every assault. I will not believe, however, that on this account General Taylor has trampled upon the rights of our brave and patriotic regiment, who were the first to rush to his relief. That regiment is composed of men of both the great political parties: they are engaged in a common cause—the noble cause of their country—and have (as we all ought to do in time of war) buried all political differences, and act as a band of brothers in the cause of their common country. The information called for may relieve General Taylor from the suspicions referred to. It is due to him, therefore, as well as to the character of the regiment, and the State to which they belong, that all these things shall be fully explained.

I am well aware, Mr. Speaker, that Alabama has not had her due share in the prosecution of the Mexican war. The people know this in the State, and they feel it. While some States, not so near the seat of war, and with less population, have been allowed to send each several regiments, Alabama has but one. Of this we do not complain. We trust there are sufficient reasons to justify the Administration, and I will not stop to inquire into the cause. I know that the people of Alabama are as ready, and I may say, as anxious to engage in the service of their country as those of any other State in the Union. I believe that instead of one regiment, twenty regiments might be obtained, if called for, in Alabama. In that State scarcely any difference of opinion exists in relation to the war; both parties sustain it. They believe it was forced upon us, and could not have been avoided without national disgrace. The able and unanswerable views upon the subject in the late message of the President, has not met with a more favorable response anywhere than in Alabama. The people of both political parties are resolved to stand upon the ground taken in justification of the war, and will cheerfully pour out their blood and treasure to prosecute it, to conquer a peace, if it becomes necessary, and bring the contest to a glorious termination. Instead of opposition to the war, or stopping to inquire how it was brought on, or might have been avoided, all parties in Alabama are surprised at, and cry out against, Congress for the delay in granting the men and money necessary to prosecute it with energy and efficiency. As far as I am concerned, I have acted upon the subject in conformity to the sentiment in my State, as well as upon my own views of sound policy. I have urged speedy action in all propositions for carrying on the war, and I have voted men and money to the full extent asked for by the Executive. Mr. Speaker, I am equally ready to vote for any measure that has been or may be proposed by the Executive to raise the money to carry on the war. I am not disposed to act the part that some professing Democrats are acting here—claiming to be in favor of the Administration, and the prosecution of the war—voting any amount of appropriation to carry it on, and refusing their support for any measure recommended to raise the money they appropriate. This course seems to me not only inconsistent, but absurd. Those who boldly oppose the war, and refuse to vote supplies to carry it on, are infinitely more consistent, and no more the real enemies of the Administration and the war. I am as reluctant to tax the people as any member on this floor, but when it becomes necessary to carry on a war, a just, an unavoidable war, and sustain the honor of the country, I will give my vote for an adequate tax. My constituents require me to do so, and will sustain me even in voting for a tax on tea and coffee, about which so much has been said.

We all know, that to carry on the war, money must be provided; and I know of no mode by which we carry on this war, if we refuse to lay any tax upon the people. Gentlemen may tell us that we can borrow money; but how can we expect to borrow, unless we make some provision to pay? War has been declared or recognized as existing, by the almost unanimous vote of Congress. It has been going on, at a heavy expense, for many months, and it is likely to continue. The President, as the head of the Government, is required to prosecute, it, and he is responsible for the manner of carrying it on. He has informed us of everything that has been done thus far, and what is proposed to be done hereafter towards bringing the war to a successful termination, relying upon the aid of Congress to enable him to carry out the plan proposed. Congress have, in effect, by their votes, approved of the measures of the Executive; but when the President calls upon us for the necessary means to carry out his measures, and recommends the mode by which the money can best be provided, some of those who gave their votes in favor of the war, and still profess to be in favor of it, vote against the President's recommendations, and it is defeated. Their objection cannot be to the particular plan recommended or they would bring forward some other—but to any plan to enable the President to prosecute the war. I do not propose, Mr. Speaker, to censure other gentlemen for their course upon this or any other subject: they are responsible to their constituents, as I am to mine; but I must say, that professing, as I do, to be the friend of the Administration, and in favor of the war, if I had, by my votes here, defeated the measures recommended by him as necessary to carry on the operations of the Government and prosecute the war, my constituents would not fail to distinguish between my professions at home and my acts here, and they would certainly act accordingly.

Mr. Speaker, having digressed somewhat from the subject immediately under consideration, I will ask the indulgence of the House, and proceed to make a few remarks on the second resolution. It is due to the House, as well as to myself, that I shall submit the facts, as far as they have come into my possession, upon which I felt myself bound to make the call upon the President proposed in that resolution. About three weeks ago, I received from Colonel John R. Coffey, of the Alabama regiment, a letter dated at Tampico, Mexico, on the subject of the arrest of Lieutenant McDuff, of his regiment. On the very day received the letter, I called upon the Secretary of War, and submitted it to him. The case, as set forth in the letter of Colonel Coffey, appears to me to be one of such enormity, so novel—the exercise of such high-handed tyranny and oppression—that I expect from the Secretary the most prompt action upon it. In this I was altogether mistaken. He did not seem to consider the case as one of sufficient magnitude to engage his immediate action. The Secretary has either become so familiar with such scenes in the course of his official duties, as not to feel, as I confess I did, for the outrages upon the rights of Lieutenant McDuff, who is my constituent; or, if he did, his manner and deportment on the occasion was so cold, so stiff, and unconcerned, as to inspire in me but little hope of obtaining redress at his hands. I then called upon the President, who very promptly, after hearing the facts, promised to see the Secretary of War, and have it speedily attended to. For this purpose I left Colonel Coffey's with him. I next heard of the letter in the hands of the Secretary of War, who promised to inform me of his actions in relation to the case, that I might, as requested to do by Colonel Coffey, communicate with Lieutenant McDuff in Alabama. After waiting some time for the promised information, without receiving any, I sent for and obtained the letter of Colonel Coffey. I have not received a reply up to this day from the Secretary of War, or from any one else, in relation to the case. And as I am requested by the colonel of the regiment, as far as possible, to protect the rights of Lieutenant McDuff, who, in his opinion, and in mine, has been most outrageously treated, and having failed altogether in obtaining any redress from the Executive branch of the Government, after several attempts to do so. I have, in the honest discharge of my duty, brought the case to the consideration of this House. That the House may be in possession of the facts, I send to the Clerk's table to be read the letter of Colonel Coffey, referred to.

It was read as follows:

Tampico, Mexico, December 28, 1846

"Dr. Chapman: General Shields, commander of this post has issued an order that Lieutenant McDuff, of the Jackson county company, should be relieved from his command until farther orders from the President, and that he shall report himself to the assistant quartermaster at this place for transportation the states: which, of course, McDuff is bound to do, or disobey an order.

"Now, I am of opinion myself, that the lieutenant is justly entitled to a court of inquiry or a court martial, without being sent from his command.

"I understand the facts to be these: a man was sent from a detachment of a working party to that company, under guard, to be guarded by it: the higher officers of the company were absent; McDuff himself was that very morning, and for sometime previous had been, reported on the morning reports sick. The prisoner was not taken charge of immediately; the general rode down, called Lieutenant McDuff from his bed in the tent, when a short conversation took place as to who was in command: McDuff telling him that he was wholly unable for duty, and was so reported daily.

"The company are loth (*sic*) to give him up; he is a good soldier, and at home a worthy young man, and a good citizen; he has raised a family of fatherless young brothers and sisters in good credit, his father having been killed in the army. This is the third campaign for himself; one in the Creek, one in Florida, and this; and before this, I have never heard aught against him.

"Now, my object is writing to you is, to ask you to intercede with the President, and get his hand of decision stayed, until the facts of the whole circumstance are fully made known, either before him or a court.

"I would be glad to hear from his case, as well as McDuff's, when you make the trial.
"Truly, your friend,
"John R. Coffey.

"N. B. Lieutenant McDuff will go from here to his home at Bellefonte, where he or any one there of your friends will be glad to hear from you. His witnesses, of course, would be those who were present at the time.   J. R. C."

I have such confidence in Colonel Coffee, knowing him to be a gentleman of unquestionable veracity, so discreet and cautious, that I rely most confidently upon the account of the transaction as stated in the letter. If the facts are as Colonel Coffey has stated them, all must agree, that the case is one as remarkable for its enormity, its tyranny, and oppression, as any that can be perpetrated against the rights of an officer. I can scarcely believe that the annuals of military operations can furnish any example of such an outrage; I have, Mr. Speaker, some acquaintance with Lieutenant McDuff; and there is now in this city, a gentleman of high character, from the same county, who is intimately acquainted with him. From my own knowledge, as well as on the information obtained from that gentleman, (Mr. Scott) I can fully corroborate the statement of Colonel Coffey, as to his good character at home. He is a man of high respectability, and as brave and patriotic as any officer in the service. Where did General Shields find his authority for thus seizing upon an officer commissioned by the Governor of Alabama, and sending him, perhaps as a prisoner, from his command, some three or four thousand miles to his home in Alabama, without giving him a trial, without allowing him the opportunity of making his defense—of being confronted by the charges, or the witnesses against him, or of producing those in his defense? Besides the violation of all the military laws and army regulations of which I have any knowledge, every principle of justice has been outraged. An officer, who (as Colonel Coffey states) was then, and had been for some days previously, confined by sickness, and so reported to him every morning as unfit for duty, to be thus dragged from his sick bed, and hastened off without a hearing, and without mercy, irrespective of his commission and his rank, is shocking to every feeling of humanity. [At that point, Mr. Douglass, of Illinois,[323] remarked (though he did not address the speaker,) in substance, that it was improper to bring such charges against General Shields, in the absence of proof.] Mr. C. resumed. Mr. Speaker, I hear it said by the gentleman from Illinois, that the resolution is unsupported by proof. Did he hear the letter from the colonel of the regiment read? Is that not proof? I consider it proof of the most certain character. The colonel undertakes to state a transaction that took place in his regiment—all the facts stated he must have known as the commanding officer officially. I cannot conceive how I could have introduced stronger proof, in the absence of the report from the War Department; to obtain which, the resolution has been offered.

Mr. Speaker, great as the outrage is against Lieutenant McDuff, that is of but trifling moment, when we consider, in comparison, the injuries influence to the public service such lawless proceeding is calculated to have. If an officer, however high in command, is to be allowed, of his own will—perhaps when under the influence of passion—thus to deprive an inferior officer, commissioned by his State, and send him home in disgrace, without allowing any trial or investigation, how can you expect to keep up the army? Who will go into the service, if such acts of oppression go unpunished? If the facts are as Colonel Coffey states, Lieutenant McDuff who has been so roughly dealt with, and for the time disgraced, was guilty of no improper conduct. But however high his offence, he had a clear right, under the military law, to a court of inquiry, or a court martial. There is not authority in the commanding general to punish an officer without trial. It is in vain to say that this injured officer can return to his regiment, and demand a court-martial. I understand Colonel Coffey to state that a court has been refused him. But he has been hurried off home, in disgrace, some three or four thousand miles from his witnesses: he is now

---

[323] Senator Stephen Douglas was from the state of Illinois and spoke in defense of General Shields, also from Illinois.

suffering all the horrors of a disgraced man, although innocent of any offence. The injury to him cannot be repaired by any proceeding now; but such scenes may, by proper action, be prevented from occurring hereafter.

Mr. Speaker, I am actuated by no unfriendly motives toward General Taylor or General Shields, in presenting these resolutions to the House; nor is it my object to prejudice the service by exposing the facts referred to. On the contrary, while I consider it to be my duty, as the Representative (and the oldest from my State on this floor) of the colonel of the regiment, of Lieut. McDuff and a large number of the Alabama volunteers, to bring these subjects to the notice of the House, after having failed in obtaining any redress or information at the War Department, I deeply regret the necessity of troubling the House at this time with them. I ask that the resolutions may be adopted.

Appendix H
Order No. 17
Major General Robert Patterson
May 5, 1847

HEADQUARTERS OF THE ARMY
Jalapa, May 5th 1847
Order No. 17

In accordance with orders from the Headquarters of the Army, the Tennessee Cavalry, the 1st and 2d Tennessee Regiments, the 3d and 4th Illinois, the Georgia and Alabama regiments of Infantry, and Capt. Williams' Company of Kentucky Volunteers, will be held in readiness to march to Vera Cruz, thence to embark for New Orleans, where they will be severally and honorably mustered out of the service of the United States, and paid off by the proper officers on duty there.

To facilitate the march, Col. Campbell, with the regiment of Tennessee horse, the 1st and 2d Tennessee Infantry, and the company of Kentucky Volunteers, will march tomorrow morning, the 6th inst.

The 2d and 4th Illinois regiments, under Col. Forman, will march tomorrow at 2 p.m. The Georgia and Alabama regiments, under Col. Jackson will march on the morning of the 7th inst.

The troops will march with their arms, ten rounds ammunition, and their personal effects, and will turn in at this place all tents, and such other articles of camp equipage, as may not be indispensable on the return march.

Each man will take in his haversack hard bread for four days, and Bacon for two days. The Brigade Commissaries will obtain from the Chief Commissary, money to purchase fresh beef, on the road, for two days.

The Quartermasters of the command will make the proper requisitions on the Acting Quartermaster General for the necessary requisitions.

In promulgating this order for these gallant regiments to return to the U. States, the Major, General, while he regrets that the term of their service will not afford another opportunity for these troops to gather additional fame in the future events of this already brilliant campaign, cannot forget that the recollections of a glorious past will be carried to their homes. The services of the twelve-month's Volunteers will always be perpetuated in their country's history with the remembrances of Monterey, Buena Vista, Vera Cruz and Sierra Gordo.

The Major General avails himself, on this occasion, to take leave of the 1st and 2nd Pennsylvania, the South Carolina and the New York Volunteers, and to tender his thanks to Brigadier General Quitman, and them, for their obedience to orders, attention to duty, and their faithful, ready and cheerful support under all emergencies since they have been under his command, and he assures these fine corps, and their gallant and accomplished commander, that he will always be happy to meet, and to serve with them.

By order of Major General Patterson

Wm. H. French, Acting Asst. Adjt General

Bibliography and Sources

Alabama Department of Archives and History, Return of Captain Zechariah Thomason (SPR 338) (Copy in possession of the author)

Alabama Historical Quarterly, vol. 20, 1985 (Alabama Department of Archives and History) pp. 188-189

Alabama Records, compiled by Kathleen Paul Jones and Pauline Jones Gandrud, v. 244, Perry County (Blewett Company, Columbus, Mississippi 1980) pp. 19 and 24

Albany Patriot, published in Albany, Georgia, June 17, 1846, December 9, 1846

American Military History, Army Historical Series, *THE MEXICAN WAR AND AFTER* (Office of the Chief of Military History, United States Army) pp. 1-16

Aycock, Jesse, Officer's Certificate of Disability, signed before Drew Ferguson, Clerk of the District Court, Claiborne Parish, Louisiana dated November 8, 1882 (unpublished) (Copy in possession of the author)

Aztec Club, *The Constitution of the Aztec Club of 1847 and List of Members* (Aztec Club, New York, 1900)

Aztec Club of 1847, Mexican War Officers Data Base—www.Aztecclub.com/search.asp; *Palmetto Regiment, South Carolina in Mexican War*, www.aztecclub.com/palmetto/pal.htm pp. 311-320; Biographies of Early Club Officers, pp. 247-253; *Contemporary Accounts of the Mexican War*, pp. 582-583, 622-627, 634-635, 668-675, 704-707 and 1014-1015.

Bailey, James Frances, Declaration of James F. Bailey in Perry County, Alabama Probate Court, dated November 1, 1850 (unpublished) (Copy in possession of the author)

Bauer, Karl Jack, *The Mexican War, 1846-1848*, The Wars of the United States Series (Macmillan, New York, NY, 1974)

The Beacon, published in Greensboro, Alabama: June 6, 1846, July 4, 1846, September 5, 1846, January 16, 1846, January 16, 1847 and March 27, 1847

Biographical and Historical Memoirs of Northwestern Louisiana (The Southern Publishing Company, Chicago and Nashville, 1890) pp. 405-406

Bonin, Martha Louise Henry, Coleman Bible Records; Pedigree Chart for Coleman ancestors; Transcript of the Mexican War Diary of William G. Coleman (unpublished) (Copies in possession of the author)

Brewer, Willis, *Alabama: Her History Resources, War Record and Public Men* (The Reprint Company, Spartanburg, S. C., 1975) Originally published in 1872, p. 588

Brooks, Nathan, *A Complete History of the Mexican War 1846-1848* (The Rio Grande Press, Inc., Chicago, 1965) pp. 92, 96-97 and 163

Booth, Andrew B., compiler, *Records of Louisiana Confederate Soldiers and Louisiana Confederate Commands*, 3 vols (New Orleans, 1920)

Butler, Steven R., *Alabama Volunteers in the War with Mexico 1846-1848* (Descendants of Mexican War Veterans, Richardson Texas, 1996) pp. 1-8, 11-18, 21-24, 42, 48-50, 57-59, 61-82, 92 and 96

Butler, Steven R., *The Eutaw Rangers in the War with Mexico* (Descendants of Mexican War Veterans, Richardson Texas, 1998) pp. 8, 11, 13-14, 20-21, 24-25, 27-28, 30-31,. 39, 40, 42-44, 51-52, 56, 59-61, 63-65, 67, 69, 72-73, 75, 80, 82, 88, 90, 92, 96-98, 100-104, 106-107, 114-117

Butler, Steven R. "ALABAMA VOLUNTEERS IN THE MEXICAN WAR" *Alabama Genealogical Society Magazine*, Volume 23, Numbers 1 and 2 (Samford University, Birmingham, Alabama) pp. 37-40

Calhoures, J. D. (M. D.), General Affidavit related to W. G. Coleman application for a Mexican War pension on the subject of the Coleman's Mexican War related disability signed November 8, 1882 before Drew Ferguson, Clerk of the District Court, Claiborne Parish, Louisiana. (unpublished) (Copy in possession of the author)

Callan, John F., compiler, *The Military Laws of the United States, Relating to the Army, Marine Corps, Volunteers, Militia, and to Bounty Lands and Pensions* (John Murphy & Company, Baltimore, 1858) p. 38.

Chance, Joseph E. ed., *The Mexican War Journal of Captain Franklin Smith* (University of Mississippi Press, Jackson, Mississippi, 1994) pp. 10-14, 17, 19-23, 27-31, 34, 39-49, 54-55, 61, 66, 80, 92, 96, 99, 110-111, 118, 138, 153 and 159.

Charleston Mercury, August 25, 1848

Christensen, Carol and Thomas, *The U. S.—Mexican War* (Bay Books, San Francisco, 1998) pp. 30-35, 38-40, 43, 46, 48, 51, 52, 58, 59, 60, 62-65, 75-78, 124, 125, 145, 164, 166-173, 178-180, 182-184, 187-189

Coffey, Colonel John Reid, Letter to Captain W. W. S. Bliss, Assistant Adjutant General, dated July 4, 1846, from Brazos Island, Texas, as quoted by Steven R. Butler in *Alabama Volunteers* in the MEXICAN WAR, 1846-1848, p. 7.

Coffey, Colonel John Reid, Letter to Brigadier General Gideon Pillow, dated September 12, 1846 in Camargo, Mexico, as quoted by Steven R. Butler in *Alabama Volunteers* in the MEXICAN WAR, 1846-1848, pp. 13-14

Coleman, Benjamin, Muster Records for Service in the South Carolina Militia dated June 6-September 1, 1812 and Company Pay Records for June, July and August 1812 (Copy in possession of the author)

Coleman, Ben R., Affidavit of Witness for Widow's Pension for the Mexican War service of William G. Coleman's spouse Mary Jane Coleman, filed in Claiborne Parish, Louisiana on December 15, 1888 before Drew Ferguson, Clerk of the District Court (unpublished) (Copy in possession of the author)

Coleman, Mary Jane, Application for Accrued Pension (Widows) Claiborne Parish, Louisiana, dated December 15, 1888, filed in Claiborne Parish, Louisiana (unpublished) (Copy in possession of the author)

Coleman, Mary Jane, Mexican War Pension, Declaration of Widow for Pension (form 3—038), dated December 15, 1888, filed in Claiborne Parish, Louisiana (unpublished) (Copy in possession of the author)

Coleman, William Goforth, Mexican War Diary (unpublished) (Transcript in possession of the author)

Coleman, William Goforth, Mexican War Muster Rolls, June 13-December 31, 1846; Muster in Roll in Mobile, Alabama dated June 13, 1846; Muster Out Roll in New Orleans dated May 27, 1847 (unpublished) (Copy in possession of the author)

Coleman, William Goforth, Application for Service Pension—War of 1846 For Captain W. G. Coleman of Capt. W. G. Coleman Company, 1st Reg't of Ala Volunteers, filed by A. W. Kenaday, Washington, D. C. dated February 4, 1887 (unpublished) (Copy in possession of the author)

Coleman, William Goforth, Letter to Colonel John R. Coffee dated June 1884 (unpublished) (Copy in possession of the author)

Coleman, William Goforth, Letter to Mary Jane Heard dated February 3, 1844, (unpublished); (Handwritten copy of the original letter in possession of the author)

Coleman, William Goforth, Declaration of Mexican War service to acquire Mexican War land bounty title in Perry County, Alabama Probate Court before Judge James F. Bailey, dated September 28, 1850 (unpublished) (Copy in possession of the author)

Coleman, William Goforth, Declaration for Service Pension, War of 1846 with Mexico, dated only 1885, the month and day being omitted in the original filed in Claiborne Parish, Louisiana and witnessed by Ben R. Coleman and J. R. Ramsey (unpublished) (Copy in possession of the author)

Coleman, William Goforth, Declaration in Claiborne Parish, Louisiana before Drew Ferguson, Clerk of the District Court, on March 28, 1887 (unpublished) (Copy in possession of the author)

Coleman, William Goforth, Affidavit of W. G. Coleman before Drew Ferguson, Clerk of the District Court in Claiborne Parish, Louisiana dated November 8, 1882 (unpublished) (Copy in possession of the author)

Columbia Encyclopedia, Sixth Edition (Columbia University Press, 2001)

Columbus Times, Columbus, Georgia, June, 9, 1846 (EXTRA), July 24, 1846, July 29, 1846

Confederate Veteran, v. XIX, October 1911, No. 10, "William Curtis Mayes"

Congressional Globe, 29th Congress 2n Session, Alabama Volunteers-Mr. Reuben Chapman, Alabama Volunteers, Speech by Mr. R. Chapman of Alabama In the House of Representatives, February 1, 1847, pp. 186-189

Cooper, William J., *Jefferson Davis, American* (Alfred A. Knopf, New York, 2000) pp. 126, 129-140, 146-156

Copeland, Fayette, *Kendall of the Picayune* (University of Oklahoma Press, Norman and London, 1943) pp. 42, 122-127, 129, 134, 147, 149-150, 152-154, 159, 161, 178, 184, 190, 195, 198

Crossroads of South Texas, Summer 1998, Volume 19, No. 2. "Ancestors of Jacques Donald Robinson"

Daughters of the American Revolution, Application for Membership in the National Society Number 527355 for Mrs. (Martha) Louise Henry Bonin a descendant of Casper Gallman (i.e., Coleman) dated July 17, 1970 (unpublished) (Copy in possession of the author)

Daughters of Colonial Wars, Inc. in the State of Louisiana, Application for Membership to the National Society of Mrs. Martha Louise Henry Bonin for Henry Gallman dated August 22, 1978 (unpublished) (Copy in possession of the author)

Davies, Wallace E., "The Mexican War Veterans as an Organized Group," *The Mississippi Valley Historical Review 35*, June 1948 to March 1949, pp. 21-38

Davis, Robert S., Jr., *Alabama Officers in the Mexican War, 1846-1848*, pp. 10-11

Del Castillo, Richard G., *The Treaty of Guadeloupe Hidalgo: A Legacy of Conflict* (University of Oklahoma Press, Norman, Oklahoma, 1990)

Dill, Harry F. and William Simpson, *Some Slaveholders and Their Slaves, Union Parish, Louisiana 1839-1865* (Heritage Books, Inc., Bowie, Maryland, 1997)

Dillon, Lester R., *American Artillery in the Mexican War* (Presidial Press, Austin, 1975) pp. 19-20, 23 and 25.

Drake, Paul, J. D., A Dictionary of Historical Terms for Genealogists (Heritage Books, Inc., Bowie, Maryland, 1994) pp. 9-10, 31, 116, 147, 180, 197

Dyer, Brainerd, *Zachary Taylor* (Louisiana State University Press, Baton Rouge, 1946) pp. 96-98, 215, 239

Eisenhower, John S. D., *So Far From God; The U.S. War with Mexico, 1846-1848* (Random House, New York, 1989) pp. 106-112, 169, 256-257, 296, and 369

Executive Document No. 65, 31st Congress, "Message from the President of the United States communicating the report of Lieutenant Webster of a survey of the Gulf coast at the mouth of the Rio Grande, " July 27, 1850, pp. 3-4

Family History Centers, Church of Jesus Christ of Latter Day Saints, Microfilms 1462788 and 1462789; International Genealogical Index

Federal Writers' Project, *New Orleans City Guide* (Boston, 1938) p. 313

Ferrell, Robert H., *Monterrey is Ours!: The Mexican War Letters of Lieutenant Dana, 1845-1847* (University Press of Kentucky, Lexington, 1990)

Flower, Mrs. C. Guiles, Mrs. Alice McKee, and Mrs. Clara Galbraith Royse Morgan, Register Generals, provided information about the genealogy and Colonial Wars records of Henry Gallman (i.e., Coleman) from information located in the South Carolina Colonial Journals and Indian Affairs records of the State of South Carolina (Not known to be published) (Copy in possession of the author)

Flynt, Wayne, *Alabama Baptists; Southern Baptists in the Heart of Dixie* (The University of Alabama Press, Tuscaloosa and London, 1998)

Frost, John, *Pictorial History of Mexico and the Mexican War* (Thomas, Copperwait and Company, Philadelphia, 1848) pp. 266-268

Gallman, Henry, Last Will and Testament, December 28, 1765 located in Charleston, South Carolina Miscellaneous Wills file for 1767-1771, Volume RR, pp. 180-182 (Not known to be published) (Copy in possession of the author)

Gandee, Leo R., 327 Carpenter Street, West Columbia, South Carolina, Letter to Mrs. Robert O. Scott, 129 Prairie Avenue, New Iberia, Louisiana, dated April 13, 1976 outlining the history of the Gallman family in Europe, Switzerland and South Carolina (unpublished) (Copy in possession of the author)

Generations, A Newsletter for the Mayes and Hatten Families, "In Search of Andrew J.," May 29, 1998, v. 1, Issue 2, p. 1, edited by Ann Mayes Golias

Georgia Telegraph, published in Macon, Georgia, August 30, 1845, September 9, 1845, May 12, 1846, June 9, 1846, September 26, 1846, August 4, 1846, August 18, 1846 and September 1, 1846, September 14, 1846

Greene, Glen Lee, *House Upon a Rock, About Southern Baptists in Louisiana* (Parthenon Press, Nashville, Tennessee, 1973) pp. 182-183

Hardee, Captain William J. dispatch to Brigadier General Zachary Taylor dated April 26, 1846 at Matamoras, Mexico

Harris, W. Stuart, *Perry County Heritage*, Volume I, "A History of Perry County" and "Memories of Perry County" (Perry County, Alabama Historical and Preservation Society, 1991) pp. 51-53, 60, 72-74, 103, 138-142, 174-175, 192

Harrison, Benjamin D., Declaration in Claiborne Parish before Drew Ferguson, Clerk of the District Court, in Claiborne Parish, Louisiana and dated March 28, 1887 (unpublished) (Copy in possession of the author)

Hawkins, Captain Edgar S. dispatch to W. W. Bliss, Assistant Adjutant-General, Army of Occupations, Texas dated May 10, 1846

Heard, John G., Affidavit of Witness for a widow's pension for Mary Jane Coleman made before Drew Ferguson, Clerk of the District Court, Claiborne Parish, Louisiana, dated December 15, 1888 (unpublished) (Copy in possession of the author)

Heitman, Francis, *Historical Register and Dictionary of the United States Army, From Its Organization September 29, 1789, to March 2, 1903* (University of Illinois Press, Urbana, 1965) vol. I, p. 265

Herbert, Colonel Hilary A., "History of the 8th Alabama Volunteer Regiment, CSA" edited by Maurice S. Fortin, *The Alabama Historical Quarterly*, v. XXXIX, 1977, No. 1, 2, 3 and 4 (Alabama Department of Archives and History, Montgomery, Alabama) pp. 56, 66, 79, 110, 139, 176, 178, 301-215, 306-317, 662

Herrera, José Joaquín, Acting President of the Republic of Mexico. A Proclamation denouncing the United States intervention to annex Texas dated June 4, 1845 in Mexico City, Mexico.

Hiney, Elias F., "Diary of Mexican-American War" Property of Susanne "Sam" Behling, the great great granddaughter of Elias Hiney; © 1997, published in the Fall/Winter Edition of the *Mexican War Journal*, a publication of the Descendants of Mexican War Veterans

Hopson, Robert, Petition of Robert Hobson, a free man of color, General Assembly Petitions 2469-01, South Carolina Department of Archives and History

Horgan, Paul, *Great River: The Rio Grande in North American History* (Holt, Rinehart, and Winston, New York, 1968) vol. 2, p. 67.

Jackson, Charles Green, Mexican War Pension, Affidavit of Witness (November 1, 1888); Declaration for Pension (February 26, 1907); Drop Order and Report dated August 4, 1911 (unpublished) (Copy in possession of the author)

Jackson, Colonel Henry R., letter to the public dated November 2, 1846 from Camp Monterrey, Mexico published in the *Savannah Republican* on December 9, 1846

James, Marquis, *The Raven, A Biography of Sam Houston* (The Paperback Library, Inc., New York, 1929) pp. 214-215, 251-254, 257-259, 262, 278-290, 292

Jerger, Dr. Jeanette L., *A Medical Miscellany* (Heritage Books, Inc., Bowie, Maryland, 1995) pp. 27, 38, 50, 152, 166

Johannsen, Robert Walker, *To the Halls of the Montezumas: The Mexican War in the American Imagination* (Oxford University Press, New York, 1985) pp. 41, 87 and 205-206

Journal of the Congress of the Confederate States of America, 1862-1865, v. I, (Government Printing Office, Washington, February 1, 1904)

Kenly, John R., *Memoirs of a Maryland Volunteer* (J. B. Lippincott and Company, Philadelphia, 1873) as quoted by Steven R. Butler in *Alabama Volunteers,* p. 45

Lasswell, Lynda J., The First Regiment of Mississippi Infantry in the Mexican War and Letters of Jefferson Davis concerning the war (Microform, Mississippi State University Library, Starkville, Mississippi)

Lea, Tom, *The King Ranch,* Volume I (Little, Brown and Company, Boston, 1952) vol. 1, pp. 36 and 247.

Lechie, Robert, *From Sea to Shining Sea, From the War of 1812 to the Mexican War, The Saga of America's Expansion* (Harper Perennial, New York, 1993) pp. 359, 401-405, 413-414, 503, 509-513, 519-524, 526-547, 564-570, 584-600

Louisiana Tombstone Inscriptions, v. VIII and v. XXIV

Lovelace, Julia Murfee, *A History of Siloam Baptist Church, Marion, Alabama* (Birmingham Press, Birmingham, Alabama, 1943) pp. 43 and 54

Malone, Dumas, *Dictionary of American Biography* (Charles Scribner's Sons, New York, 1933) vol. 3, pp. 371-372; vol. 14, pp. 306 and 603; vol. 15, pp. 15-16 and 315-316; vol. 17, pp. 106-107; vol. 19, pp. 19 and 83; and vol. 20, pp. 536-537

Map 3, Congree River Plat dated 1759, copy supplied by Ben E. Coleman, Shreveport Louisiana, displaying early Gallman family land acquisitions in South Carolina (unpublished) (Copy in possession of the author)

Matamoros Gazette, April 11, 1846

McCaffrey, James M., *Army of Manifest Destiny: The American Soldier in the Mexican War 1846-1848* (1942)

McCord, Howard F., *Baptists of Bibb County*, A Denominational Salute to the People Called Baptists in Cahawba (Bibb) County, Alabama, 1817-1974 (Printed in U. S. A., 1979) pp. 11, 28-29

McCraw, Carol Joyce, compiler, *Its McCraw not McGraw*

Meyer, Jack Allen, *South Carolina in the Mexican War—A History of the Palmetto Regiment of Volunteers, 1846-1917* (South Carolina Department of Archives and History, 1996) pp. 7, 15, 18-19, 29*fn*, 33-34, 41, 49, 55*fn*, 57-65, 88-91, 112-114, 179-182, 191, 201, 257 and 272-273.

Meyers, William Starr, ed., *The Mexican War Diary of George B. McClellan* (Princeton University, Princeton, 1917)

Miller, Robert Ryal, *The Mexican War Journal and Letters of Ralph W. Kirkham* (Texas A & M University Press, College Station, 1991) pp. 10-11 and 19

Mobile Daily Advertiser, Saturday, May 23, 1846

Monroe, Haskell M., Jr. and James T. McIntosh, Editors, *The Papers of Jefferson Davis* (Louisiana State University Press, Baton Rouge, 1971) vol. I, 1iii-1xv, vol. 3, pp. 22-52, 123-162; vol. 3, II, pp. 16-19, 66 and 250.

Moore, Caroline T., *Abstracts of the Wills of the State of South Carolina, 1760—1784*, pp. 96 and 121

Muscogee Democrat, published in Columbus, Georgia, June 13, 1846

National Archives, Washington, D. C., copy of muster rolls of Company C, First Regiment of Alabama Volunteers; War of 1812 muster rolls for Benjamin Coleman dated June 16 to 30, 1812 and June 30 to August 31, 1812 and June 29 to September 1, 1812 and June, July and August 1812 (unpublished) (Copy in possession of the author)

National Society of the Dames of the Court of Honor, Application for Membership of Martha Louise Henry (Bonin) dated February 23, 1981 related to the Mexican War Service of William Goforth Coleman of Claiborne Parish, Louisiana (unpublished) (Copy in possession of the author)

National Society of United Daughters of 1812, National Number 22588, Application of Membership of Mrs. Paul (John) Bonin, dated July 25, 1982 related to the War of 1812 service of Benjamin Coleman (unpublished) (Copy in possession of the author)

Nevin, David, *The Mexican War* (Time Life Books, Inc. 1978) and Polk, *The Diary of a President 1845-1849* (Longmans, Green and Company, New York, 1952) pp. 60-72, 126, 133-136, 159 and 162

Nevins, Allan, *The Diary of a President* (Second Edition, Longman's, 1952) pp. 155-156

New Orleans Delta, September 12, 1846

New York Sun, May 7, 1847

Niles' National Register, Baltimore, Maryland, July 18, 1846, November 21, 1846 (pp. 183-184), May 1, 1847 (pp. 132-133), May 8, 1847 (p. 159)

Ocmulgee Church Book, Perry County, Alabama, (unpublished, pages not numbered) (Copy of the handwritten original in possession of the author)

Owen, Thomas McAdory, *History of Alabama and Dictionary of Alabama Biography* (S. J. Clarke Company, Chicago, 1921) p. 986

Owens, Gilbert C., *Aycock* (unpublished)

Parrish, T. Michael, *Richard Taylor, Soldier Prince of Dixie* (University of North Carolina Press, Chapel Hill and London, 1992) pp. 6-14

Pauley, Robert D., "Pack Mules and Surf Boats: Logistics in the Mexican War," *Army Logistics*, November and December, 1997

Paxton, Rev. W. E., *A History of Baptists in Louisiana From the Earliest Times* (C. R. Barnes Publishing Company, St. Louis, 1888) pp. 615-616, 580-582

Perry County Heritage, Volume II (The Book Committee and Friends of the Perry County Historical Preservation Society (printer and date of publication not stated) pp. 6-7

Perry County, Alabama Marriage Records Books: 1820-1832, 1832-1839 and 1839-1851

Peters, Martha Ann, "The St. Charles Hotel: New Orleans Social Center, 1837-1860," *Louisiana History*, vol. I, 1960, pp. 191-211

Peterson, Roger T., *A Field Guide to the Birds of Texas and Adjacent States* (Houghton Miffin Company, Boston, 1963) pp. 69, 75 and 169

Pettit, Madge, *Pioneers and Residents of West Central Alabama* (Heritage Books, Inc., Bowie, Maryland, 1988) p. 165

Polk, James K., President of the United States at Washington, D. C., to the Congress of the United States, A Special Message Calling for a Declaration of War against Mexico dated May 11, 1846

Riley, Reverend Benjamin, *History of Conecuh County, Alabama* (1881)

Robinson, Jacques Donald, Ancestral Charts (unpublished) (Copy in possession of the author)

Rogers, Warren, *Alabama; The History of a Deep South State* (The University of Alabama Press, Tuscaloosa and London, 1994) pp. 151-152, 155

Salley, A. S. Jr., *History of Orangeburg County, South Carolina, From Its First Settlement to the Close of the Revolutionary War* (Regional Publishing Company, Baltimore, 1964) Colonial war service of Henry Gallman (i.e., Coleman)

Salley, A. S., Jr., compiler and editor, *Marriage Notices in The South-Carolina Gazette; and Country Journal (1765-1775) and in The Charleston Gazette (1778-1780)* (The Walker Evans & Cogswell Co., Charleston, S. C., 1904) p.12

Sanchez, Mario, *A Shared Experience's Historical Survey*, www.rice.edu/armadillo/past/book/part2/steambot.html

Savannah Georgian, October 28, 1846, January 7, 1847

Scott, General Winfield report to William L. Marcy, Secretary of War dated March 29, 1847, Vera Cruz, Mexico

Scott, General Winfield report to William L. Marcy, Secretary of War dated April 19, 1847, Plan de Rio, Mexico

Scott, General Winfield, Supplementary Report on the Battle of Cerro Gordo dated April 23, 1847

Singletary, Otis A., *The Mexican War* (The University of Chicago Press, Chicago, 1960) pp. 41 and 128

Smith, George W. and Charles Judah, editors, *Chronicles of the Gringos: The U. S. Army in the Mexican War, 1846-1848, Accounts of Eyewitnesses and Combatants* (The University of New Mexico Press, Albuquerque, 1968) pp. 287-289, 341

Smith, Justin Harvey, *The War with Mexico* (Macmillan Publishing Company, Gloucester, Mass., 1963 [c. 1919]) vol. I, pp. 204-215, 225-238, 240-256, 263-264, 276-283, 347-369, 357, 364-365, 416, 417, 430-431, 512-513; vol. II, pp. 17-58, 332-355

South Carolina Archives, Royal Grant to Henry Coleman, Volume 4, page 267 and Pre-Revolutionary Loose Plats (Copy in possession of the author)

South Western Baptist, March 24, 1852

Stauffer, Dr. Alvin P., "The Quartermaster Department and the Mexican War" (*Quartermaster Review,* May-June 1950)

Stewart, John Craig, *The Governors of Alabama,* 1975

Tampico Sentinel, March 24, 1847

Taylor, Richard, *Destruction and Reconstruction* (Da Capo Press, New York, 1879)

Taylor, General Zachary report to Roger Jones, Adjutant General of the Army dated September 25, 1846 from Monterrey, Mexico

Taylor, General Zachary to General Mariano Arista dated April 25, 1846

Thirteenth Congress, 2d Session, House Executive Document No. 1: Message from the President of the United States (Washington, D. C.: Wendell and Van Benthuysen, 1848) pp. 1183-1185

United States Congress, Joint Resolutions for the Admission of the State of Texas dated March 1, 1845 and December 29, 1845

United States Congress, House Select Committee on Assault upon Senator Sumner, Thirty-fourth Congress, Report No. 182, Washington, 1856

United States Pension Agency, Pensioner Dropped –Form 3—1081 dated April 10, 1906, reporting the death of Mary Jane Coleman (unpublished) (Copy in possession of the author)

Vargo, Louis, "When Lincoln Lived By The Sword," *Civil War Times Illustrated* (Primedia Publication, Vol. XL, No. 7, February 2002) pp. 24-29

Walker, James H. and Robert Curren, *Those Gallant Men of the Twenty-Eighth Alabama Confederate Infantry Regiment* (Heritage Books, Inc., Bowie Maryland, 1997) pp. 21, 315, 323, 329-330

War Department, Adjutant General's Office, Washington, D. C., dated January 18, 1883 summarizing the Mexican War service of William G. Coleman for the muster rolls from June 13, 1846 through April 30, 1847 requested by the Commissioner of Pensions in Washington, D. C. (unpublished) (Copy in possession of the author)

War Department, Adjutant General's Office, Washington, D. C., dated March 20, 1885 summarizing the Mexican War muster rolls records of John G. Heard, B. D. Harrison and Jesse Aycock from December 31, 1846. (unpublished) (Copy in possession of the author)

Webb, Walter P., *The Handbook of Texas* (The Texas State Historical Association, Austin, 1952) vol. I, pp. 795-796; vol. 2, pp. 13-14.

Weems, John Edward, *To Conquer a Peace, The War between the U. S. and Mexico* (Texas A & M Press, College Station, Texas, 1988)

White, Virgil D., *Index to Mexican War Pension Files* (The National Historical Publishing Company, Waynesboro, Tennessee, 1989) There is a revised addition of this source published in 1993.

Wilcox, Cadmus M., edited by his niece, Mary Rachel Wilcox, *History of the Mexican War* (Church News Publishing Company, Washington, 1892) pp. 610, 614, 618, 634-635, 659, 682 and 687.

Will of William S. Johnson, Edgefield County, S. C. dated December 27, 1834, Book D, pp. 148-150, recorded by Oliver Towles, on November 8, 1841 and distribution of the assets of William S. Johnson by executors, dated September 14, 1846. (unpublished) (Copy in possession of the author)

Winters, Richard, *Mr. Polk's Army; The American Military Experience in the Mexican War* (Texas A & M University Press, College Station, 1997) pp. 5-13, 15-29, 37-41, 46-47, 60, 66-78, 80-87, 114-116, 121, 126, 140-144, 146-147 and 180

Index

Cos, General Martín Perfecto de, 66, 162*fn*
Covar, Elizabeth, 137
Covar, Isabella, *137fn*
Covar, J. L., 137 *fn*
Covar, John, 137*fn*
Covar, Nancy, 137 *fn*
Cowley, James, 122
Cowley, Mary Ann, 109
Crawford County, Alabama, 25
Crawford, Amarintha, 122
Crawford, Louisa,
Crawford, Reverend Peter, 4
Crawley, Nancy, 123
Cross, Colonel Truman, 9, 58*fn*
Cross, Elizabeth W., 124
Cross, Mary Ann, 24*fn*, 123
Crossman, Captain, 113
Crow, Jane F., 123
Crow, Martha Jane, 19, 124
Crow, Reverend Charles, 17, 18, 19, 123
Crow, Silas Harlan, 124
Crowley, John, 115, 122, 123, 129, 161
Cunningham, Captain Hugh M., 21, 53*fn*, 185
Curry, Berkley Perry, 115
Curry, Jabez, 51*fn*
Curry, James H., 115
Curry, John, 18
Curry, Margaret Caroline, 115
Curry, Martha, 115
Curry, Milo Cincinnati, 18, 19, 94, 97, 102, 115, 129
Curry, Sally, 115
Curry, Thomas, 18, 115

D

Dacus, James T., 64, 99, 116, 129, 160
Dacus, John W., 29, 116, 129
Dacus, Rufus W., 102, 108, 116, 129
Dacus, Susan E., 102, 116
Dale, Thomas J., 21*fn*
Dallas County, Alabama, 1*fn*, 13, 18, 19, 50, 51, 116, 117, 121, 122, 132
Danford, John, 27*fn*
Darrow, Christopher, 25
Davenport, J. L., 180
David, a slave, 28*fn*
Davis, Colonel Jefferson, 28*fn*, 44*fn*, 54, 73, 97, 149*fn*
Davis, Colonel Reuben, 52
Davis, Dr. James, 91, 173, 174
Davis, Elizabeth Ann, 125
Davis, Joseph, 28*fn*
Davis, Hugh, 4
Davis, Leroy E., 102, 104, 116, 129
Davis, Martha J., 102, 116
Deas, Captain George, 86, 172
DeKalb County, Alabama, 21, 24*fn*, 25*fn*, 26, 29, 30, 57*fn*, 81
Demorest, Elizabeth, 119
Dennis, Amanda, 116
Dennis, Charles R., 80, 116, 129

Dennis, John R., 16, 95, 100, 116, 129
Dennis, Joseph G., 15, 19, 59, 65, 74, 96, 100, 102, 108, 116, 129, 154, 162, 166
Dennis, Reverend John, 17*fn*
DeRussey, Colonel Lewis G., 66, 162*fn*
Descendants of Mexican War Veterans, xiii, 46
Desha, General Robert, 25
DeSoto Parish, Louisiana, 18, 96, 109, 110, 122, 123, 124, 177, 179
Devot, Prescott, 41
Diario, newspaper, 53
Dominguez, Manuel, 87
Douglass, Representative Stephen, 190

E

Earle, Lt. Colonel Richard G., 24, 25, 32, 49, 50, 51, 54, 81, 92, 120, 132, 134, 152, 178
Edgefield District, South Carolina, 15, 16, 71, 72, 91, 98, 114, 144*fn*, 164
Edwards, Sarah, 113
Edwards, William N., 64, 100, 116, 129
Eighth Alabama Infantry Regiment (CSA), 103-105, 107, 109, 110, 113, 119-121, 125, 127
Eighth U. S. Infantry Regiment, 36*fn*, 44
Eiland, Dr. M. A., 35, 36, 64, 65, 117, 129, 139, 143, 151, 160
El Telégrafo, Mexico, 83, 85*fn*
Elder, John, 16*fn*
Elections, xv, xvi, 7, 8, 14, 15, 16, 24, 31, 54, 111, 133
Eleventh Alabama Infantry (CSA), 105
Eleventh Mississippi Infantry (CSA), 108
Encino, Mexico, 90
England, 7, 8, 10
England, Joel W., 13
Enterprise, steamboat, 40
Eutaw Rangers in the War with Mexico, xiii
Eutaw Rangers, xiii, 21*fn*, 25*fn*, 28*fn*, 31, 53, 70, 92, 96*fn*, 167*fn*, 169
Everett Institute, 117
Everett, Charles H., 117
Everett, Dettie E., 117
Everett, Edward, 117
Everett, James D., 117
Everett, John Pickney, 15, 19, 80, 95, 102, 113, 117, 129, 170
Everett, L. Etta, 117
Everett, Laura E., 117
Everett, Reverend George, 117
Everett, Sarah J., 102, 117
Everett, Sarah M., 117

F

Fagan, Lt. William Long, 107
Farley, Lavina Sophronia, 102, 117
Farley, Robert, 64, 80, 100, 102, 108, 117, 118, 129
Farrar, Elizabeth, 18, 108, 118
Farrow, Amon, 137
Fashion, steamship, 27, 28, 91, 134, 173
Ferguson, Drew, 178

Twenty-Second Texas Cavalry (CSA), 107, 114
Twenty-Sixth Alabama Infantry (CSA), 108
Twenty-Third U. S. Infantry Regiment, 36*fn*
Twiggs, General David E., 37, 57, 65-67, 69,
    75, 79, 90, 160, 163, 165, 169, 173
Tyler, President John, 7, 8
Typhoid fever, xvi, 59, 119, 120, 156*fn*

U

Uniforms, xvi, xvii, 22-24, 43, 90, 93, 132
Union Parish, Louisiana, 96, 114, 116, 117,
    119, 123, 124
United Confederate Veterans, 110

V

Vance, Lafayette, 65, 80, 101, 127, 130, 155,
    160
Vasquez, General Ciriaco, 84
Vera Cruz, 14*fn*, 15fn, 48*fn*, 57, 64-81, 83,
    85-87, 89-93, 100, 101, 103, 104, 113,
    114, 116, 120-124, 126, 163, 164-173,
    177, 155*fn*
Virginia, steamship, 39, 60, 92, 93, 141, 155,
    156
Vixen, steamship, 165

W

Walker, Benjamin F., 34, 100, 102, 127, 130,
    140
Wallace, William, 110, 127, 128, 130
Walthall, John N., 18, 112, 149, 150
Walthall, Richard Booker, 13, 14
War for Southern Independence, 16, 17, 21*fn*,
    47, 54, 95-97, 103, 105-107, 109, 110,
    112-114, 116, 118-122, 124-127, 145*fn*
War of 1812, 15, 35*fn*, 36*fn*
Watson, Hugh P., 24, 172
Watson, Lt. Colonel William H., 44
Watson, Mrs. Grace T., 115
Watters, Elizabeth, 126
Weaver, Colonel P. J., 176
Weger, Lucinda, 126
West Point, Military Academy, 24*fn*, 30*fn*,
    36*fn*, 54, 75, 133*fn*, 150*fn*
West, Alfred W., 128, 130
White, Isaac, 1
Willis, Anna H., 16
Willis, Captain William T., 47*fn*
Wilson, Asa Ann, 128
Wilson, Colonel Henry, 89
Winship, Captain Oscar F., 47*fn*, 50, 150,
    151*fn*
Witter, J. A., 96
Wolfe, Adolph, 172*fn*
Wood's Texas Cavalry, 11
Woodruff, Dr. C. A., xvi*fn*
Worth, General William Jenkins, 36, 54, 65,
    66, 69, 70, 71, 76, 165, 166
Wright, Captain, 39
Wyatt, Lucy E., 113

Y

Yeates, Clara, 123

Yellow Fever, v, 5, 42, 63, 80, 83, 86, 89, 117
Youngblood, Captain John B., 21

About the Author

J. HUGH LEBARON has a bachelor's degree in history and is a former history teacher. He was led to Perry County in search of information for family history and has been exploring the primary records in that county for over a decade. The results of his efforts were two narratives centering on Perry Countians: "Sketches from the Life of Charles Crow—1770-1845," published in *The Alabama Baptist Historian* in June 1998 and "Abraham Wyche Jackson, A Biography." He is also the author of "James Monroe Nash Military Service in the War for Southern Independence." Another result of his searching through dusty county records, studying mind numbing microfilms, consulting with volunteer descendants, conferring with Mexican War specialists and poring over published volumes is *Perry Volunteers in the Mexican War*. While the sources used by the author inspire confidence in his writing, the diary of Captain William G. Coleman and the journals of two other men serving in the Alabama regiment give this narrative an inimitable quality by using descriptions provided by men who were there and described what they saw.

Made in the USA
Coppell, TX
02 June 2021